Introducing Character Animation with Blender

TONY MULLEN

BICENTENNIAL
1807
WILEY
2007
BICENTENNIAL

WILEY PUBLISHING, INC.

Acquisitions Editor: Pete Gaughan
Development Editor: Jim Compton
Technical Editor: D. Roland Hess
Production Editor: Eric Charbonneau
Copy Editor: Nancy Sixsmith
Production Manager: Tim Tate
Vice President and Executive Group Publisher: Richard Swadley
Vice President and Executive Publisher: Joseph B. Wikert
Vice President and Publisher: Neil Edde
Media Project Supervisor: Laura Atkinson
Media Development Specialist: Kate Jenkins
Book Designer: Caryl Gorska
Compositor: Kate Kaminski, Happenstance Type-O-Rama
Proofreader: Jen Larsen
Indexer: Nancy Guenther
Anniversary Logo Design: Richard Pacifico
Cover Designer: Ryan Sneed
Cover Images: Mauro Bonecchi, Sacha Goedegebure, the Blender Foundation's Orange Project, Yuichi Miura

Acknowledgments

First and foremost, I would like to thank all the developers of Blender who, under Ton Roosendaal's very capable leadership, have created what I consider to be the most powerful and reliable piece of open-source software available to artists of any kind. Blender's open development model means that most of these developers are working purely out of love for the project, and they deserve credit for their tremendous efforts and prodigious skills. You can find a complete list of the contributors to Blender's code for each release on the appropriate release notes pages at www.blender.org. In addition to the developers of the code, I would like to specifically thank the Orange Project team for its hard work on creating the ideal showcase for Blender's capabilities, *Elephants Dream*, and for its generosity in releasing it as an "open movie" for everyone to enjoy and learn from. I would also like to extend special thanks to Claudio "malefico" Andaur and all involved in the *Plumiferos* project for supplying me with material from that very promising production. ■ Because classes and textbooks on Blender have so far been difficult to come by, becoming a skilled Blender user is almost by necessity a community endeavor. For this reason, I owe a huge debt of gratitude to the Blender users who regularly post at the BlenderArtists forum (http://blenderartists.org/forum/) and enable less-experienced users to benefit from their knowledge. The users and developers posting in this forum ensure that it remains the single most useful resource for Blenderers of all levels, and I learned most of what I know about Blender from people there. I would like to single out a few regular posters there who, knowingly or unknowingly, have been particularly helpful to me in my work on this book: Andy Dolphin (AndyD), Mike Stramba, (mstram), Roland Hess (Harkyman), Jason Pierce (Sketchy), Aligorith, Calvin, Jason van Gumster (Fweeb), Jonathan Williamson (mr_bomb), Derek Marsh (BgDM), Fligh, Jorge Rocha (Toloban), TorQ, Greybeard, Tom Musgrove (LetterRip), Campbell Barton (cambo), Andrew Cruse (Basil_Fawlty), Enrico Valenza (Env), Gimble, broken, and Nozzy. These are a few of the true Blender gurus, and I highly recommend readers of this book to take advantage of their knowledge and their willingness to share it. I also would like to extend my gratitude to the moderators of that forum who help to make it such a great environment. And of course, I am very grateful to all of the extraordinarily talented artists who supplied me with renders for the gallery and animations or .blend files for the accompanying DVD. Their excellent work provides a compelling showcase of what Blender is capable of. ■ This book wouldn't have seen the light of day without the support and expertise of editors Pete

Gaughan and Jim Compton, marketing manager Kelly Trent, as well as the efforts of all at Sybex who had a hand in putting the book together and getting it out. I would like to thank them all very much. Many thanks also to Bassam Kurdali and especially Roland Hess for enabling me to benefit from their Blender expertise through their comments and corrections as technical editors on the book. I would also like to express my gratitude to all of my colleagues at Tsuda College in Tokyo for their support for this book and to my students for allowing some of my enthusiasm for Blender to rub off on them. ■ On a personal note, I would like to express my gratitude to Yuka Haraguchi for her encouragement, support, and patience throughout my work on this book and all my time-and-attention-consuming Blender-related activities. I would also like to extend very special thanks to my mother for taking me along on her trips to the art supply store when I was a child—especially for the day when she acquiesced to the pleas of six-year-old me and bought me my own copy of Preston Blair's *Animation* (which I still own to this day). ■ Finally, I'd like to dedicate this book to the memory of my father, whose impressive collection of vintage *Pogo* books helped to instill in me a love of cartooning in all its forms, and whose keen interest in the evolution of computer graphics would have made him a natural Blender fan.

About the Author

Tony Mullen, Ph.D., has a broad background in CG-related work. He currently teaches in the Department of Computer Science at Tsuda College in Tokyo, in which his courses have included modeling and animation using the Blender open-source 3D software package and courses on the Python programming language (the language used for scripting in Blender). He has worked as a newspaper cartoonist, illustrator, animator, computer programmer, researcher, and university lecturer.

As a freelance animator, Mullen has created animations for several independent filmmakers and for the Jido Kanji educational software project. As an independent filmmaker himself, he worked on several short films, including the award-winning Super-8 short *The Devices of Gustav Braüstache, Bachelor of Science* (co-writer), and the recently completed 16 mm live action/stop motion animated film *Gustav Braüstache and the Auto-Debilitator* (co-writer and co-director with Rob Cunningham, lead animator), which is currently in submission at several international film festivals. Mullen is currently completing work on an animated short of his own in Blender.

Contents

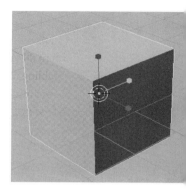

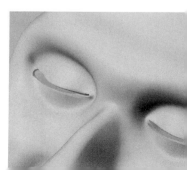

Foreword

It is now exactly four years ago that Blender was released as free software on the Internet, and I can only say that this was the best thing ever to happen with Blender! Not only has Blender attracted hundreds of active developers and volunteers worldwide but the amount of users has also been growing beyond a number we can't even count any more.

Last year, Blender development got a big boost with our project, *Elephants Dream,* the world's first "3D open movie." With the team of artists and developers that was involved, two key issues were defined that had to be tackled to make Blender suitable for serious animation movie production. One of them was the rendering pipeline, but we decided to start with the most crucial issue: improving character animation tools.

During the second half of 2005, most of the animation system in Blender was rebuilt from scratch, speeding up the system and enabling a solid foundation for exciting new development. This is a process that still goes on. Many more teams and individuals now work on animation and movie creation with Blender, providing valuable feedback for design of better tools.

With so much work done in this area, I was very happy to hear from Tony Mullen about his plans to write a book on character animation with Blender. And even more delighted when Sybex decided to accept his proposal and work on publishing this book.

Tony is an experienced author and has been an enthusiastic Blender artist for a long time, so I'm very proud he decided to bundle his knowledge in a book to share with everyone. Looking at a selection of finished chapters now, I can say that this will definitely be the guide for artists who want to understand 3D character animation in general and how to achieve this in Blender.

I wish everyone a lot of pleasure reading this book!

—Ton Roosendaal
Chairman, Blender Foundation
Amsterdam, November 2006

Foreword

In the last year, it was my great pleasure to work on a short animated movie called *Elephants Dream.* One of our goals was to test the use of entirely free and open-source tools for graphics and animation. Our primary 3D application was Blender, which proved to be an amazingly capable and friendly tool to use in a production environment. Since then, I have heard about various totally courageous studios using Blender around the world—both for fully animated movies and to add effects to traditionally filmed elements.

It might come as a surprise to many that Blender, a program that is free and open, is capable of producing 3D character animation and rendering as well as its commercial siblings (that can cost anywhere from hundreds to thousands of dollars). This should not be so shocking; there are many excellent open-source applications, but it is true that relatively few of them are graphics production tools. Blender has a very consistent, fast, and customizable interface, with options to create a production pipeline almost entirely in one application—a boon especially for small productions without a huge technical team.

I hope that Blender will continue to democratize the process of making computer animation and computer art, and it is for this reason that I was glad to hear of Tony Mullen's project to write a book about using it for character animation. Building a production pipeline—even in one application—goes far beyond understanding the basics of the interface. Most users will find themselves able to understand the basic data types, constraints, and deformers very easily just by reading online documentation or from experimentation; but understanding these things is just a first step, and character animation involves putting together the elements in rather elaborate ways that are not so easily discoverable.

Character animators learning Blender—especially as their first 3D package—often find themselves at a bit of a disadvantage compared to those using other software. The program itself is quite capable, but going from the low-level objects provided by the interface to the high level of rigged and animatable characters is far from obvious. What they need is a guide that can bridge that gap by teaching the fundamentals—not just descriptively but also by showing how to put them together in a character animation pipeline. Here is that guide!

—Bassam Kurdali
Director, *Elephants Dream*

Introduction

In the past decade or so, 3D modeling and animation technology has made huge leaps in terms of power and availability. Resources that were until recently available only to well-financed production houses and movie studios have come within reach of ordinary computer users, both in terms of hardware computing power and in terms of quality software. These days anybody with a personal computer has the potential to create high-quality 3D imagery, and when it comes to software, no package better represents this revolution in accessibility than Blender.

The Open-Source Advantage

Blender is a powerful 3D modeling and animation software package available for Windows, Macintosh, and Linux. Like other similar packages such as Lightwave, 3D Studio Max, and Maya, Blender offers a wide range of modeling, animation and rendering tools. It also has a number of distinguishing features of its own, including its excellent cross-platform portability, the ability to run scripts in the Python programming language, a unique and intuitive user interface for efficient workflow, and extraordinary flexibility in importing and exporting files, scenes, and objects for use with other programs, including a variety of high-quality ray tracers. It has advanced physics simulators, and its new, lightning-fast implementation of UV unwrapping has already become the envy of the industry. These features alone are enough to make Blender a strong competitor in the world of 3D tools, but its biggest single distinguishing feature is that it's free.

That's not simply to say that somebody's giving out free samples that you can use in some capacity without paying for. Blender is licensed under the GNU Public License, the foremost license for open source software. This means that Blender source code is freely available for anybody to download, use, copy, alter, and distribute for any purpose, provided they abide by the guidelines laid out in the GPL. These guidelines require that changes made to the code be explicitly identified and that resulting released code remain open and freely available. In short, Blender is truly, fully free, and the license is designed to make sure it stays free for good.

For people with a computer science background, the idea that top quality software can be free is not new. Open source projects such as the GNU/Linux operating system, the Apache web server, and the MySQL database have amply demonstrated the robustness and quality possible with an open-source development model. All of those are examples of widely used, high-quality, and *commercially viable* free software. Furthermore, software such as the TeX/LaTeX typesetting package, widely used for academic typesetting in technological fields, stands as a clear testament to the potential for innovation in open source software; TeX/LaTeX remains unrivaled in what it does by any proprietary consumer-oriented software package. Richard Stallman, the author of the GPL and longtime advocate of free software, likes to emphasize the notion of "free as in free speech, not as in free beer," and many Blender users are quick to stress that their fondness for Blender is not based on cost.

Nevertheless, in the realm of consumer-oriented and graphics software, it remains true that most of the best industrial-strength software applications are proprietary. Even the best open source applications in these areas tend to come across largely as underdog imitations of their proprietary counterparts. For this reason, it is reasonable to wonder what the catch is with something like Blender. And the good news is that as far as the software itself is concerned, there really is no catch. Blender is a robust, fully-fleshed-out piece of software, remarkably free of bugs, and more stable than some proprietary packages with similar functionality. Its development is rapid, with new features and fixes being released at a steady clip. Development is overseen by Ton Roosendaal, the creator of Blender and head of the Blender Foundation, and the core programming team is passionate and committed to holding the Blender code to high standards. The Blender Foundation regularly participates as a mentoring organization in Google's Summer of Code program, in which young programmers are given the opportunity to contribute to an open source project. So in the case of Blender, as with the best open source programs, being free does not imply a lack of quality in the software itself.

Furthermore, in addition to allowing programmers from all over the world the ability to contribute code and bug fixes to the software, the open source model also encourages a sense of community among users. The free nature of the software itself encourages users to share their expertise and abilities where they can. Aside from the core programmers, there are numerous users contributing useful Python scripts to the community, to say nothing of the countless high-quality tutorials created by users.

What we are left with is a first-rate, professional quality 3D animation package which is available to everybody completely free. You don't have to pay thousands of dollars for the software and commit to many more for upgrades, you don't have to risk getting nabbed pirating software, you don't have to worry about your chosen package falling out of favor or the vendor going out of business, you don't have to mess around with watermarks on your work or hobbled, semi-functional shareware. With Blender, *you're* free to get right down to what's important: creating.

Depending on your needs, Blender may be the only 3D animation package you ever have to bother with. If you are a hobbyist, or a freelancer, or the head of your own production company, you may be able to do fine without ever touching another 3D modeling and animation application. However, Blender in its current incarnation as a first tier 3D animation tool is comparatively new. Before the recent recode of the armature system in version 2.40, Blender suffered from a number of shortcomings as an animation tool. Even then, it was highly regarded for its modeling abilities and its versatility, but with the recent improvements in its animation capabilities, Blender has come into its own in the realm animation. It is now fully capable of producing high quality animation, and with time it will surely begin to be adopted into more and more professional studios and production houses impressed by its flexibility and workflow.

At present, of course, Blender is not the industry standard. If you are hoping to get work in the field of animation, it would be a good idea to aim for basic proficiency in at least one other 3D application. You can't really predict which application you may be asked to work with in a job setting, but prospective employers will appreciate the fact that you are familiar with more than one environment. Even so, there are advantages to using Blender. For building portfolio pieces and show reels, any quality software will do, and the freedom and flexibility of Blender is as much an advantage for students and job-seekers as it is for anybody else. Most of the skills you will need in the industry are general 3D and animation skills, and these can be learned with any fully functional software package. The skills you master in Blender will transfer to other software packages and greatly speed up your ability to pick up new applications.

Who Should Buy This Book

As the title implies, this book is intended for people who want to learn to create quality character animation using the Blender 3D software package. Such people probably fall into three basic groups:

- Blender users who have experience with modeling and rendering, but have not yet seriously explored Blender's character animation capabilities. It is likely that a lot of Blender users fall into this category, since Blender has been heavily used for years as a 3D illustration tool.

- Experienced character animators who are considering making a transition to using Blender instead of, or in addition to, another software package. These people can expect to be quite familiar with the concepts dealt with in this book, but need to know how the concepts are implemented in the Blender software.

- Highly motivated newbies to both Blender and the field of character modeling and animation. These are the people who will be picking the bones of this book. I hope to supply these readers with all they need to use Blender to get started in character modeling, and also to give them some good pointers on where to go from here to develop their skills more fully.

For all of these people, the learning curve can be steep. At the time I'm writing this, there are no published, up-to-date books on Blender available in English. There is some excellent new introductory documentation available at the Blender Wiki page, thanks to the Blender Foundation's Summer of Documentation project, and I strongly recommend looking at it. Aside from this, however, cohesive learning resources for Blender are still hard to come by. Until now, the way to learn Blender has been to scour the Web for free tutorials and online documentation, and to participate in discussion groups such as the BlenderArtists group at blenderartists.org/forum. The fact that so many people have become adept in Blender is a testament to the extraordinary quality of the tutorials and the documentation available, all created by people who have donated their time and expertise to supporting the Blender community.

These resources remain invaluable, and in this book I will make an effort to point you to the best of them. Nevertheless, it requires some real effort to seek out up-to-date, quality tutorials and to teach oneself from so many diverse sources, and it is difficult for scattered tutorials, even very good ones, to get into sufficient detail and depth on a specific topic. For this reason, I have taken a very broad view of what the topic of character animation encompasses. Modeling, texturing, and animation are all part of what I cover here, and you can use most of the information in this book to apply to other forms of modeling and animation than character animation. Likewise, although it is very much a part of this book, I do not go into great depth on the art of animation per se. In Chapter 18, I recommend several books to help you deepen your knowledge and skills in this regard.

With *Introducing Character Animation with Blender,* I aim to provide a clear, cohesive overview of character creation and animation as implemented in Blender. I hope that this encourages people to make the most of Blender's capabilities, to exercise their own creativity, and to support the fantastic community that has developed around this software.

There are several ways you can use this book. The most straightforward (and demanding) is to start at the beginning and follow all the steps to model and animate the rigged character described over the course of the book. Alternately, you can skip around from chapter to chapter and follow only the steps of the individual chapters. For this, I have included .blend files on the accompanying DVDs representing various incomplete stages of the character rig. You can find the appropriate .blend file for the starting point of the chapter and then work through the chapter using that file.

What's Inside

Here is a glance at what's in each chapter.

In **Part I: Creating a Character with Blender**, I take you through the Blender program, its tools, and the complete foundational process of building a character.

Chapter 1: Blender Basics: Interface and Objects will introduce you to the Blender desktop and show you how to navigate the various windows you'll be using throughout the book. This chapter also explains the basics of how Blender handles 3D objects and what this will mean to you as you work with them.

Chapter 2: Working with Meshes covers the most important mesh modeling tools, and shows several approaches to organic modeling. The chapter culminates with the completion of the Captain Blender character mesh, which we will use throughout the rest of the book for animation tutorials and examples.

Chapter 3: Materials and Textures continues with modeling the Captain Blender mesh, now focusing on creating clothing, skin, and hair using such tools as material shaders, UV mapped textures, and the particle system for hair.

Chapter 4: Armatures and Rigging introduces the armature system with simple examples, and then moves on to creating a high-quality armature for the Captain Blender character.

Chapter 5: Shape Keys and Facial Rigging moves beyond the basics of armature deformations to show how more precise animation of mesh shapes can be accomplished with shape keys, and how the behavior of these can be associated to armature poses to create easily controllable facial expressions and improved joint deformations.

In **Part II: Bringing It to Life: Animation**, we turn to animating the character we have created in Part I.

Chapter 6: Basics of Blender Animation looks at the simple example of a bouncing ball to introduce the ideas of interpolation (Ipo) curves and keyframes, which are the underlying components of all animation in Blender.

Chapter 7: Armature Animation shows how posing, keyframing, and pose ipos work with the character rig we created in Part I to create our first real character animations. We look at creating actions such as jumping, walking, running, as well as others.

Chapter 8: Facial Animation and Lip Sync turns attention to the facial rigging we did in Chapter 5. Using these methods of facial posing, we see how the character can be made to express emotion, and how lip movements can be created to sync with a sound file.

Chapter 9: Nonlinear Animation looks at Blender's powerful Nonlinear Animation Editor, in which multiple independently created actions can be edited together to create a single complex animation.

Chapter 10: Further Issues in Animation covers a number of worthwhile topics in character animation which have not been addressed in other chapters, such as interacting with props, and using features such as lattices, soft body simulation, and metaballs.

Chapter 11: Rendering and Editing tells you what you need to know to output your animations to fully-realized, finished works using Blender's built-in rendering engine. In this chapter you will learn how to use the Sequence Editor to edit separate animated segments together to create a complete animation.

Chapter 12: Using Python Scripts shows you how to use the Python scripts included in the standard Blender distribution and highlights some of the most useful scripts for character animation.

In **Part III: Blender in Production** we look at real-world cases of Blender being used in professional level animation projects.

Chapter 13: Full-Scale Productions: *Elephants Dream* **and** *Plumiferos* introduces the two best known Blender-based animation projects: the world's first "open movie," *Elephants Dream*, and *Plumiferos*, the eagerly-anticipated CG feature film from Argentina.

Chapter 14: A Look Into *Elephants Dream* peeks into the *Elephants Dream* production files to see how the characters of that film are modeled and rigged, and highlights some of the interesting approaches to character animation taken by the creators of the film.

Chapter 15: Feifi the Canary: *Plumiferos* **Takes Wing** presents a very special look at a fascinating character rig from *Plumiferos*, an inspiring behind-the-scenes glimpse at this exciting project.

Chapter 16: Blender in the Pipeline takes a step back and looks at Blender's place in these production's pipelines; we look at how the projects are organized and where Blender fits into the workflow.

Part IV: Blender and Beyond wraps up by giving you some pointers to where you can go to continue deepening your skills and understanding beyond what's contained in this book.

Chapter 17: Other Software and Formats gives a brief overview of the import and export possibilities of Blender to and from other 3D formats, and surveys a variety of open source software which will likely be of interest to Blender animators.

Chapter 18: Resources directs you to some recomended books, tutorials, and other resources for deepening your knowledge of animation and CG techniques in general.

What's on the DVD

First and foremost, the companion DVD is home to a complete Blender 2.42 program installation for Windows, Mac OSX, and Linux, and all the project files you'll need to follow along with the book's tutorials and exercises, organized into folders by chapter. Among these are the `.blend` files for the Captain Blender character you see throughout the book. These files represent Captain Blender at various points in his creation. You will find the plain mesh, the mesh with textures, material, and hair, the fully armature-rigged character, and several files representing different animations. Using these files, you should be able to jump into the book at any point and begin following tutorials without having worked your way through previous chapters, if you so desire. In addition to the `.blend` files, you will also find rendered videos of the Captain Blender animations discussed in the text.

We've also included a high-res version of the animated short *Elephants Dream,* the world's first open-source movie. The source and project files for *Elephants Dream* are available from `www.elephantsdream.org`, so you can remix and reuse the movie to make your own creation, under a version of the Creative Commons license.

In addition to *Elephants Dream*, we have collected an impressive gallery of short animations created by Blender artists around the world to demonstrate the potential of Blender's animation capabilities. Be sure not to miss these fantastic pieces of work by Roland Hess, Enrico Valenza, Eric Terrier, Martin White, Stephan Rodriguez, Jason van Gumster, Sacha Goedegebure, Peter Hertzberg, Trevor Jacobs, Nathan Dunlap, Niels Philipsen, David Revoy, Jason Pierce, Philippe Roubal, and the *Plumiferos* production team. Also, several excellent sample rigs are included for your use and study, among them Bassam Kurdali's *Mancandy* rig, Jason Pierce's *Ludwig* rig, Jorge Rocha's clothed female figure, David Revoy's *Little Fairy,* and Nathan Towle's cartoon mouse character.

On top of this, we've assembled an excellent collection of third-party software to help you with your Blender work and education.

GIMP 2.2 is the premiere open-source graphics application, for Windows, Mac OS X, and Linux. This 2D image manipulation software is an invaluable tool for creating textures for use with 3D models.

Audacity 1.2.4b is a simple to use, but very powerful sound processing application which will allow you to edit and manipulate audio files for use in your animations.

VirtualDub 1.6.16 is a simple but very useful video editing application which allows you to edit video and sound together.

InkScape 0.44 is a vector drawing application which is useful for 2D image creation.

Python 2.4.3 is the scripting language of Blender.

YafRay 0.0.9 is a high-quality open source ray tracer for use with Blender, which is capable of rendering a number of sophisticated light effects not possible with Blender's internal renderer.

BlenderPeople 0.8 is a poweful Python-based plug-in, created by D. Roland Hess, which enables the simulation of large-scale crowd scenes, including battles, using Blender's character animation functionality in conjunction with a MySQL database (an open source database application which can be freely downloaded from `www.mysql.com`).

VLC Media Player is a multi-platform video player which should enable you to play any of the media files included on the DVD.

Look on the DVD for a coupon toward rendering services from ResPower. Finally, the DVD also includes a page of web links, connecting you to all these software sources, the Blender Foundation, various Blender community sites, and much more.

How to Contact the Author

I welcome feedback from you about this book or about books you'd like to see from me in the future. You can reach me by writing to blender.characters@gmail.com. You can also find me among the regular posters in the BlenderArtists forum at blenderartists.org/ forum. For more information about my animation work please visit my website at www.tonymullenanimation.com.

Sybex strives to keep you supplied with the latest tools and information you need for your work. Please check their website at www.sybex.com, where we'll post additional content and updates that supplement this book if the need arises. Enter **Blender** in the Search box (or type the book's ISBN—**978-0-470-10260-2**), and click Go to get to the book's update page.

PART I

Creating a Character with Blender

Before you do *any actual character animation, you need a character to animate. The goal of the first part of this book is to get you comfortable enough with the modeling and rigging tools in Blender to translate your own ideas into actual 3D characters. Blender has powerful mesh modeling tools and a very flexible system for creating materials and textures. It also boasts a state-of-the-art armature system that will enable you to create complex, highly poseable rigs for your characters. By the end of this part of the book you will have a fully-rigged character completed, which you can use to follow the animation tutorials in the following part. More importantly, you will have gained the skills to create your own.*

CHAPTER 1

Blender Basics: Interface and Objects

Blender is similar to other high-end 3D software packages. Users experienced in other 3D software should find learning Blender relatively straightforward after they internalize its underlying concepts. Although some might seem quirky at first, many of these distinguishing points are deliberate design decisions that help to make Blender a very intuitive and usable package. (If you're already familiar with Blender's interface and underlying concepts, feel free to start with Chapter 2.)

Blender wears its underlying design on its sleeve. For users familiar with the ideas behind object-oriented programming, many aspects of Blender's organization will be especially intuitive, such as the use of objects, function overloading, and the reuse of data-blocks. Getting a good feel for these ideas and how they are implemented in Blender will greatly increase your proficiency at accomplishing what you want. Nevertheless, it's not necessary to be a programmer to use Blender, and this book doesn't assume any programming knowledge.

Blender's idiosyncrasies begin with its interface, and so will this book. With some practice, you will come to find the interface to be remarkably intuitive and efficient, but it takes a little getting used to at first. Mostly, you'll learn by doing over the course of this book, but in this chapter, we'll take a quick overview of the most salient points of the Blender interface.

- ▓ **Work Areas and Window Types**
- ▓ **Navigating the 3D Space**
- ▓ **Objects and Datablocks**
- ▓ **User Preferences**

Work Areas and Window Types

When you first open Blender, one or two windows will open on your system's desktop, depending on the operating system you use. In Windows, your main Blender window appears in front of the Blender Console window. In Linux, the Console is hidden unless you open Blender from the command line in a terminal window, in which case the Blender Console is the terminal itself. In Mac OS X, the console does not appear initially, but it can be accessed from within the Applications → Utilities directory. The Console is a solid black window with white text, as shown in Figure 1.1. It should read Using Python version 2.4 if Python has been installed properly. If not, don't worry about it for now; Blender runs fine without it. The console is used to display output from Python scripts and other plugins and integrated software, such as renderers. Eventually, you will probably want to be sure that Python is installed to take advantage of the tools described in Chapter 12 such as the pose handler and the BlenderPeople crowd-simulation script. For the purposes of the material covered in this book, however, the only thing you need to know about the Console is that you should not close it. If you do, Blender shuts down unceremoniously, which might result in losing some of your work.

Blender *does not* prompt you to save changes before closing. If you accidentally close Blender without saving, simply open a fresh session and select Recover Last Session from the File menu. The most recent Blender session is automatically saved in a file in your /tmp/directory by default.

The other window is the main Blender window (see Figure 1.2). If it's not already maximized, maximize it. Blender can use all the screen real estate you can give it.

Figure 1.1
Console

Figure 1.2

Blender desktop

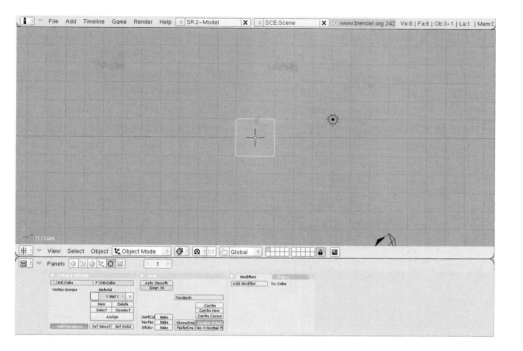

What you're looking at now is your Blender desktop, which should appear a lot like the illustration in Figure 1.2. By default, you will be looking at Screen 2, a preset desktop configuration intended for modeling. Your desktop is divided into three separate work areas, although it might appear to you to be divided into two. The biggest area, filling the middle of the screen, is the 3D View window. The area along the bottom of the desktop is the Buttons window. And at the very top, along the edge of your desktop, is the header of the User Preferences window.

The User Preferences window is hidden, but you can see it by putting your mouse over the border between the 3D View window and the User Preferences window until you see the mouse change into a black double-arrow shape. With the mouse in this position, hold the left mouse button and drag the mouse downward. Doing this increases the area of the User Preferences window so that you can see what's inside it. Your desktop should now look like Figure 1.3. Notice that each of the three work areas now has a header and the area itself. In the case of the User Preferences, the header is at the bottom of the work area. In the other two areas, the header is at the top. If you place your mouse anywhere over the headers and right-click, you are given the option to change this. You can have the header at the top of the area, at the bottom, or you can get rid of the header entirely. You won't to be dealing with the User Preferences window at the moment, so you can drag the border back up and rehide that area.

Figure 1.3

The desktop with the User Preferences window in view

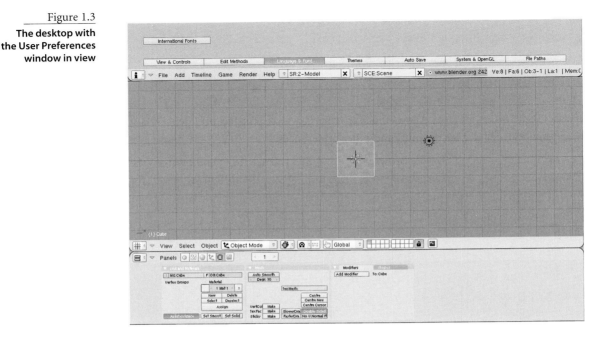

If you roll your mouse over the border between two work areas (or between a work area and the edge of the desktop) so that your mouse pointer switches to the black double arrow, you can right-click for options for work area layout. Any work area can be split vertically or horizontally, resulting in two identical work areas. Likewise, any two areas can be joined together, provided that their borders are aligned. By splitting and joining work areas, you can lay out your desktop in whatever way suits you. Every window also has a *header*, which is the bar full of drop-down menus and buttons that runs along the top or bottom of the window. By right-clicking on the header, you can access a menu to select whether the header is displayed at the top of the window, at the bottom of the window, or not at all.

All work areas are created equal. Blender's various functions are accessed through specific window types, any of which can be displayed at any time in any work area. Notice the icons in the leftmost corner of each work area header. These icons indicate which window type is currently being displayed in that work area. If you left-click the icon, you see a drop-down menu with all the Blender window types. You can select a window type from this drop-down menu or you can select a window type by pressing Shift and the appropriate function key over an active work area (the work area that your mouse pointer is over is the active one). The window types are as follows:

3D View ⊞ Displays 3D objects and scenes in various modes, including the Object, Edit, and Pose modes, among others. Allows a variety of viewing options, including toggled perspective/nonperspective drawing (NUM5). Accessed with Shift+F5.

Buttons ▤ The main area for buttons, fields, and other controls for a variety of modes and functions. Button groups and panels available for display in the Buttons window depend on the current mode and the selected object type. Accessed with Shift+F7.

Outliner ▦ Allows a graphical overview of all datablocks and the links between them, with multiple display options. Accessed with Shift+F9.

Information/User Preferences ℹ Allows the user to specify look-and-feel preferences, language preferences, file location defaults, and other preferences.

File Browser/Data Browser ✎ In File Browser mode, allows the user to open files from the hard drive. In Data Browser mode, allows the user to import or append Blender datablocks from within files on the hard drive.

Timeline ◷ Displays the progress through time of an animation; allows starting, stopping, and scrubbing through the animation; and allows the user to input the start, end, and current frame directly.

IPO Curve Editor ﹃ Allows selection and editing of IPO curves and keyframes. Which kinds of IPOs are available depends on the selected object and the type selected in the drop-down menu in the IPO Curve Editor header. Accessed with Shift+F6.

Action Editor ✄ Allows sequences of armature poses to be stored together as actions for subsequent use in nonlinear animation. Accessed with Shift+F12.

NLA Editor ☰ Allows actions and other animations to be combined in a nonlinear way to form complex animations.

Image Browser ◙ Allows browsing of images and textures from the hard drive with thumbnails.

Node Editor ◲ Allows editing and configuring of material, texture, and shading nodes.

Scripts ✿ Allows the user to browse and execute installed Python scripts.

Text Editor ▤ Allows text editing. Often used as an area for notes about the blend file or for Python scripting. Python scripts might be executed from the Text Editor using the Alt+P hotkeys. Accessed with Shift+F11.

Video Sequence Editor ▦ Allows nonlinear editing, compositing, and playback of video sequences. Can take still frame or video sequences as input. Accessed with Shift+F8.

Image/UV Editor ◲ Allows editing of UV face information and image-based textures. Accessed with Shift+F10.

Audio ∿ Allows audio playback and matching of audio to animation.

In this book, the term *window* usually refers to a work area with a specific window type active. For example, the term *3D View window* will mean a work area with the 3D View window type selected. It's perfectly possible to have more than one of the same type of window open doing different things at the same time. You can have, for example, two 3D View windows open at once—one looking at a side view and one looking at a front view of your character.

Buttons Window

For new users, a first look at Blender's buttons can be intimidating. Indeed, there are a lot of buttons, but you'll soon get used to ignoring the ones you don't need to use. Aside from the character animation system you will be looking at in this book, Blender has a fairly huge amount of functionality; from a fully implemented game engine, to sophisticated physics simulations, to advanced rendering and lighting effects. For the purposes of this book, you'll be focusing on the functionality you need, so you can expect to ignore a lot of the buttons you see for now. Nevertheless, just to get oriented, we'll take a brief look at the entire buttons area here.

The buttons area is divided into six *contexts,* several of which are further divided into *subcontexts.* The contexts and subcontexts can be entered by clicking the corresponding button in the Buttons window header or sometimes by pressing a corresponding function key (not all contexts have function key shortcuts). If a context has a shortcut key, you can cycle through its subcontexts by repeatedly pressing the shortcut. The contexts and their subcontexts are as follows:

- Logic (F4)
- Script
- Shading (F5)
  - Lamp buttons
  - Material buttons
  - Texture buttons (F6)
  - Radiosity buttons
  - World buttons
- Object (F7)
  - Object buttons
  - Physics buttons
- Editing (F9)
- Scene (F10)
  - Render buttons
  - Anim/Playback buttons
  - Sound block buttons

This book does not cover the Logic or Script buttons contexts at all; they are mainly of concern to game creators. You will spend a great deal of time with Edit buttons, Object buttons, Scene buttons, and Shading buttons, although you won't be getting into all the subcontexts. Even within the buttons contexts you will be learning about, there will be functionality you won't have call to use. You'll look more closely at the buttons areas themselves as you use them over the course of the book.

Context-Sensitive Menus

Blender contains a number of menus that are accessible in certain window types and in specific modes. Throughout this book, we will use these menus to add objects in Object mode, to perform special operations in Edit mode, and to key values for animation, among other things.

Navigating the 3D Space

The first thing you need to get used to when using Blender, as with any 3D app, is navigating the 3D space. Three main tools to do this are the following:

> **Middle mouse button (MMB):** Freely rotates the 3D space. By default, the 3D space is rotated around the zero point of all axes. You can choose to have it rotate around the active object by changing the Rotate View setting in the View & Control preferences in the User Preferences window.
>
> **Ctrl+MMB (or mouse wheel):** Zooms in and out in the 3D space.
>
> **Shift+MMB:** Pans 3D view.

The middle mouse button can be emulated by Alt+left-clicking, which can be useful for laptops that have no middle button or whose "middle button" is a difficult-to-push combination of right and left buttons. In the case of a one-button Mac mouse, the mouse click is equivalent to left-clicking. The middle button is Alt+Mouse, and you simulate the right mouse button with Apple(~)+Mouse.

In many cases, hotkeys and mouse movements have analogous results in different contexts. A good example is the behavior of the Ctrl+MMB and Shift+MMB hotkeys. As just mentioned, these keys allow zooming and panning in the 3D window. However, if the mouse is over the Buttons window (at the bottom of the default screen), they have results analogous to zooming and panning. Ctrl+MMB allows the user to enlarge or reduce the size of the button display, and Shift+MMB allows the user to move the entire button display around within the work area.

You will use the 3D cursor (see Figure 1.4) frequently. It can be positioned by left-clicking where you want it in the 3D viewport.

Figure 1.4
3D cursor

Blender Units

Blender uses one unit of measurement, unsurprisingly called a Blender Unit (BU). A Blender Unit is the size of a single square on the background grid in the Blender 3D viewport. If you are working on scale models, you need to decide what real-world measurement to assign to a single BU and then proportion your work accordingly. There are several nice Python script tools available for scale modelers who want more measurement precision than Blender offers natively, but you won't have any need for this kind of precision here.

Using Hotkeys

One thing that any new user can't fail to notice is that Blender favors the use of a lot of hotkeys. Memorizing and becoming comfortable with the various hotkeys and their specific configurations on your own machine is one of the first hurdles to learning to work with Blender. The most important Blender hotkeys are listed in Tables 1.1 and 1.2.

Table 1.1

Hotkeys Common to All Modes

HOTKEY	ALL MODES
Spacebar	Global/Context menu
R	Rotate
S	Scale
G	Translate (move)
X	Delete
A	Select all/Deselect all
B	Border select
BB	Circle select
Ctrl+P	Make parent
Alt+P	Clear parent
Shift+D	Duplicate
I	Insert animation key
Alt+C	Object conversion menu
Right arrow	Move forward one frame
Left arrow	Move backward one frame
Up arrow	Move forward 10 frames
Down arrow	Move backward 10 frames
Shift+right arrow	Go to the last frame
Shift+left arrow	Go to the first frame
~	Show all layers
1-9	Show numbered layer
F12	Render
F11	Display rendered image
W	Special menu
X, Y, Z	Constrain transformation to [selected global axis]
XX, YY, ZZ	Constrain transformation to [selected local axis]

HOTKEY	ALL MODES
Shift+X, Shift+Y, Shift+Z, Shift+XX, Shift+YY, Shift+ZZ	Constrain transformation to take place in the selected plane
N	Display transform properties
Shift+S	Snap menu
Numeric 1, 3, 7	Front, side, and top view
Numeric 0	Camera view
Ctrl+lt+Numeric 0	Move camera to current view
Ctrl+Numeric 0	Use selected object for camera view:

HOTKEY	OBJECT MODE	EDIT MODE
Tab	Go into Edit mode	Go into Object mode
F	Go to Face mode	Make Edge/Face
P	Play game	Separate mesh selection into new object
L		Select linked vertices
M	Move object to new layer	
U		Undo
E		Extrude
V		Rip mesh
K		Loop cut/Knife menu
Ctrl+J	Join meshes/curves	
Ctrl+A	Apply scale and rotation	
Alt+R, Alt+G, Alt+S	Clear rotation, clear translation, clear scale	
Ctrl+N		Recalculate normals outside
Ctrl+E		Edge specials
Alt+S		Fatten/shrink
Ctrl+S		Shear

Table 1.2

Hotkeys Specific to Object and Edit Modes

This information is also available from the Blender.org wiki site:

`http://mediawiki.blender.org/index.php/Reference/Hotkey_Map`

You can find this information within Blender by running the "Hotkey and Mouse Action Reference" script from the Help menu. For users of laptops or one- or two-button mouse devices, some further key combinations are also necessary. The instructions in this book assume that you have a three-button mouse and a separate number keypad, but I will point out how to simulate the key combinations if you don't. You can also find a rundown of the various necessary key combinations for your hardware configuration in the appendix of this book. With a little time following the instructions in this book, the hotkeys will begin to come naturally, and the speed and ease with which you can work with Blender will greatly increase. If you've done animation in other 3D software, you probably have a good idea which of these keys you'll use most often. If you're new to the field, expect to become very familiar with the R, S, and G keys for rotating, scaling, and moving things around; and with the I key for keying frames for animation.

Layers

In the header of the 3D viewport there are 20 small square buttons, divided into 4 rows of 5 buttons. These buttons toggle the visibility of individual layers in a scene .

Layers enable you to separate objects in your 3D view so that you can see some objects, but not others. Unlike layers in most 2D animation and graphics software, layers in Blender are mainly used simply to hide certain items. They can be useful to organize your work during editing and also during animation itself; the layer an object is on can be animated, enabling you to make objects appear and disappear by switching from an invisible layer to a visible layer. In addition to making objects visible and invisible, layers have other uses as well. Lights can be restricted to illuminate only objects on the same layer as the light, which is an indispensable tool in lighting. Also, forces such as wind effects and curve guides, which will be discussed later in this book, are limited to affecting only objects on their own layer.

You can toggle the layers that are visible in the 3D viewport and to the renderer by using the buttons mentioned previously or by using the keyboard number keys (not the numeric keypad). You can toggle multiple layers at once by Shift+clicking the buttons. The top row of layers corresponds to the keyboard number keys 1 through 0. The bottom row of layers corresponds to Alt+1 through Alt+0. In general, the numeric keypad is used for changing views, and the keyboard numbers are used for changing layers. Either can be used for inputting numbers into a text field, for example.

> Accidentally pressing a keyboard number key other than the layer you are working in can provide an alarming shock for the beginner when all objects suddenly disappear from the 3D view window! Don't panic; simply return to viewing the layer your work was on by using the layer buttons.

You can send an object to a different layer by selecting the object and pressing the M key. A dialog box displays with the layer buttons in the same order as they appear in the 3D viewport header. Simply click the layers you want to send the item to, holding Shift to select multiple layers, and click OK. An object can reside on as many layers at once as you choose.

Views and Perspective

There are various ways to view your scene. When you open Blender initially, the view is by default along the Z axis ("top view" for the purposes of this book). This default view is also an orthographic (flat) view, in which lengths and sizes are not affected by their distance from the viewer. To toggle into Perspective mode, press 5 on the numeric keypad. This mode gives a more realistic perspective view.

It is possible to zoom too far forward in Perspective view, and find yourself trapped. If your viewpoint seems frozen or difficult to control, this is probably the problem. Simply press 5 on the numeric keypad to toggle into Orthographic view and then zoom your viewpoint out.

Using the number pad, you can switch your view to follow the *X, Y,* or *Z* axis. The default view is along the Z axis and it corresponds to 7 on the numeric keypad. The numeric 1 key changes the view to look down the Y axis, and numeric 3 will change the view to follow the X axis. Holding down the Ctrl key while pressing these numbers changes the view to their respective opposites, looking up the axis from the negative direction. Numeric 2 and 8 rotate the scene vertically with respect to the 3D viewport, and numeric 4 and 6 rotate the scene horizontally.

Camera

The 0 key on the numeric pad switches to the active camera viewpoint. Dotted rectangles frame the view, indicating the video safe areas, as you can see in Figure 1.5. If the camera is on a visible layer, a solid rectangle also appears, representing the camera itself. You can right-click this rectangle to select the camera, like any other object. From other views, you can place the camera at the current view by pressing Ctrl+Alt+numeric 0, which will also put you automatically into camera view. You can also use Ctrl+numeric 0 to make *any object* into the active camera. This can be used to switch cameras, but it can also be used to check on the "viewpoint" of other objects as well, which can be useful for directional objects such as spotlights.

Figure 1.5

Camera view

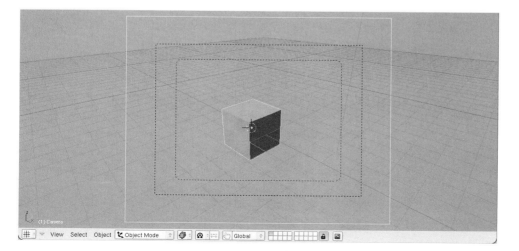

Preview Window

A quick way to get a preview of your scene that is near render-quality is to use the Preview window in the 3D viewport. To open this window, use Shift+P. The preview takes a few seconds to generate, and is updated in close to real time when you move the Preview window or the view in the window (see Figure 1.6).

> There are several common hotkeys that incorporate the P key, but the P key itself can be startling if pressed inadvertently because it activates Blender's Game mode. If this happens, exit the mode with the Esc key.

Interacting with 3D Objects

In the header bar of the 3D View window, there is a drop-down menu for selecting the mode. The default mode to begin with is Object mode, in which you can select and manipulate objects and relationships between them.

There are several ways to select objects. The simplest way to select a single object is by right-clicking it. If you hold Shift, you can add individual objects to the selection. Selected objects are outlined in pink. The last object you selected is outlined in a lighter pink, indicating that it is active. To make one of the other selected objects the currently active object, Shift+right-click it. Shift+right-click the active object to remove it from the selection. By pressing the Z key you can toggle between the wireframe and solid views. In solid view, you cannot select objects that are completely obscured from the view by other objects. You must either move your view to a place where you can get to the object or enter wireframe view. In this view, Alt+right-clicking a spot where more than one selectable object is present allows you to select from a list of those objects.

Another option for selecting objects is by using the Box Select tool, accessed by pressing the B key once. This tool allows you to drag a box over an area of the screen and then select all visible objects within the box. Hold down the left mouse button while dragging the box to cover the selection. Pressing the B key and then dragging the box with either the right or middle button uses the box for deselection. There are several ways to manipulate the location, rotation, and size of objects, and it is entirely a matter of personal preference which one to use.

Figure 1.6
Preview window

Hotkeys

- To rotate, press the R key once and rotate the object with the mouse. The default rotation axis is the current angle of the 3D View. After you rotate the object the way you like it with the mouse, left-click to accept the new rotation; otherwise, right-click to quit the rotation without making the change.

- To translate or change an object's location in 3D space, the hotkey is G. Press this key once and move the object around with the mouse. As with rotation, left-clicking finalizes the move, and right-clicking aborts it.

- To scale an object, the hotkey is S. When you have pressed the S key, moving the mouse closer to the pivot point reduces the scale of the object, and moving the mouse farther from the pivot point enlarges the object. Again, left-click finalizes; right-click aborts.

Mouse Movement Shortcuts

As an alternative to the hotkeys mentioned previously, you can rotate, translate, and scale an object by using mouse movement shortcuts. In Object mode, with your object selected, hold down the left button and drag your mouse in the following patterns to enter the corresponding manipulation modes:

- **Circular motion** enters Rotation mode

- **Straight line** enters Translation mode

- **Sharp V** enters Scale mode

After you enter these modes, you'll perform the manipulations in the same way as with the hotkeys.

Manipulators

Blender also provides the manipulator widgets shown in Figure 1.7 for rotation, translation, and scaling. These three manipulators can be toggled on and off independently of each other by using the buttons in Figure 1.8. To use a manipulator, left-click on the colored portion of the manipulator of the axis along which you want to perform the operation. In the case of translation, click the colored arrow on the appropriate axis; in the case of scaling, click the colored rectangle; and in the case of rotation, click the colored curve that circles the axis you want to rotate the object around.

Figure 1.7

The manipulator widgets: (A) rotation, (B) translation, (C) scale

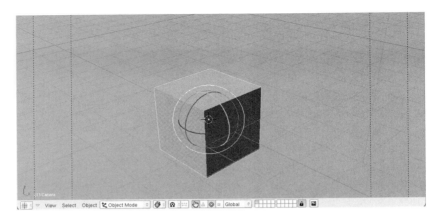

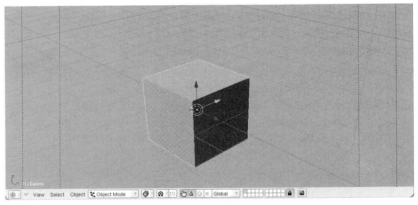

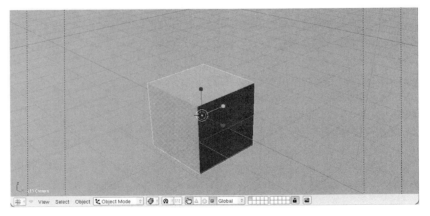

Figure 1.8

The manipulator selection buttons

Restricting to Axes

When performing rotation, translation, or scaling, it is often desirable to restrict the operation to a particular axis or to fix one axis while operating in the other two. To select an axis to rotate, scale, or translate along, press X, Y, or Z after pressing the R, S, or G key. This restricts the operation to the global axis. Press the axis key twice to restrict the operation along the object's local corresponding axis. To scale or translate along a plane, press Shift and the key corresponding to the axis you do not want changed. For example, to scale an object along its X and Y axes, press S followed by Shift+Z.

Pivot Point

The *pivot point* is the point around which rotations are calculated, and it is also used as a reference point for scaling. You can choose what to use as your reference point in the drop-down menu shown in Figure 1.9. The default, Median Point, is a point calculated to be in the center of your entire selection. If you have multiple objects selected, the median point is somewhere in between them all. You can choose to have objects rotate independently around their own centers, around the active object, around the 3D cursor, or around the center of the object's bounding box. The default median point pivot, which can be set with the Shift+comma hotkey, is the most commonly used, but we will occasionally switch the pivot point to be the 3D cursor for specific purposes, which can be set with the keyboard period key.

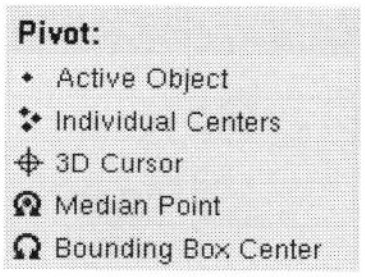

Figure 1.9

**Pivot selection
drop-down menu**

Object Centers

Every object has a center. The *center* is the point around which the object rotates by default, and the location of the center is considered to be the location of the object. Translations and rotations done in Object mode are carried out on the entire object. However, in Edit mode it is possible to move the 3D portion of the object (for example, in the case of a Mesh object, by selecting and moving the entire mesh in Edit mode) without moving the center. When doing a lot of editing, it is easy for this to happen and can result in poorly placed centers that can cause unexpected behavior with objects. The best way to reposition the center automatically is to simply click the Center New button in the Edit Buttons area, with the object selected and in Object mode.

Parenting

Parenting is an important way to create relationships between objects (and some other entities, as you will see). You will use parenting often in modeling, animating, and texturing. When one object is *parented to* another, we refer to the first object as the *child* and the second object as the *parent*. In this case, the child object's movements are all considered only in relation so the parent. Any translation, rotation, or scaling performed on the parent object is also performed on the child object. However, the relationship is not symmetrical.

Like a moon around a planet, the child object can move or rotate in relation to the parent object without influencing the parent object. To define a parent relationship, select more than one object. The *active* object is the last object selected, and by default it is highlighted with a lighter pink than the previously selected objects. Press Ctrl+P to parent all selected objects to the active object; that is to say, the selected objects all become child objects to the active object. In the case of two objects, the first object you select is parented to the second object. To delete a parent relationship, select the objects and press Alt+P.

Parenting is not restricted to just object/object relationships. It is possible for vertices or bones to be parents to objects. There are two types of *vertex parenting*: single-vertex parenting and triple-vertex parenting. With *single-vertex parenting*, the parented object follows only the location of the parent vertex. *Triple-vertex parenting* allows the object to follow both the location and the rotation of the vertex triad it is parented to. You will see an example of vertex parenting in Chapter 3.

Similarly, *bone parenting* allows an object to be in a parent relationship with a single bone in an armature. In bone parenting, the parented object inherits the location, rotation, and other qualities (such as squash and stretch) from the parent bone. You will see examples of bone parenting in Chapter 4.

Objects and Datablocks

Objects and datablocks are the fundamental building blocks for everything you will do in Blender. It's not a complicated system, but having an understanding of how it all hangs together will make it much easier to work efficiently. This chapter describes objects and object data, and introduces the ideas of datablocks and linking. Later on in the book, you'll see a lot more of datablocks—indeed, just about everything you see will be some kind of a datablock—so it helps to have an idea of what the concept means in Blender.

It's often necessary to make adjustments to the modeling of a character in the middle of an animation. There are a number of reasons why you might want to do this. To reduce animation or rendering time, you might want to block a scene with a simpler version of the character you will ultimately use. You might need to fix texturing or modeling problems that you didn't notice before beginning to animate. Also, with involved, team-based animation projects, a certain degree of flexibility is probably required in terms of task ordering—so that all the participants can make efficient use of their time. Allowing animators to work with armature deformations of Mesh objects while other artists are modeling, rigging, and refining the meshes themselves can save considerable time. In particular, using linked datablocks can eliminate the need to re-edit or reappend the same datablock into different scenes or shots. For these reasons, an understanding of Blender's underlying object and datablock organization can be very useful.

In Blender, the basic 3D entity is an *object*. There are a number of different types of objects, each of which has different characteristics and different kinds of data associated with it. All objects have the characteristics of location, rotation, and size. 3D object types include the following:

- Meshes
- NURBs curves/surfaces
- Bezier curves
- Meta objects
- Armatures
- Lattices
- Text objects
- Empties
- Cameras
- Lamps

In addition to location, scale, and rotation, each 3D object is associated with a datablock of specific information to its type. In the case of the Empty object, there is no other information besides this basic 3D object information.

All objects have certain properties. Every object has a *location*, which is the point in space of the object's center. Every object has a *size* defined in terms of the percent of its size at the time of its creation. Every object has a *rotation*, which is the difference between the angles of its local axes and the global axes of the 3D space.

All objects of a particular type also have type-specific *datablocks* associated with them. A Mesh object requires a Mesh datablock, for example, and a Lamp object requires a Lamp datablock. This datablock contains information pertinent to the thing itself. The properties specific to a mesh, such as the placement of its vertices and faces, are contained in the Mesh datablock. A Lamp object datablock likewise contains information about the kind of light source and its properties.

Meshes and Mesh Objects

It is easy to get confused between the object itself and the object's type-specific datablock, but the distinction is important. It is common shorthand, for example, to refer to a Mesh object simply as a *mesh*, but strictly speaking, a mesh in Blender refers to the *Mesh datablock* associated with the *Mesh object*.

To see an example of Mesh objects and their datablocks, open Blender and look at the Links and Materials tab in the Buttons window. You see two drop-down menus: one reads ME:Cube, and the other reads OB:Cube. These are the names of the mesh and the object, respectively. Because objects and datablocks have separate namespaces, it is not a problem for them to be named identically; in fact most of the time it is intuitive that they should be.

Now, in Object mode, place your 3D cursor off to one side of the default cube, press the spacebar, and add a mesh. A cone is a good choice. The default number of vertices for a new cone is 32 and we'll go with that, so click OK. Note that the mesh name and the object name, predictably enough, are Cone, as you can see in Figure 1.10. (If you add another object of the same type, Blender automatically appends the suffix .001 to the end of the new name and increments for each subsequent new object.)

Whenever you add a new object to a scene, you automatically enter Edit mode for that object. Press Tab to switch back into Object mode, and select the Cube Mesh object. In the Links and Materials tab, left-click the small double-arrow icon at the left of the mesh name drop-down menu where ME:Cube is written. In the drop-down menu, Cone will be there as an option. Select this option, and your Cube object is now a cone! Not only is it a cone, but it's the exact *same cone* as the Cone object. If you edit the mesh on one of these objects, both objects' meshes will be edited, as you can see in Figure 1.11. On the other

Figure 1.10

Adding a cone

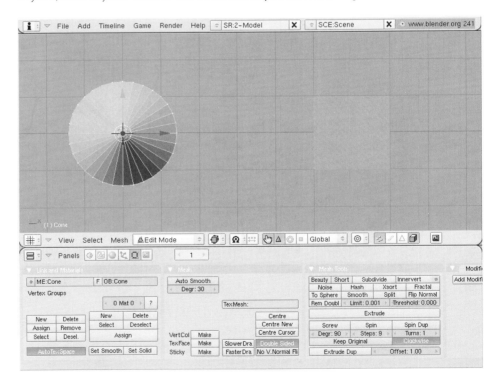

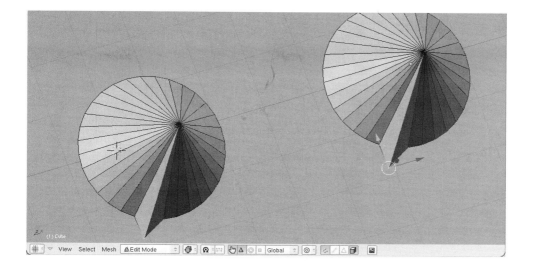

Figure 1.11

Editing the mesh

hand, the objects are still very much independent. To see this, in Object mode select the Cube object. Press S and scale the object to about twice its size. Now you have a big cone and a small cone because mesh edits are made to the Mesh datablock, which is now shared between the objects, and overall scale is an object-level property. Go back to the mesh drop-down menu on the Cube object and look at the options.

In the drop-down menu, there are two options: Cone and Cube. Select the Cube mesh from the drop-down menu. Now your Cube object is again associated with a Cube mesh. However, the cube is now twice the size that it was before because the scaling you did in Object mode applied to the object instead of the mesh.

Exploiting this distinction between Mesh objects and the meshes themselves can be very useful for character animation because it helps maintain a flexible and modular workflow. An armature modifier, as you will see later in the book, operates on a Mesh object, which means that it is possible to replace the mesh itself in the middle of an animation simply by swapping a new Mesh datablock as the object data for the animated object.

You will learn more about these meshes in Chapter 2, so it is a good idea to save this .blend file now so that you can come back to it later.

Managing Datablocks

Datablocks are used to describe most aspects of modeling and animation in Blender. Materials, textures, IPO curves, and actions are all examples of datablocks that can be freely associated with any number of different objects after they're created.

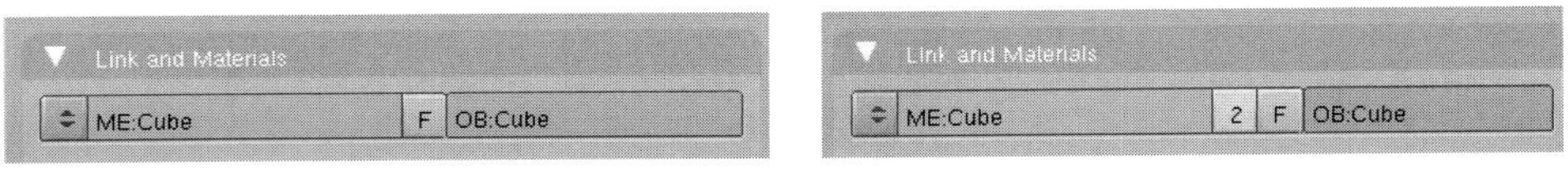

Figure 1.12

(A) The default Cube mesh has one user, the Cube object. If it is unlinked from this object, it is not persisted after the file is closed because it has no users. (B) By toggling the F button, a fake user is added (the displayed number 2 refers to the number of users for that datablock). Now, even if there are no real users of the datablock, it persists because its user count is not zero.

In the preceding example, when you looked in the drop-down menu for the name Cube, you might have noticed a small circle to the left of the word. This circle indicates that Cube is currently an unused datablock—a datablock that is not associated with any object. Blender discards unused datablocks when it shuts down, so if you save the file and then shut down and restart Blender with things in that state, this mesh is gone. In fact, there is no way to actively delete such datablocks; they remain "alive" until Blender quits. If you want to purge unused datablocks without completely quitting Blender, you can save and then reopen your file.

Sometimes, it might be necessary or desirable to keep some datablock on hand, even though it does not have a "user" object. If you want an unused datablock to persist after saving, it is necessary to create a "fake" user for it. For datablocks that can be retained in this way, including the ones mentioned previously, there is be a button next to the datablock drop-down menu with the letter F, as shown in Figure 1.12.

Selecting the datablock you want to make persistent and clicking F creates a fake user for the datablock so that it will not be discarded at shutdown.

In some cases, such as actions, Blender creates a fake user automatically when the datablock is created. In this case, it might be desirable to remove a fake user to delete the undesired datablock. To do this, it is necessary to enter the Data Browser window (by clicking Shift+F4 in any window). In the Data Browser window, you can browse the various types of datablocks in your .blend file. The ones that have the letter F next to them are associated with fake users. You can toggle fake users on and off by selecting the datablock and pressing the F key.

Outliner Window

To see a graphical representation of the datablocks in a scene, select Outliner from the Window-type drop-down menu on any window or press Shift+F9 over the window. The Outliner window opens in the default OOPS Schematic view. In the example in Figure 1.13, you see the schematic for the scene you created earlier with the cube and the cone. In the Outliner window, the various datablocks and their relationships are laid out graphically. The layout here changes predictably when you link the Cube object with the Cone mesh, as in Figure 1.14. You cannot edit anything in the Outliner window, but you can select objects, which are selected simultaneously in any 3D view of the scene (in which they can be deleted, moved, or edited).

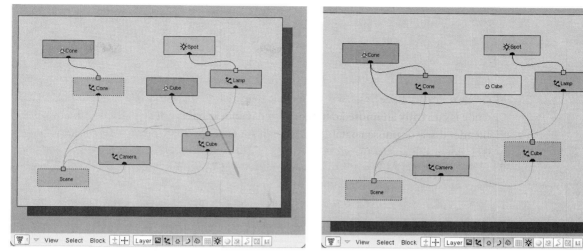

Figure 1.13

OOPS schematic for the original case

Figure 1.14

OOPS schematic with the Cube object associated with the Cone Mesh datablock

You can choose which kinds of datablocks are displayed in the Outliner window by toggling the row of icon buttons in the Outliner window header representing scene, object, mesh, curve, metaball, lattice, lamp, material, texture, IPO, image, and library datablocks (see Figure 1.15). You can also use the Layer button to toggle the Outliner view to display only visible layers or to display all layers.

Figure 1.15

Toggle buttons for viewing object types in the outliner

In the View menu in the drop-down header of the Outliner window, you can select the Outliner view, which gives a different visualization of the data in your file, as can be seen in Figure 1.16. As in the OOPS schematic view, you can select the datablocks, and you are put in the appropriate mode to edit the datablock you selected.

Figure 1.16

Outliner view

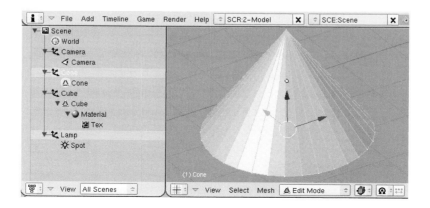

Accessing Data from Different Files

It is often necessary to have access to objects or datablocks from other files. Animation projects can quickly get far too big to want to store in single .blend files, and yet many different scenes and shots are likely to share the same main elements. There are several ways to access datablocks between separate files in Blender.

The first and simplest way is to use *append.* To append a datablock from another file, select Append from the File menu or press Shift+F1. A Data Browser window opens, in which you can access .blend files stored on your computer and their contents. In the Data Browser window, when you click the name of the file, you see a list of datablock types, just as if they were directories. Enter the appropriate type directory; you see a list of the datablocks of that type available for appending. Here is another place to be aware of the difference between objects and object type datablocks. If you want to append a Mesh object from another file, for example, you find the object in the Object type directory instead of the Mesh type directory.

Another approach to using data across separate files is by linking the datablocks. Linking can be done similarly to appending, except that in the Data Browser header, the Link button is selected instead of Append. In this case, the data can be edited only in the file from which it was originally linked, and all edits appear in the files that linked to the data.

Groups

Objects can be collected together into named groups using the Add to Group button in the Object Buttons area, seen in Figure 1.17. Groups themselves can then be treated as an object type when appending, allowing you to append whole collections of objects easily.

User Preferences

At present, it's not possible to configure your own hotkey bindings in Blender. However, a number of interface options exist, and you can look at these in the User Preferences window that you had a glimpse of earlier. By default, the ToolTips option is turned on, so hovering your mouse over the various buttons and options brings up a brief explanation of each. Under View & Controls, you can select from a number of options that affect how the interface works. Most of them are self-explanatory, and you should experiment with which kind of controls suit your workflow best. The Themes button allows you to select from two button shape options and create a color scheme for your Blender desktop. The Edit Methods panel allows you to adjust your levels of undo. The auto-keyframing option can also be accessed here (it will be discussed in more detail in the animation section of this book). Most of the other preferences panels are not of direct interest to you for the purposes of this book.

Figure 1.17

Add to Group button

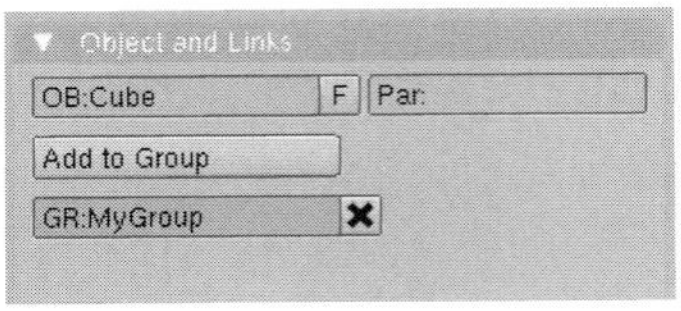

After you have the configuration the way you like it, press Ctrl+U. You are prompted to Save User Defaults. If you say yes to this, a file will be created in your `.blender` directory called `.B.blend`. From that point on, when you open Blender it will be in the same state that you saved the user defaults, including which windows are open, and even includes the contents of the 3D window. If you start up Blender ordinarily and find something amiss each time you start up, it is possible that you inadvertently saved a user default file that you had not intended to. To return everything to its default state, simply delete the `.B.blend` file in your `.blender` directory. On my system, that directory is here:

```
C:\Program Files\Blender Foundation\Blender\.blender
```

You can experiment with all these user options. There's a lot to play around with, in terms of look and feel. As long as you don't press Ctrl+U, all settings will return to default on your next startup. For the rest of this book, we assume most things to be in their default configuration, and the screen shots will all show the default theme.

Now that we've covered the basics of the Blender interface and the datablock system, you're ready to get your hands dirty and begin to do some modeling.

CHAPTER 2

Working with Meshes

In Blender, as in many 3D animation programs, the basic object type for use in character modeling is the mesh. Two of the main methods of character animation, armatures and shape keys, are best-suited for use with meshes. For this reason, although you can use other modeling techniques, such as NURBS, Bezier curves, and metaballs, they should be converted to meshes eventually to make the best use of these techniques. Perhaps because of this, Blender's mesh modeling tools have attained a higher level of usability than its other modeling tools. At the time of this writing, improvements are planned for Blender's NURBS modeling tools, but at present Blender favors polygon modeling.

This chapter looks at Blender's main tools for character modeling. You'll look at several different approaches, and by the end you will have built a fairly complex character mesh, which you will texture, rig, and animate in later chapters. If you prefer to skip these modeling tutorials and get straight to the next step, check the DVD for the appropriate `.blend` file to start with. The tutorials in this chapter should result in the same mesh that you will find in the `CB-Model-base_mesh.blend` file, so you can use that file to start on the next chapter's tutorials. However, if you are interested in learning to model characters in Blender, follow the tutorials in this chapter before moving on and use the `.blend` file as an additional reference.

- **Polygons and Subsurfacing**
- **Blender Modifier System**
- **Extrusion Modeling and Box Modeling**

Polygons and Subsurfacing

Polygon modeling refers to modeling shapes defined as collections of vertices connected by straight edges, which in turn form polygonal faces. These shapes are called *meshes*. Editing a mesh involves adding, removing, or moving vertices, edges, and faces.

The time it takes the computer to calculate 3D information about a mesh depends primarily on the number of vertices (verts) in the mesh. For this reason, it is best to use the fewest possible vertices to accurately represent the desired shape of your mesh. There is also another reason to do this: meshes with fewer vertices are easier to edit. If you have too many vertices, it becomes difficult to keep the surfaces of your mesh as smooth and even as with fewer vertices.

Because it requires a very large number of flat polygons and straight edges to give the illusion of rounded, organic surfaces, Blender uses another method of calculating the surface of a mesh based on its polygon structure, called Catmull-Clark subdivision surfacing (also called *subsurfacing* or simply *subsurfing*). Subsurfacing in this manner involves breaking each polygon in the mesh into smaller component polygons—subdivisions—to greatly increase the appearance of smoothness of the surface. The calculations are simple enough that the computer can do them on the fly much more quickly than it would take it to keep track of an equivalent number of real vertices.

Let's return to the two objects from Chapter 1, Cube and Cone, and their associated meshes. Select the Cube object. Subsurfacing is done in Blender by adding a subsurface modifier to a mesh object. In the Modifiers tab in the Buttons window, click Add Modifier and select Subsurf from the drop-down, as shown in Figure 2.1.

As you can see, with the subsurf modifier turned on at level one, the cube's surface takes on a different, smoother shape. In the Levels field on the subsurf modifier panel, change the value to 2. Now you have something that begins to resemble a sphere. Optimal values for subsurfacing are 2 for the Levels field and 3 for the Render Levels field. This means subsurfacing will be smoother when you actually render, which is appropriate. Higher values for these fields are unnecessary and can lead to serious slowdowns and even freeze your computer.

Although the cube now looks a lot smoother than it did before, it still looks like flat surfaces forming a sphere. To change this, it is not necessary to add more subsurface levels. Rather, you can simply change the way Blender calculates shading, giving the illusion of a smooth surface, by selecting Set Smooth in the Links and Materials tab in the Buttons window. Do this on the Cube object and you will see how much smoother it appears.

Let's try the trick from Chapter 1 again, and replace the Cube mesh data with the Cone mesh data on the Cube object. A couple of things are worth noting. First of all, the Cone shape is now subsurfaced. The subsurf modifier acts on the mesh *object* and therefore swapping in new mesh data will not change the subsurfacing. You now have a subsurfaced Cone shape.

Figure 2.1

Adding a subsurf modifier

The second thing, or maybe the first thing, you'll notice about this subsurfaced Cone shape is that it doesn't look very good. At any rate, it's not what you would call smooth, as you can see in Figure 2.2. This is an illustration of the problem that one often hears about with regard to triangles and subsurfacing. Because of the nature of the subsurfacing calculation, triangles often do not subsurface smoothly, and the more elongated the triangles are, the more pronounced this problem is.

Figure 2.2

A subsurfed cone made of triangles

In general, conventional polygon modeling wisdom holds that triangles are to be avoided. As you can see in Figure 2.3, the same cone subsurfaces much more smoothly when you make some cuts and change the geometry to quads. In fact, equilateral triangles subsurface reasonably well in many situations, but the reality of mesh deformations means that any triangle on your mesh in a place that is animated cannot stay equilateral all the time. For this reason, triangles should be avoided in places on your mesh that are visible and intended to be animated. As for the use of other n-sided polygons, which are an option in some modeling software, Blender makes the choice easy. You can't use them. Quads and triangles are the only polygons that Blender supports. Which means you'll be using a lot of quads.

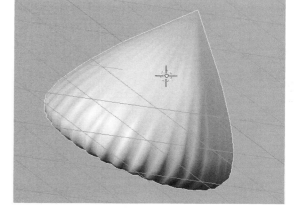

Blender Modifier System

As you just saw in the case of subsurfacing, certain qualities can be imposed on a mesh object by use of modifiers. A variety of modifiers are available to create special effects, but you will only be looking at the modifiers most pertinent to character modeling and animation. In addition to the subsurf modifier, these modifiers include the following:

Figure 2.3

A cone modeled with quads

Mirror This modifier displays a virtual mirror image of the mesh across a selected axis (the default is X). This is very useful for modeling symmetrical objects such as faces and bodies.

Lattice This modifier associates a mesh with a lattice object, allowing for simple deformations of the mesh. This is often used for distorting the shape of a mesh in unrealistic ways, and is useful for cartoon effects such as stretching and squashing and bugging eyes.

Armature This modifier associates a mesh object with an armature object for figure posing.

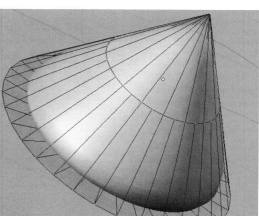

Modifiers all share certain options. You can toggle the display of the modified form of the mesh with these buttons, which are located to the immediate right of the modifier's name:

The leftmost button toggles the display of the modified mesh in the rendered view, the middle button toggles the display in the 3D View window in general, and the rightmost button specifically toggles the display of the modifier in the 3D View in Edit mode.

All modifiers also have the options to "copy" and "apply" the modifier. Copy simply means to create an identical modifier at the same place in the modifier stack as the original. Apply deletes the modifier and applies its effects to the mesh, creating a new, unmodified mesh, which is identical to the modified form of the original mesh. Care should be taken with this option. It is usually not necessary to apply a subsurface modifier, for example, and a mirror modifier should be applied only when all edits requiring mirroring have been finished.

NURBS MODELING

NURBS (non-uniform rational B-splines) are a way to define curved lines and surfaces that are more precise, more compact, and more restrictive in terms of modeling than subsurfaced meshes. NURBS is an older method for creating organic shapes using CG, but since the rise of subsurface modeling, NURBS modeling has fallen from favor somewhat for character modeling purposes, depending upon the specific 3D application. Current uses of NURBS tend to focus on industrial design, where precision is more important than it is in character animation. (Precision measurement in general is not a strong suit of Blender, making it inadequate at present as a CAD application.) Blender has NURBS modeling capabilities, but it has much better support for mesh modeling. The only real reasons for a character modeler to use NURBS in Blender are to apply specific, personally preferred modeling methods or to follow habits acquired using more NURBS-oriented software. Another drawback of using NURBS for character modeling in Blender is the limitations on armature modification available for NURBS. Although NURBS surfaces can take armature modifiers, it is not possible to create vertex groups or do weight painting on NURBS surfaces, and armatures are limited to using envelopes to influence the surface. I'll talk more about what this means and why it is so restrictive in Chapter 4. For now, it should suffice to say that meshes in Blender can be much more responsive to armatures than NURBS surfaces are. This all might change in the future because Blender's possible development plans include improvements in the NURBS modeling interface, and if there is a demand for it, someone might improve the NURBS rigging system as well. Even if such improvements are made, however, it is likely that this would mainly improve Blender's usefulness to industrial designers, rather than significantly affecting how character modeling is best done in Blender.

Several NURBS primitives can be created by hitting Space to add an object and selecting Surface or Curve. The donut primitive available for NURBS is the one shape that is not available as a mesh primitive (although a donut shape is trivial to create with mesh modeling by adding a circle to represent the donut's cross-section and spinning it around the 3D cursor with the Spin modeling tool).

The tools available for modeling with NURBS are largely analogous to those available for mesh modeling (although there are far fewer).

As you create modifiers, they appear in order in a stack, which determines the order in which the modifiers are applied. The up and down arrow buttons on the modifier panel allow the modifier to be moved up or down in the stack. To the left of these arrows in some modifiers is a gray circle. This button toggles the application of the modifier to the edit cage, which you will see more of later in this chapter.

To see an example of how the resulting mesh can differ according to the order in which the modifiers are applied, create a new file in Blender and select the default cube. In the Modifiers tab, choose Add Modifier → Mirror. Now enter Edit mode. Select all vertices by pressing the A key. Move the entire cube one Blender unit (BU) to the right along the X axis. To do this, press G and X in succession, and hold down Ctrl while you move the object with the mouse to turn on incremental snapping. As you move the cube to the right, you will see the cube's mirror image moving to the left. When you have moved the cube one BU, the cube and its mirror image will be flush with each other, as in Figure 2.4(a). Now, add a subsurface modifier in the same way that you added the mirror modifier. Set the levels at 2. You should end up with the peanut-like shape you see in Figure 2.4(b). In this case, the mesh being subsurfaced is not the original cube, but the mirror-modified cube. If you want to subsurface the original cube and mirror-modify the resultant mesh, you need to bump the subsurface modifier up so it is applied before the mirror modifier. Do this by clicking the up arrow on the subsurface modifier (or the down arrow on the mirror modifier, of course). The resulting modified mesh, as you can see in Figure 2.6, is two separate sphere shapes. Note now that if you go ahead and apply both of these modifiers (you must apply modifiers in top-down order), you wind up with a single mesh object, whose mesh consists of two sphere shapes, as in Figure 2.7, which can no longer be edited in the same way as the previous mirrored cube.

You will look more closely at the various modifiers and their uses later in the book.

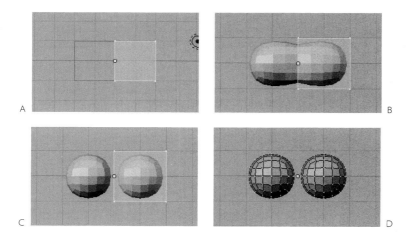

Figure 2.4

The effect of modifiers on meshes: (A) a mirrored cube; (B) the cube mirrored and then subsurfaced; (C) the cube subsurfaced and then mirrored; (D) the mesh with the modifiers applied

Extrusion Modeling and Box Modeling

Although there is a fairly fixed set of basic tools used in polygon modeling, there are several possible approaches to take to modeling. Broadly speaking, the various approaches fall into two main classes: *extrusion modeling* (often referred to as "poly by poly" modeling) and *box modeling.* In extrusion modeling, the modeler starts with a small portion of a model—which could be a polygon, or an edge, or even just a point—and works outward from this starting point using extrusion and other tools. In box modeling, the modeler begins with a simple 3D object, often a cube, and uses subdivision and cuts to mold the shape into the desired model.

These approaches are not mutually exclusive. In fact, construction of even a marginally complex model usually incorporates elements of both approaches. All polygon modeling makes use of extrusion and subdivision, so drawing a clear distinction between these modeling approaches is of limited value. Nevertheless, although it is largely a matter of personal preference, whether you choose to start with a cube to build your model or start with a single polygon or vertex will determine the subsequent steps you need to take to create your model.

Because the two methods differ in the emphasis they place on various tools, it is good practice to go through concrete examples of both.

Modeling a Human Head with Extrusion Modeling

Although it is necessary to keep in mind how the geometry will develop, extrusion modeling allows for a lot of freedom in where you place vertices at the beginning of the modeling process. In this example, it enables you to trace the outline of a photograph closely.

The first thing you need to do is set up the work areas so that you can see the background images you want to use to guide your modeling. First, you delete the default cube with the X key and split the 3D View window into two halves by right-clicking on its top or bottom border and choosing Split Area; then moving the vertical line to the middle of the 3D View and left-clicking to split the area into two equal-sized 3D viewports.

In the left window, click 1 on the numeric keypad. In the right area, click numeric 3. This puts you in the position of viewing along the Y axis and the X axis, respectively, which are considered here to be front and left side views.

You will now load the front view image and the right side view image you have into the corresponding viewports. To load a background image, go to the View menu in the 3D View window header and select Background Image. Clicking on this opens a widget with a

Figure 2.5
Loading the background image

button reading Use Background Image. If you click this button, the widget will appear as shown in Figure 2.5. Click the file icon highlighted in the image to select an image, which opens a File Browser window in which you can select the image from your computer's file system. The File Browser is relatively straightforward, but it has a few quirks. The P (parent directory) button is used to move up in the directory hierarchy, to the parent directory of the present directory. Clicking on the double dot entry in the directory listing itself has the same effect. The button directly below the P button, with the up and down arrow icon, enables you to select a different drive to read from. (On the accompanying DVD, you can find the images in the Chapter 2 folder.) You will load the image `front.tif` in the viewport on the left and `side.tif` in the viewport on the right.

In the Background Image widget for the front view, note the X offset value. The default is zero, but it might need to be adjusted to get the photograph to line up as closely as possible to the centerline. Because you will begin modeling with a mirror modifier, the model will be perfectly symmetrical. Real faces are not perfectly symmetrical, so over the course of the modeling it might be necessary to adjust this X offset to account for the difference and to keep the model as close to the overall face as possible. Non-symmetrical modeling has to be done later.

If you plan to create your own background images, keep in mind that Blender calculates the default size based upon the width of the photograph. For this reason, it is simplest to work with photographs that have both the same height and width. The best thing is to crop your background image in an image manipulation program such as Gimp or Photoshop in such a way that the eye line, nose, and lips line up as closely as possible. There will always be inconsistencies in the view caused by perspective and slight shifts in the position of the subject.

Now that you have the background image in place and the views organized, you can get started. You'll start by adding a plane. Your 3D cursor should still be in the center of both views; if it isn't, left-click the center of the view to put it there, and then click Shift+S and select Snap Cursor to Grid to get it centered. The location of the 3D cursor determines where newly created objects will be. To create the plane, press the spacebar and select Add → Mesh → Plane from the menu that appears. Your work area should look like the one in Figure 2.6. You won't be using the manipulator right now, so you can toggle it off by clicking the small white hand icon on the header of the 3D window.

Next, apply a mirror modifier, as you did earlier in the chapter during the discussion on modifiers, and move the plane along the X axis until the plane's edge is flush with the mirror image's edge (see Figure 2.7). Do this by pressing G followed by X to constrain the translation to the X axis. To get a better view of the reference image, you can toggle the object's transparency by pressing the Z key.

Select and delete the vertical edge furthest from the center. You'll be left with a single mirrored edge up the center of the nose.

While editing with a mirror modifier, select the Do Clipping option to ensure that your center verts stay flush with the mirror axis. This process also ensures that overlaps do not occur when you scale or extrude portions of the mesh.

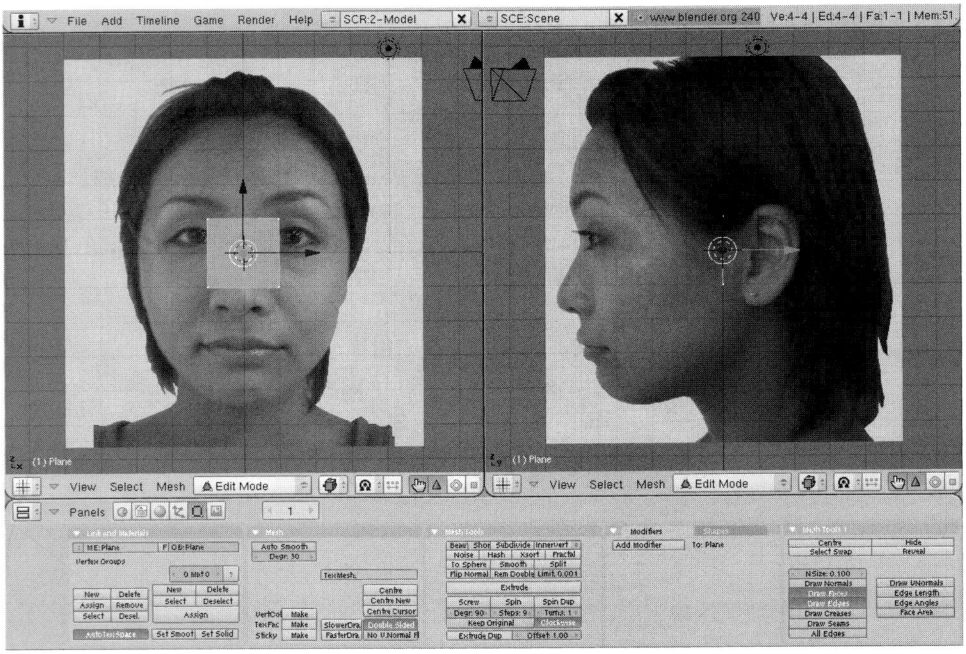

Figure 2.6

Adding a plane over the background image

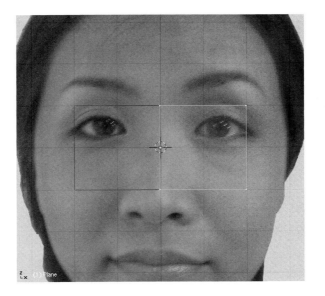

Figure 2.7

Mirroring the plane

Now you will use the Extrude tool to trace the outline of the profile. Be sure to do the next steps in the side view window, so that the vertices you create remain on a plane with relation to the X axis and that the line up the middle of the face remains straight. First move the edge forward (G, Y) until it is in the vicinity of the front of the face and then extrude from its end points. To do this, select one of the end vertices of the edge and Ctrl+left-click. You can also extrude with the E key, but for extrusion like this, Ctrl+LMB is much more efficient. Note that if you do not have any vertex selected, Ctrl+left-click creates a new vertex unconnected to the rest of the mesh. You'll be using that later, but for now you want to keep the verts connected.

Create the profile of the face (see Figure 2.8) by extruding vertices and moving them around with G.

In the front view outline, create the lips by extruding single verts out from the center-line's upper lip vert. Connect the last two verts by selecting them both and pressing F to create an edge between them, resulting in something like Figure 2.9.

When you are extruding the lip outline, it might be possible that you don't see your changes mirrored on the left side of the model. If this is the case, you are probably viewing in Solid mode, which displays only mirrored faces. Pressing the Z key shows the wire frame model properly mirrored.

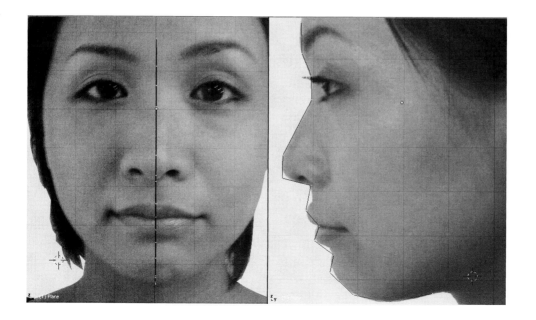

Figure 2.8

Outlining the profile of the face

Figure 2.9

Outlining the lips

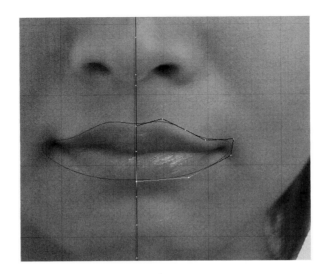

The lip outline you made here lies on the plane of the current view. You want the lips to follow the curve of the face and you'll use the proportional editing tool for this. This enables you to edit certain vertices and have other vertices follow along in proportion to how close they are to the verts you're working on. This is a very handy tool for creating curved surfaces in meshes, among other things. Proportional editing can be turned on and off with the O key or by selecting from the drop-down menu in the 3D viewport header. You also have the option to select connected proportional editing in the drop-down menu. This method allows proportional editing for verts that are within the area of influence but only if they are connected directly to the edited verts by edges that are also within the area of influence. Turn proportional editing on now, and from the falloff options drop-down menu that appears, select Sharp Falloff.

Select the two verts on the edge of the mouth outline, and in side view click G and Y to move them to match the shape of the lips. The gray circle you see represents the area of influence of the proportional edit. You can change its size using the mouse wheel or by using the + key and – key. It should be about the size you see in Figure 2.10. If you can't see the gray circle, it might be too big to see. Double-check that proportional editing is turned on and try it again, hitting the – key repeatedly to bring the circle into view.

After you finish, turn proportional editing off. In the same way you defined the edge of the lips, extrude the vertices to create the basic geometry of the face. As you go, adjust the vertices position along the Y axis so that they conform approximately to the shape of the face in the side view. Also, check your shape from other angles. (When not in a straight-on angle, the background image is invisible. When you return to one of the number-key views, it comes back into view.) Continue to extrude and move verts until you have a shape like the one in Figure 2.11. Be sure that you have the same number of verts and that they are placed exactly as you see them in the figure because their placement becomes important later on in the modeling.

Take note of the geometry you've begun to construct at this point. Several important features are already established, which are important regardless of what modeling technique you use. Both the eyes and the mouth are already being constructed of loops. As you continue to model, you will keep the eyes and mouth in this form. Even when you model

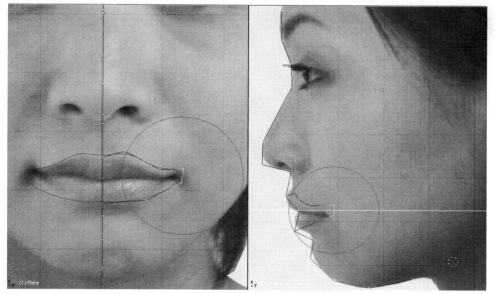

Figure 2.10

Moving multiple verts with proportional editing

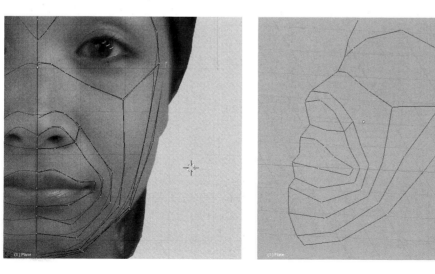

Figure 2.11

The basic geometry of the face should look like this

a different character later using box modeling, you will still make sure that the mouth and eyes are loops and that the loops extend and overlap in a way that includes the nose and cheeks within an unbroken pattern of loops. This is important from an animation perspective. You might be able to get away with different underlying geometry for a still model, but if you intend to animate facial expressions, you'll find that the human face is unforgiving in terms of the necessary geometry.

You need to make the eye outline now. To do this, create a vert in front view by Ctrl+left-clicking with no verts selected. You can extrude from this vert to create the outline of the eye, as in Figure 2.12. Once again, the number of verts shown is important because you will later need to connect the eye to rest of the face, so be sure to follow the example exactly.

LOOPS AND GEOMETRY

The term "geometry" is used to refer to the underlying structure of the mesh. Identical-looking meshes can have different underlying structures, and for beginning modelers it is easy to get caught up in making the shape look right, at the expense of paying attention to the actual structure. When making models for animation, however, it is very important to consider the underlying structure because it will determine how the mesh deforms when you begin to add shapes or poses.

Geometry is important because of the way the edges and vertices provide "tension" by holding the surface in place. Think of an umbrella: an open umbrella is shaped something like a hemisphere, made of cloth and held in its shape by a geometry of edges extending from the tip. It is possible to construct a similar hemisphere of cloth by using concentric rings, for example, but such a structure clearly does not fold like an ordinary umbrella. This is somewhat analogous to how edges influence the deformation of a mesh. To get the correct geometry, it is important to take into consideration what deformations you want from the mesh.

Loops are continuous sequences of edges ("edge loops") or faces ("face loops") that define the surface of a subdivided form. Loops might completely encircle some section of the mesh, but this is not necessarily the case. Not all edges or faces are part of a loop. Edge loops can be selected in their entirety by using Alt+RMB; you should try selecting a few edges in your model in this way to get a sense for what Blender recognizes as edge loops. Loops are very important in facial modeling; without correct loop structure in the face, it is very difficult to get good facial deformations. Good loop structure is especially critical in the mouth and nose area.

For the best deformations, the flow of the loops should approximately follow the shape of the muscles of the face because they determine how the shape of the face will change and the directions along which the skin will stretch. As you progress through this tutorial, you should pay close attention to the way edges and faces create loops. Further study of facial anatomy and musculature can also be very helpful.

Figure 2.12

Outlining the eye

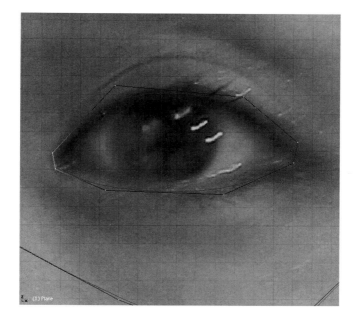

Fix the shape of the eye outline to follow the eye in the background image by translating the appropriate verts along the Y axis, as with the rest of the face.

Begin to fill in the faces. To fill in faces, select four verts at a time and press the F key.

The faces you fill in will also appear in the mirrored portion of the model. Fill in the faces, four verts at a time. You'll also extrude a bit more up from the eyebrow, by selecting the series of verts over the eye and pressing the E key followed by the Z key to extrude straight upward. For these steps, follow Figure 2.13 to ensure that you are creating faces in the correct places. It doesn't matter in what order you make the faces, but it does matter which vertices you select to make faces with. Make sure that your facial geometry matches that of the figure. Then, under modifiers, press Add Modifier and select subsurf. Put levels at 2 and render levels at 3. Select all vertices with the A key and click Set Smooth on the Link and Materials tab. Your face should look something like Figure 2.14. Make sure that your edges are laid out in the same way as the figure. If the solid view of your model shows some strangely shaded areas and seams, try pressing Ctrl+N (Recalculate Normals Outside).

To create the nose and nostrils, you extrude the region formed by the five faces from the current tip of the nose and draw them forward along the Y axis, as shown in Figure 2.15. After doing this, move the resulting vertices into place to form the shape of the nose (see Figure 2.16).

Figure 2.13

Creating the facial geometry from sets of four vertices at a time

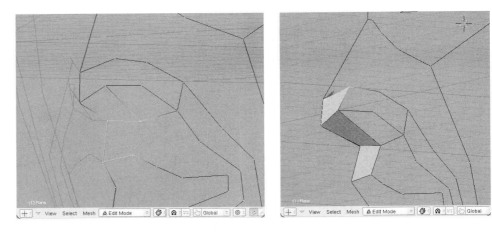

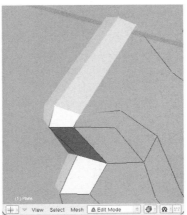

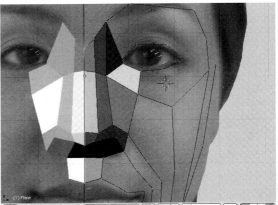

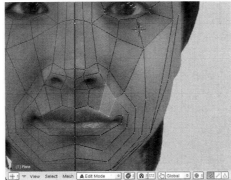

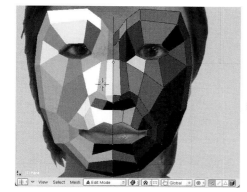

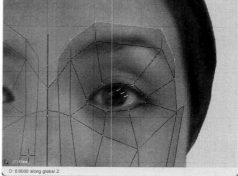

Figure 2.13
continued

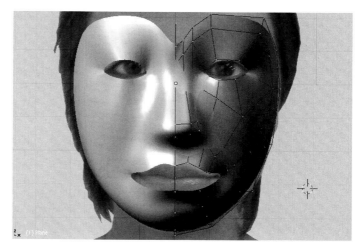

Figure 2.14
The subsurfaced face mesh

Figure 2.15
Extruding the region on the tip of the nose

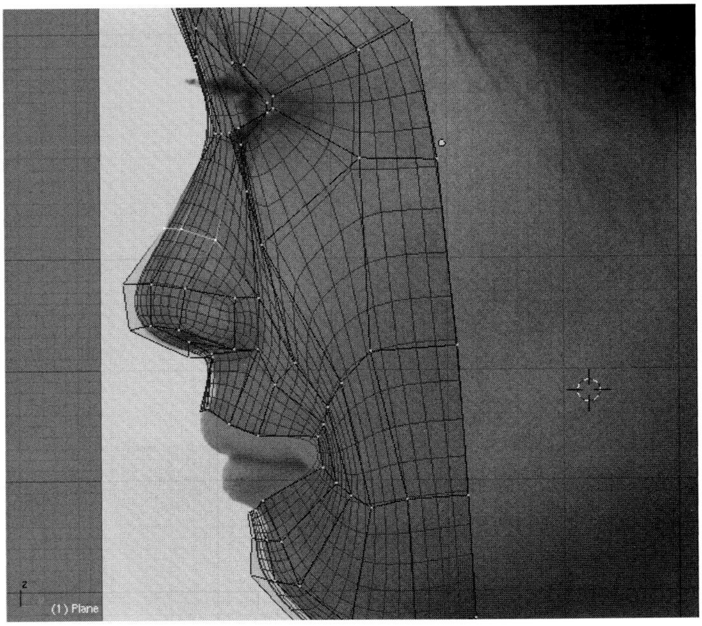

Figure 2.16

Pushing verts to shape the nose

After you have a clean mesh for the nose, extrude the two faces at the bottom of the nose and scale them down, as in Figure 2.17. Merge the three verts at the base of the nostril into a single vert as in Figure 2.18 by selecting them and using W→Merge. Choose the Merge Center option, which creates two pairs of triangles. Create quads by selecting the pairs of triangles and using the F key to create a four-sided face in their place.

Figure 2.17

Extruding to form the basis of the nostril

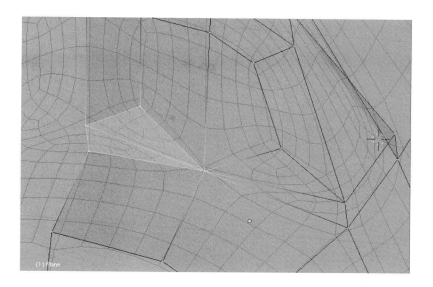

Figure 2.18

Merging excess verts

Extrude the nostrils twice and draw them upward into the nose, resizing them appropriately.

You'll create the indentation around the outside edge of the nostrils now. First cut the two faces over the tip of the nose using K → Knife (Exact). Draw the knife across the faces to cut them, as in Figure 2.19. This process results in several triangles being created. Select the two triangular faces that are flush against the cheek and press F to create a quad, as shown in Figure 2.20.

Select the side of the nose and the attached faces up into the nostril, and then cut these faces with K → Knife (Midpoints), as in Figure 2.21. This results in two triangles on the side of the nose. Select both of these faces and press F to create a quad.

Figure 2.19

A knife cut across the top of the tip of the nose

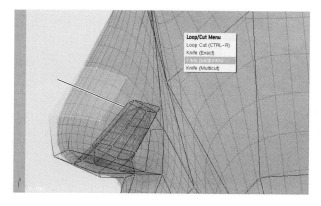

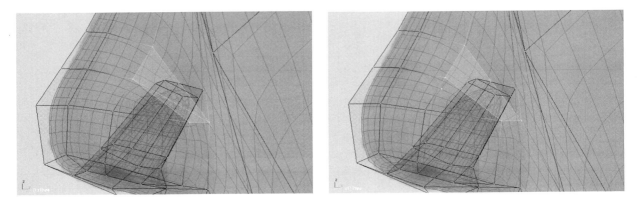

Figure 2.20

Creating a quad from the resulting triangles

To create the lips, snap the 3D cursor to the vert in the middle of the mouth area, as in Figure 2.22. After you snap the cursor there, delete the vert with the X key, but be sure not to move your 3D cursor off that spot. Select 3D Cursor from the Pivot Point drop-down menu in the 3D viewport header. Using the circle select tool (B B), select the verts around the edge of the mouth. (Alternatively, you can loop select the vertices in one step by using Alt+RMB on any edge of the mouth.) Extrude these edges three times. Each time, press the E key, followed by S, to scale the extrusion. You should scale each extrusion slightly in all directions; then scale it again slightly more in the Z direction only, which you can do with S, Z. After you extrude and scale the edges three times, you should have something similar to the lips in Figure 2.23. In side view, model the lip shape to conform to the background image. Don't forget to put your pivot point back to the Median Point. It might be confusing later if you forget that your pivot point is at the 3D cursor.

With the Loop Cut tool (Ctrl+R), add a loop around the lips and then add another one vertically from the bottom lip down the chin, as in Figure 2.24. Then make a loop cut around the eye and position it in side view, as in Figure 2.25.

Figure 2.21

A knife cut around the side of the nose and into the nostril

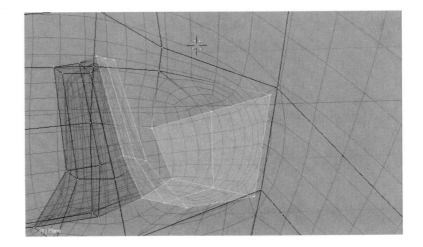

Select the edge of the eye and extrude and scale down slightly; then extrude again and move the new edge back along the Y axis, as in Figure 2.26.

You now add some eyeballs. In Object mode, snap the cursor to the face object and add a UV sphere with 12 rings and 12 sections, as in Figure 2.27. Apply a mirror and a subsurf modifier to the sphere, set it smooth, and move it into the place of the eyeballs. As you can see in Figure 2.27, you now need to edit the face mesh around the eyeballs to make sure that they are convincingly housed inside the face. Do this by moving the vertices of the eyelid forward little by little so the eyelid covers the eye and by adjusting their position as necessary. It can be a challenge to edit the eyelid's shape to match the eye nicely, so it is best to be patient and do it incrementally.

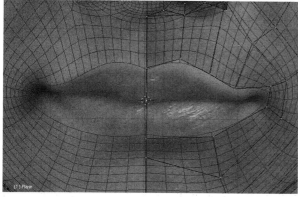

Figure 2.22

Snapping the cursor to the vert in the middle of the mouth

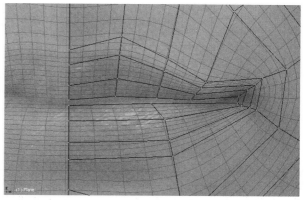

Figure 2.23

Extruding the edges of the lips

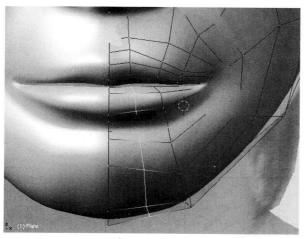

Figure 2.24

A few loop cuts added to the mouth area

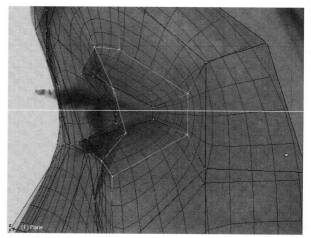

Figure 2.25

Positioning another loop around the eye

Figure 2.26

**Forming the edges
of the eyelids**

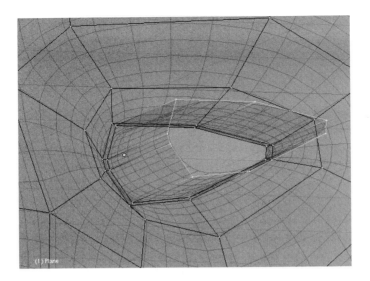

Extrude and edit the edge of the face as in Figure 2.29; then separate two verts at the
bottom and extrude a new vert with Ctrl+RMB (see Figure 2.30) to transition to the neck.
The remainder of the head can be constructed simply by extruding edges and filling in
faces to create the structure seen in Figure 2.31. The final model should look something

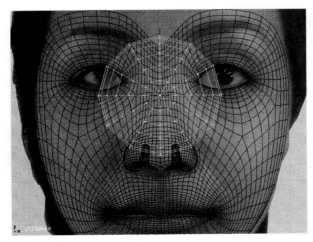

Figure 2.27

Adding a sphere to create eyeballs

Figure 2.28

Positioning the eyeballs

like Figure 2.32. For space reasons, I won't go into modeling the ear. You can experiment yourself with drawing an outline of the ear with verts and filling in and extruding to create the full shape. You can use a separate mesh object on a separate layer to do the ear and then join the ear with the head later. If you run into problems modeling the ear, see Chapter 18 for a list of online modeling tutorials that will help you out.

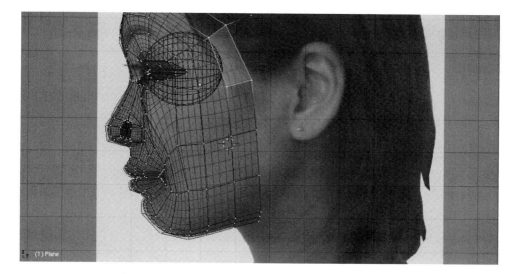

Figure 2.29

Extruding the edge of the face

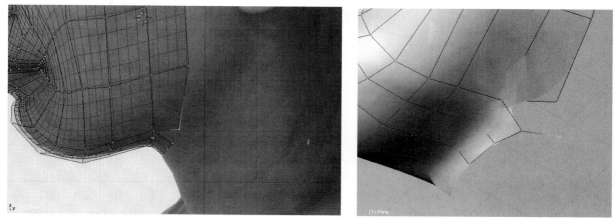

Figure 2.30

Editing verts to transition to the neck

Figure 2.31

A wireframe view of
the structure of
the head

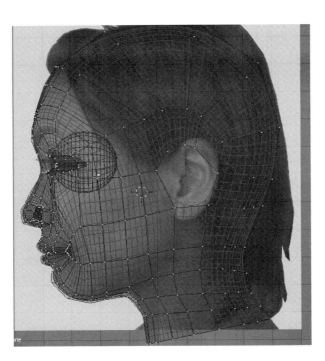

Figure 2.32

The finished mesh of
the head (sans ears)

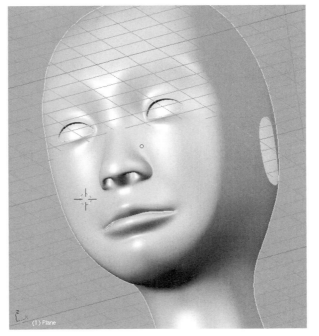

The mirror modifier works by making a mirrored duplicate of the mesh you're working on. After it is applied, these vertices become real. Adding another mirror modifier creates a new set of mirrored verts. If this is edited, the original unmirrored mesh remains unchanged, resulting in a variety of mesh problems. For this reason, it is not advisable to add a new mirror modifier after you have already applied one. One way around this limitation is to delete half the mesh before applying the second mirror modifier. However, it is best to try to get all your symmetrical editing done before applying the mirror modifier. If you're not sure you've done this, it might be best to save a backup file before applying the modifier.

Introducing Captain Blender: from Mild-Mannered Cube to Superhero

The next tutorial will follow the creation of a whole cartoon-style character using box modeling and will give you the basis for the character model that you will continue to work with and build on throughout the book. There is no reason why you could not use some variation of extrusion modeling, but because you want to focus on the overall shape of the body early on, box modeling is a good option. In contrast with the previous tutorial's example of starting with the details of the face and working outward to the shape of the head, box modeling enables you to quickly work out the proportions and then to focus on smaller and smaller areas of detail. Note again that these methods are not exclusive to each other. It is possible to model the head using extrusion modeling, model a body using box modeling, and then attach the head to the body. After you become accustomed to mesh modeling in Blender, you will find your own favorite approaches to modeling various kinds of objects and characters.

Getting Started: Legs and Feet

You will begin modeling in the same way as you did with the face in the previous tutorial, except you will not delete the default cube. Load the background images `capblend_front.tif` and `capblend_side.tif` from the DVD and set up your workspace similarly to in the previous example: with a front view and a side view 3D viewport open. Add a mirror modifier to the cube and move it off to one side, as in Figure 2.33. Again, be sure to select the Do Clipping option. Scale it up along the Z axis (S, Z) so that it extends from the top of the shoulder to about flush with the groin, and move the outside edges toward the center so it forms a rectangular box approximately the same size as the character's torso. With all verts selected, bring up the Specials menu with the W key and select Subdivide. Temporarily toggle Do Clipping off; extrude the bottom face down and scale it to create the thigh, as in Figure 2.34. Toggle Do Clipping back on.

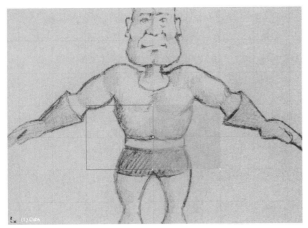

Figure 2.33

Applying a mirror modifier to the default cube

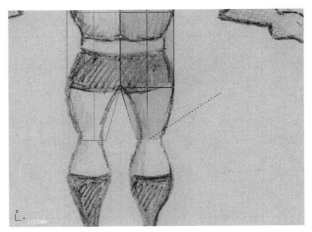

Figure 2.34

Extrude and scale to form the thigh

You'll apply the subsurface modifier now. There are several options for displaying the subsurface. By clicking the small gray circle to the right of the modifier name, you can enter Cage mode, which applies the subsurface model to the editing cage as you model. The editing cage is what you actually edit; with Cage mode option selected, it conforms tightly to the subsurfaced form of the mesh. Extrude and scale the loops of the legs until you get the basic shape shown in Figure 2.35. With Cage mode toggled off, the editing cage retains the shape of the unmodified mesh. You can toggle Cage mode on and off as the mood takes you; I do. Editing with Cage mode on or off is entirely a matter of personal preference.

Figure 2.35

The torso and legs so far, with subsurface applied to the editing cage

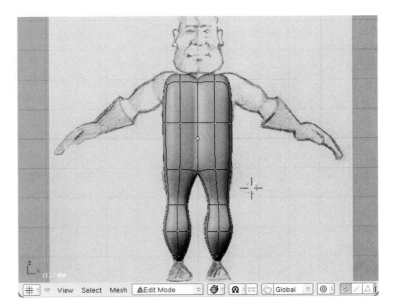

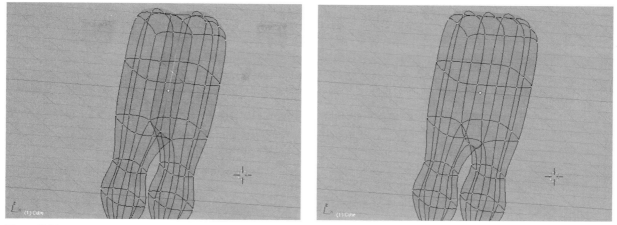

Figure 2.36

The torso with internal faces and with the faces removed

If you are viewing your model in Solid mode (Z key), notice that there is an indentation running down the mirror line of the model. This means that there are faces along the mirror line that must be removed. Use the Z key to enter into Wireframe mode and delete the vertex in the middle of the chest so that the shape looks like Figure 2.36.

Push verts around to get the mesh to conform generally to the shape of the background image in side and front view. Add a loop cut with Ctrl+R around the belt area and scale it down to create the outline of the waist (see Figure 2.37).

Figure 2.37

A loop cut at the belt area

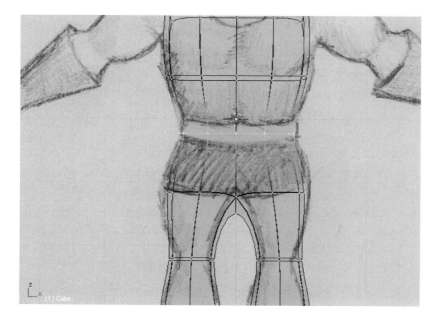

The method you used so far has produced some rather boxy legs, so round them out by selecting the verts shown in Figure 2.38 (a) and scaling them inward. (Alternately, you can loop select each circle of vertices and then use Ctrl+Shift+S to spherize them.) Select the bottommost vertex loop and extrude downward along the Z axis three times to create the ankles and begin the feet; then select the front two faces of the nubs, as shown in Figure 2.38 (b), to prepare to extrude the feet.

Extrude along the Y axis and scale along the X and Z axes three times in to create the shape of the feet, as in Figure 2.39. Then select the faces on the bottoms of the feet and flatten them by scaling in the Z axis to 0 (S, Z, 0); then extrude the soles downward, resulting in Figure 2.40.

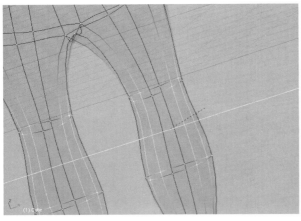
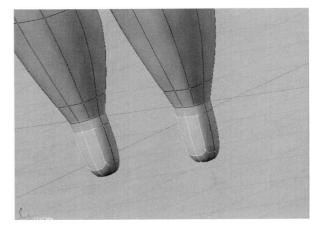

Figure 2.38
Rounding out the leg shape (A) and preparing to extrude the feet from the ankle area (B)

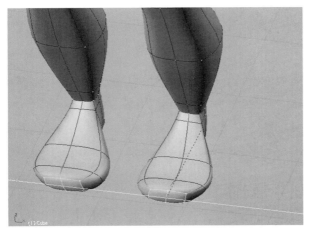
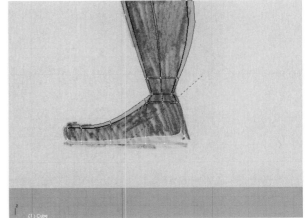

Figure 2.39
Extruding and shaping the feet

Figure 2.40
Scaling and extruding the soles of the feet

Scaling to zero along an axis is a very useful, general-purpose trick for lining up a collection of selected verts along a particular axis. Select the verts and scale with the S key and an axis key; then simply press 0 and finalize the transformation with a left click. A related trick: you can scale to -1 along any axis to "scale" the verts into a mirror image of their original formation!

At this point, your character's legs and hips should look something like Figure 2.41. You'll need to add some loops and pay attention to the form from several different views to get your model to look like Figure 2.41, but you should be able to do it by now. Your model doesn't need to look identical to mine, but try to get it as close as possible. I made the knees and ankles relatively narrow to simplify the rigging. Thick joints can require some extra attention when rigging, as you will see in the case of the shoulders in Chapter 5. Also, make sure that you have enough loops around the joints. Note that the edit cage in these illustrations is no longer fitted to the subsurface.

Torso and Arms

This section will focus on Captain Blender's upper body. As before, you will make a lot of use of loop cuts and extrusion, but you will also see the use of the knife tool to create new edges within selected faces. It is important to keep in mind what kinds of deformations you will want from the character when you come to animating him. This decision will influence how you model the arms.

Make another loop cut with Ctrl+R around the chest and another one just below the belt area, as shown in Figure 2.42; then select the eight faces shown in Figure 2.43. Using K → Knife (Midpoints), cut an oval path through the midpoints of the edges connecting these faces to result in a pattern of cuts (see Figure 2.44).

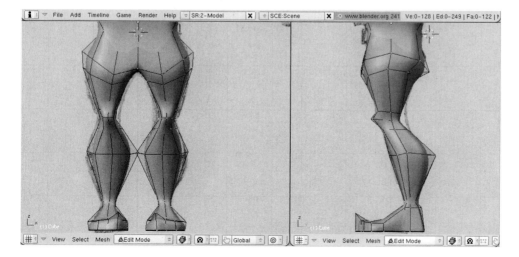

Figure 2.41

The lower body so far

Select the four faces at the shoulders and extrude outward twice (see Figure 2.44), scaling down and rotating slightly along the Y axis, to create the base of the arms. Add an edge loop around where the bottom of the rib cage should be, as shown in Figure 2.45, and begin to form the shape of the pectoral muscles and define the stomach muscles by selecting the edges shown in Figure 2.46 and drawing them forward along the Y axis.

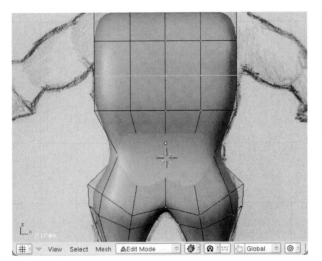
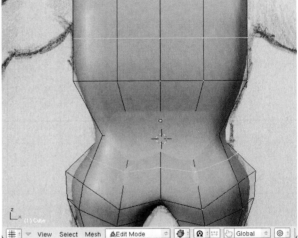

Figure 2.42

Loop cuts around the chest and waist

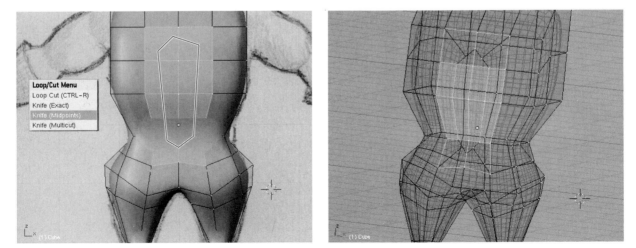

Figure 2.43

(A) Some more loop cuts on the torso and waist; (B) Using the knife tool to cut a pattern of edges

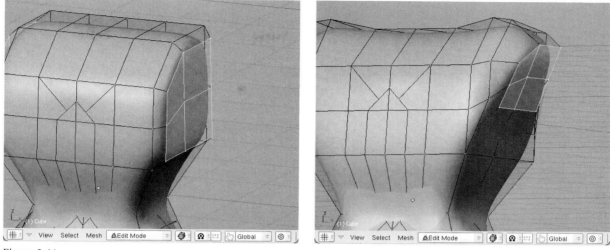

Figure 2.44
Extruding the shoulders

Extrude out the arms down to the wrist, as shown in Figure 2.47. Because Captain Blender is posing with his palms down, you want the arm mesh to be structured to deform nicely when rotated palms forward. You can prepare for this deformation by twisting the arm mesh slightly now. With the forearm section selected, move your view so that you are looking directly up the arm from the wrist, straight on, and rotate the forearm about 45 degrees counterclockwise. Then select the edge loop at the very end of the arm and rotate it another 45 degrees further. Now extrude the segments, which will become the hand (see Figure 2.48).

Hands and Gloves

This section looks at the details of creating the hands and the flared gloves. Once again, you will use all the techniques of the previous sections, while adding a few new ones, such as separating polys using the rip tool and stitching mesh segments again by creating faces.

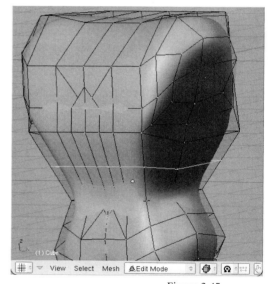

Figure 2.45
Add an edge loop around the bottom of the rib cage

Make two loop cuts in the hand and extrude the thumb, beginning as shown in Figure 2.49, and extruding several times, as shown in Figure 2.50.

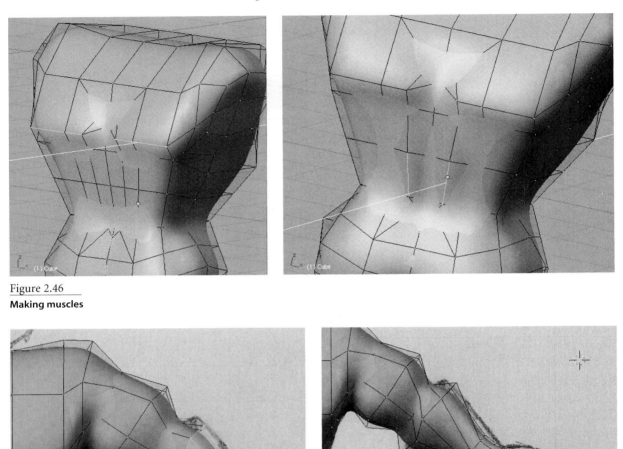

Figure 2.46

Making muscles

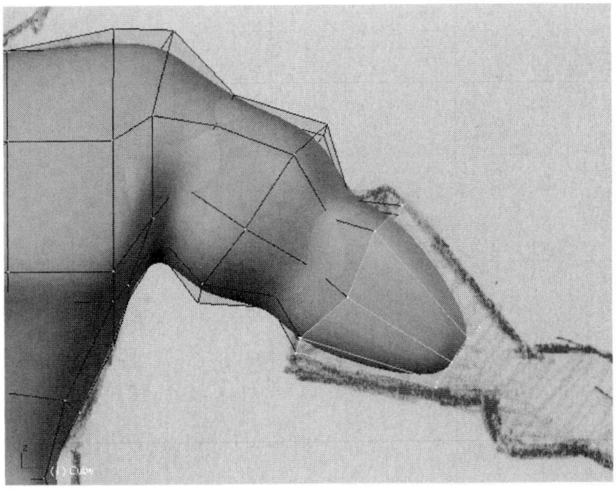

Figure 2.47

Extrude and scale to form the arm

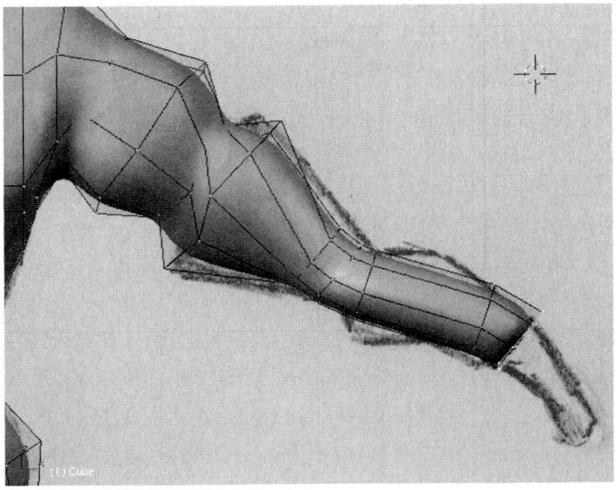

Figure 2.48

Extruding the basis of the hand

To make the basis for the fingers, use the Knife (Exact) tool (K key) to cut the through the four faces on the back of the hand, creating the edges shown in Figure 2.51. Delete the faces on the edge of the hand and make a similar knife cut in the palm of the hand, using six faces instead of four, resulting in the edges shown in Figure 2.52.

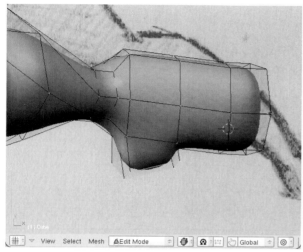

Figure 2.49
Extruding the base of the thumb

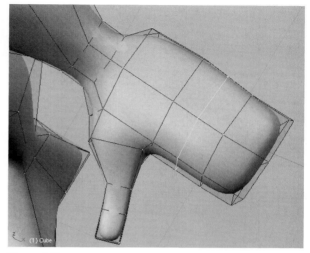

Figure 2.50
Beginning to form the hand

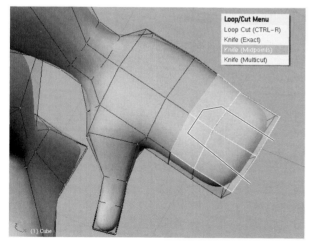

Figure 2.51
Cutting edges in the back of the hand

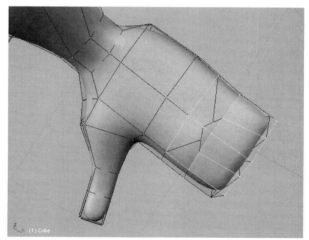

Close the open end of the hand by creating four quads; then cut the quads with the loop cut tool. Draw the new edge outward slightly along the X axis and then close up the open quads at either side, as shown in Figure 2.53. Extrude fingers from the four pairs of faces at the edge of the hand, as in Figure 2.54. You must do at least the first extrusion for each finger separately. Try doing all four sets of faces at once and see what happens. Don't worry if you have to spend some time pushing vertices around to get this just right; it's good practice. Try to get your model to look as similar to mine as you can.

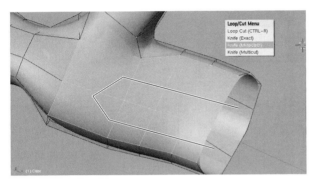

Figure 2.52
Cutting edges into the palm

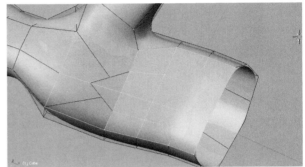

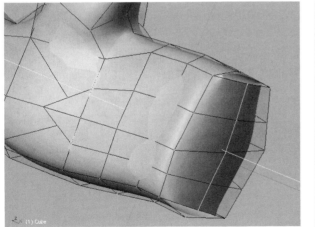

Figure 2.53
Closing up the hand mesh

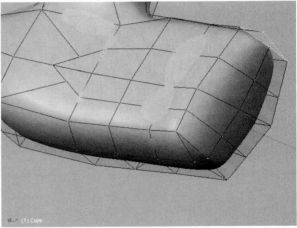

Get rid of the two diamond shapes at the base of the index finger by selecting the two verts shown in Figure 2.55, pressing the W key, selecting Merge, and then selecting At Center. Do the same thing to remove the diamond shapes at the base of the pinky. Your resulting mesh should look something like Figure 2.56.

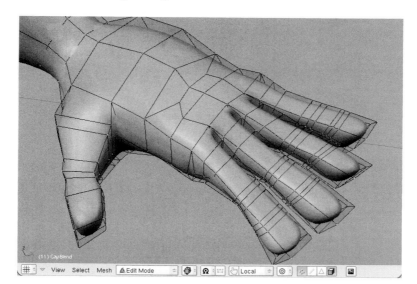

Figure 2.54

Forming the fingers

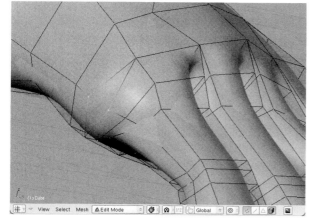

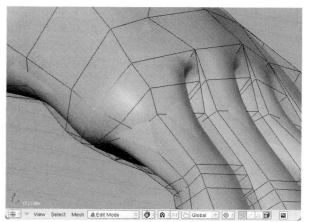

Figure 2.55

Merging excess vertices

Figure 2.56

The full hand

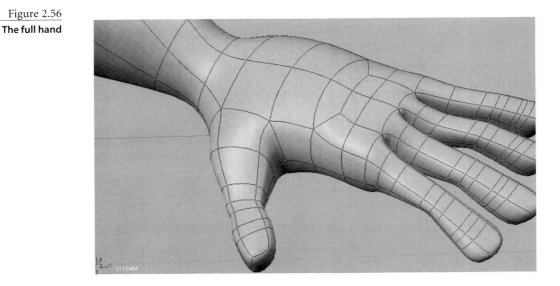

To make Captain Blender's gloves, select the loop just above the wrist with Alt+E and split it with the V key, resulting in a separation (see Figure 2.57).

Figure 2.57

Ripping the edge around the wrist with the V key

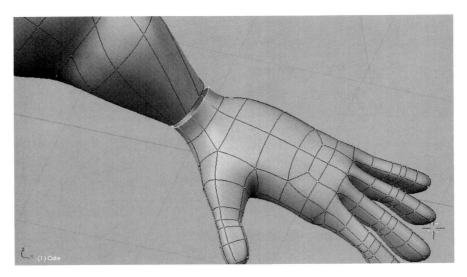

Extrude and scale the outer portion of the glove up, as in Figure 2.58; then do the same with the inner part. Connect the two together by selecting four verts at a time and using F to create quads.

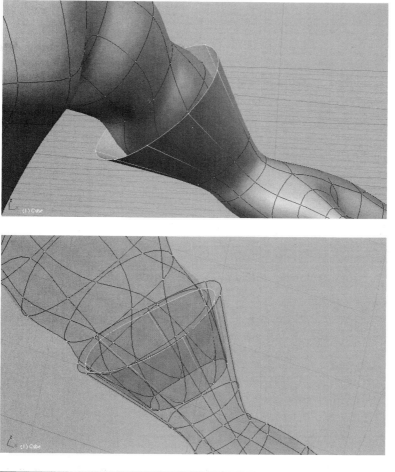

Figure 2.58

**Modeling the flare
of the glove**

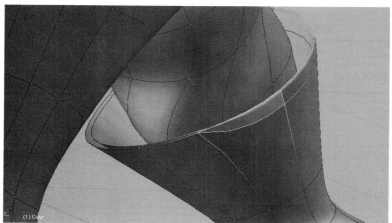

Collar and Belt

In this section, you'll model the collar and the belt. The collar will give you the chance to see how extrusion can be used to create tightly creased forms, such as the place where Captain Blender's neck meets his suit. The belt will be a separate mesh object that you will join to the body.

Turning to the point where the head will join the shoulders, select the top and center two (four, when mirrored) faces and cut edges in them with the Knife (Midpoints) tool, as shown in Figure 2.59. Delete the vertex in the center and widen the hole that remains to the size of the suit's neckline. Extrude twice straight down the Z axis and then again twice straight up the Z axis, as in Figure 2.60, to create the edge of the suit. Reposition all these new verts so that the extruded portion lies flush with the top of the shoulder area and extends flat back under the suit, as in Figure 2.61.

You will create the belt as a separate object and then join it to the main mesh. Press the Tab key to leave Edit mode on the mesh you are making. To create the belt, press numeric 7 to go into top view and add a cylinder with 12 sections. Add a subsurface modifier; then make two loop cuts around the perimeter: one near the top and one near the bottom. The extra edges created by the loop cuts give the belt a slight bevel. Position the belt and adjust it to follow the contours of the character's midsection, as in Figure 2.62. In this example, you created the belt as a separate object, so you must now join the meshes by selecting both mesh objects in Object mode and pressing Ctrl+J.

Figure 2.59

Cutting a hole in the suit

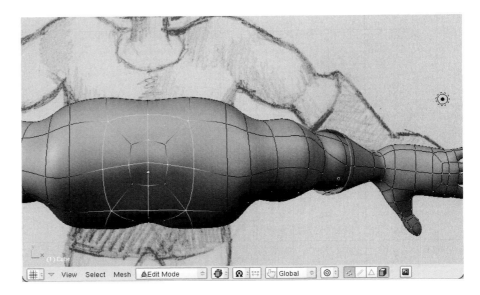

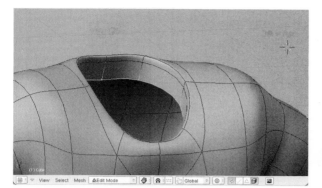
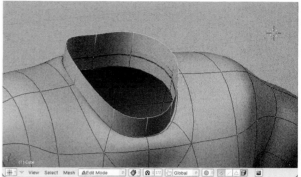

Figure 2.60
Extruding to create the edge of the suit

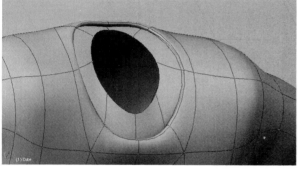
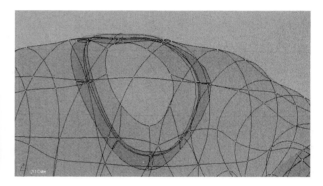

Figure 2.61
Forming the neckline

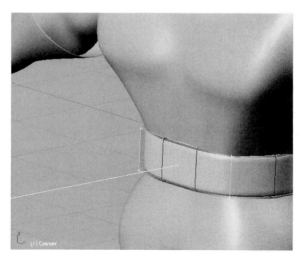

Figure 2.62
Making the belt

Figure 2.63

The body so far

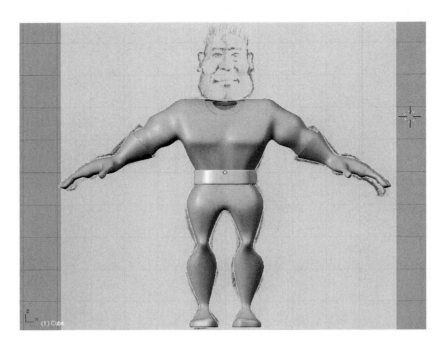

Figure 2.63

The body so far

You now have the body mostly finished, as can be seen in Figure 2.63. You'll model the head separately to begin with, so change to a different layer and add a new cube mesh object over the head of the background image. Use Shift+S → Snap Cursor to Grid to get the cursor properly centered before adding the cube.

Modeling the Head

Now turn to the head. You should try to have a balance between creating the face and head shape that you want and maintaining an underlying geometry structure that will make it easy to animate facial expressions later. The basic approach is to begin with a few loop cuts in a simple shape and to gradually add more and more detail using loop cuts, knife tool cuts, and other techniques. You begin by forming the general shape of the head and making the first few cuts to sketch out the layout of the facial features.

Use W → Subdivide Smooth (accepting the default smooth value of 1) to subdivide the cube into a shape like that shown in Figure 2.64. Select and delete the left side (your left, the character's right) of the head, leaving the right half and the center row of vertices; then add a mirror modifier. Scale and shape the head and add edge loops as in Figure 2.65.

Select the front area where the eyes will be and cut edges with the Knife (Midpoints) tool, as in Figure 2.66. From there, follow the series of illustrations beginning in Figure 2.68, making cuts with the K key tools (loop cut, exact knife, and midpoints knife), ripping the mesh with the V key where shown, and merging verts with the W key menu and moving verts as necessary to follow the illustrations. Often, after using the knife tool, you will find

Figure 2.64
The head cube subdivide smoothed

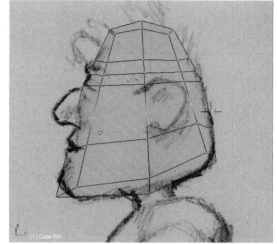

Figure 2.65
Shaping and loop-cutting the head

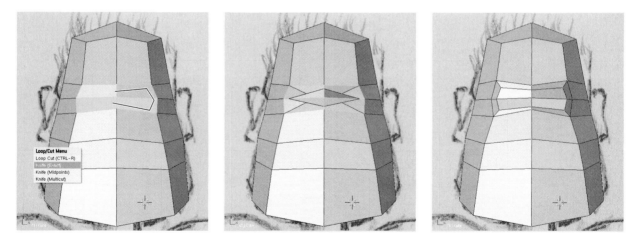

Figure 2.66
Cutting edges where the eyes will eventually be

that vertices need to be repositioned to give the shape you're after. Modeling a head can be tricky, so I have included .blend files for several intermediate stages of the head modeling process on the DVD, which you can refer to if you get lost following these steps. These files are called partial-head1.blend and partial-head2.blend. I identified the points that these files correspond to in the text. The final, full character mesh can be found in the file named CB-Model-base_mesh.blend on the DVD.

You now have a rough idea of the shape of the head and the locations of the features. You can begin to model the features, starting with the area around the mouth (Figure 2.68).

Now, you'll open up the neck by cutting a hole in the bottom of the mesh and deleting the appropriate area, as in Figure 2.69. You then concentrate on adding detail to the head (see Figure 2.70).

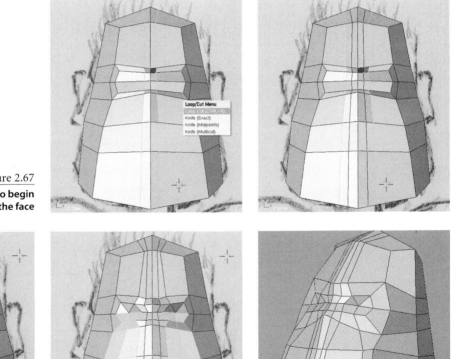

Figure 2.67

Follow the sequence of images to begin creating the face

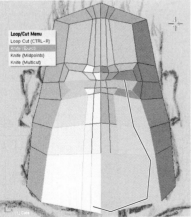
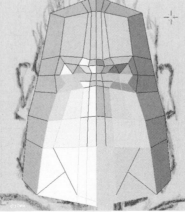
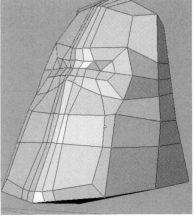

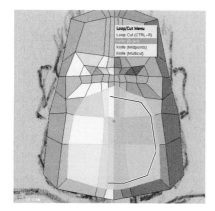

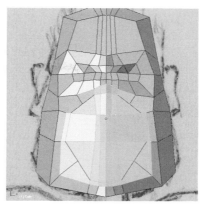

Figure 2.68

Forming the mouth area with several cuts

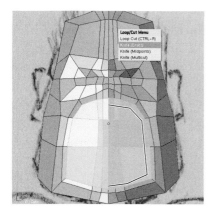

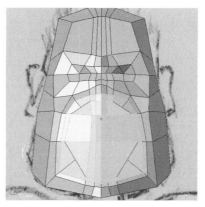

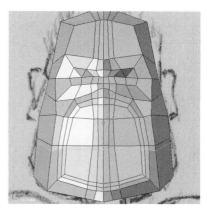

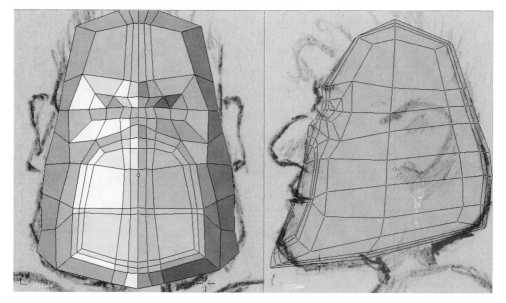

At this point, if you are having trouble following the steps, you might want to take a look at the `partial-head1.blend` file on the DVD, which will show you exactly how your mesh ought to look up to now. You now turn to modeling the nose, which is almost ready as it is. You just need to add one loop cut and pull the correct faces forward to give the nose its shape, as in Figure 2.71.

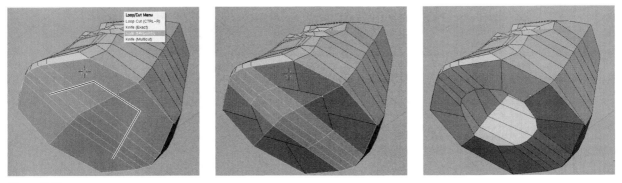

Figure 2.69
Opening up the neck

Figure 2.70
Adding detail to the head

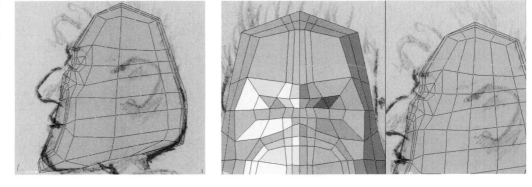

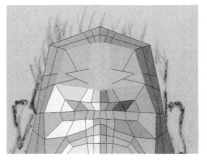
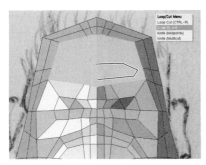

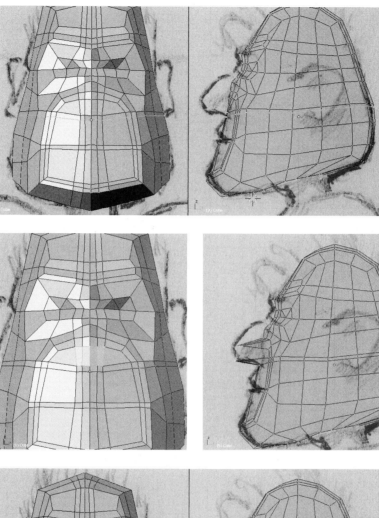
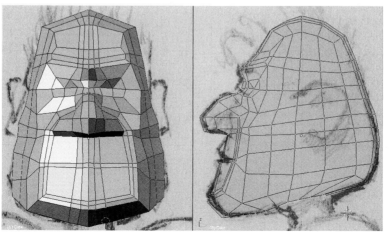

Figure 2.71
Modeling the nose

Now you'll make a few more loop cuts around the head, as in Figure 2.72.

You want to model the mouth a little bit differently than it is now. You do this by adding a knife cut to define the general area of the mouth and then deleting the faces inside this area, adding a few more edge loops, and extruding inward while scaling down several times, as in Figure 2.73. Then it is a matter of making some loop cuts and adding more and more detail (see Figure 2.75).

Figure 2.72

Loop cuts

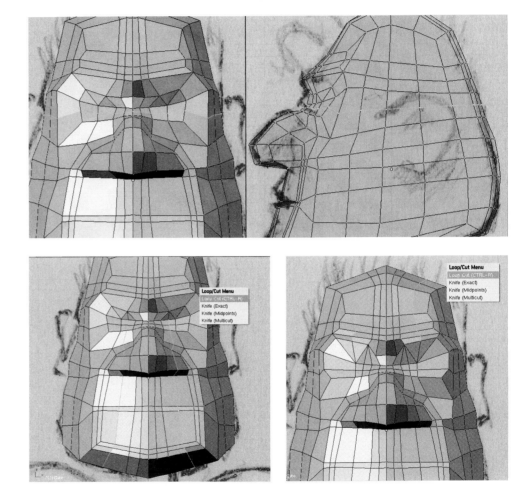

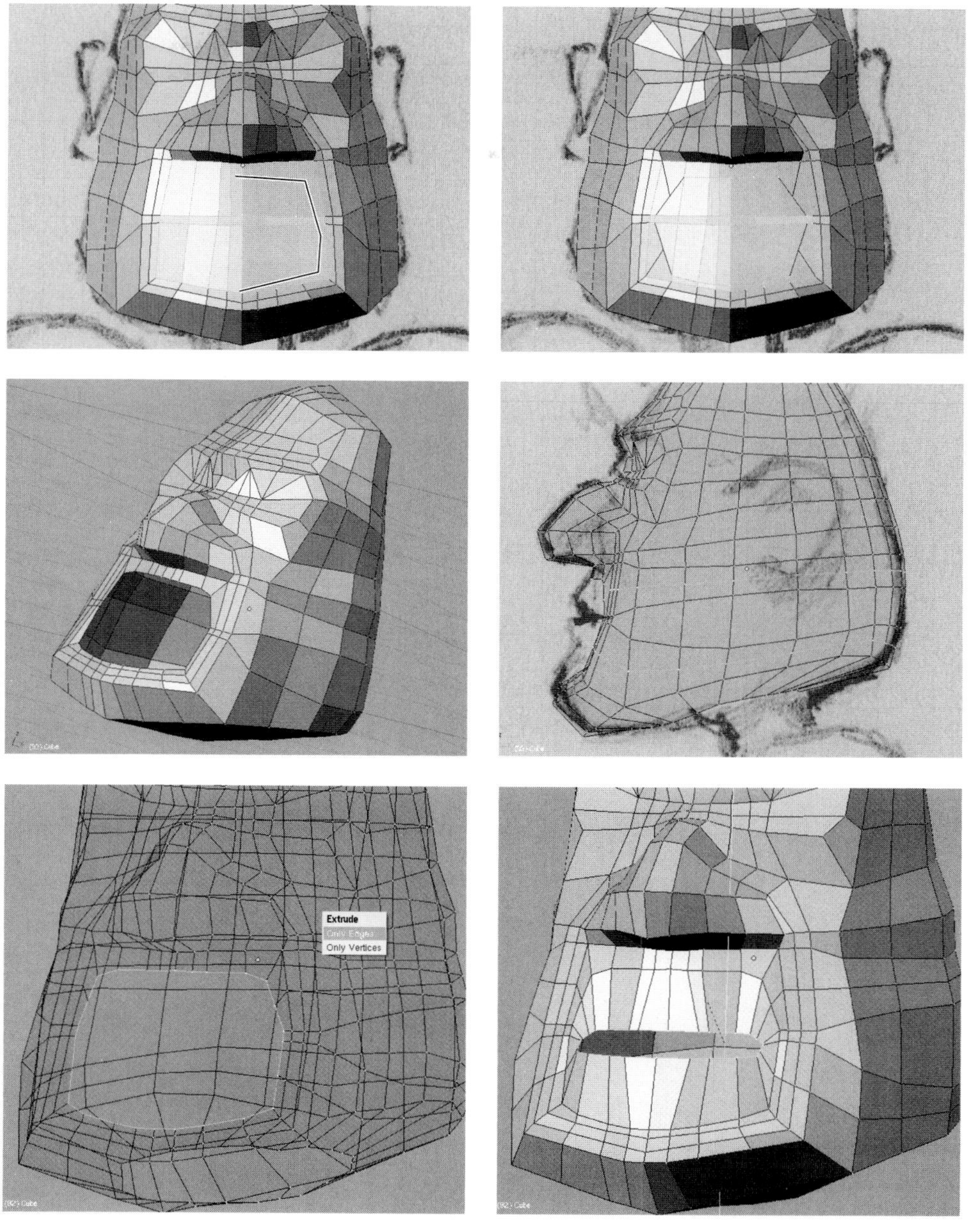

Figure 2.73

**Creating the
mouth area**

Figure 2.74

Adding detail to the mouth area with loop cuts and vertex pushing

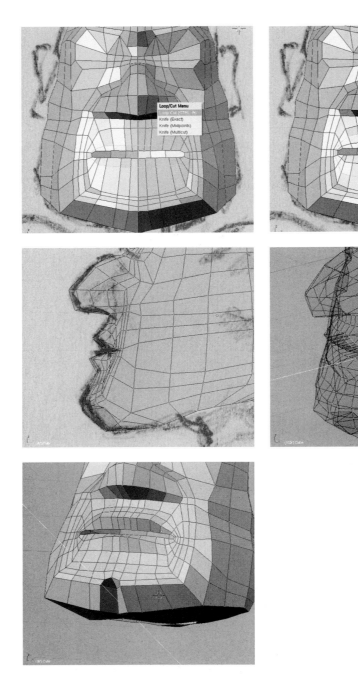

Now you turn your attention to the eye area. You need to reorganize the faces in the eye area slightly by deleting some faces and making some others with the F key. Then you need to make a few cuts and extrude inward to create the eye sockets, as shown in Figure 2.75.

Figure 2.75
Creating the eyelids and eye sockets

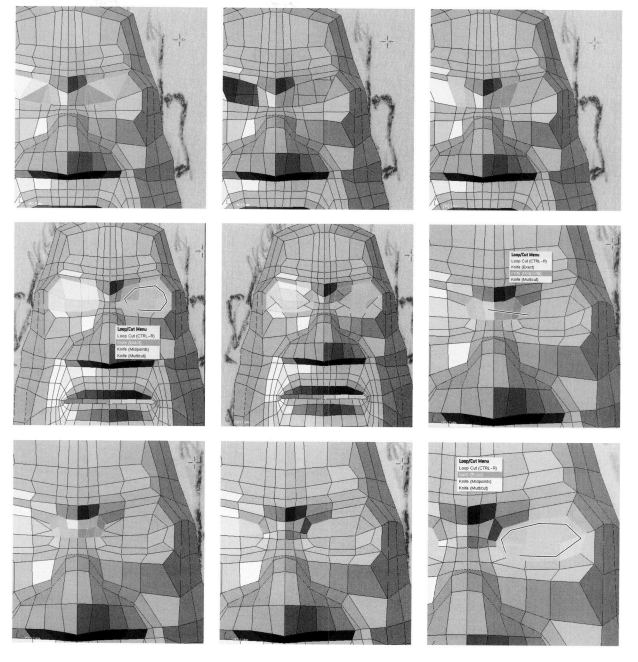

Figure 2.75 cont.

**Creating the eyelids
and eye sockets**

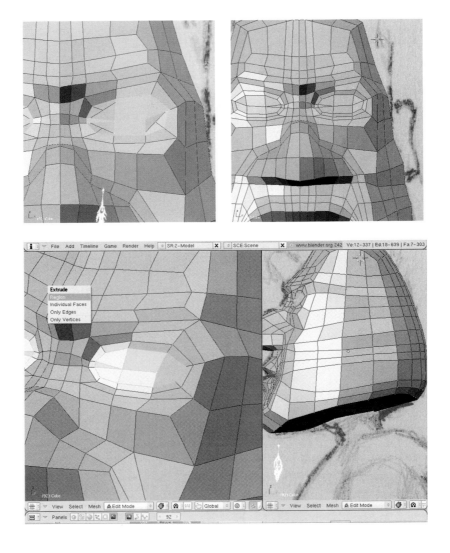

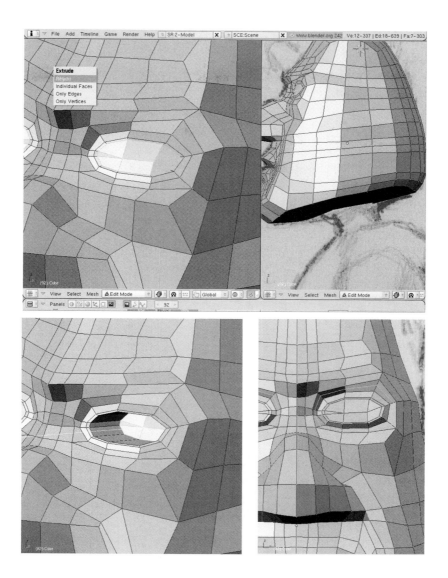

Figure 2.75 cont.

Creating the eyelids and eye sockets

The file `partial-head2.blend` shows what the state of the mesh should be when you've progressed to this point in the tutorial. If you're having any trouble following the process now, that file should help to get you back on track.

To model a bit more detail in the face, you will now add a vertical loop cut that will extend from the eye socket down the cheek. However, to control the edge loop structure around the mouth, it is necessary to rip a few edges extending from the neck up the lower side of the face. To rip edges or vertices from each other, use the V key with the vertex or the edge you want to rip selected. After you make the required rips, you will add the loop cut and then stitch the mesh together: first by merging verts with the Merge option (press the W key to bring up the menu for this) and then by adding faces with the F key. These steps are illustrated in Figure 2.76.

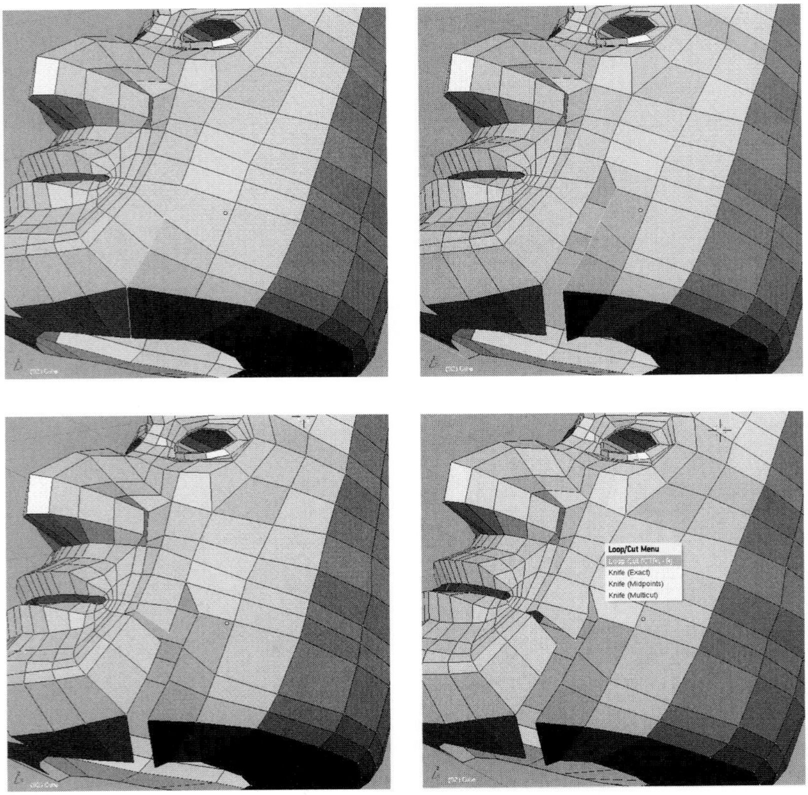

Figure 2.76

Controlling a loop cut with rips and merging

Figure 2.76 cont.
Controlling a loop cut with rips and merging

You take a very simple approach to modeling the ears—basically just a couple of extrudes and some vertex pushing, as in Figure 2.77. In the final image, note that you have applied a subsurf modifier in Cage mode to get a better idea of how the vertex pushing is affecting the form of the ear.

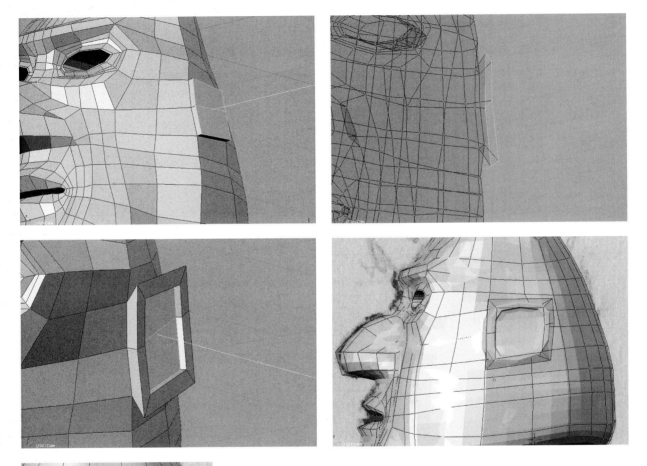

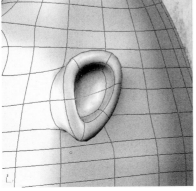

Figure 2.77

Making ears by extruding and moving vertices

To get a good place to attach the head, create a circle with eight vertices at the base of the head and connect the head mesh to it, as in Figure 2.78.

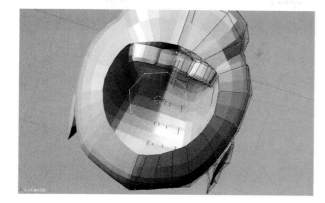 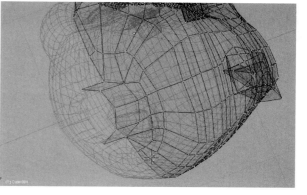

Create eyes in the same way as you did in the face example earlier in this chapter. Then add a subsurface modifier to wind up with a head along the lines of Figure 2.79. Send the head to the same layer as the body by pressing the M key and selecting layer 1. Join the two meshes by selecting both objects and using Ctrl+J. The head can be attached now by simply creating faces between the neck and the shoulder area with four verts at a time, as in Figure 2.80, resulting in the neck shown in Figure 2.81.

Figure 2.78

Finishing off the base of the head

Figure 2.79

The finished head, subsurfaced with eyes

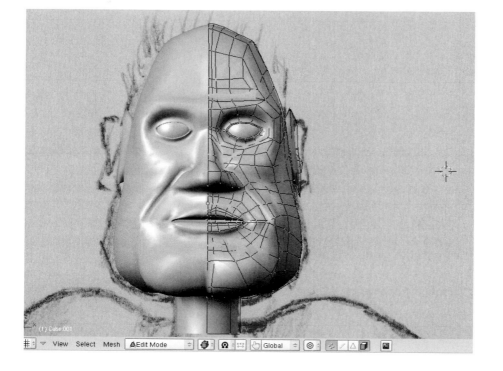

Figure 2.80

**Attaching the head
to the body with
the F key**

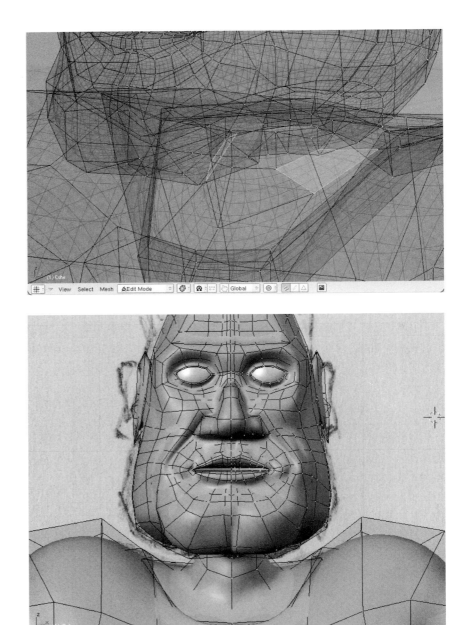

Figure 2.81

**The head fully
attached**

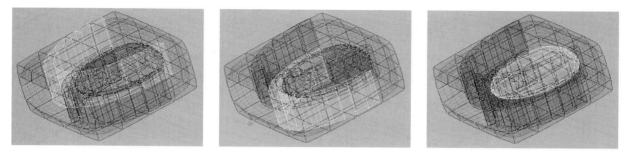

Figure 2.82
Mouth setup

Create the inside of the mouth with the cube subdivided twice, and create the top row of teeth by adding a tube with 32 verts, removing half of it, scaling it to the shape of a row of teeth, and extruding it inward.

Copy this by pressing Shift+D and scale to create the bottom row of teeth. The tongue is a UV sphere with 12 segments and 12 rings, scaled to the shape of a tongue. The mouth setup can be seen in Figure 2.82. Place the mouth as in the cutaway image in Figure 2.84 and attach by creating faces between the inside edge of the lips and the edge of the mouth structure. When the mouth has been fully attached, select the entire mesh with A, remove any doubles that might have cropped up with the W key → Rem Doubles, and recalculate the normals outside using Ctrl+N.

That wraps up the mesh modeling for Captain Blender. If all went smoothly, you should have a character mesh looking something like the one in Figure 2.84. If not, read the next section to see whether any of the problems your mesh is having are covered. Also, open up the file `CB-Model-base_mesh.blend` on the accompanying DVD and compare the places where your model is different from this one.

Figure 2.83
Placement of the mouth in the head

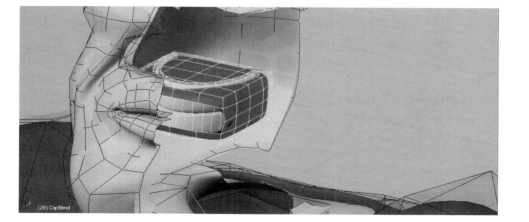

After you've given your model a good going over and have decided that you're satisfied with the model, apply the mirror modifier. This will make the whole mesh into a symmetrical, unmodified, single mesh. When you make edits now, you will no longer have the mirroring effect. It is possible to make mirrored edits on a symmetrical mesh without the mirror modifier by selecting the X-mirror edit option in the Mesh Tools 1 panel, but it is still a good idea to wait until you are pretty much finished with the symmetrical modeling before applying the mirror modifier.

After you do this, save your model. In the next chapter, you will move on to adding materials, textures, and hair to the Captain Blender character, so you'll want to have your mesh handy.

Common Problems and Solutions in Mesh Modeling

Many of the most common problems that arise during mesh modeling are easy to spot and have straightforward solutions. This section looks at a few that are sure to arise if you do extensive mesh modeling.

Inconsistent Normals

A telltale ugly black shadow-like seam like the one in Figure 2.85 indicates mismatched normals. If you select Draw Normals in the Mesh Tools tab, you can see which direction the normals in your mesh point, as in Figure 2.86 (normals are displayed in blue by default in Blender). Most often, normals point outward, and in all cases they should be consistent throughout a mesh. In this

Figure 2.84

The completed Captain Blender mesh

instance, the normals on the left half of the mesh are pointing outward, as they should be. Because the mesh in the figure is in solid view, you cannot see the normals on the right side because they are reversed and are pointing inward.

This problem is very simple to solve. Select all verts and hit Ctrl+N. A dialog box displays, asking whether you want to Recalculate Normals Outside. Click OK, and the problem should vanish. If it doesn't, there could be more serious problems with the structure of your mesh.

Overlapping Faces

This problem is often not apparent in the 3D window in Blender; it becomes visible only when the image is rendered, showing up as a pattern of dark artifacts on the surface of the mesh, as in Figure 2.87. This problem is caused by multiple faces sharing the same coordinates. It is most often the result of inadvertently duplicating a mesh or portion of a mesh, and leaving the duplicated portion in the same spot as the original.

There are two likely possibilities. First, you might have duplicated the object. In Object mode, right-click once on the mesh object and move it with G to see if it is a duplicate or not, as in Figure 2.88. If it is a duplicate object, delete the unwanted copy. If it is not a duplicate object, the verts and faces of the mesh were probably accidentally duplicated in Edit mode. This might show up as a strange pattern of selected edges, as in Figure 2.89, but it might also not be evident at all. In any case, the solution is to select all verts in the mesh and choose Rem Doubles in the Mesh Tools panel to remove doubled vertices.

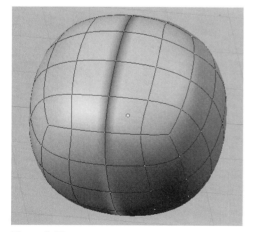

Figure 2.85
Inconsistent normals

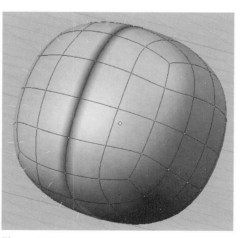

Figure 2.86
With Draw Normals turned on, they don't all point outward

Figure 2.87

**Overlapping faces
create artifacts
when rendered**

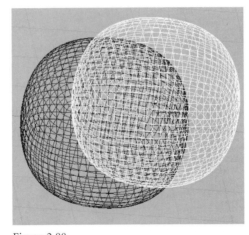

Figure 2.88

Move an object aside to see if it is hiding an identical object

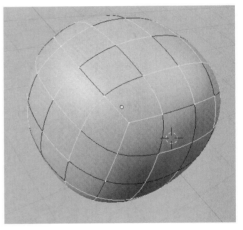

Figure 2.89

A strange selection pattern in Edit mode might indicate overlapping faces

Internal Faces

Unwanted pinching in your mesh is often the result of having unnecessary faces connecting parts of the mesh that should not be connected. Generally, a mesh should be hollow, without separate compartments inside it. The pinched mesh in Figure 2.90 is a result of having internal faces connecting the middle loop of vertices.

This can be solved by selecting all unwanted internal faces (see Figure 2.91) and deleting them with the X key, choosing Faces from the Delete menu.

Unwanted Doubles

Another common problem is the appearance of a creased seam on your mesh, as in Figure 2.92, which is usually caused by doubled edges.

Use the Box Select tool (B) to select the seam, as in Figure 2.93, and do Rem Doubles (this can be found in the Mesh Tools tab and also in the W specials menu). If the vertices are not exactly in the same place, it might be necessary to adjust the Limit field to the right of Rem Doubles. Raising this value increases the area within which verts are considered doubles of each other. Raising this value too high results in merging vertices that should not be merged, so be careful.

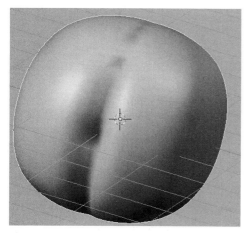

Figure 2.90

A pinched effect caused by internal faces

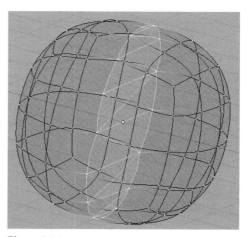

Figure 2.91

Delete unwanted internal faces to solve the problem

In some cases, if there is a seam in which the corresponding verts are too far from each other to be merged using remove doubles, it might be necessary to "weld" the seam shut two verts at a time. Select the two verts you want to merge, press W and choose Merge. You might need to do this for all the verts in the seam in some cases.

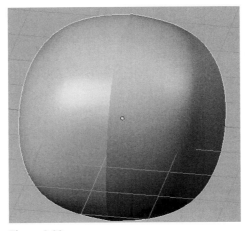

Figure 2.92

An unwanted crease caused by doubled-up verts

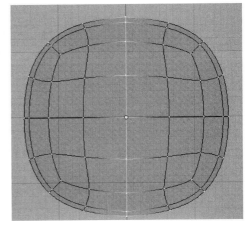

Figure 2.93

Select all verts in the offending area using the Box Select tool

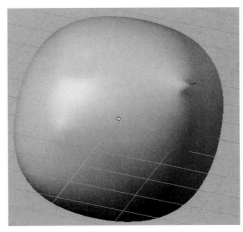

Figure 2.94

Problems caused by unwanted extrusion

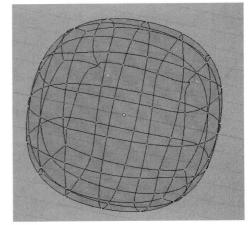

Figure 2.95

Unwanted extrusions in Wireframe mode

Unwanted Extrusions

Accidentally pressing Ctrl+LMB with a single vertex selected is a common cause of unwanted extrusions, which can show up in a mesh in a variety of ways, creating pimples and pockmarks on the surface of your mesh, depending on the nature of the extrusion. You can see the surface results of this problem in Figure 2.94. The cause of the problem is clearer when the mesh is viewed in Wireframe mode, as in Figure 2.95.

The solution is simply to delete the extruded verts. In the cases in which the verts have been extruded far enough to be clearly identifiable, as in the top two cases where the verts are extruded into and out from the surface of the mesh, the verts can be selected and deleted.

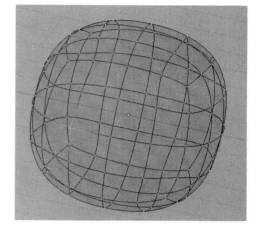

Figure 2.96

A doubled vertex

In the more subtle case in Figure 2.96, the extruded vert was not displaced, and so resides at the same coordinate as the original vert. This is actually just another case of unwanted doubles, and the solution is to select the doubled vert using the Box Select tool and to remove doubles.

Now that you have covered the basics of mesh modeling and created the mesh of the character, you can begin to add details. The next chapter will look at creating materials and textures, and using static particles to make hair. There will be a few more points at which you will put the modeling skills to use to make small adjustments and additions to the mesh, but most of the mesh modeling is now done for this character.

CHAPTER 3

Completing the Model with Materials, Textures, and Particles

Previous chapters covered the basics of using Blender's various modeling tools to build organic shapes. But this is only the first step of creating characters. By default, all the shapes you build begin as a uniform, dull gray, slightly glossy material. To make characters interesting and lifelike, or even just to change their color, you need to delve into the world of materials, textures, and static particles to complete the model.

- Material Datablock

- Textures and UV Mapping

- Using Static Particles

Material Datablock

Let's begin by starting up a fresh session with Blender. When an appropriate object (in this case, the default cube) has been selected, the following *material index* widget can be seen in the Links and Materials tab in the buttons window:

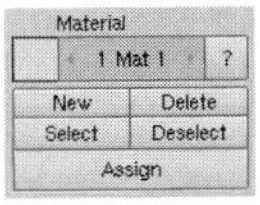

Pay close attention to what this index shows because it is an important point in working with materials. The set of materials available for you to work with is determined here, and you also select which specific material index you are working with. Materials are assigned to portions of the mesh based on their index, so if you accidentally alter a material index, you might wind up with different results than you want. The interface in the materials area, as you will see shortly, can be slightly confusing in this regard, so make a note to always confirm that you are working with the correct material index to avoid confusion. The material index is also displayed in the Links and Pipeline tab in the materials buttons area.

The widget now tells you that there is one material available and that the current active material index is 1, so if you go into the Materials editing panel, you will be editing material number 1. The little square in the upper left shows the color of the material to make it easier to distinguish materials at a glance. The question mark button enables you to set the active material to be the material assigned to faces you have selected on the 3D object (this is available only in Edit mode).

The buttons below the material index selection widget are mostly self-explanatory. New creates a new material index and sets it as active. The material associated with this new index is the same material as the previously active index. If you click New now, the field will read 2 Mat 2, and the gray square will be identical. If you go into Edit mode, select some portion of the default cube, and then click the question mark button, the field will read 2 Mat 1 because the cube is assigned material 1.

To edit the material at the current material index, you enter the materials buttons panel (see Figure 3.1), either by clicking the buttons highlighted below the index selection widget or by pressing F5 once.

The current material index is 1. The material associated with this index is called Material, as you can see in the drop-down menu under Link to Object (see Figure 3.2). Remember, when you created index 2, the material link was duplicated, so this material is also associated with index 2. If you edit this material now, you will edit the material that both indices are associated with.

Figure 3.1
Materials buttons panel (F5)

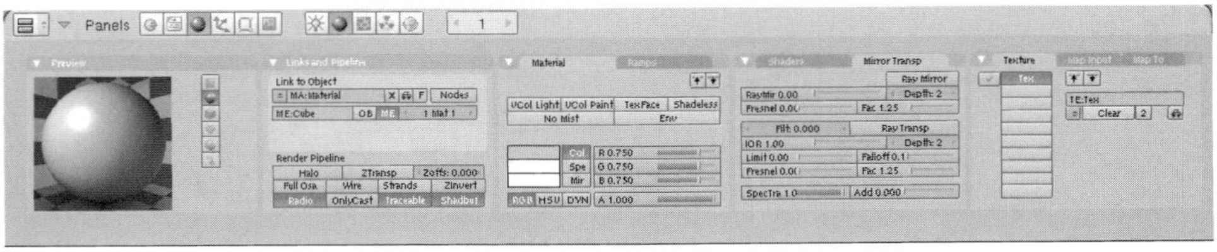

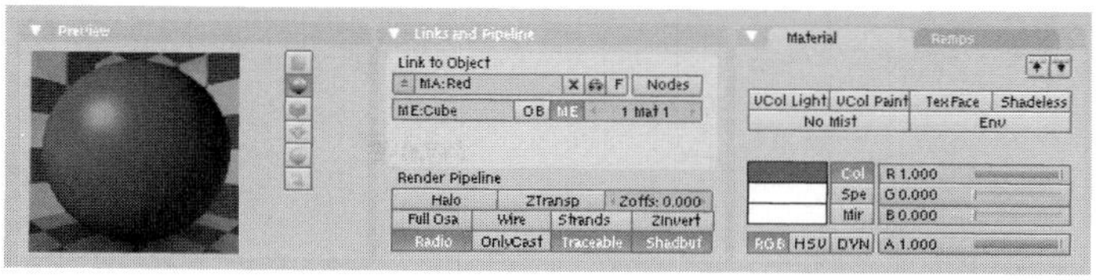

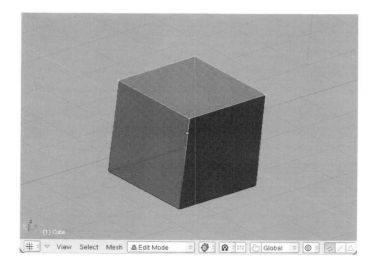

Figure 3.2

Preview, Links and Pipeline, and Material tabs in the materials buttons area

Let's start by giving the material a name that means something. You do this by simply changing the name in the drop-down menu beside MA. You'll change that to Red. Note that this does *not* create a new material; it simply changes the name of the material you are working with. Now material indices 1 and 2 are both associated with Red. There is no longer any material called Material.

The only editing you'll do here is to change the base color of the material. Under the Material tab, move the slider for R up to 1.000 and move the sliders for G and B to 0. In the 3D viewport, the cube should be red now.

Go back to the editing buttons by pressing F9. Using the arrow buttons in the material index field, set the active material index as 2. The field should read 2 Mat 2. Now, in the 3D viewport in Edit mode, select the top face of the default cube, as shown in Figure 3.3. In the materials widget, click Assign. You won't see a change, but there is one. The top face of the cube is now material index 2. But because material indices 1 and 2 are both pointing to the same material, Red, their appearance in the viewport is the same.

Go back to the Materials editing panel. You're now working on material index 2, the active material index. Click the small arrow icon to the left of the Material drop-down menu and choose Add New. The new material is now called Red.001 and it is a duplicate of Red. However, it's a completely separate material now, and you can edit it freely. Rename this material **Green** and adjust the RGB values accordingly.

Figure 3.3

The cube with the top face selected. All faces appear red on your monitor.

Figure 3.4

The cube with two distinct materials. The top face should appear green on your monitor.

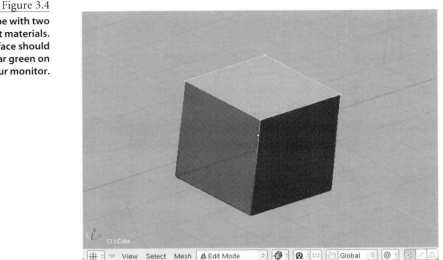

Now you can see a difference on the default cube (see Figure 3.4). If, as recommended, you're doing this exercise on your computer, the top face is now green. You have two distinct materials that can be edited independently of each other.

As with other datablock links, the links between material indices and materials can be switched around freely. You can easily link material 1 with Green and material 2 with Red, reversing the placement of materials assigned to the cube's faces. Simply make the appropriate index active, and then in the editing panel select the material you want to link it to from the Material drop-down menu.

Material Properties

Now that you've seen how to keep the material datablocks organized, let's look more closely at what you can do with them. For the purposes of this book, it's enough to think of materials as essentially colors and shading properties. You will learn more about texturing, but you will not be looking at some of the more exotic material properties and functions available in Blender. For more exhaustive information on materials, as with all subjects, you should consult the official documentation.

As you saw in the first section, one important property of a material is the color. R, G, and B values can be set using sliders or by clicking the value and editing the number directly. The alpha value (A) can be set in the same way. This value determines the opacity of the material.

Shaders influence how light reflects from the surface of an object. In nature, this is determined by the physical properties of the material's surface. Shaders are algorithms for simulating the reflective effects of these physical properties. By default, the Shaders tab is set as shown in Figure 3.5. There is a drop-down menu to choose a diffuse shader (set to Lambert in the example) and, below that, a drop-down menu to choose a specular shader (set to CookTorr here). The diffuse shader has a slider to determine the amount of light reflected from the surface (reflectivity), and the specular shader has a slider to determine the degree of specularity or shininess and (in most cases) a slider to determine hardness. By selecting different shaders and adjusting their parameters, you can simulate a wide variety of physical surfaces.

Figure 3.5
Shaders tab

TOON AND ANIME STYLE SHADING

A shader is generally used to create a realistic simulation of some specific physical surface. In character animation, one common exception to this use of shaders is in toon shading, which creates a cartoon or traditional 2D anime style appearance. Toon shaders divide gradations into several levels of shading that can be smoothed together or not, resulting in a sharp, cartoony distinction between lit parts and shaded parts of the object. Toon shaders are often used in conjunction with the Edge feature in the Render buttons panel, which adds an outline around the object as part of the rendering process, further enhancing the traditional 2D look. In the image shown in the following graphic, the old man rendered on the right is made of toon-shaded materials with the Edge feature turned on, in contrast with the more realistically shaded and rendered old man model on the left. In this case, the materials in the old man on the right were all set to toon shading for both diffuse and specular shaders, with the Smooth value set to 0 for maximal sharpness between shaded and nonshaded areas. Specularity and size values varied between the materials, and you should experiment for the effect you want.

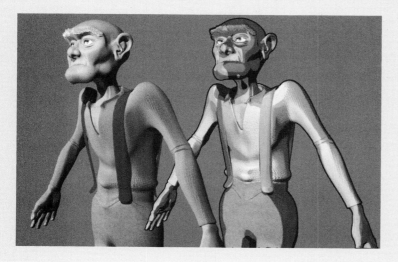

MATERIAL NODES

Blender has a powerful node system that can be used to create materials as well as to do advanced image compositing. Nodes behave similarly to the way layers behave in some 2D image processing applications, enabling effects and inputs to be laid over one another and be combined in various ways. Nodes are much more powerful than layers in this sense because they can be combined in nonlinear ways. With material nodes, you can have complete control over every aspect of a material by combining fundamental components of materials and shaders in a flexible way. Nodes form a network of linked inputs and outputs, which can be viewed and edited in the Node Editor window; the basic node setup for the default material is shown in the following graphic.

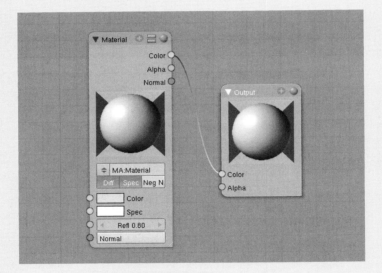

It is beyond the scope of this book to discuss nodes in detail, but the knowledge you gain by working with Blender's ordinary materials system will not be wasted when you move on to using material nodes because materials that use nodes are always composed of at least one basic material that is the input to the network of nodes. The understanding you have of color, shaders, mirroring, transparency, and textures will all remain pertinent when you work with nodes. In this sense, material nodes do not replace the basic material system, but rather extend it.

You can find thorough documentation and some excellent tutorials on using nodes by following the links listed in Chapter 18.

Shading and Materials for Captain Blender

Let's return to the superhero model you were working on in the previous chapter. You want to now give him a colorful suit, not to mention some skin and hair.

Orange seems like a good color for Captain Blender's tights, and blue is good for his gloves, boots and britches. You'll make his belt black for a little variation, and then there will need to be at least one more material for his head. For now, press New three times in the materials index panel so that you have four material indices.

The next few steps can be done in any order. You need to associate vertex groups on the mesh with material indices, and you have to create and name a new material for each index. By default, the entire mesh is assigned material index 1, which will be the orange material. Let's begin by selecting the portions of the mesh you want to be blue, as shown in Figure 3.6.

In the materials index field, click to Mat 2, and click Assign. Now go to the materials editing buttons and select Add New from the Materials drop-down menu. The default name will be Material.001. Rename this to **Blue**.

For the blue material, set the RGB values as R:0.2, G:0.2, and B:0.6. In Blender, color values range from 0 to 1. If you are accustomed to working with a scale of 0 to 255, you should simply think of 1 as the equivalent of 255, the maximal value of the color, with 0 the same in both cases. Captain Blender's gloves, boots, and britches are made out of super-strength PVC, and Lambert shaders are good for plastics, so you'll use a Lambert diffuse shader with reflectivity set at 0.8; for the specular shader, you'll use the Wardiso shader with specularity set at 0.8 and rms set at 0.215.

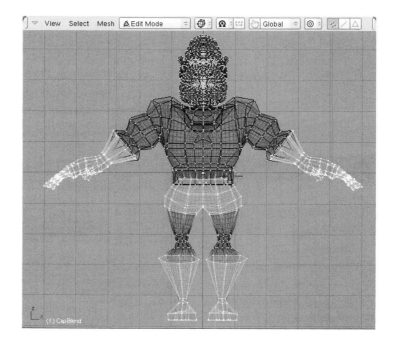

Figure 3.6

Captain Blender mesh with boots, gloves, and britches selected

Now switch the active material index to Mat 1, rename the material to **Orange**, and set the RGB values to 1.0, 0.29, and 0.0, respectively. Captain Blender spends a lot of time in this suit and it needs to be easy on the skin, so you'll give it a nice velvety surface by using a Minnaert shader with reflectivity at 0.55 and the darkness value set to 0.42. There's basically no specularity on this material, so for the specularity shader, you'll stick with the default CookTorr shader with specularity set to 0.

Run a render to see how these shaders are looking on your mesh. Check Chapter 11 for tips on how to set up your camera and lighting for a good-looking render.

Now select Captain Blender's belt. To do this, place the mouse near one of the vertices of the belt and press L. Because the belt is not connected by any edges to the rest of the mesh, it can be easily selected in this way. Assign the belt to Mat 3. Go into the materials editor and create the material for the belt (you can experiment a bit with the settings). You'll need to do the same thing with the inside of Captain Blender's mouth and his teeth. You can select them by using the L key and the vertex groups you defined in Chapter 2. Keep the color dark and reflectivity pretty low on the inside of the mouth because it will be noticeable if it is too bright. You'll be looking more closely at the head shortly, but give it a skin-colored material for the time being (so that it's not all orange).

At this point, you should have a mesh with six materials: one each for the orange suit; blue gloves, boots, and britches; belt; skin; mouth; and teeth.

Basic Texturing

No superhero's outfit is complete without a big splashy logo across his chest. You will use an image texture for this. Before you go any further, you need to go into Object mode and add an Empty object. You want it to be placed squarely in front of the chest, as shown in Figure 3.7. Press Shift+S to snap the 3D cursor to the grid before adding the Empty by pressing the spacebar and selecting Empty from the menu.

You'll put the texture directly onto the orange material, so you need to make sure the appropriate material index is active. Go to the materials edit buttons and then to the Texture panel.

Now you'll create a new texture, which you can do in the same way you create new materials. Just go to the drop-down menu shown in Figure 3.8 and select Add New from the drop-down menu to the left of the Clear button. Name the new texture **logo**.

After you've created the new logo texture, you'll go to the texture editing buttons by clicking the leopard skin texture button or by pressing F6. Select Image from the Texture Type drop-down menu. An Image buttons panel will appear. The first thing to do here is to load the image. Click Load Image and find the logo.png file from the accompanying DVD on your file system.

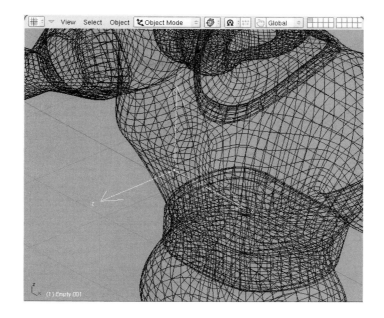

Figure 3.7
The Empty you will use to control the placement of the logo

You'll leave most of the default settings alone, but you'll select UseAlpha and ClipCube, as you can see in Figure 3.9. Using alpha means that the image's alpha channel will be considered (in this case, it will make the area around the outside of the logo transparent). ClipCube is an option that defines how you want the texture to cover the surface. In another case, you might want to extend or repeat the texture to cover the surface. Clip and ClipCube both place a single copy of the texture on the surface and surround it with zero alpha, which leaves the remainder of the surface unchanged. The difference is that Clip clips the image in only two dimensions, which means that the material will exhibit the texture on all its surfaces, along the depth axis. In practice, this means that the logo will show up not only on Captain Blender's chest, but also, in reverse, on his back. You don't want this, so use ClipCube, which limits the texture's influence to a cube-shaped area.

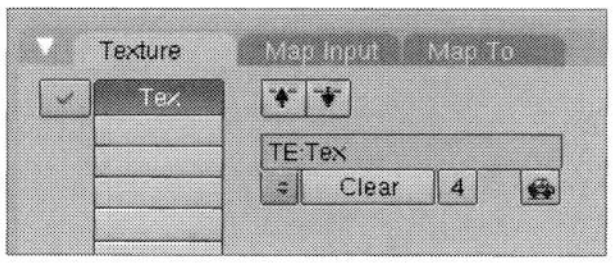

Figure 3.8
Texture tab

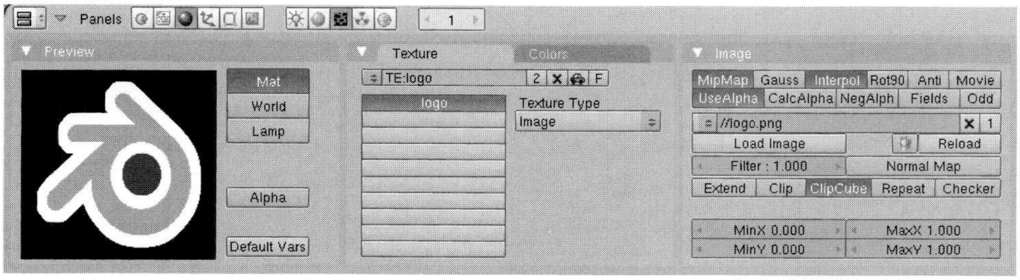

Figure 3.9
Loading the logo image as a texture

After you've loaded the image, it's time to work on the texture mapping. First, go to the Map Input tab. You'll base the mapping of this texture on the location of the Empty you created earlier. To do this, select Object and enter the name **Empty** in the available field.

The next tab you'll look at is the Map To tab (see Figure 3.10), in which you specify which properties of the material will be affected by the texture, and to what degree. Obviously, you want color to be affected 100 percent, so select Col and leave the Col slider at the default 1.0. You could leave it at that, but it would be nice to give the logo a nice glossy iron-on look. You can do this very simply: bump up some other values, in particular the reflectivity, specularity, and hardness, which are all very low or 0 in the base orange material. Select them as shown in Figure 3.11. You can control the degree to which the texture influences these using the variation (Var) slider. You don't want to overdo it here, or else the result won't look good at all. A modest 0.3 for this slider will do fine.

And that's almost all for the logo. You can render it out to see how it looks or you can simply press Shift+P in the 3D view window to see the render preview window, as shown in Figure 3.11. Probably the logo is not quite right, but no worries. That's what the Empty is for. You've set the mapping of the texture to depend on the Empty, which means that you can now move the texture around, even resize or rotate it, by manipulating the Empty. Nudge the Empty up along the Z axis to raise the texture and scale the Empty up slightly to enlarge the logo. When you're satisfied with the placement and size of the logo, render it out by pressing F12 to see the result, which should look something like Figure 3.12.

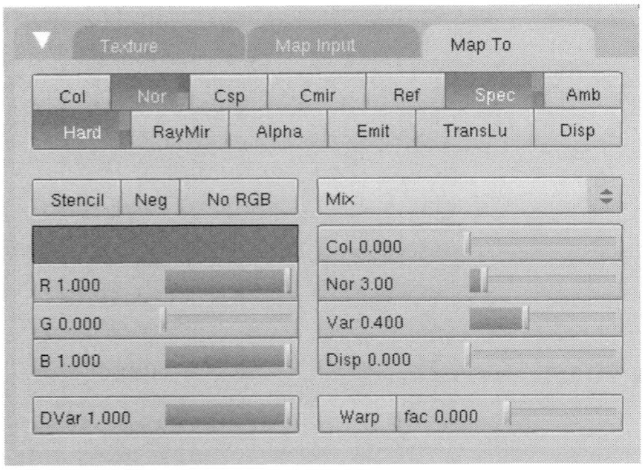

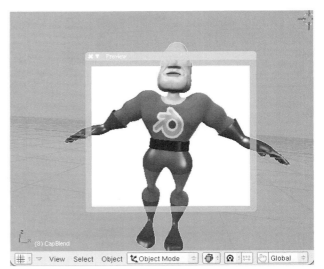

Figure 3.10
Map To tab

Figure 3.11
The preview window in the 3D viewport (Shift+P)

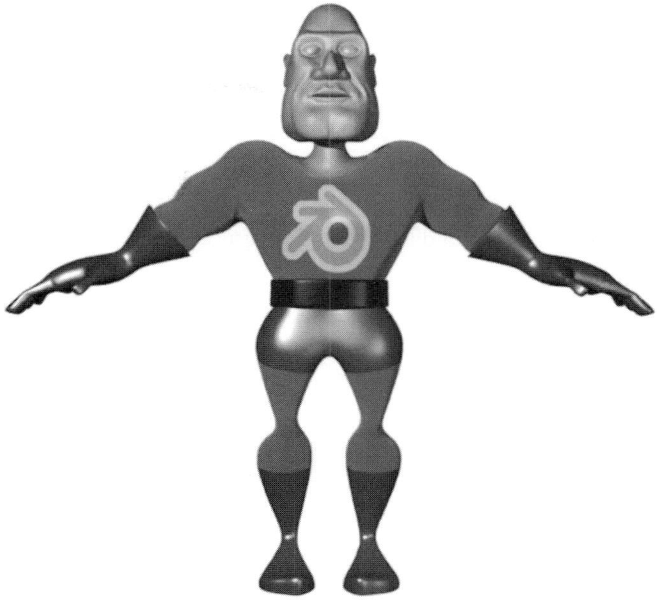

Figure 3.12
A full render with materials

Textures and UV Mapping

Next you'll turn to Captain Blender's head and face. Using material and shader options is not really enough to give you the kind of look you want for human skin. The best way to get convincing-looking skin is by applying two-dimensional textures to the surface of the mesh, much as you did with the logo, although you'll use a more sophisticated approach to mapping. In the case of Captain Blender, you're not going for an especially realistic look, but the same methods you'll use here to apply the texture are applicable to much more realistic styles. Of course, a realistic style generally requires much more detailed textures than a more cartoony style.

UV mapping provides a way to apply a two-dimensional image or texture onto the surface of a three-dimensional object. The name *UV* refers to the two-dimensional coordinates, U and V, which are mapped into the 3D (X, Y, and Z) coordinate space. Blender has powerful tools for creating this mapping, which make it fairly straightforward to unwrap any 3D object after you get the hang of it.

The first step of UV texturing an object is to create a representation of the surface you want to apply the texture to in UV coordinate space—similar to the way maps of the world are sometimes represented in a flattened, orange-peel style. Creating this 2D image is called *unwrapping*. By default, Blender uses a method of unwrapping called *Angle Based Flattening*.

Because Captain Blender's head is a more or less a closed surface, you need to prepare the object for unwrapping a bit by providing seams along which it can be split. The unwrapper will first cut the surface along these seams and then flatten it. Do this by selecting the edges that should be seams and pressing Ctrl+E for the Edge Specials menu. Select Mark Seam. Do this for the edges shown in Figure 3.13. It is a good idea to mark the seams in places that are likely to be unobtrusive later; for example, parts of the mesh that are covered by hair, are visible only from behind, or that conform to creases or concealed places in the mesh.

Next, select the entire head by selecting the Head material index and clicking Select. (Before doing this step, make sure to press A once or twice to make sure all other verts [vertices] are deselected.) With your head selected, take a close look and make sure that the selected area includes the entire head. This is the area that will receive the UV mapped texture. Also, make sure that your seam goes all the way to the edge of this selected area.

With this area selected, in the Mode drop-down menu, select UV Face Select mode. Your mesh will appear as shown in Figure 3.14. The faces that were selected in Edit mode will remain selected in UV Face Select mode, so the faces of the head should appear in a very light purple while the rest of the mesh appears white.

Figure 3.13

Several views of the seams for unwrapping the head

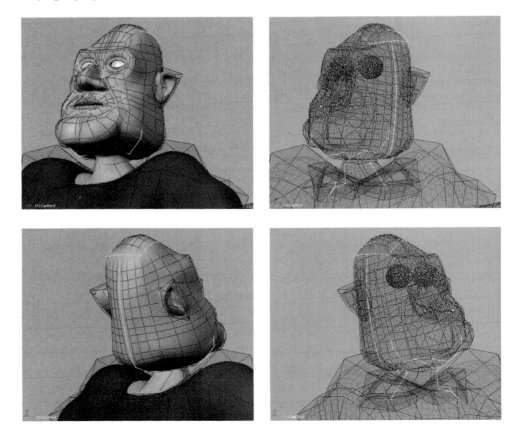

You can also create seams while in UV Face Select mode, and there are a number of tools that can make this even easier than creating them in Edit mode. You can mark a seam that borders selected faces using Ctrl+E (this will also clear seams in the same way), you can mark or clear a seam on the edge under your mouse cursor using Alt+RMB, and you can mark or clear seams along the most direct path from the last marked seam using Shift+Alt+RMB.

Now you're ready to unwrap. In a separate work area, change the window type to UV/Image Editor. You'll see a black and gray grid pattern. Press E and select Unwrap. If nothing appears, it is because you didn't have the faces selected in the UV Face Select window. Go back to this window, switch to Edit mode, make sure that the head is selected, switch back to UV Select mode, and try unwrapping again with the E key. Alternately, select Unwrap from the UV menu in the UV editor header. The result should look something like Figure 3.15.

Blender's automatic unwrapping calculates the angles between the faces to minimize the distortion of the 2D image when wrapped around the 3D surface. For this reason, the generated mapping that you see here should not be edited directly. However, it might be desirable to adjust the shape of the mapping to better reflect relative sizes or locations of individual faces, or to get rid of overlapping faces in the automatically generated mapping. The way to do this is to *pin* certain points into place and then to unwrap the faces again. When you do this, the pinned points remain in a fixed position, whereas the rest of the mapping is recalculated according to Blender's algorithm.

You can use the Box Select or Circle Select tool to select points to pin here (or simply right-click on the points). The first thing you do is select the middle points on the top and bottom of the mapping and then pin them to the middle of the grid. To do this, select the point, move it by pressing G to the position where you want it, and press P to pin it. Pinned verts appear highlighted red.

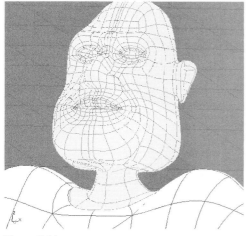

Figure 3.14

The head in UV Face Select mode

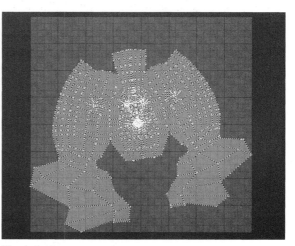

Figure 3.15

The UV surface as it appears when first unwrapped

As shown in Figure 3.16, you have selected six points around the sides and center of the mapping and pinned them where you want them. Be sure that your pinned verts are approximately symmetrical; otherwise the mapping will turn out lopsided. If you unwrap again, you will see that the previously pinned verts are now nicely incorporated into the unwrapping (see Figure 3.17). However, it is not necessary to unwrap every time you move verts around; instead, select Live Unwrap Transform from the UVs menu in the UV window. This allows you to move a pinned vertex freely and have the unwrapping update automatically in real time.

Figure 3.16

The UV texture with six points pinned into place

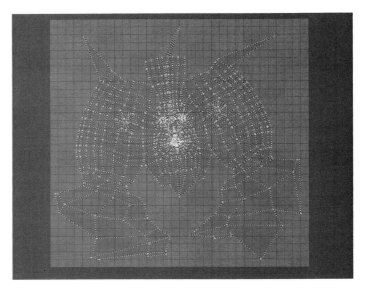

Figure 3.17

The UV texture as it appears after being unwrapped with the pinned verts

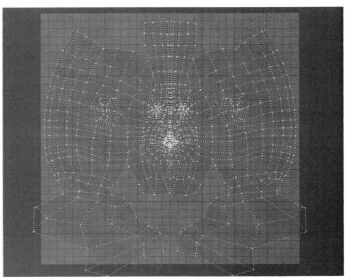

You'll pin a few more verts, as shown in Figure 3.18, and unwrap again (see Figure 3.19).

Because your mesh is slightly different from mine, the details will be different. In my case, for some reason, the mouth is coming out a bit misshapen. I want to get the mouth to be more symmetrical. Also, it is often the case that overlapping faces need to be pulled off each other. To get the mouth symmetrical without any overlapping, I pinned the verts around the mouth, as shown in Figure 3.20.

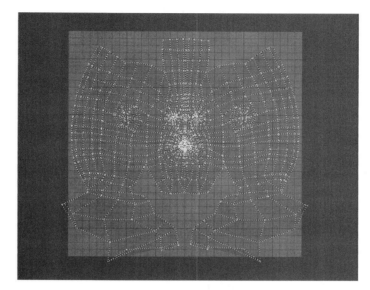

Figure 3.18

Pinning some more verts…

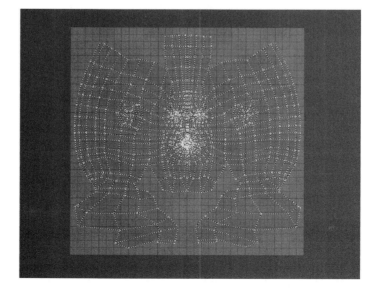

Figure 3.19

…and unwrapping again

Figure 3.20
**Pinned verts around
the mouth**

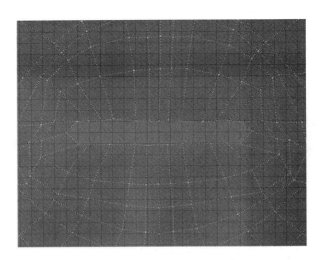

Finally, you want to export the mapping to an image so that you can use it in the 2D image manipulation program of your choice as a guide for painting the texture you want to use. From the UV menu, choose Save UV Face Layout. The default options are mostly fine, but you should choose a larger size. Put **2000** into this field and click OK. A file browser window will open, and you can choose a location and a name for the output file, which will be in Targa format and will look something like Figure 3.21.

Figure 3.21
**The exported
mapping**

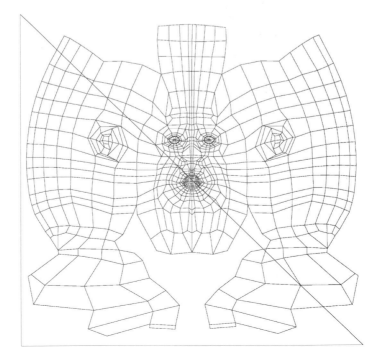

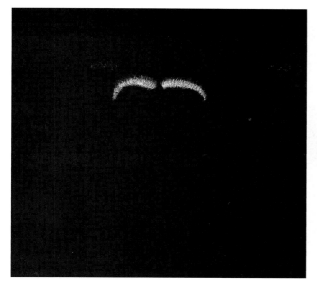

Figure 3.22

A bump map image for the eyebrows

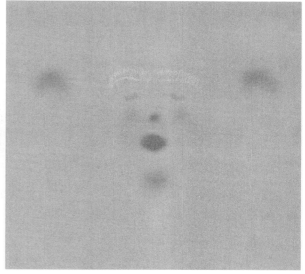

Figure 3.23

The color map for the face

The next step involves some basic knowledge of how to use a 2D image manipulation program such as Adobe Photoshop or the open source Gimp (which is included on the DVD accompanying this book). The basic idea is to create an image file with the UV mapping on one layer, paint your desired colors and textures on other layers, and then save the image file with the UV mapping layer hidden.

The first thing you'll do is map the colors. You'll create an image for the color of Captain Blender's skin. which will include the slight color change around his lips and cheeks, and you'll draw the color of the eyebrows directly onto the image. For this skin image, I took a chunk of skin from a photograph and used the rubber stamp tool to spread it over the surface, and then I drew the details by hand. For more realistic skin tones and splotches, you can incorporate more photographic detail. Be sure to paint each detail on a separate layer in your 2D software. In particular, you'll use the layer with the eyebrows on it (see Figure 3.22) elsewhere, so keep a document around with it separated. The final output color map can be seen in Figure 3.23. It can be in any of several image formats, although PNG is recommended if there needs to be an alpha channel (which is not the case in this example). Its lossless compression is also an advantage over JPEG.

To apply the texture, first load the image into the UV/Image editor. To do this, select Image → Open from the header menu and find your color map on the hard drive (this process associates the image with a UV mapping). The next step is to create a new texture on the material. From the materials edit buttons, choose the Textures panel, select Add New from the drop-down menu, and rename the new texture **faceskin**, as shown in Figure 3.24.

Figure 3.24

Creating the faceskin texture

Now go into the texture editing buttons. Select the texture type Image and load the image in the Image tab. Return to the materials editing buttons and go to the Map Input tab. Select UV. Finally, go to Map To, select Col, and make sure that all the other buttons are unselected. The Col slider should be at 1. You now have the color of the face mapped. Do a render and see how things look (see Figure 3.25).

As you can see from the render, simply painting the eyebrows on with color alone is really not adequate because the eyebrows are completely flat against the skin of the brow. To give them a little bit of shape, you'll use a bump mapped texture, which is used to give the appearance of bumps or gouges on a surface. To do this, you need a separate image to use as the bump map texture. In 2D image software, you can do this by copying the eyebrow layer from the color map and creating a solid, high-contrast, black and white image such as the one shown in Figure 3.22.

To apply the eyebrow bump map, go through the same steps as with the color map. First, in the UV Editor, go to the Image menu and open the bump map image file. This creates the mapping. Next, go back to the materials editing buttons and add a new texture to the material for the brow bump map. Do this by clicking the first empty box below faceskin and clicking Create New Texture. Name the texture something like **brow**. Your texture tab should now look like Figure 3.26. Press F6 to go to the texture editing buttons from here.

These texture boxes are analogous to the material indices in the Link and Materials tabs. Each one is associated with a texture, and the selected box determines which texture you'll edit when you enter the texture editing area. If you change the texture you are working on in the editing area, you automatically assign the new texture to the current box. To keep your textures organized, it is best to always use the Texture tab to select the texture to be edited.

Figure 3.25

A first render of the head with the color map

As you did with the face color map, go into the texture editing area, select the texture type Image and load the image. Return to the materials area and select UV in the Map Input tab, as before. In the Map To tab, a few things are different. First, deselect Col because you're not interested in using the colors of this image. Select the second option for Nor by clicking twice. The first click will select Nor, and the second click will turn the text in the box yellow. If you click Nor once, dark areas will be bumps, and light areas will be indentations. Because the eyebrow map is white on black, you want the white areas to be bumps, so choose the second mapping option. Set the Nor slider at 3.00. The label *Nor* refers to the fact that bump mapping influences the texture in the direction of the normals. (Bump mapping is not the same as normal mapping, which is another way to obtain a similar effect in certain cases. Normal mapping is not discussed in this book because it has restrictions on its use that make it impractical for texturing characters.)

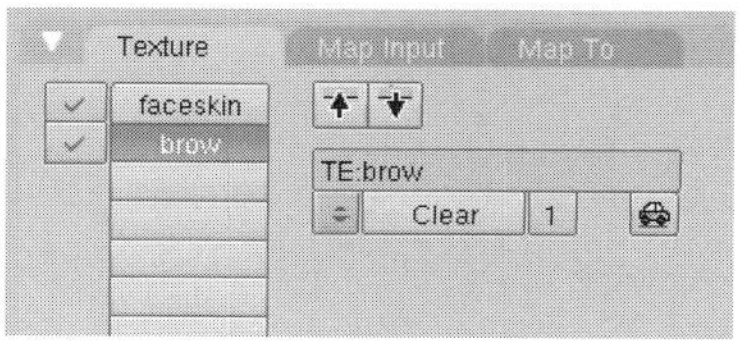

Figure 3.26

Adding the brow texture

You also want to add a little bit of shine to the eyebrows, which you can do by mapping some other values with the same texture. Click Spec and Hard to have this texture control those values as well. As you saw with the chest logo, the Var slider controls how much effect the texture has over these values. You'll set that now at .4. You can now run another render to see the results (see Figure 3.27). The zero point for the texture map is 50% gray, so although the white areas increase in Spec and Hard values, the black parts of the texture actually have their Spec and Hard values reduced. This is all right for your purposes here, but it is something to be careful of. The eyebrows look more convincing now that you have differentiated their specularity and hardness from the rest of the face.

Figure 3.27

A render with bump mapped eyebrows

Eyelashes

So far, you have considered mesh modeling and texturing to be separate tasks. In some cases, however, the two tasks become especially interrelated. In the case of eyelashes, for example, it is desirable to use a texture itself to create the shape of the lashes. Because a texture must be applied to a mesh, it is necessary to return briefly to mesh modeling to create a surface on which to apply the texture. (This is the first of two occasions in this chapter when you'll do some mesh modeling specifically with the intention of creating a suitable base to apply a texture to.)

Modeling convincing eyelashes can be a challenging task, and there are a variety of ways to go about it, from painting them directly onto the surface of the face, to using static particles such as those you'll use for hair later in this chapter, to modeling them directly with meshes. Always consider what kind of quality you need for eyelashes when deciding how to model them. If you plan to have extreme closeups, it will be necessary to use one of the more sophisticated and painstaking approaches.

For the present purposes, you'll take a fairly simple approach to creating and texturing a mesh surface for each set of eyelashes, four in all. You'll start by selecting and duplicating the edge loops around the eyelids, which will be approximately where you want the lashes to be. Move the duplicated edges out a bit along the Y axis to make them easier to work with, as shown in Figure 3.28.

Next, you'll extrude the edge along the Y axis to give you the surface. After extruding, press S, Y, 0. This takes the front edge and lines all the verts up flat on the Y axis, as shown in Figure 3.29.

Figure 3.28

Duplicating the edges around the eyes

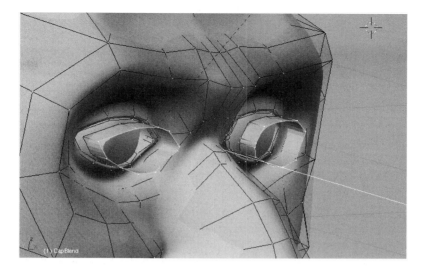

Figure 3.29

Extrude along the Y axis to create the plane of the eyelashes

You'll do a little tweaking now, separating the outer edges of the surface by selecting each edge and hitting the V key and also deleting the face closest to the nose. Also, move the faces back toward the face and position them in the way you want the eyelashes to be. Another important step here is to select all the faces and press Ctrl+N to recalculate the normals outside. If you skip this step, your UV map will not come out right. Your results should look like Figure 3.30.

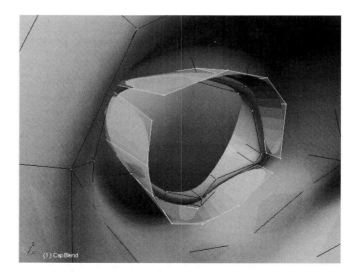

Figure 3.30

Separate the top from the bottom lashes and give them a natural shape

Next, assign a new material, which you can call Lash, to these faces. Set the material color to R:0615, G:0.289, B:0.0. This will give us the reddish-brown color of the eyelashes. Set alpha (A) to 0, set specularity to 0, and select Ray Transp in the Mirror Transp tab. You use Ray Transparency to allow shadows to be cast by the lashes themselves when Ray Shadows are used on a lamp. This will increase the time needed to render, but it will make the lashes a bit more visible. Using Z Transparency will speed up rendering, but will not allow shadows (which help us recognize the shape of the lashes). In the Lash material, create one texture called **LashAlpha**. Create your UV mapping for the lashes in the same way you did for the full head, although in this case you won't have to add seams. Each lash is separate from the others and will be handled by the UV mapper individually: The UV mapping I wound up with can be seen in Figure 3.31. I did not need to tweak it at all in this case. The 2D image I used for the texture can be seen in Figure 3.32. This is a PNG image, and what appears in the figure as white is actually alpha zero. You can create an image like this in Photoshop or Gimp.

Select the LashAlpha texture and go to the texture editing buttons. Select the texture type Image and load the lashes texture image provided on the DVD. With the image loaded, click Use Alpha. Back in the materials buttons, go to the Map Input tab and select UV; then go to Map To, unselect all the buttons on the top, and select only Alpha.

Now select LashColor in the Texture tab and go into texture editing. This texture type will be a blend texture and will use only one color. In the Colors tab, click Colorband. Click Del to get rid of one of the colors. The current color index window will read Cur:0. Render a closeup of your eyelashes. They should be looking something like Figure 3.33.

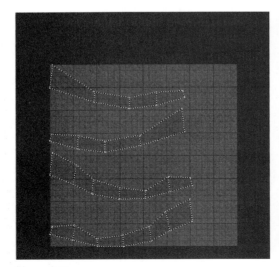

Figure 3.31
The UV unwrapping for the eyelashes

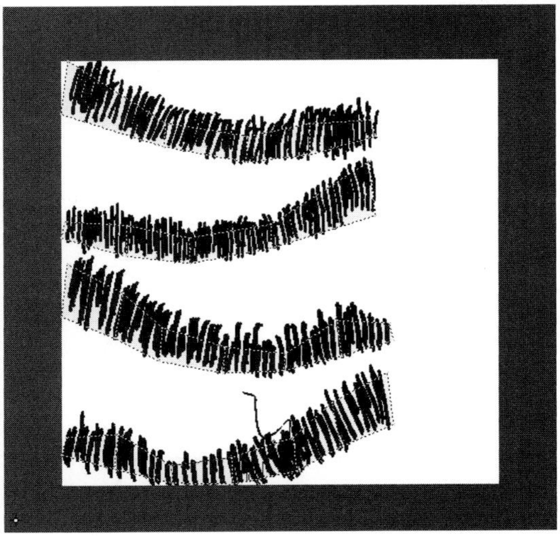

Figure 3.32
A simple image for texturing the lashes

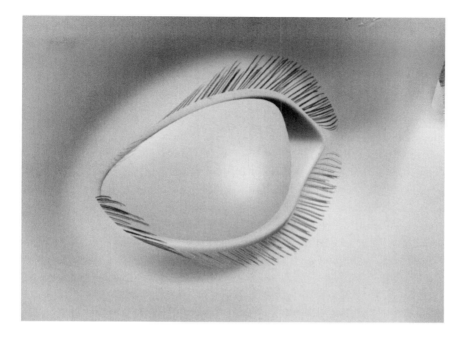

Figure 3.33

The finished eyelashes

Modeling Eyes

So far, the superhero has been lacking one of the most important parts of a convincing human face: eyes. Now you'll replace the blank gray orbs he currently has with some actual eyeballs. This process also involves a few additional steps of mesh modeling.

You'll begin with those very orbs, because they are already the right size. To view the eyeballs on their own, select them in Object mode and press the numeric keypad slash key to enter Local mode. You'll now view only the eyeballs and you can work with them without seeing anything else until the next time you press the number pad slash key.

Figure 3.34

A loop cut for the iris

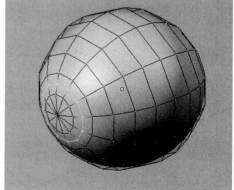

Also, you'll make only one eye and then copy it, so you can remove the mirror modifier and recenter the object center on the single orb object. To remove the mirror modifier, simply click the x in the upper-right corner of the modifier on the modifiers tab. To position the object center, refer to "Object Centers" in Chapter 1.

So now you're working with a single UV sphere with 12 segments and 12 rings. Use the Loop Cut tool (Ctrl+R) to make a loop cut around where the iris will be (see Figure 3.34).

The eyeball is made up of two spheres, one inside the other. The outer sphere is transparent and models the clear lens in front of the iris and the specularity over the surface of the eyeball. The inner sphere will contain the colors and textures you want for the various parts of the eye. To make the two spheres, go back into Object mode and duplicate the orb with Shift+D. Scale the new sphere down one percent by pressing S and immediately entering **.99**.

You'll work with one sphere at a time, so let's put them on separate layers for the time being. Select the outer sphere, press M, and select any of the currently invisible layer buttons to put the sphere on that layer.

With the inner sphere selected, go into Edit mode and create a concave indentation where the iris will be. Make sure that you have proportional editing turned on with the drop-down menu in the 3D window header and set to sphere falloff. Then select the vertex at the pole of the sphere and use G, Y to move the point inward. Make sure to adjust the influence of the proportional editing tool with the + and - keys (or the mouse wheel) so that only the nearest vertices are affected. You can see the influence of the proportional editing tool as a very light gray circle. If you try to move the vertex and the whole eyeball moves, it is because the proportional editing tool's field of influence is very wide. It might be too wide for you to see the circle in the 3D viewport. You might need to move the view out a bit to see the circle. Also, remember that you can adjust the proportional editing tool's field of influence only while you are actually editing. You must press the G key first; then you can adjust the size of the circle. You should wind up with an indentation like the one shown in Figure 3.35.

That's all the modeling you need to do on the inner eye. The real work here is done in the material, and specifically in textures. Create a new material index in the Materials Index tab and name it **EyeBall** in the materials editing area. Turn the RGB values all up to 1, making the eyeball pure white. In the Shaders tab, set specularity to 0.

Figure 3.35

Indenting the iris area with G and Y

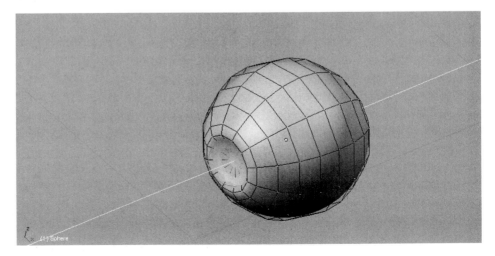

The iris and pupil will be made up of three procedural textures layered on top of each other, which will together create the color, texture, and lightness and darkness of the eye. You'll start with the basic color. Create a new texture in the top texture slot and name it **IrisColor**.

In the texture editing area, select Blend as the texture type. From the options that appear in the Blend tab, choose Sphere. Now select the Colors tab and click Colorband, which enables you to add and remove colors along a gradated band. In the case of a spherical blend, the left and right of the band correspond to the outside edge and the center of the circular blend, respectively. Colors in the color band are associated with an index value, beginning with 0, and you can see the current index you are working within the window labeled Cur (for Current).

When you first open the color band, you are editing color index 0. The default is black with an alpha value of 0. You'll change this to white, but leave the alpha value the same. Do this by moving all RGB sliders to 1.

Next, click the right arrow button in the Cur: field to move to color index 1. You want this white with a 1 alpha value, so slide all the sliders to 1. Notice that you can also slide the barriers between colors to control the location and steepness of the gradation between colors.

Now click Add to add a new color. You'll now be editing color index 2, which will be the base color of Captain Blender's irises. I've selected a mild green with R:0.266, G:0.509, and B:0.081. Add another color index, index 3, and make it solid white with an alpha of 1. Finally add one more color index, index 4, and make it solid black, again with an alpha of 1. This last color index will represent the pupil. Now move the barriers between colors around in the colorband until you have a gradation that looks something like Figure 3.36. Note that the outermost edge is not actually black, but appears so because you have the leftmost color's alpha value set to 0.

Go back to the materials editing buttons. In the Map To tab, choose Col. In the Map Input tab, choose Orco for the mapping. Select Sphe (spherical) as the shape of the mapping and select Y, blank, and X for the axes along which to apply the mapping. Finally, adjust the size of the texture to -2.50 along the X and Z axes. All these options can be seen selected in Figure 3.37.

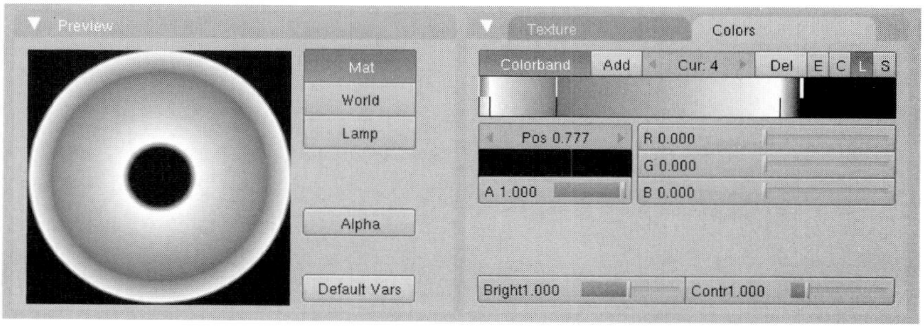

Figure 3.36

Creating the iris and pupil color with a colorband

In the materials preview tab, you can view your texture as it will appear on differently shaped surfaces by pressing the button with the appropriate shape. Press the button with the sphere to see how this texture looks on a sphere. If your model is the same size and rotation as mine, it should look something like Figure 3.38. If not, you might have to wrestle with the Map Input values some.

Another tool for getting an idea of how things are coming along with textures and lighting is in the 3D viewport's preview window. For this, simply click Shift+P in the 3D window. Try this now and verify that your eyeball looks something like Figure 3.39.

You'll now add some texture to this iris. Normally, human irises aren't solid green, but instead are flecked with other colors, such as brown, and so you'll add a brown noise texture to the material to get this effect. You'll need another texture on the EyeBall material, so click on the texture slot and Add New. Name this texture **IrisTexture**.

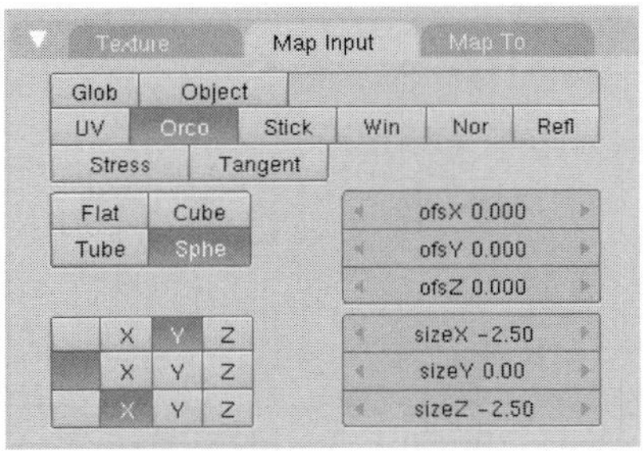

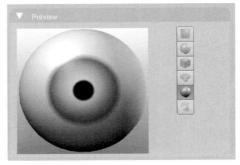

Figure 3.37

Map Input options for the iris texture

Figure 3.38

Your material preview should look like this

Figure 3.39

The eyeball as it looks in the preview window

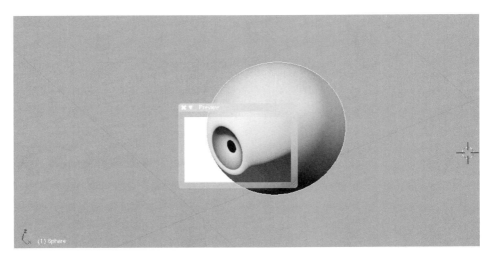

In the texture editing area, select the texture type Clouds. In the Clouds panel, select Hard Noise and set the NoiseSize value at 0.122, which is about half the size of the default, so the cloud texture will be fine enough to give some interesting patterns in the iris.

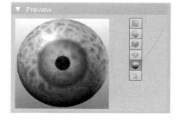

Figure 3.40
The eyeball with cloud texture applied

Go back to the materials editing area. In Map To, select Col and set the mix color to brown by setting R:0.513, G:0.278, and B:0.000. Leave the Map Input values at the default. Your materials preview tab should now be showing something like Figure 3.40, which is textured all right, but not very healthy looking.

To fix the eyeball, insert a stencil texture over the cloud texture to make sure that the cloud noise peers only through the places where you want it. To do this, you take the IrisTexture texture and put it into the third slot instead of the second slot by using the little arrows next to the slots (see the graphic in the margin).

These arrows represent something like Blender's version of copy and paste. The up arrow loads a datablock up into the Blender internal Clipboard. The down arrow brings the datablock down from the Clipboard into the active slot for the datablock. So you will first select the IrisTexture slot (the second box down) and click the up arrow. Then you will select the first empty slot, select the third box down, and click the down arrow. Select the second slot again and click the Clear button; then you'll create the new texture with the Add New button. Name the texture **IrisStencil**.

The IrisStencil texture will again be a spherical blend type texture, and you'll need to set up the color band as you did for the first texture. In this case, you'll have four color indices. Color 1 will be the default alpha 0 black. Color 2 and color 3 will both be alpha 1 white, and color 3 will be alpha 0 black again. Set the position markers as in Figure 3.41.

For the mappings, set the Map Input values exactly the same as the IrisColor texture. For Map To, set Spec and click on Stencil. Check the progress with the Shift+P preview window in the 3D area. The brown cloud texture should now be limited to the iris area and fading toward the center.

Figure 3.41
Colorband for IrisStencil

Now go to the layer in which you left the outer eyeball object and put it back into the same layer with this object using the M key. In Edit mode, with proportional editing turned

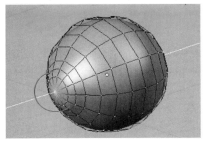

Figure 3.42
Making the lens convex

on (the field of influence should be about the same as it was the last time you used it), select the pole vertex over the iris area and pull it outward along the Y axis to create the slight bump of the eye's lens (see Figure 3.42).

Create a new material for this object and name the material **OuterEye**. Set alpha at 0, and in the Shaders tab, set specularity at 1.100 and hardness at 275. This time, you do not need the material to cast shadows, so ray tracing is unnecessary. If you can avoid it, it will save render time to use Z Transparency instead of Ray Transparency. Z Transparency calculates transparency simply by making things visible that are farther from the camera instead of by following the paths of photons through the material. To turn on Z Transparency, select the ZTransp button under Render Pipeline in the Links and Pipeline panel of the Material buttons.

Your finished product should look something like Figure 3.43 when you render it out. You can join the outer mesh and inner mesh by selecting both in Object mode and hitting Ctrl+J. Name the object **Eyeball.L** and place it in the left eye socket. Then copy the object with Shift+D and press the X key to move the new eyeball directly over to the right eye socket. Place it properly and make sure it's got the correct name.

Figure 3.43
The completed eyeball

In the next section, you'll use particles to give Captain Blender some hair.

Using Static Particles

Blender's particle system is a powerful tool with a wide variety of uses. Particles provide a way to represent and animate clusters of objects that are too small to be practical to simulate in other ways. Dust, powder, swarms of insects, and the like are often suited to simulation with particles. Particles can also be given a blurry quality and used in conjunction with textures to create convincing flame and smoke effects. This book, however, won't be looking at these uses of particles. Instead, it focuses on a specific method of using particles, namely *static particles*, which can be used very effectively to generate convincing fur and hair.

Like all particles, static particles are emitted from a mesh, which is referred to as the emitter. The emitter can be visible or not, and can be made of any material. The static particles also have a material. You can control a number of qualities, such as length and suppleness, by using particle parameters and you can also influence the movement and position of the particles with external forces. Other qualities of the hair are determined by material settings.

Creating Hair with Static Particles

You now want to give Captain Blender some hair. There are a variety of ways to do this: you could model the hairstyle directly with a mesh and use texturing to give it a convincing appearance. With what you've learned so far about texturing and mesh modeling, you should be able to come up with some interesting approaches to doing it. However, the most realistic method of creating hair in Blender is by using particles, which is what you'll do here.

As mentioned previously, particles are emitted from a mesh. Because you want the hair to come from Captain Blender's head, it might seem sensible to have the Captain Blender mesh itself be the emitter. It is possible to control the amount of particles emitted from each face on a mesh, so you could make sure that the particles were only emitted from the hair area on the head. However, this isn't the best approach. Because particle emission is based on vertices and faces, it winds up being closely tied to geometry. To have the maximum control over the particle emission, you will want to freely adjust the geometry to do so. You might want to subdivide the mesh or move verts around. The best geometry for particle emission might well not be the best geometry for the mesh model. For this reason, you'll create a separate mesh to be the particle emitter, but you'll do so based on the original mesh by duplicating the portions of the head you want to emit hair and creating a separate object from the new mesh. Select the verts shown in Figure 3.44 and press Shift+D. Immediately press P to separate the new portion of mesh into a separate object.

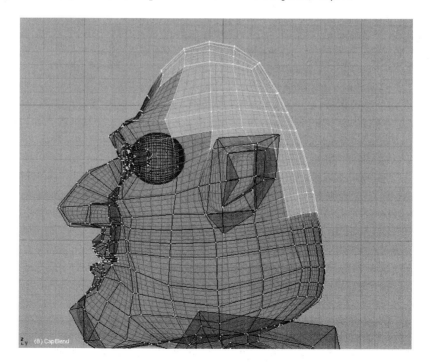

Figure 3.44
Select verts to create a scalp

You'll focus on this new object, a caplike shape that will be the hair emitter. You can fill in a few missing faces around the edges so that you have a nice shape for the hair to emit from, as shown in Figure 3.45.

Because this new mesh object was a copy of the body mesh object, the center is still in the same place. You want to put the center more where it belongs for this object, so position the center in the middle of the mesh, as described previously in Chapter 1. Now reduce the size of the emitter slightly, as shown in Figure 3.46. Also, you need to triple vertex parent the emitter to the head mesh. As explained in Chapter 1, this parenting enables the object to follow both the location and the rotation of the vertex triad to which it is parented. To implement it, choose three vertices in the head that are symmetrically distributed approximately around where the emitter is. Put the hair emitter mesh on a separate layer, but keep both layers visible for the time being. Finally, apply the subsurface modifier, which will make the subsurfaced shape real with an attendant increase in the number of vertices. That is what you want.

Next, go to the edit buttons for this mesh and create a new material. Call the material **Hair**. Set R:0.907, G:0.615, and B:0.213. Set reflectivity at 0.90, specularity at 1.55, and hardness at 195. Click Shadow and TraShadow. Make a note of which material index this material is on.

Figure 3.45
Adjusting the verts and edges in the scalp object

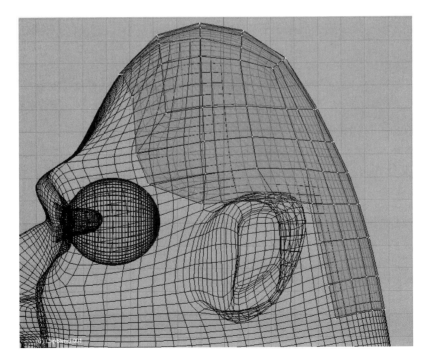

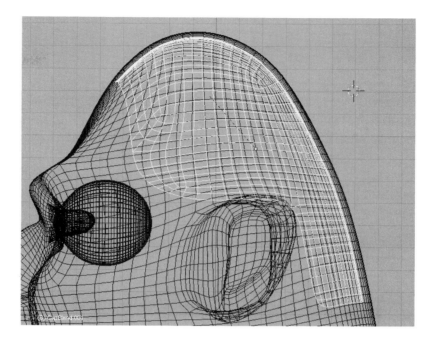

Figure 3.46

The scalp object is reduced to be just under the surface of the actual head.

Now you can turn on the particles. Go to the Object buttons with F7 and into the Physics buttons area, represented by the graphic in the margin.

Under the Particles tab, click New. Select Static. Input the values Emit: 15000, Step: 1, Life: 50, and Disp: 100. Emit is the number of particles that will be emitted; in this case, the number of strands of hair. Step is something like the resolution of the hair. Smaller step values make for more smoothly curving hair. The smallest possible value is 1. Life is the duration of the particle in the case of nonstatic particles. With static particles, it indicates the length of the strand (although this length is also influenced by other factors, as you will see). Finally, Disp is the percentage of particles that will be displayed in the 3D window. I have this set to 100, but if your computer seems slow with this setting, you can reduce it to whatever value your machine can handle. It has no effect on the rendered result.

In the From buttons, select Verts, Faces, and Even. In Display, click Vect and select the appropriate material index for the Hair material in the Material: field.

Now go to the Particle Motion tab. Enter **Keys:24**. In the Normal field, enter **0.005**. In Random, enter **0.001**. These values determine the initial direction of the hair strands.

If you run the preview window over your image now, you see that, sure enough, Captain Blender has sprouted hair. However, to make the hair a little bit more convincing you'll make some adjustments to the hair material. First, go to Links and Pipeline and click Strands. Set the sliders at the values Start:1, End:0.269, and Shape:-0.57, which affects the shape of the particle strands, giving them a concave taper.

Next set the alpha value of the material at 0. You'll control this value with a texture to give the hair a tapered wispy look at the ends. Because the material alpha is the baseline on which texture alpha builds, you want it set to 0.

Create a new texture on this material, which you can call **StrandAlpha**. In the textures editing area, select a linear blend texture type. Go to the Colors tab, click Colorband, and set the values as shown in Figure 3.47. In fact, the color doesn't matter here; all that matters is the alpha value, which should be at 1 for the color index on the left and gradated to 0 for the color index on the right.

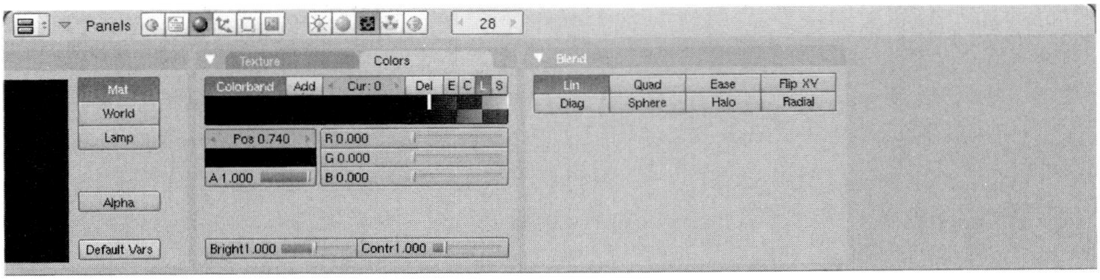

Figure 3.47
Colorband for the hair strand alpha value

Back in the materials editing buttons, select Strand in the Map Input tab. In Map To, select Alpha and unselect all other buttons. Set the Var value at 1.

If you do a render now, you should get something along the lines of Figure 3.48. It is hair all right, but it looks a little like the hero stuck a fork in a toaster. You'll want to do something about his hairstyle.

Figure 3.48
Captain Blender's hair going straight out along the normals of the scalp

Controlling Hair Emission with Vertex Groups and Weight Painting

The particle settings give you a certain amount of control over the length, density, and direction of the particles, but there are ways to control these properties much more precisely. For density and length, a good way to do this is to use vertex groups and weight painting.

You'll be seeing a lot more of both vertex groups and weight painting in the next chapter because both play a crucial (and closely related) role in skinning a mesh to an armature. But there are a variety of other uses as well. You'll look at one here.

Essentially, vertex groups are named collections of vertices. There are no limits on which vertices can belong to what groups. In addition to membership in a group, each vertex also has a weight between 0 and 1 with respect to the group. You can think of the weight as being something like the strength of the vertex's membership in the group. In fact, the weight can have various meanings depending on how you are using the vertex group. A zero weight is for all practical purposes the same as nonmembership in a group (this will be discussed in more depth when you look at weight painting for skinning in Chapter 4). A vertex can be a member of any number of vertex groups at the same time and have a different weight in each group.

To use a vertex group to give Captain Blender a haircut, you first need to create a vertex group on the hair emitter mesh. In Edit mode, click New under Vertex Groups on the Link and Materials tab. Call the vertex group **HairLength**. Now go to the Particle Motion tab. In the Vgroup field, enter **HairLength**.

If you go back into Object mode now, you will see that Captain Blender is bald again because you have made the hair velocity dependent on vertex weights in the vertex group HairLength. At the moment, none of the vertices is members of that vertex group. There are a couple of ways to put these verts into the group. You can do it by hand, in Edit mode, by simply selecting the verts to assign (in this case, all of them) and clicking Assign in the Vertex Group area. The default weight is 1, so if you did that, you would assign all the verts a weight of one. This would put us back in the same state you started in, with all points on the mesh emitting hair at full power.

A more flexible way to assign weights to vertices in a vertex group is to use *weight painting*. With weight painting, zero weights appear as blue, 1 weights appear as red, and weights in between 0 and 1 range from blue-green to yellow to orange. You use the mouse to basically airbrush weights onto the mesh. You can adjust the size of your brush and the opacity of the paint, meaning how many times you need to go over the same spot for the paint to have the full effect. You'll try this now.

Hide the other layers so you can focus on the hair emitter object. (Or you can use the numeric slash key [/] to enter local mode for the emitter object.) Select the object and go into Weight Paint mode using the same drop-down menu from which you select Edit and

Object modes. You should see your object appear in solid blue. In the buttons area, you get a new buttons tab called Paint. Turn Weight and Opacity all the way up to 1 and spray a bit onto the mesh by left-clicking. As shown in Figure 3.49, you should see the hair emerge from the point you're spraying as the underlying color turns red.

You can set the weight however you like. At the bottom portion of the mesh, use a very low weight to get the hair to emerge very short. The vertex paint color gradient is a color spectrum from red (value of one) to blue (zero) which passes through orange, yellow, green, and so on. On the top of the head, the weight should be 1, so the top of the mesh should be fully red. In the middle area, you want green and yellow and orange strips.

Another option in the Paint tab is X-Mirror. Click that to mirror your weight painting along the X axis, which will be very handy in this case.

After a bit of painting, you should come up with something along the lines of Figure 3.50. Although it's not as clearly visible in the grayscale printed figure, on your own screen you'll see that the gradations in weight paint color are visible from the inside of the mesh.

Styling with Curve Guides

The haircut is an improvement, but you can control the hair even more by using *curve guides*, which are curve objects that have a force field activated on them. It's important to realize that Blender's hair styling tools are in their infancy, and an improvement in them is

Figure 3.49

Painting hair onto the mesh in Weight Paint mode

one of the most-often requested features from long-time and new users alike. Although a lot is possible with the present tools, the level of effort and time required to get complex hair effects is quite high, and hair styling can be a source of considerable frustration. It is likely that you'll find yourself among the many users eagerly anticipating improvements to these tools. In the meantime, you'll work with the powerful but painstaking methods presently available.

To make a curve guide, add a Bezier curve object in Object mode with Space → Add → Curve → Bezier Curve. Reduce the size of the curve to approximately the length of one of the longer hairs on Captain Blender's head. In the Object buttons area (F7), go to the Fields and Deflection tab and select Curve Guide from the drop-down menu. Enter **MinDist:0.10** and **Falloff:0.100** and then click Additive. This defines the minimum distance from which the curve guide will have an effect, the distance at which its effect diminishes, and the property of being additive with other curves.

Move the curve around the hair area. You should be seeing the effect of the curve guide on the hair now. If you don't, you probably have the curve on a different layer from the particle emitter. The effects of force fields are always limited to the layer they are on.

Copy this curve and position the two curve guides around the head to get a good basic hairstyle effect. The placement of my hair guides can be seen in Figure 3.51, and the resulting hairstyle can be seen in Figure 3.52.

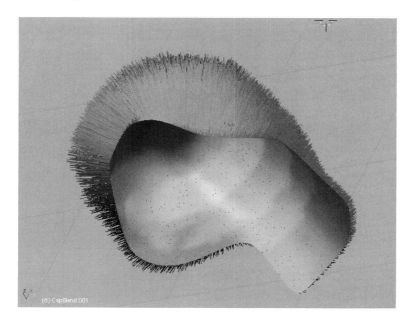

Figure 3.50
Fully weight painted scalp mesh

Figure 3.51

Placement of the curve guides for this hairstyle

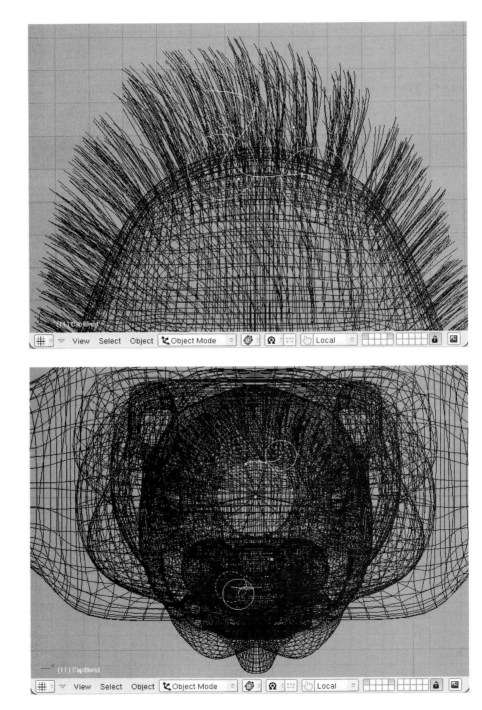

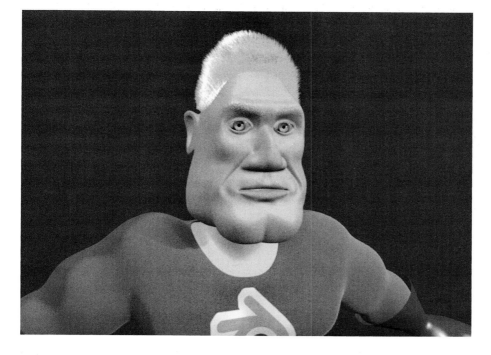

Figure 3.52

A simple hairstyle with curve guides

Curve guide placement can be tricky, and a lot more than two curves may often be necessary to get the hairstyle effect you're after. Furthermore, additive guides are limited the precision with which they allow you to control the hair.

To give an example of a more precise and painstaking way to control hair, you'll give Captain Blender a jaunty heroic cowlick. This is also an example of how hairstyles might be controlled by using multiple overlapping meshes for emitters. To do this, you will duplicate a chunk of the forehead of the current hair emitter mesh, as you can see in the top view image in Figure 3.53.

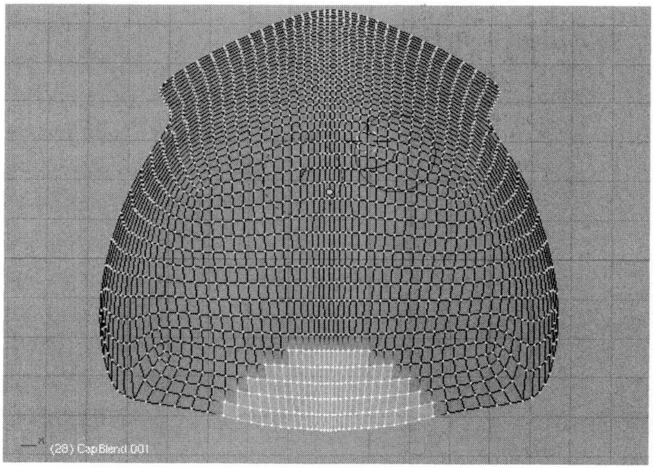

Figure 3.53

Separate a section from the front of the scalp mesh to create a second hair emitter

Duplicate this section with Shift+D and separate it into a separate object with P, as you did with the original hair emitter mesh. You'll see that hair will leap out of the mesh immediately when it becomes a new object. It has inherited a copy of the particle system of the first mesh. You need to make a few adjustments to the particle system here. In Object mode, select the new forehead hair mesh and put it on a separate layer.

Now go to the Particles tab for this object and change the Amount value to **2000**. Go to Particle Motion and set Normal to 0. Also, for visualization purposes, I have Disp set to 0 in the Particles tab, so you can see clearly what I'm doing with the curve guides. This means that the particles will not be drawn in the 3D window. Setting this low can help speed things up if your 3D window display becomes sluggish, but it will not have an effect on how the particles are ultimately rendered.

Create a Bezier curve on the same layer as the forehead hair mesh. Be sure to select 3D button in the Curve and Surface tab of the curve object. Extrude a second segment from one end of the curve using the E key, yielding three control points (This can also be done by subdividing the curve using the menu accessible with the W key.) Add a curve guide force to this curve, but in this case select Use MaxDist and enter a MaxDist value of **0.04**. In this case, you will want the hair to follow the guides closely and each guide's effect to be localized, so don't select Additive. Shape your curve something like that shown in Figure 3.54. Copy the curve in Object mode three times. Place the curves with the small dotted circle against the forehead mesh. This circle indicates the exact area within which hair particles will follow the curve. Edit each curve to be somewhat different from the others, so that you wind up with a cluster of four similar but different curves, like those shown in Figure 3.55. Note that the particle display value has been set to 0 on the mesh so that the curves can be seen clearly.

With the display value set back to 100, you can see what the hair looks like as it follows these curves. The cluster of fuzz on the surface of the mesh is due to the 0.001 value you left in the random field in the Particle Motion tab. This will be hidden under the head mesh in any case, and it is helpful to have a slight random influence in the hairs following the guide. Position the forehead hair mesh and curve guides with respect to the head mesh, as shown in Figure 3.56.

Preview and tweak until you've got Captain Blender's hair looking like you want it. It should look something like the render shown in Figure 3.57.

Figure 3.54

A 3D Bezier curve to guide the cowlick

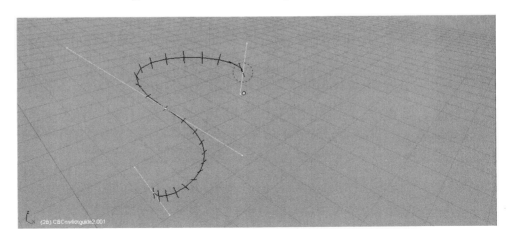

(28) CBCowlickguide2.001

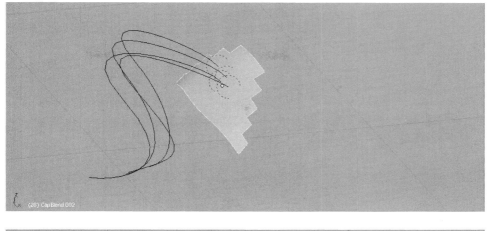

Figure 3.55
A cluster of curves is used to create the cowlick

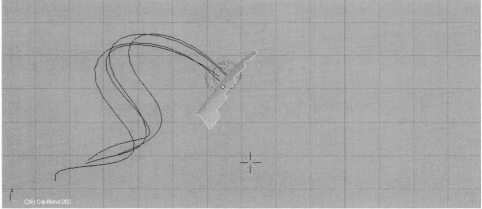

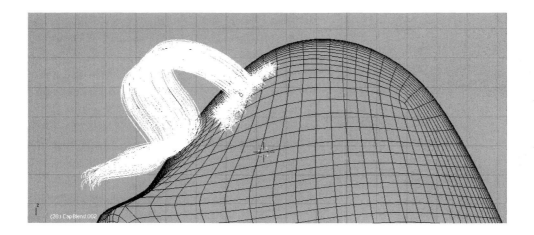

Figure 3.56
Particle strands following the cowlick curve guides

Figure 3.57

**Captain Blender
with a full head
of hair**

Using curve guides can be a painstaking endeavor. Particularly with characters with long hair, a hairstyle can easily require 100 or more carefully positioned curves and several emitter meshes. The case here is a comparatively simple example, intended to give you an idea of what's possible and how to use the tools. If you're new to using hair guides, hang in there and have patience. Hopefully, improvements will be along soon.

You now have completed the creation of the Captain Blender mesh. The next step is to rig and skin the mesh with an armature that will enable you to pose and animate the character. You'll learn how to do this in the next chapter.

CHAPTER 4

Armatures and Rigging

Most 3D character animation, both CG and traditional, relies on armatures to manipulate the characters' body parts. Armatures behave as the characters' skeletons, and their segments are referred to as bones. Of course, the mechanics of motion and posing are very different for a 3D mesh than they are for a flesh-and-blood human, so the bones of a CG character do not generally correspond to actual bones in a live person. Nevertheless, they are very similar conceptually. Building an armature can be very simple or very complicated, depending upon how much control the animator wants over the character's body parts and how many constraints and restrictions are desired on the character's movement. An armature in which the knees can be bent sideways, for example, is likely to be a simpler armature than one in which the joints have natural limitations. The degree of complexity necessary in an armature depends upon the requirements of the animation. A good armature should result in an easy-to-manipulate character with convincing movements.

The process of "rigging" a character means setting up an armature and its associated constraints. "Skinning" refers to connecting a mesh to an armature so that manipulating the armature results in the desired deformations of the mesh. The mesh should follow the movement of the armature in the appropriate way. Simply put, this is accomplished by having each bone influence the movement of certain vertices. There are several ways to assign influence to vertices, which are discussed in this chapter.

- **Blender Armature System**
- **Building a Simple Armature**
- **Rigging Captain Blender**

Blender Armature System

An armature in Blender is made up of bones and their parent relationships, connections, and the various constraints that control their motion and interaction. A well-put-together armature can be used to create very realistic poses quickly and easily. You now look briefly at the basic types of bones and constraints used in creating sophisticated armatures.

Bones

The armature system in Blender includes a variety of options for the behavior and the display of bones. Depending on the options selected for each bone, it is possible to identify a number of basic bone types used in rigging.

Deform bones This is the default for bones. Deform bones are allowed to influence the vertices of a mesh.

B-Bones B-bones are bones that can be broken into multiple segments, enabling them to bend and twist. B-bones work like bezier splines (the "B" stands for "bezier"), and each bone acts as a curve handle, allowing for curvy poses. They can be useful for creating flexible spines and curving limbs. They can also be used to distribute torque over a larger area than just the joint, which can be useful for ball-and-socket joints such as shoulders, which provide special challenges for rigging.

IK solvers IK solvers are used to control the endpoint of an inverse kinematic (IK) chain, in which the position of the chain of bones is calculated based on the location of the tip of the chain.

Stride bone The stride bone is used to associate an armature's progress along a path with the movements of the bones in the armature. It is used to ensure that the down foot is fixed relative to the ground as the armature moves forward during a walk cycle.

Ipo drivers Bones can be used to control any animatable property by creating an interpolation (Ipo) driver associating the bone's position or rotation with the appropriate Ipo.

Custom controls Custom controls aren't so much a type of bone as just a special way of customizing the appearance of bones. You can have bones appear in Pose mode in the form of specially assigned meshes, which can be useful for visually distinguishing special-use bones such as Ipo drivers from other bones.

A variety of options exist for bone display and editing. Many of these options are discussed in this chapter.

Constraints

Constraints are essentially restrictions and controls that make movements by an object or bone dependent on another object or on some other factor. Setting up an armature with well-applied constraints can make posing the armature much easier than simply controlling every bone's movement completely by hand.

Important constraints in armature design include the following:

IK Constraint Works with an IK solver to create a chain of bones whose position can be determined by the location of the tip.

Copy Location/Rotation/Scale Restricts the location, rotation, or scale of one bone or object to that of another. It is more restrictive than parenting in that the constrained object or bone cannot be translated, rotated, or scaled independently of the other.

Track-to Constraint Forces an object or bone to point in the direction of ("track to") a specified object. This is useful for eye tracking and also to control the movement of the camera by tracking the camera to an empty.

Floor Constraint Defines an object or bone beneath which another object or bone won't go. This is often used in conjunction with IK solvers to prevent feet from going beneath the level of the ground.

Stretch-to Constraint Causes a bone or object to stretch or squash to an object or bone that is set as the target constraint. It can also manage the displacement of volume, which results from the stretching or squashing.

Action Constraint Enables a bone's movement to be controlled by an action that has been animated in advance and that in turn is linked to the rotation around a specific axis of another bone.

Building a Simple Armature

To get a look at the basics of building, displaying, and posing an armature, you'll build a quick and simple armature for the figure shown in Figure 4.1. If you followed the modeling tutorials in Chapter 2, you should have no problem box-modeling the figure yourself. If you prefer to skip the modeling, you can find the mesh of this figure on the accompanying DVD, in the file `figure.blend`. In the following example, front view is the view displayed by pressing numeric 1, top view is the numeric 7 view, and numeric 3 displays the view from the left side of the figure, as in the other examples in this book. If you model the mesh yourself and use a mirror modifier, be sure to apply the modifier to make the whole mesh real before proceeding to rig the mesh.

Figure 4.1
A simple figure

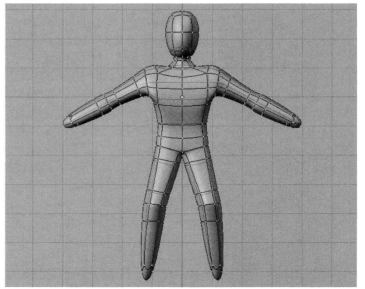

Figure 4.2

Adding an armature

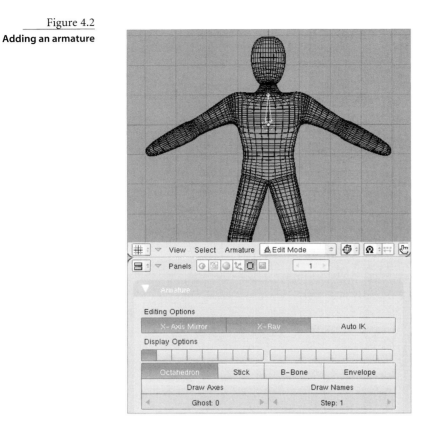

The first step is to create the armature. The 3D cursor should be placed at the center of the mesh object. In Object mode, press the space bar and select Add → Armature. A bone will appear in Edit mode with its root at the 3D cursor.

There are a number of editing options for armatures. For this exercise, select X-Ray and X-Axis Mirror to make the armature visible through the mesh and to enable mirrored editing across the X axis, which is very handy when creating symmetrical armatures such as this one.

Editing armatures and bones is analogous to editing most kinds of objects in Blender. The G, R, and S keys have the same effect of translation, rotation, and scaling as they do elsewhere. Likewise, the E key is used to extrude, which in the case of bones creates a new connected bone from the tip or the root of the original bone.

You begin by using a variant form of extrusion that is enabled by X axis mirroring, and press Shift+E to do a mirrored extrude from the tip of this first bone. Draw the extruded bone out to your right and notice that a mirrored bone also emerges, resulting in the shoulder portion of the armature you see in Figure 4.3.

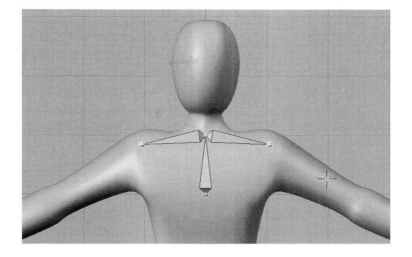

Figure 4.3

Using mirror extrude (Shift+E) to form the shoulders

From the endpoint of the bone you extruded, extrude two more bones for the arms by pressing the plain E key. It is no longer necessary to specify a mirrored extrusion with Shift+E. Any bones you extrude from these mirrored bones now have all edits, including extrusions, mirrored across the X axis.

Adjust the center bone downward somewhat with the G key and Z key to put the base of the neck at a better position. Then extrude upward from that bone by pressing the E key once, followed by the Z key once, to ensure that the extrusion is straight along the Z axis. At the top of the neck, extrude again in the same way for the head.

Figure 4.4

Extruding the arms

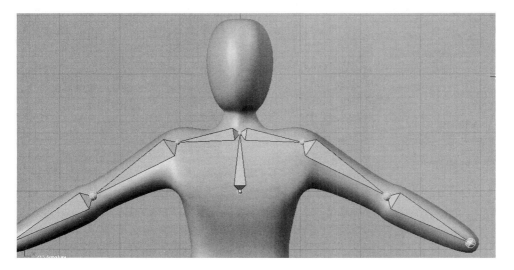

Figure 4.5

**Extruding down-
ward to create the
lower abdomen**

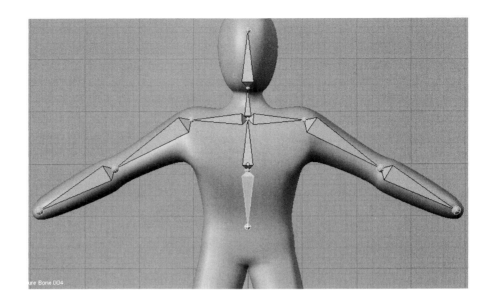

For the lower body, select the root of the first bone. (The root is the lower portion here, the short portion of the octahedron. The longer end is called the tip.) Extrude another bone straight down from this point by pressing the E key and Z key, as shown in Figure 4.5.

Press Shift+E to mirror-extrude the hips and then continue extruding down the character's left side (your right side). Extrude two bones for the leg, connected at the knee. Then, extrude one more bone straight down by pressing E and Z. These two final bones, extending beyond the edge of the mesh, have a special use, and they should not be connected to the rest of the bones. Select them *both* and press Alt+P and select Clear Parent. This operation is not handled by the mirror-edit function, so it is necessary to make sure that both bones are selected.

Arms and legs should be bent slightly in their rest position to facilitate proper bending during IK posing. You should bear this in mind when modeling your mesh and when setting up your armature.

Adjust the bones' endpoints from front and side to get them approximately similar to the setup shown in Figure 4.6. When you have them properly placed, select them all with the A key and press Ctrl+N to recalculate the bone roll angles, which will correct for the rolling that the bones did when you edited them.

It is a good idea to always do this (and most rigging tasks) before you begin to animate. When you have done this, select the mesh and add an armature modifier. This process is done in the same way as any other modifier, such as the subsurf and mirror modifiers you have seen previously. The difference here is that you must specify the name of the modifier object you want to use. In the Ob. field, enter **Armature**, which is the default name of the first armature created. Also, make sure that the Vert Groups button is unselected and the Envelopes button is selected, as shown in Figure 4.7.

Envelopes

The main point of rigging is to associate the influence of bones in the armature to vertices on the mesh. As mentioned previously, there are several ways to do this. The most sophisticated way is to use vertex groups and weight painting, which is the method you will spend time on later in this chapter. For very simple cases, an expedient way is to use envelopes. When you use envelopes, you allow each bone to influence all vertices within some specific area around the bone, defined as the bone's envelope. You can scale both the primary influence within the envelope and a secondary area of gradated influence.

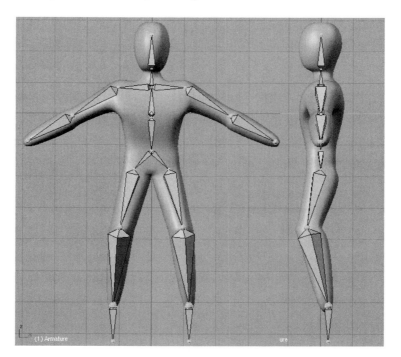

Figure 4.6

Front and side views of the completed armature

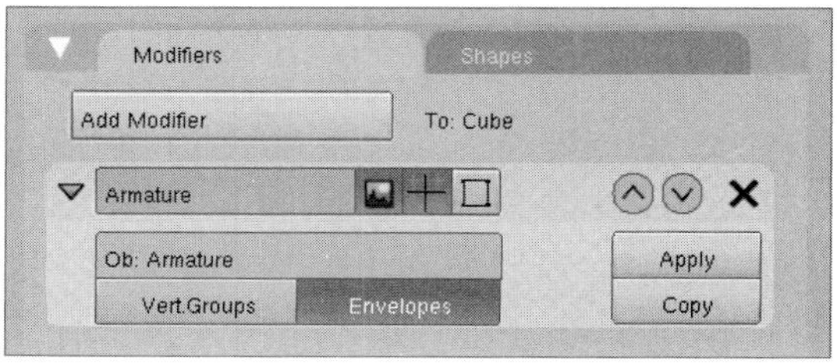

Figure 4.7

The Armature modifier panel

If you switch the bone display option from Octahedron to Envelopes, you see the bones' envelopes represented graphically, as shown in Figure 4.8. The tubelike shapes you see are the envelopes themselves. Portions of the mesh within their area will be influenced fully by the bone's movement. The translucent white areas around the envelopes are their areas of gradated influence. The influence here diminishes from 1 to zero, and vertices that fall inside these areas will be partially influenced by the bone.

You must be in Envelope Display mode to scale the envelopes. If you are, you can scale them by selecting the envelope or the bone tip (envelopes show up purple; tips show up yellow). The secondary influence area can be scaled by pressing Alt+S. In Edit mode, you can scale the secondary envelope on multiple bones at a time, but the bones must be selected in their entirety, either by clicking the bone or by Shift+clicking both endpoints. To scale these, switch to Pose mode using the Mode drop-down menu. You want to scale the envelopes so that they completely enclose the mesh, and so the appropriate portions of the mesh are contained within the envelope of the bone that should move them. This process will result in the envelopes looking something like Figure 4.9.

The figure can now be posed (see Figure 4.10). Switch the armature display option to Stick to make things a little easier to see. Enter Pose mode and try out some poses. Simply select a bone and rotate it in Pose mode. You might notice some problems. Some areas might not be moving along with the bone, as in the case of the elbow in Figure 4.11. That section of the mesh is probably not adequately covered by the envelope. Increase the size of the envelope around that spot.

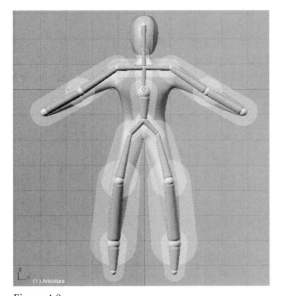

Figure 4.8
The armature in Envelope Display mode

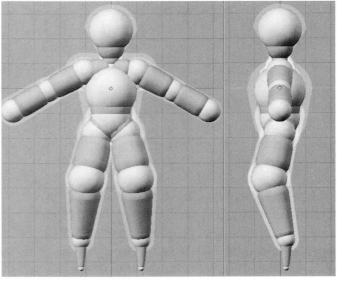

Figure 4.9
Envelopes edited to enclose the mesh

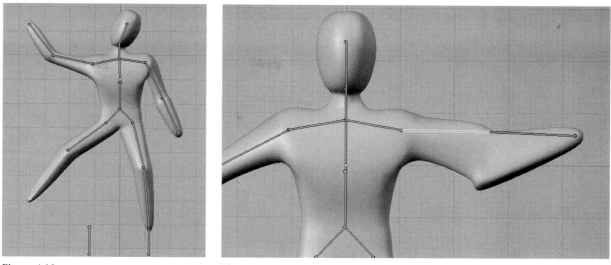

Figure 4.10

Posing the armature

Figure 4.11

A deformation problem caused when an area of the mesh is not covered by an envelope

Before continuing, reset your mesh into the rest pose. You can do this by selecting all the bones in Pose mode and pressing Alt+R to clear rotations (if necessary, Alt+G and Alt+S will clear locations and scaling as well, but that shouldn't be necessary here).

Inverse Kinematics

The type of posing you did in the last section when you rotate a bone—for example, the upper arm or leg—and the bones which are parented to the posed bone follow along is called *forward kinematics*. The posing motion is controlled at the root of the limb to be posed. Another way to pose is called *inverse kinematics*, in which the posing is done by positioning the end of the limb and letting the computer calculate the various angles the limb has to take to get there. Inverse kinematics can be a very powerful tool, but both methods have their appropriate uses, as you will learn later. For now, you will look at a quick example by applying an IK constraint to the left leg of the model. The unconnected bone at the very end of the leg chain will be the IK solver bone. Let's give it a name that makes a little more sense than the current name: call it **IK.L**. You can name it by selecting it in Edit mode and entering the name in the BO: field in the Armature Bones tab, as shown in Figure 4.12. You have already unparented it, so there should be no bone visible in the Child Of drop-down menu. Also, Deform should be unselected. I have given meaningful names to the other bones as well.

Next, you want to apply an IK constraint to the final bone of the IK chain, which is the sequence of bones that will move to follow the IK solver. In the case of this leg, it is the lower leg bone, named LowerLeg_L, which needs the constraint. In Pose mode, select this bone and choose Add Constraint in the Constraints tab. Select IK Solver and set the values, as shown in Figure 4.13. For the OB: value, enter **Armature** because you are constraining it to a bone in the Armature object. When an Armature object is entered in this field, a BO: field will automatically appear, and you can enter the name of the IK solver bone in that field. Make sure that Use Tip is selected and that ChainLen is set to 2. You can also use a convenient shortcut for setting IK constraints. To do this, simply select the target of the IK constraint, Shift+select the bone you want to apply the constraint to, press Ctrl+I, and select the appropriate choice in the drop-down menu. This will save a number of steps in setting up your IK constraint, but you will still need to edit the chain length in the Constraints panel.

> The default chain length is defined as 0, which actually means that the entire chain of bones, up to the root, is included in the IK chain. This is often not what you want and can lead to strange behavior of the armature when you pose the IK solver. Be sure to set your ChainLen value to end at the point where you want your IK chain to stop.

And with this, the IK constraint is in place. Now move the left leg IK solver around and observe the effect, illustrated in Figure 4.14. If you want to return the armature to its rest position, press Alt+G.

Vertex Groups and Weight Painting

Simply using envelopes is fine for simple meshes; in particular, limbs that are relatively narrow and uniformly shaped can be satisfactorily deformed by using only envelopes. However, envelopes are very limited in the amount of control they allow over the placement

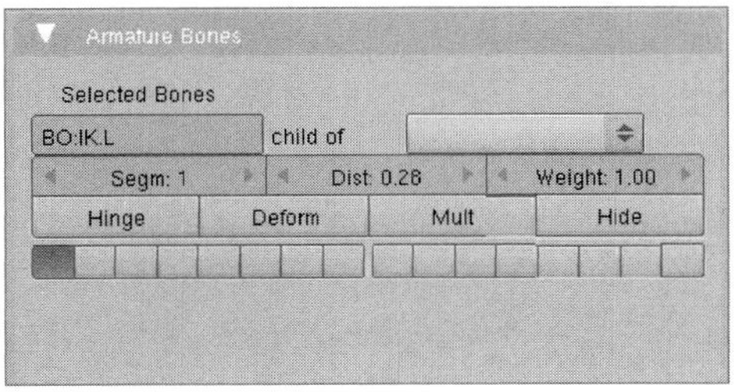

Figure 4.12

Armature Bones panel for IK.L

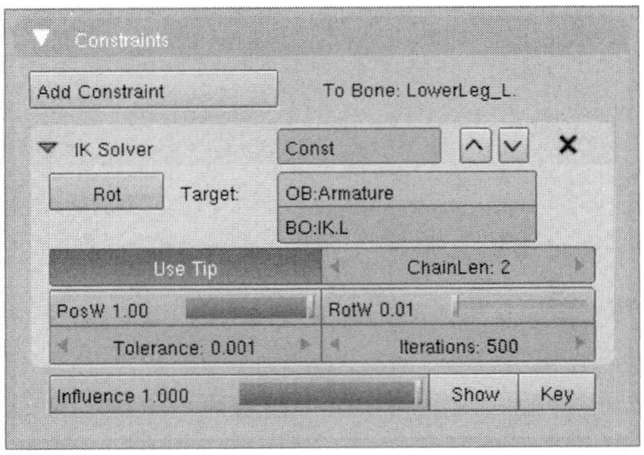

Figure 4.13

IK Constraints panel

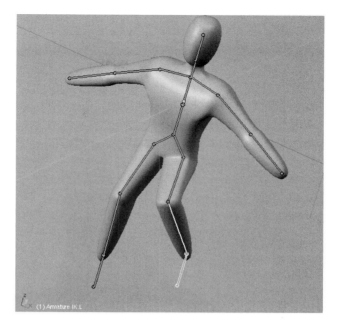

Figure 4.14
Posing with the IK solver

and strength of bone influence on a mesh. For more complex rigs, it will be necessary to define vertex groups for each deform bone and to assign weights to the verts within these groups, similarly to the way you controlled the hair length in Chapter 3.

You can create vertex groups automatically by converting the envelopes influence to vertex group weights. First select the armature and ensure that it is in Pose mode. Next, select the mesh and enter Weight Paint mode. The entire mesh is solid blue regardless of which bones are selected because there are no vertex groups defined on the mesh.

When naming bones, always ensure that the bone names end with .R and .L (or _L and _R) for left and right, respectively, because a number of useful automatic functions in Blender rely on this convention. To name the bones, in Edit mode name one side's bone in the Armature Bones tab (for example, **UpperArm.L**). Then move your mouse over the text field for the name *without clicking* and press Ctrl+C. Select the corresponding bone on the right side, and again move over the text field without clicking and click Ctrl+V. This will paste the same name into the field, and Blender will automatically add the .001 suffix because it is a duplicate name. Now, with the right bone selected in Edit mode, press W while in the 3D window and select Flip Left-Right Names. Blender automatically renames your bone UpperArm.R.

Select the upper-left arm bone, press the W key, and click Apply Bone Envelopes to Vertex Groups. As you'll see on your monitor, the area around the bone will turn red (in grayscale illustrations such as Figure 4.15, the red area appears as lighter gray, whereas the blue area appears as dark gray). To recall the discussion of weight painting in Chapter 3, this indicates that the vertices in this area have a weight of one for the vertex group associated with this bone. You will also find that the new vertex group has appeared in the vertex group drop-down menu for your mesh.

Figure 4.15

Weight paint on the shoulder of the mesh

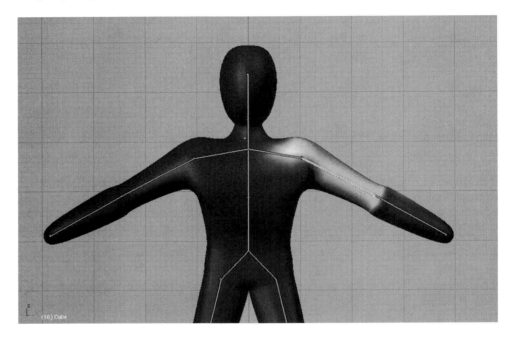

Do the same for the other bones and then go to the armature modifier and turn off Envelopes and turn on Vert.Groups. You can now adjust the influence of the bone in the same way as you adjusted the hair length in Chapter 3, using weight painting. You can also pose bones while you are in Weight Paint mode, enabling you to see how your weight painting is affecting the deformations in specific poses. An example of the improvement in deformations that can be attained by applying just a little bit of weight paint on the two arm bones can be seen in Figure 4.16.

A common source of deformation problems is to have the wrong deformation option selected. If you are using vertex groups, you should be sure to have Envelopes deselected in the armature modifier. It is possible to use both at once, but in most cases this is not what you will want.

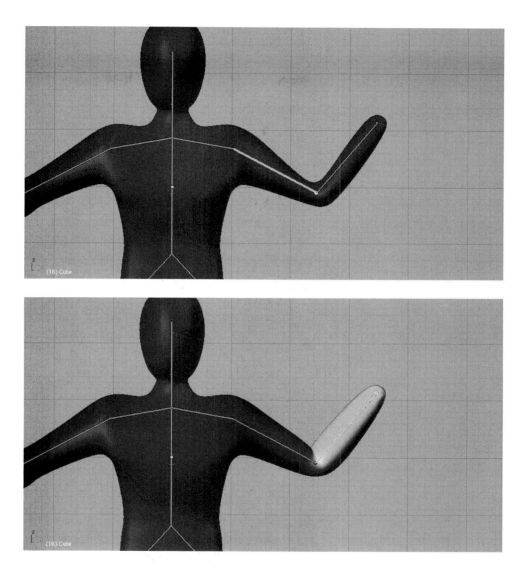

Figure 4.16

An example of improved deformation using weight painting

Rigging Captain Blender

Now that you've learned some of the most basic concepts of armatures and rigging, you'll return to our hero and get down to putting together a high-quality, full-featured rig to control him. The rig you'll be building is a slightly adapted version of the freely available Ludwig rig by Jason Pierce. You can find Jason's complete Ludwig character on the DVD in the file `ludwig.blend`. This is a very nice rig that makes use of a variety of interesting features.

You begin in Object mode with the Captain Blender mesh on layer 1 and start working with the armature in layer 2. Select the mesh object, press Shift+S, and select Cursor to Selection to center the cursor on the mesh to start creating the armature. Press Space → Add → Armature. You now have a single bone in Edit mode. In the Armature tab in the buttons area, select X-Axis Mirror and X-Ray for editing options. You should now be seeing something like Figure 4.17.

This first bone will be the armature's Root bone. All the other bones will be directly or indirectly parented to this bone, so that when you move this bone the entire figure will move with it. Place the Root bone as in Figure 4.18 by rotating the bone 90 degrees along the global X axis (press R, X, 90) and translating it down along the Z axis (press G, Z). In the Armature Bones tab, find the field that says BO: Bone. This is the name of the bone. If you continue without changing this name, each new bone is automatically named Bone.001, Bone.002, Bone.003, and so on, which is not very descriptive. At least for now, try to name your bones more or less as soon as you create them. Change this bone's name to **Root.**

With your 3D cursor in the same spot it was before, create a new bone. With the pivot point set to the 3D cursor, size the bone down so that it is as it appears in Figure 4.19. It will be the base of Captain Blender's spine.

Figure 4.17

Adding an armature to Captain Blender

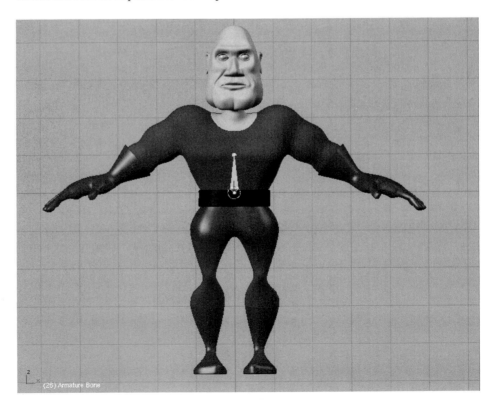

Figure 4.18
Positioning the Root bone

(28) Armature Bone

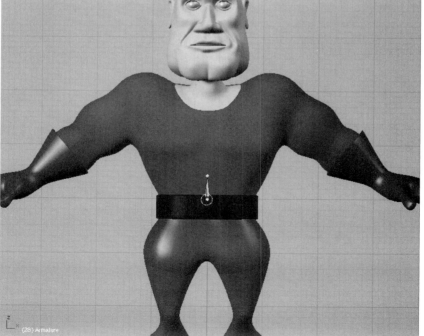

Figure 4.19
Base of the spine

(28) Armature

Extrude straight up three times to create the basis of the spine. Do this by pressing E, Z to constraint the axis. From the bottom up, name these bones **Spine.1**, **Spine.2**, **Spine.3**, and **Spine.4**. Add another bone by pressing the spacebar. With the pivot point set to the cursor, rotate the bone 90 degrees and size it up a bit, as shown in Figure 4.20. Name this bone **Torso**, and parent Torso to Root. There are two ways to do this. In the Selected Bones panel in Edit mode with Torso selected, select Root from the Child Of drop-down menu and be sure that the Co button to the right of the drop-down menu is unselected. You don't want these bones connected. The other way to parent the bones is to select both bones in the 3D window (first Torso and then Root) and then press Ctrl+P. Select Keep Offset. Figure 4.21 shows the result.

From the tip of Spine.4, extrude a bone called UpperBody straight back along the Y axis. Reparent this bone to Torso in the same way you parented the Torso bone to Root, as shown in Figure 4.22.

Extrude another bone forward from Spine.4. Name this bone **Shoulders** and parent it to UpperBody. If it's not already there, snap the cursor to the base of Spine.1 and add a bone with the spacebar. Rotate the bone -90 degrees with the 3D cursor as pivot point, so that it looks like Figure 4.23. Name this bone **Pelvis** and parent it to Torso.

Figure 4.20

Side view of Torso and the four spine bones

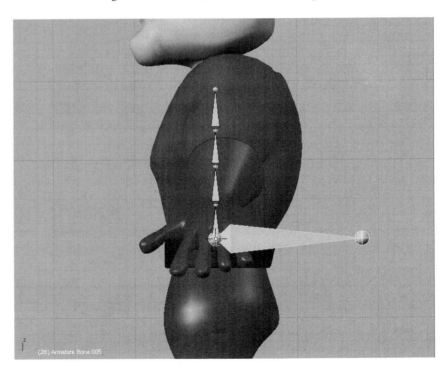

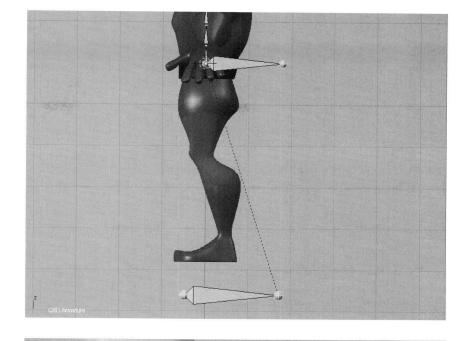

Figure 4.21

Torso bone parented to Root

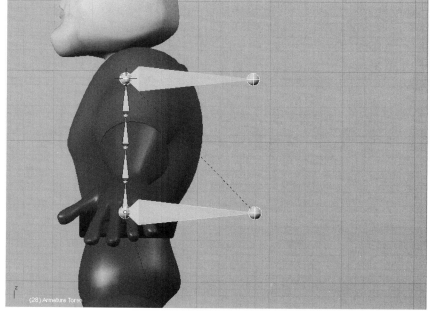

Figure 4.22

UpperBody is parented to Torso

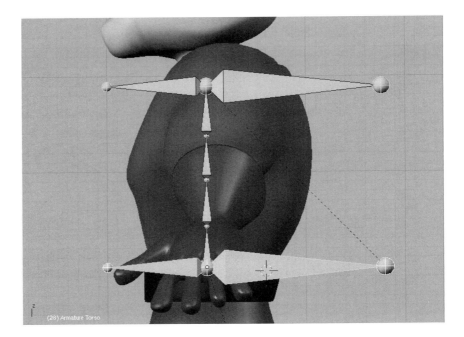

You'll now put the X-mirror editing to work for you. From the tip of Spine.4, mirror-extrude the shoulder bones. Do this by pressing Shift+E and then add the X key to constrain it to the X axis; the resulting bones should look like Figure 4.24. From now on, any extrusion or movement of one side of this extruded chain will be mirrored on the other side.

> X-mirror armature modeling applies to extruding and moving bones, but not to duplicating, parenting, or unparenting bones. When you do these things, it is necessary to explicitly select both sides' bones to have the change apply to both sides.

Name the left bone **Shoulder.L** and follow the bone-naming instructions at the beginning of this chapter to name the right shoulder bone appropriately (it should wind up with the name **Shoulder.R**). From the tip of Shoulder.L, extrude a small bone straight back along the Y axis. This extruded bone should be mirrored on the right side, as shown in Figure 4.25.

Select *both* of these bones and press Alt+P to disconnect the bones. Do not clear the parent. Now displace the bones back slightly along the Y axis, as shown in Figure 4.26. Name these small bones **ShoulderLoc.L** and **.R**. You will use them to fix the location of the base of the arms, so that you can position them independently of the neck and spine. However, first you'll take advantage of the mirrored extrusion by extruding the bicep bones directly from the shoulder bones, as shown in Figure 4.26. Name these bones **Bicep.L** and **.R**.

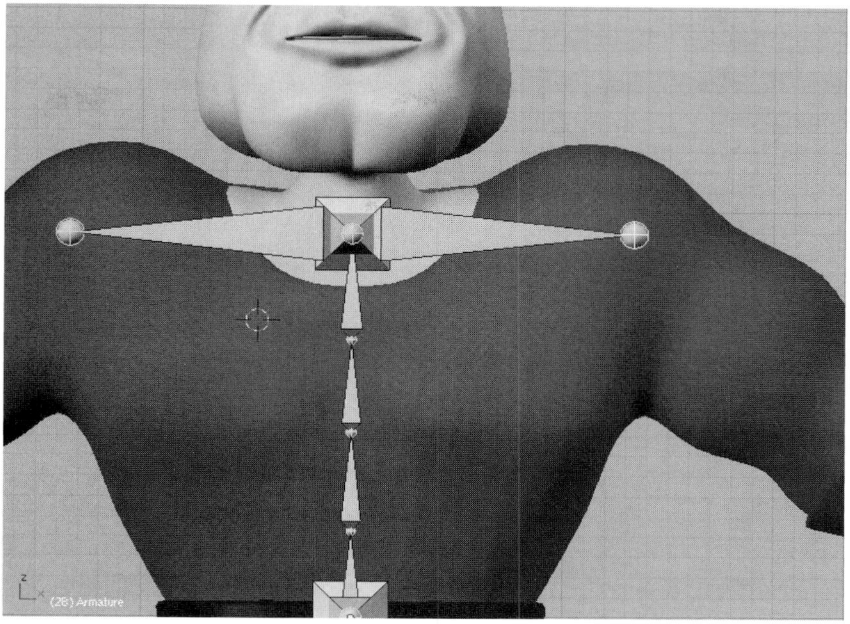

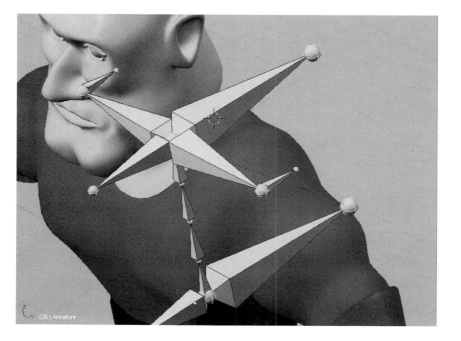

Figure 4.24

Mirror extruding the shoulders

Figure 4.25

Extruding location bones for the shoulders

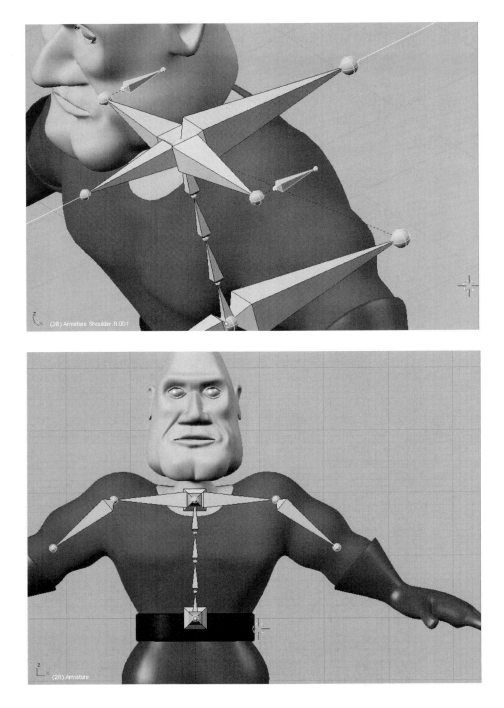

Figure 4.26

Displace the shoulder locators slightly

Figure 4.27

Extruding the biceps from the shoulder bones

You'll reparent each bicep to the Torso bone. This will automatically separate them from the shoulder. To keep the biceps anchored in place, you'll use a copy location constraint and have each bicep copy the location of the corresponding ShoulderLoc bone. To create a constraint, go into Pose mode and go to the constraints tab in the edit buttons. Click Add Constraint and select Copy Location. The constraint name does not really matter; it just helps to distinguish them if there is more than one on a particular bone, so you can leave that as Const. Fill in the rest of the fields, as shown in Figure 4.28, for both the right and the left bicep. Whatever you decide to name your constraint, you should decide before you begin animating; after you key a constraint's influence, as you will begin to do in Chapter 7, you shouldn't rename the constraint.

Figure 4.28

The copy location constraint

If you flip back and forth between Pose mode and Edit mode now, you will see the bicep bone jump over to meet the ShoulderLoc bone in Pose mode. You want the rest pose be identical to the Edit mode pose, so you have to make sure that the bones are already where the constraints will force them to be. You can do this now by simply moving the biceps back along the Y axis until their roots are squarely on top of the roots of the ShoulderLoc bones, as shown in Figure 4.29. It might help to go to the side view (press numeric 3) and toggle into wireframe view (press Z) before doing this to make sure the bones' roots line up.

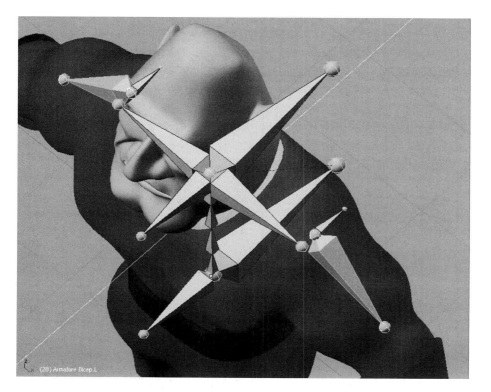

Figure 4.29

Positioning the biceps in Edit mode to match their constrained rest position

Constraints influence the pose in Pose mode, but not in Edit mode. To return a bone in Pose mode to its rest pose, select the bone and clear its rotation, location, and/or scale by pressing Alt+R, Alt+G, and Alt+S, respectively. If bones are still positioned differently in Pose mode than in Edit mode after doing this, it is the result of some constraint acting upon them. For maximum control and clarity while working, it is a good idea to try to keep the rest pose in Pose mode as close as possible to the Edit mode pose. This can be done in part by planning ahead where your constraint target bones are placed so that their influence in rest pose does not alter the unconstrained rest pose position.

From the tip of the bicep, continue to extrude down the arm, extruding bones you'll name **Forearm.L** and **Hand.L**, as shown in Figure 4.30. Mirror the names.

Extrude the base of the thumb, select both right and left bones and disconnect them by pressing Alt+P. Move them forward along the Y axis and rotate them into place at the base of the thumb, as shown in Figure 4.31.

Figure 4.30

Extruding the fore-arms and hands

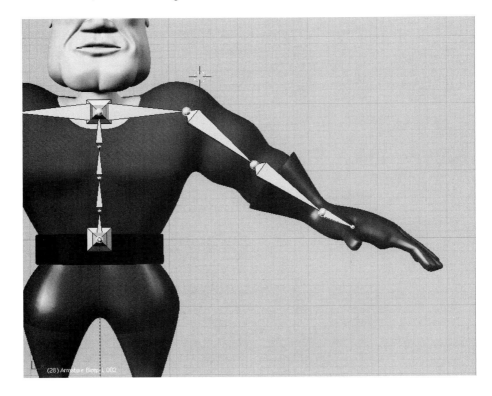

Extrude twice to form the segments of the thumbs. Now select all three bones on both sides, six in all, and press Shift+D to duplicate. Offset the duplicated bones slightly and duplicate in the same way three more times to create the rest of the fingers. Position the fingers as shown in Figure 4.32. Counting outward from the hand, give the bones the following names (suffixed with .L and .R, accordingly):

fin_thumb_1	fin_thumb_2	fin_thumb_3
fin_index_1	fin_index_2	fin_index_2
fin_middle_1	fin_middle_2	fin_middle_3
fin_ring_1	fin_ring_2	fin_ring_3
fin_pinky_1	fin_pinky_2	fin_pinky_3

Figure 4.31
Extrude the thumbs and select both to disconnect

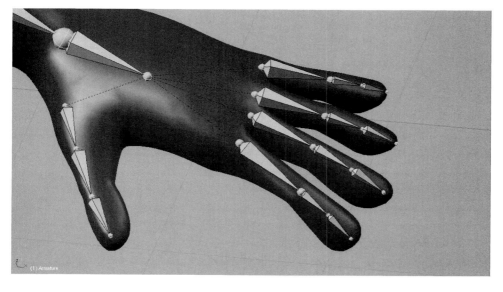

Figure 4.32
Copy and position all five fingers on each hand to match the mesh.

You turn now to the hips. By pressing Shift+E, mirror-extrude the hips downward from the base of Spine.1, as shown in Figure 4.33. Select them both and disconnect them by pressing Alt+P and position them as shown in Figure 4.34. They should be called **Hip.L** and **.R**. Continue to extrude from their tips to create bones that you'll name **Thigh.L/.R** and **Shin.L/.R**.

> You might find that some of your bone roll angles are different from those in the illustration. To recalculate the bone roll angles, select the bones in Edit mode and press Ctrl+N. Doing this now is not necessary, but it doesn't hurt. It is a good idea to recalculate all bone angles after you have finished editing the armature and before adding the armature modifier to the mesh. Be careful, though; after you begin animating with the armature, recalculating bone roll angles changes the appearance of the animation.

Extrude the Foot.L/.R bone and toeDeform.L/.R, as shown in Figure 4.35. You will be using a slightly sophisticated setup to control the motion of the foot, employing several constraints. You will return to setting this up shortly.

IK Constraints

One of the most frequently used constraint types is the IK constraint. As mentioned earlier, IK constraints apply to an IK chain—a chain of bones (for example, a limb)—and enable posing of this chain by simply positioning the point where the chain should end and having the computer calculate the angles of the bones necessary to achieve this. You can also place restrictions on these angles (for example, restricting certain joints to particular axes or restricting allowable angles to within a particular range).

Figure 4.33

Extruding the hips

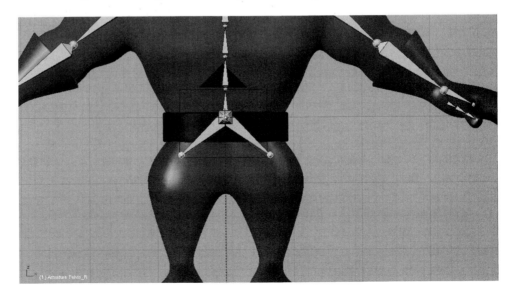

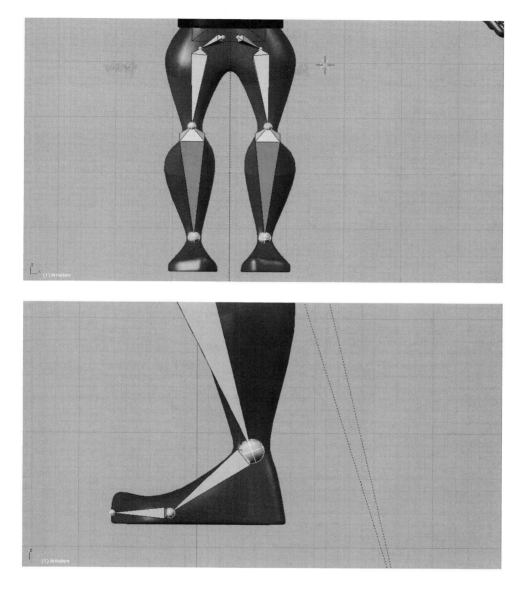

Figure 4.34

Hip and leg positions

Figure 4.35

Extruding the feet

IK constraints are very good for legs. They enable easy control of the leg movement and because the positioning of the leg often depends on the endpoint (namely the floor), it is an intuitive way to rig legs. For arms, IK posing can be useful when the placement of the hand is the main thing you are animating, such as when the character is grabbing an object. However, there are times when it is best to turn off the IK constraint and pose the arm using forward kinematic (FK) posing, which is the standard way (FK is basically the way one traditionally poses a plastic doll, for example). Arm motions, such as throwing or waving, are characterized by an arc. These motions come naturally when using FK posing, but not when using IK posing, which would move the hand in a straight line from one point to the next. In addition, FK gives you specific control over each joint in the armature, resulting in much more precise control over the general line of action of your pose. Fortunately, you can control the influence of an IK constraint on the fly over the course of an animation (as you will see in Chapter 7), so there is no problem using both FK and IK posing. You can use whatever posing method is appropriate for each movement.

IK constraints are sometimes used for fingers. This is a matter of personal preference, but you will be using FK in the fingers in this model and controlling complex but frequently recurring motions by using action constraints, as you will see later in this chapter. You will be using IK to control the motion of the neck, head, and spine; in the latter case, you will be using it alongside stretch constraints.

An IK constraint is generally set up on the last bone of a connected chain of parented bones.

By default, the entire sequence of a chain of bones is controlled by an IK constraint, which is why it is called an "IK chain." You will set the length of the IK chain yourself when you set up the constraint. The constraint lists a target bone, which is the bone whose location determines the point to which the IK chain extends. This bone is not part of the IK chain, and it should generally not be parented to a bone in the IK chain, although it is possible to do this (doing so will usually result in unpredictable behavior and/or paralysis). Keeping this restriction in mind will help to explain some of the armature design decisions made in this armature. Aside from this, any object can be the target for an IK chain. Some people also prefer to use empties as IK targets, but this is not advisable in Blender because at present only armature poses can be animated into reusable *actions* (as will be discussed further in this chapter and in Chapter 7).

You'll start with the simplest IK chain in the rig: the neck. First, you need to add a bone to anchor the neck at its base. This bone will be called **neckloc**. Add this bone as shown in Figure 4.36 and parent it to UpperBody.

Using the 3D cursor to place the new bone at the base of neckloc, add the bone Neck, as shown in Figure 4.37. This bone also should be parented to UpperBody. Extrude another bone directly forward on the Y axis, as shown in Figure 4.38. This bone will be called **HeadController**.

HeadController will be the bone to which you will parent other bones in the head, so that they follow the motion of the head. Because you want it to move naturally at the end of the neck, it is necessary that it be connected to the neck. For this reason, you cannot use HeadController as the IK target for the neck; you must make another bone for that purpose. So from the same point where you extruded HeadController, extrude another bone, which you will call **Head**. Extrude it in the same direction, constrained to the Y axis, as HeadController. Make it somewhat larger than HeadController, as shown in Figure 4.39. Parent Head to UpperBody.

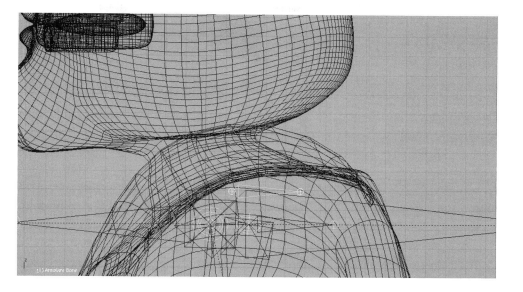

Figure 4.36
Adding the neck location bone

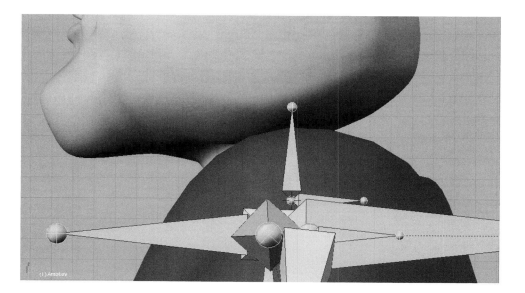

Figure 4.37
Extruding the neck

Figure 4.38
Extruding the Head-Controller bone

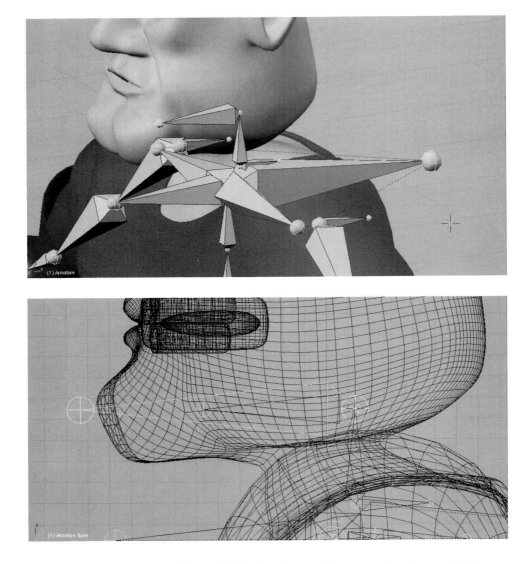

Figure 4.39
Adding the Head bone

You now put two constraints on Neck. The first will be a copy location constraint, targeted to neckloc. To add a constraint quickly and easily, select the constraint target, Shift+select the bone on which you want to put the constraint, and then press Ctrl+Alt+C, which will bring up a menu of constraints. In this case, select Copy Location from this menu, which will anchor the neck in place at the base. The other constraint you want is an IK constraint, targeted to Head. In both cases, the OB: field should say Armature.

This is the object the constraint is targeted to; in this case, the default-named Armature. After you enter an armature's name in the object field, a new field will appear in which you can enter the target bone. The Neck bone's Constraints panel should now look like Figure 4.40.

Move the Head bone around a bit and observe how the Neck responds. In the case of an IK chain of one, there is not a lot going on; the bone simply tries to follow the motion of the IK target. However, as you have it now, the HeadController bone is not moving in a very natural way. It would be much nicer if you could control the angle of that bone with the same bone that you use to control the head's movement—namely, the Head bone. And indeed you can, by using a copy rotation constraint on HeadController, targeted to Head, as shown in Figure 4.41. After you finish, try moving the Head bone around again and rotating it; notice the improvement in the head movement. You can see the difference in Figure 4.42.

Next, you will add the IK solver for the spine. You can extrude this straight up out of Spine.4 in Edit mode, as shown in Figure 4.43. You must reparent it because Spine.4 will be in the IK chain. Name the bone **IK_Spine** and parent it to Shoulders. In Pose mode, add an IK constraint on Spine.4 targeted to IK_Spine. Set the chain length to 4. For the spine's IK, you also want the constraint to take the rotation of the IK target into consideration, enabling you to control the sway of the spine directly with the IK target. To make this happen, select Rot as an option for this constraint.

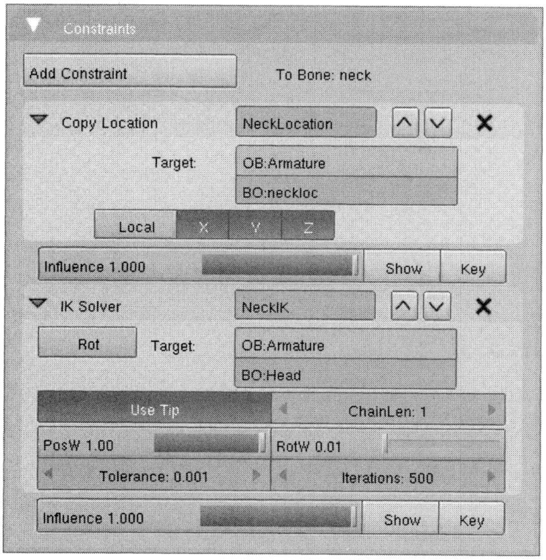

Figure 4.40

Constraints panel for the Neck bone

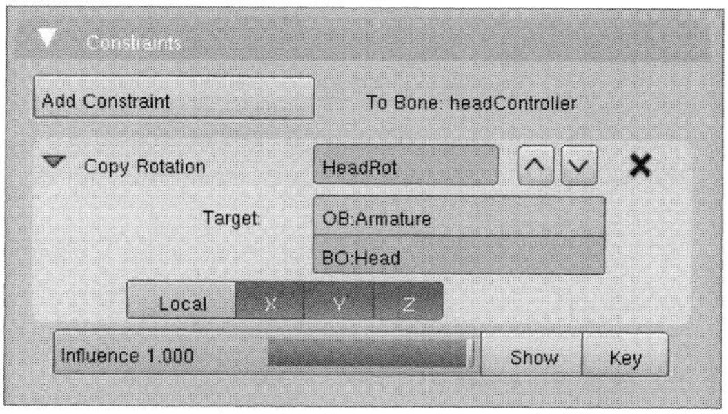

Figure 4.41

Constraints panel for the HeadController bone

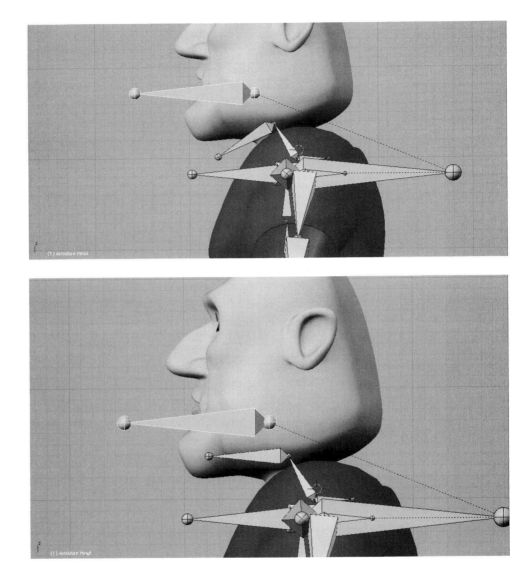

For the arms, you can create the IK bones by copying the hand bones by pressing Shift+D and slightly enlarging them with the 3D cursor as a pivot point placed at the base of the bone. The new bones thus continue to share the same rotation and location as the original Hand bones, as shown in Figure 4.44. Name these bones **IK_Arm.L** and **.R**. Create an IK constraint on the forearm bones targeted to these IK bones.

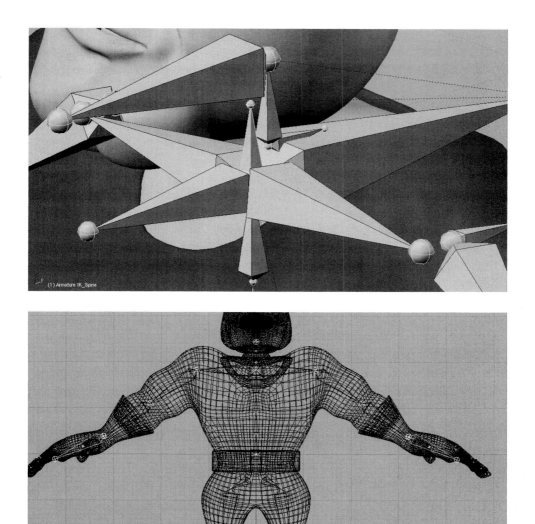

Figure 4.43
Extruding the IK target for the spine

Figure 4.44
Creating IK targets for the hands

You can now control the motion of the arm, but the angle of the hand remains independent of the IK target bone. You can simplify the control of the hand by copying the rotation of the IK target bone onto the Hand bone. To do this, set up copy rotation constraints on Hand.L and Hand.R to IK_Hand.L and IK_Hand.R, respectively. The improved motion can be seen in Figure 4.45.

The hand motion without and with the copy rotation constraint to the IK target

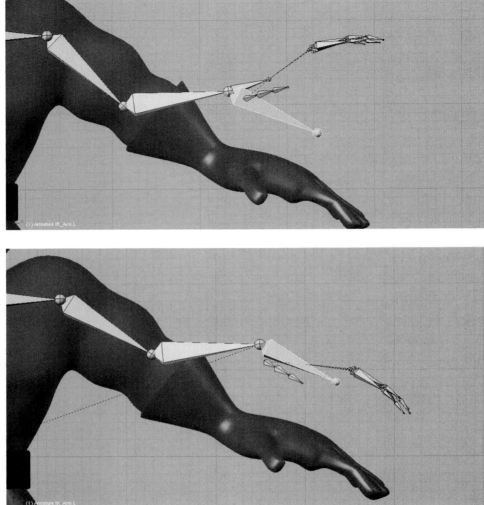

For the foot, you begin by selecting the Foot bone and copying it by pressing Shift+D. You leave the copy exactly where it is—occupying the same place as Foot—so you have two bones in an identical position. Name the new bone **FootMech.L** and **.R**. Press Alt+P to clear the parent (see Figure 4.46). Later you will reparent this bone, but for now it is necessary to unparent it from the shin bone, so that you can make it into an IK target bone. Add that IK constraint now to the shin bones. Make the chain length 2. Then, as you did with the head and the hands, add a copy rotation constraint on the Foot.L/.R bones, targeted to FootMech.L/.R.

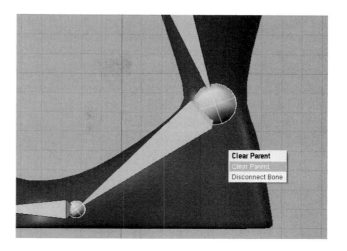

Figure 4.46
Copy the Foot bone and clear the parent. There are actually two overlapping bones in this illustration in the position highlighted.

You'll now extrude two more bones straight down from the tip of the shins and reparent these bones to the Root bone, as shown in Figure 4.47. Call these bones **FootRoot.L** and **.R**. These bones will be used to do much of the positioning of the feet.

Next, copy toeDeform.L/.R and clear the parenting on the resulting bones. Name the new bones **Toe.L/.R**. They should occupy the same place as toeDeform.L/.R. From the base of these bones, extrude two bones back along the Y axis, as shown in Figure 4.48: **ball.L/.R** and **heel.L./R**. Rotate the heel bones 180 degrees around the X axis. Parent the heel bones to the FootRoot bones, and parent the ball bones and the Toes bones to the heel bones. Parent FootMech.L/.R to the ball.L/.R bones. Create a copy rotation constraint on toeDeform.L/.R with the target of Toe.L/.R.

Figure 4.47
Extruding the FootRoot bones

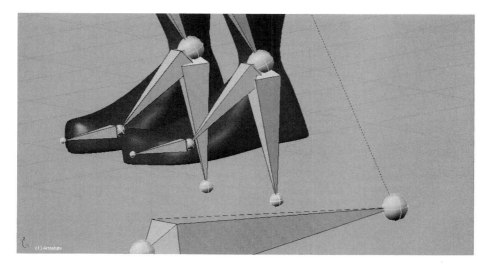

Selecting and deselecting parts of overlapping bones can be tricky. There are several ways to make this easier when multiple bones must share a single position in an armature. One way is to create custom shapes for the bones, as you will see how to do in Chapter 5. You can see good examples of this technique in Bassam Kurdali's Mancandy rig on the accompanying DVD. Another approach is to use the B-bone display in the armature, which enables you to give bones arbitrary thicknesses. You can then fatten or shrink one of the bones down by pressing Alt+S in Edit mode or Pose mode. You can see an example of bones displayed in this way in the foot rig in Chapter 14.

Figure 4.48

Extrude the ball and heel along the Y axis and then rotate the heel 180 degrees.

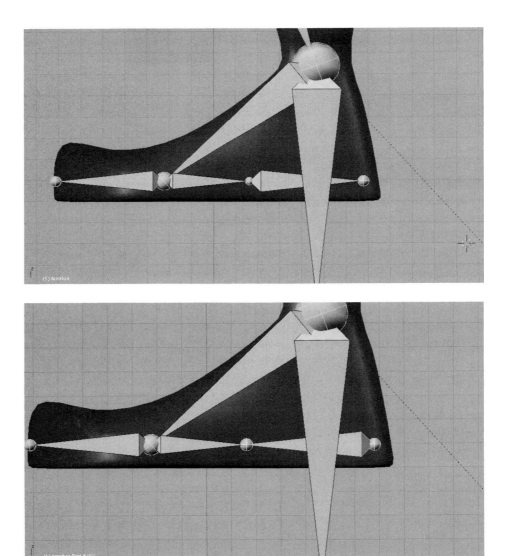

Add one more bone, up the back of the heel, as shown in Figure 4.49. Call this bone **heelDeform.L/.R**. Parent this bone to FootMech.

Finally, extrude another bone from the tip of the shin bones directly back along the Y axis and reparent these bones to the root bone (Figure 4.50). Name these bones **Ball_Heel_Rotation.L/.R** and put a copy location constraint on them targeted to their corresponding FootRoot bone.

Figure 4.49

Adding the heelDeform bone

Figure 4.50

Adding the Ball_Heel_ Rotation bone

You should now be able to move the foot using FootRoot.L/.R, as shown in Figure 4.51. There is more to be done with the foot (you will learn about it later in the chapter when action constraints are discussed).

Stretch Constraints

As the name suggests, stretch constraints enable you to give a bone a rubbery behavior that stretches out thin and squashes fat. Furthermore, the portion of the mesh that is modified by this stretch-constrained bone (and any objects parented to the bone) will also inherit these characteristics. You can determine how realistic or exaggerated the conservation of volume is, for example, when you stretch or squash the object. The effect of the stretch constraint tends to be cartoony when applied to body parts that do not normally stretch, such as bones or heads. However, stretch constraints also have a number of uses in more-realistic rigs. They can be used to help simulate muscles or to help deform hard-to-rig areas such as the front of the neck or the shoulder/chest area, among other uses.

However, when used sparingly for cartoon rigs, stretching and squashing can be a very good way to exaggerate emotions or the effect of motion and physical forces (for example, stretching a character to exaggerate his reaction of surprise or fear or squashing him slightly when he lands hard on his feet).

To give squash and stretch to the character's head, extrude directly upward along the Z axis from the tip of the Neck bone twice, as shown in Figure 4.52. The longer of the two bones should be named **HeadStretch**, and the bone on the end should be **HeadStretch-Control**. Both bones should be parented to HeadControl. Extrude a third bone downward at an angle from the tip of HeadStretch and then disconnect the bone but do not clear the parent relationship. This will be the bone that the mesh will actually be deformed by, so name it **HeadDeform**.

Figure 4.51

Moving the foot using the FootRoot bone

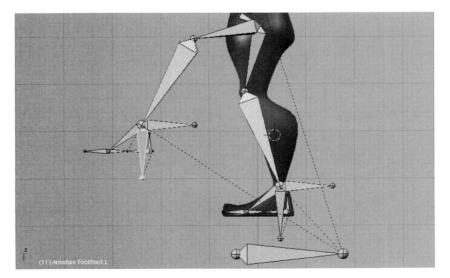

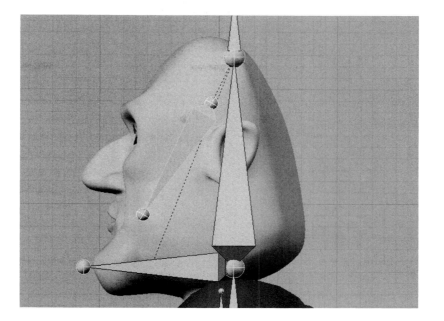

Figure 4.52
**Setting up the head
deformation bones**

In Pose mode, apply a stretch-to constraint to the HeadStretch bone with HeadStretch-Control as the target. You can leave the default values as they are. Blender calculates the rest distance on its own. If you move the bone in Edit mode after adding the constraint, you need to click the R button to the right of the Rest Length field to have Blender recalculate the bone's rest value.

The Volume Variation field enables you to set the degree to which the bone and the mesh's volume distort. A higher value gives a more rubbery, exaggerated effect. Finally, select the HeadStretchControl bone in Pose mode and press the N key to see the Transform Properties tab. You want to lock transforms on LocX and LocZ by clicking on the lock icons for those axes, as shown in Figure 4.53. This will restrict the bone from moving only lengthwise, straight along its local Y axis. Now experiment with moving the HeadStretchControl bone. Note that the HeadDeform bone also stretches because it is parented to the bone with the stretch constraint.

The stretch constraint works similarly to the IK constraint in that it forces the tip of the constrained bone to follow the movement of a target object or bone, which should not be in a direct parent relationship with the constrained bone. Rather than calculate angles for an IK chain, however, it calculates the deformation of the bone itself. Because IK chains and stretch constraints calculate the way a bone should extend to the target in different ways, it does not work to simply apply stretch constraints in sequence to each bone in an IK chain. However, it is possible to get a stretch-and-squash effect on an IK chain by building a sequence of bones which combines an ordinary IK chain with other bones that have stretch constraints applied, as you will do for the spine.

Figure 4.53

Restricting the motion of the Head-StretchControl bone in the Transform Properties window

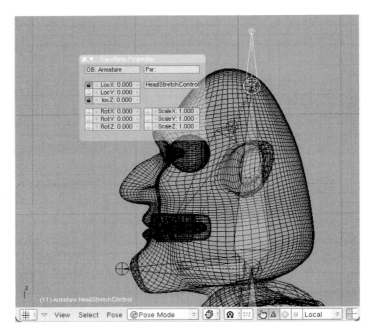

Figure 4.54

Constraints panel for SpineStretch.2

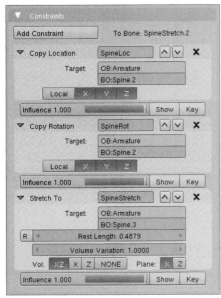

You already have the IK chain set up for the spine. What you will do now is to duplicate the top three bones in this chain: Spine.2, Spine.3, and Spine.4. Copy the bones in place by pressing Shift+D. Name the bones **SpineStretch.2**, **SpineStretch.3**, and **SpineStretch.4** to correspond with the bone each was copied from. Parent all these bones to Torso.

Now, for each of the SpineStretch bones, add copy location and copy rotation constraints targeting the corresponding Spine bone. SpineStretch.4, which is located exactly in the same place as Spine.4, should be constrained to copy the location and rotation of that bone, for example. This ensures that as the Spine bones move, the SpineStretch bones stay with them and follow the motion.

Next, for each of the SpineStretch bones, add a stretch to constraint targeting the *nonstretch constrained* bone directly above it. SpineStretch.2 should be stretch constrained to Spine.3, SpineStretch.3 should be stretch constrained to Spine.4, and SpineStretch.4 should be stretch constrained to IK_Spine. For example, Figure 4.54 shows how the Constraints panel should look for SpineStretch.2.

Finally, the bones in the actual IK chain must be set to allow some stretchiness. While in Pose mode, for each of the bones in the IK chain, go to the Armature Bones tab and enter **0.100** in the Stretch field. You can increase that value to make the effect "stretchier" if need be.

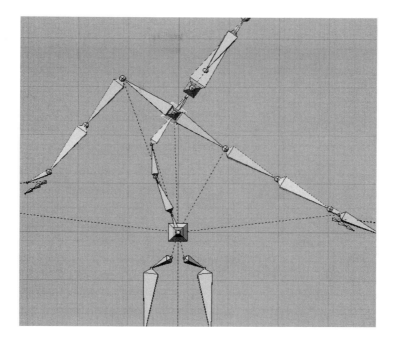

Figure 4.55

A pose using the stretch constrained spine

You should now be able to control the upper body's motion by moving and rotating the UpperBody bone. Experiment with the effect. You should be able to produce a pose something like that shown in Figure 4.55.

Action Constraints

An action constraint is a powerful and versatile method of restricting a bone to assume a specific position or make a particular movement based upon the position or movements of the target bone. Setting up action constraints enables you to control frequently used complex movements by associating them with a simple movement, such as the X-rotation of the target bone.

Action constraints can be an important part of rigging, but to create them you need to jump ahead a bit and dip into animation. This book assumes that you have a basic familiarity with an animation Timeline, frames, and the idea of keyframing. If so, you should have no trouble following along with the next few steps. If you are not familiar with these ideas, it might be better for you to skip ahead and read a bit about posing, keyframes, and actions in Chapters 6 and 7 before proceeding with this section.

For this rig, you will be using action constraints to set up the hands and feet. In fact, there are other good ways to set up both hands and feet, which do not require action constraints. Because you are modeling this rig based upon Jason Pierce's widely used Ludwig rig, you will follow that rig's approaches to hands and feet. Using them here also provides a good example of action constraints in general and should give an indication of how useful they can be. For some very nice alternatives to the action constraint approach to rigging hands and feet, see Chapter 14, and the discussion of the rigging techniques used in *Elephants Dream*. Also see Bassam Kurdali's Mancandy rig, which is included on the DVD of this book.

The first step of creating an action constraint is to create an action. You can think of an *action* as a unit of animation. It is a series of movements that goes on for a set number of frames. It can be a wave or a step taken in a walk cycle. When you get into nonlinear animation, you will see how actions can be combined to produce more-complex animated sequences. For now, it's enough to focus on single actions. You will create three action constraints for this rig. One is for the feet, and it will enable you to roll the feet forward and backward in a natural way by rotating a single bone. The other actions are for the hands. One action will curl the hands into fists, and the other action will spread the fingers.

You edit actions in the Action Editor window. Split your screen up now so that you have a layout something like the one shown in Figure 4.56. You want a 3D viewport open, an Action Editor window (the window type with the "drowning man" icon), and a Timeline.

To create a new action, click the ⬍ button and click Add New. Give the new action a name. Because the first action you will create is the roll of the foot and you intend to use it as a bone-driven action, name the action **drvToeHeelRoll**.

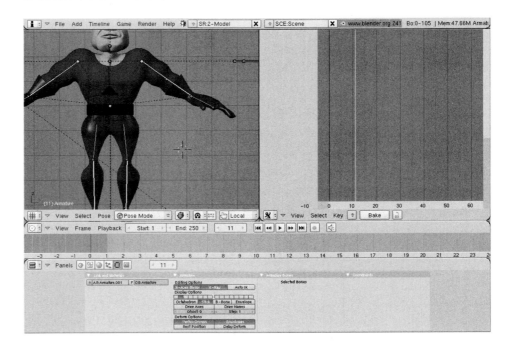

Figure 4.56
Blender screen with a 3D viewport, Action Editor, and a Timeline open

When you create a new action, the currently active action (if there is one) is duplicated to create the new action. If you want to create a completely blank new action, you must first remove the active action from the Action Editor by clicking the X to the right of the Action drop-down menu. Another way to do this is to keep an empty action on hand and select this action before creating a new action.

Actions consist of keyed positions along the Timeline. The drvToeHeelRoll action begins in an exaggerated forward roll, rolls back into the rest position after 10 frames, and continues into an exaggerated roll backward onto the heels. Because the rest position will occur at frame 11, go to frame 11 first and key the rest position. In the Current Frame field on the Timeline, enter **11**. Then, in Pose mode, select ball.L, ball.R, heel.L, and heel.R. Press I and select Rot to key the rotations of these bones, as shown in Figure 4.57.

Next, go to frame 1. Rotate both the left and right ball bones counterclockwise just slightly past the point that looks like a natural forward roll for this character's feet. With those two bones selected, once again key their rotation by pressing I. Your screen should now look something like Figure 4.58 (top), with two bones keyed at frame 1 and four bones keyed at frame 11. Finally, go to frame 21. This time, rotate the right and left heel bones together clockwise, again just past the point that would be a natural pose. Key the rotation of these two bones.

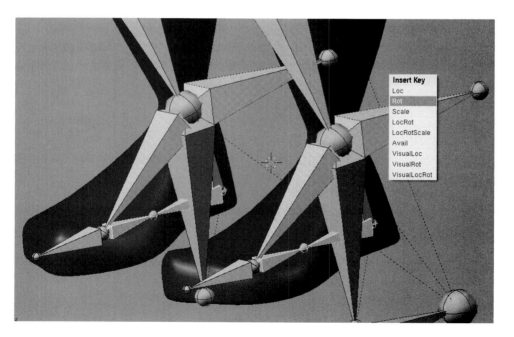

Figure 4.57

Keying the rotation of the ball and heel bones with I

Figure 4.58

Setting keyframes for frames 1 and 21

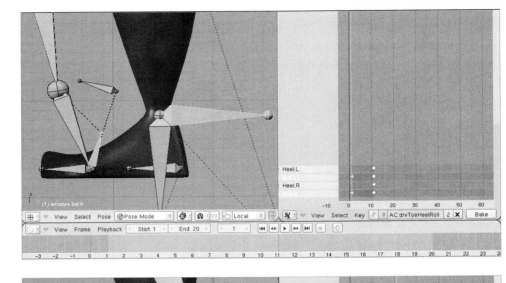

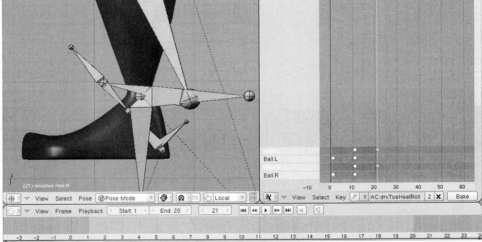

That's all you need to do for this action. You can play it back by pressing the play button on the Timeline or by pressing Alt+A in the 3D viewport. (You might want to set the end frame to something less than 250, so you don't have to wait 10 seconds for each repetition of the action.) The next thing you want to do is to associate this action with a driver bone. For the driver bone, use the Ball_Heel_Rotation.L/.R bones you created earlier for this purpose. You want to associate the action with the X axis rotation of the Ball_Heel_Rotation bones so that when the driver bone is in rest position (that is, at frame 11 of the action), the foot is also in rest position, and when the driver bone rotates up and down, the foot position moves backward and forward through the range of motion described in the action. The top point of the driver bone's rotation should be rotated straight upward, and the low point should be rotated straight down, so you want to associate frame 1 and frame 21 with these top and bottom positions, respectively.

To do this, you must create a separate action constraint on *each* of the bones you want to be affected by the movement of the driver. In this case, it means that both the left and right ball and heel bones, four in all, need to have action constraints placed on them, all with the same action. Like other constraints, these action constraints take a target object or bone; in this case, the driver bone for the appropriate foot. They also require an action to be inputted in the AC: field. In this case, the action is drvToeHeel-Roll. You want the action to be based on the driver's X rotation, so you can leave it as-is, but you must unselect the Local button, or else the constraint will calculate based on rotations inherited from the parent (in this case, the Root) bone, which can be confusing. The start and endpoint refer to the frames within the action that should constitute the range of the action constraint's motion; in this case, start is frame 1 and end is frame 21. The Min and Max values indicate the range of driver bone rotation angles between which the action constraint will range. Enter **-90.00** for Min and **90.00** for Max in these fields to correspond with the positions in which you want the driver bone at the beginning and end of the action. The same values should be entered in constraints for each of the four constrained bones. After they have been entered, experiment with posing the foot using the Ball_Heel_Rotation bones. An example of an action constraint panel can be seen in Figure 4.59.

The next action constraints you will create control the major movements of the hands. Although for this tutorial, I include this section with the other action constraints, in a real project it would probably be a good idea to create these poses after the mesh has already been fully rigged to the armature, to be sure that the poses work well with the deformed mesh. If you want to do this, you should skip ahead to the last section of this chapter to rig the mesh and then come back here to finish creating the action constraints. If you prefer, though, it is also fine to go straight through and create the actions here with just the armature. In either case, it is possible to adjust the poses later if they don't turn out to be exactly what you want with the mesh deformations.

To create the action constraints for the hand, you first need to create control bones for the drivers. You will place these bones on a simple hand-shaped control setup. Add a small new bone at the top of the spine called HandActuatorLoc, as shown in Figure 4.60. Parent this bone to UpperBody.

Figure 4.59

Action constraint on the Ball bone

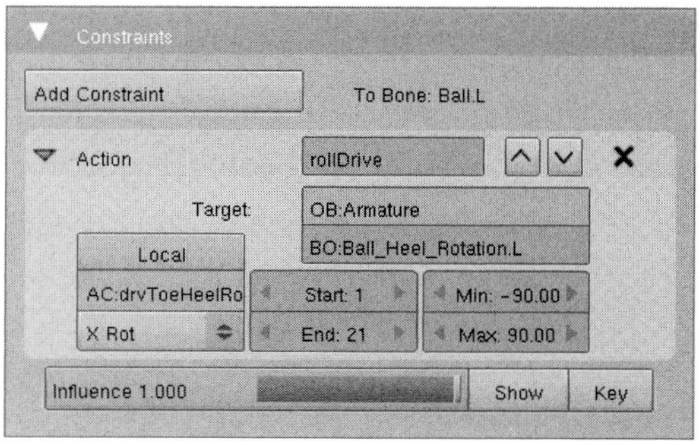

Figure 4.60

**Positioning the Han-
dActuatorLoc bone**

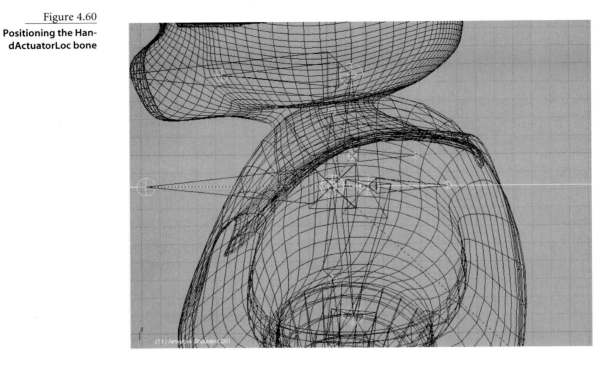

Mirror-extrude two bones along the X axis from HandActuatorLoc. Select both of these bones and disconnect them from their parent. Move them outward over the hands area, as shown in Figure 4.61. Name these bones **HandActuator.L/.R.** Extrude another bone from them and disconnect it to create the thumb control, as shown in Figure 4.62. Select both right and left bones and copy them four times, adjusting the position of each subsequent finger control, as shown in Figure 4.63. Name these bones as follows:

FingerThumb.L/.R

FingerIndex.L/.R

FingerMiddle.L/.R

FingerRing.L/.R

FingerPinky.L/.R

Now you will create the action drvFingersCurl. Again, you will have the action range from 1 to 21, with the rest position at 11. First, go to frame 11 and select all the actual finger bones (not the controller bones)—15 in all for each hand. By pressing I, keyframe the rotation of these bones. Frame 1 is an exaggerated open hand. Go to this frame, pose the left hand (as shown in the first image in Figure 4.63), and keyframe the left hand's finger

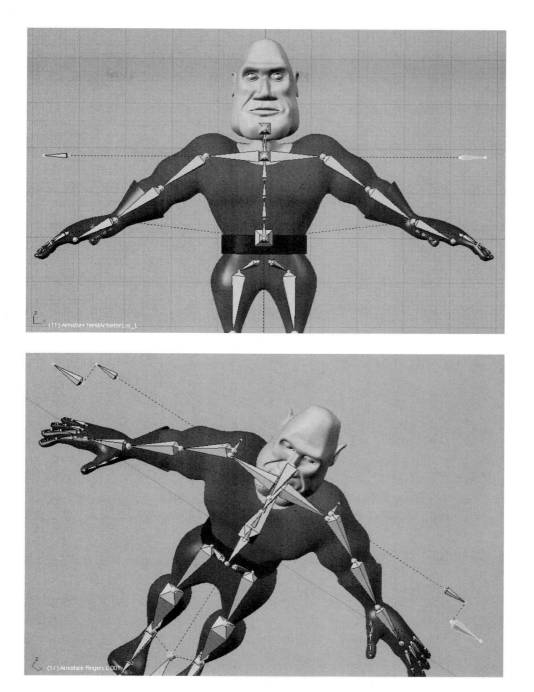

Figure 4.61

Disconnecting and bringing the HandActuators out along the X axis

Figure 4.62

Extruding and disconnecting the thumb actuator

Figure 4.63

Copying and positioning each finger's actuator

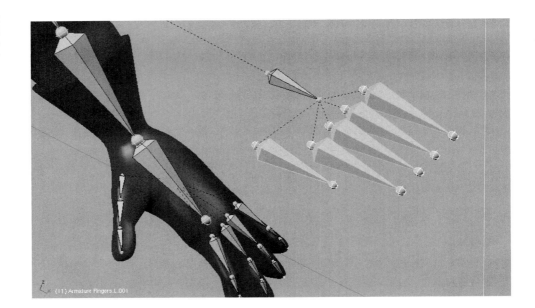

bones. Now find the up and down arrow buttons in the header. (You might have to slide the header over a bit by pressing Ctrl+MMB to see these buttons.) Recall the method of "cutting and pasting" in textures introduced in Chapter 3. There are actually three arrows: one pointing down, one pointing up, and one pointing up with a second arrow wrapping around it. Once again, you use these arrows to move information to and from the Blender Clipboard. For poses, this is an especially powerful tool because it enables you to intelligently flip poses from right to left. With the left hand posed and the finger bones selected, click the down arrow. This copies the pose to the Clipboard. Now click the up button with the wrapping arrow. This arrow takes the pose from the Clipboard and flips it right to left to apply it to the model. Blender bases this on the names of bones, which is one reason why the .L/.R naming convention is important. You will find that your right side bones now mirror the pose of the left side. Select the finger bones in the right hand and key their poses at frame 1. Follow the same process at frame 21 to form a fist, as shown in the third picture in Figure 4.64.

You'll apply these action constraints to each bone in each finger in the same way that you applied them to the two bones in the feet. For each bone, you want the action constraints to target the corresponding finger controller. The settings are similar to those in the foot bones you used, except that you can drive the action by rotation on the Z axis. An example of the settings for these fingers can be seen in Figure 4.65. You will need to apply a similar constraint to each finger bone on each hand. Once again, be sure to deselect Local. Note that the Min and Max rotation values will be different on the right side from the left because the control bones will be rotating in the opposite direction. You should experiment and try to come up with the correct values yourself.

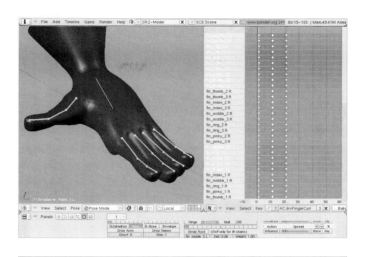

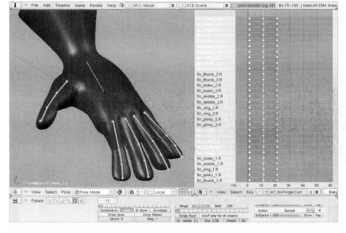

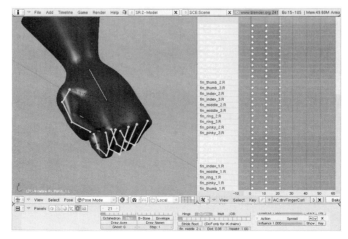

Figure 4.64

The three keyframes in the drvFingersCurl action

Finally, you set up similar constraints driven by the same controller bones' X axes. They correspond to the spread of the hands. Once again, you create a similar action to drvFingersCurl and call this one **drvFingersSpread**. Frame 1 should have the fingers tightly squeezed together, frame 11 should have the fingers at rest position, and frame 21 should have the fingers spread apart, as shown in the illustrations in Figure 4.66. In this case, it is necessary to pose and key only the first bone of each finger.

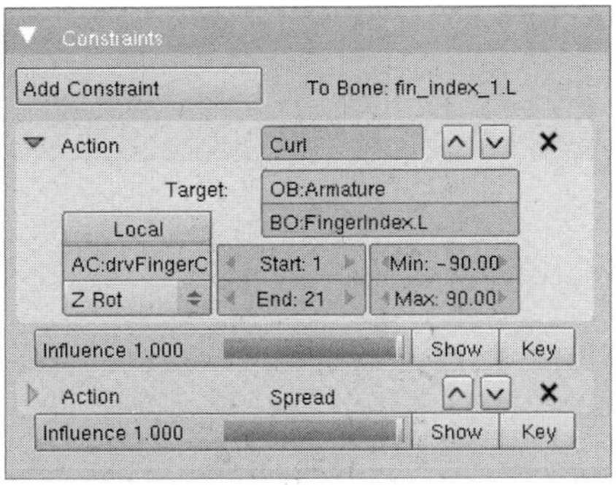

For this action constraint, you do not need to have the driver bones rotate a full 180 degrees to cover the range of the action. It is probably sufficient to have the 1 and 21 frames correspond to 20 degrees up and down from the rest position on the X axis, so that the fingers more or less follow the spread of the controllers. Note that spreading the ring and pinky figures will involve rotating the driver bone in the opposite direction from the middle and index fingers. Finally, because you posed and keyed only the first bones of each finger, you likewise need to apply action constraints to only those bones.

Now that you have the action constraints set up on the hands, you see that the hands are quite poseable. Although the actions themselves involve spreading or clenching the whole hand, with separate control bones you can now activate these actions on individual bones independently, resulting in a wide range of possible hand positions.

Armature Summary

Table 4.1 sums up the basic points of this armature. For the sake of brevity, I list only the left-side bones, and for fingers I list only the first bone of the thumb and the action driver for the thumb. For each bone, the table identifies its parent, whether that bone is connected, whether it should be deformed, and which constraints are active on each bone and the target of the constraints.

Attaching the Mesh

Before you go any further, it would be nice to separate the bones out a little bit so you could look at only the bones you're interested in at any given time instead of having to deal with the entire armature at all times. When posing, you need to be worried only about bones that control movement: IK solvers, action drivers and other constraint targets, and sometimes limbs in the case of FK posing. When rigging the mesh, you will mainly be concerned with bones that deform the mesh—the ones you have the "deform" option turned on for. In some cases, you might want to do some posing while rigging the mesh to make sure that the mesh deforms properly when posed. But there are also bones that serve an important purpose in the armature, but are not directly pertinent to anything you will want to do from here on. You'll use armature *layers* to control the display of bones.

Figure 4.65
Curl action constraint for the left index finger

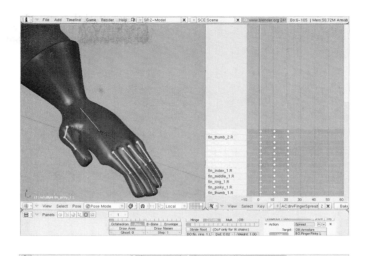

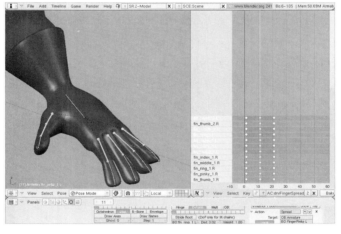

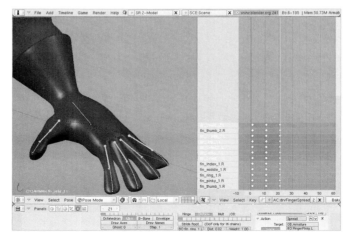

Figure 4.65
Keyframes for the drvFingersSpread action

Table 4.1

Elements of the Captain Blender Armature Structure

BONE	PARENT	CONNECTED	DEFORM	COPY LOC	COPY ROT	IK	STRETCH	ACTION
Head	UpperBody	No	No	No	No	No	No	No
HeadStretchControl	HeadController	No	No	No	No	No	No	No
HeadStretch	HeadController	No	No	No	No	No	HeadStretchControl	No
HeadDeform	HeadStretch	No	Yes	No	No	No	No	No
headController	neck	No	No	No	No	No	No	No
Hand.L	Forearm.L	Yes	Yes	No	IK_Arm.L	No	No	No
Forearm.L	Bicep.L	Yes	Yes	No	No	IK_Arm.L	No	No
IK_Arm.L	Torso	No	No	No	No	No	No	No
Bicep.L	UpperBody	No	Yes	ShoulderLoc.L	No	No	No	No
ShoulderLoc.L	Shoulder.L	No	No	No	No	No	No	No
UpperBody	Torso	No	No	No	No	No	No	No
Shoulder.L	Shoulders	No	No	No	No	No	No	No
Shoulders	UpperBody	No	No	No	No	No	No	No
IK_Spine	Shoulders	No	No	No	No	No	No	No
necknull	neck	No	No	No	No	No	No	No
neckloc	UpperBody	No	Yes	No	No	No	No	No
neck	UpperBody	No	Yes	neckloc	No	Head	No	No
handActuatorLoc	NONE	No	No	IK_Spine	No	No	No	No
spineStretchNull	Spine.4	Yes	No	No	No	No	No	No
Spine.4	Spine.3	Yes	No	No	No	IK_Spine	No	No
Spine.3	Spine.2	Yes	No	No	No	No	No	No
Spine.2	Spine.1	Yes	No	No	No	No	No	No
Spine.1	Pelvis	No	No	No	No	No	No	No
Pelvis	Torso	No	No	No	No	No	No	No
Rib3.L	SpineStretch.002		Yes	No	No	No	No	No

BONE	PARENT	CONNECTED	DEFORM	COPY LOC	COPY ROT	IK	STRETCH	ACTION
Rib2.L	SpineStretch.003		Yes	No	No	No	No	No
Rib1.L	SpineStretch.004		Yes	No	No	No	No	No
SpineStretch.002	Torso	No	Yes	Spine.4	Spine.4	No	No	No
SpineStretch.003	Torso	No	Yes	Spine.3	Spine.3	No	No	No
SpineStretch.004	Torso	No	Yes	Spine.2	Spine.2	No	No	No
Hip.L	Pelvis	No	Yes	No	No	No	No	No
Thigh.L	Hip.L	Yes	Yes	No	No	No	No	No
Shin.L	Thigh.L	Yes	Yes	No	No	FootMech.L	No	No
Foot.L	Shin.L	Yes	Yes	No	FootMech.L	No	No	No
ToeDeform.L	Foot.L	No	Yes	No	Toes.L	No	No	No
HeelDeform.L	Foot.L	No	Yes	No	No	No	No	No
FootRoot.L	Root	No	No	No	No	No	No	No
Heel.L	FootRoot.L	No	No	No	No	No	No	Ball_Heel_Rotation
Ball.L	FootRoot.L	No	No	No	No	No	No	Ball_Heel_Rotation
FootMech.L	Ball.L	No	No	No	No	No	No	No
Ball_Heel_Rotation.L	Root	No	No	No	No	No	No	No
Toes.L	Heel.L	No	No	Ball.L	No	No	No	No
Fingers.L	HandAcutatorLoc	No	No	No	No	No	No	No
FingerThumb.L	Fingers.L	No	No	No	No	No	No	No
Fin_Thumb1.L	Hand.L	No	Yes	No	No	No	No	Finger Thumb.L
Root	NONE	No	No	No	No	No	No	No

Although there are options to hide bones in Pose mode using the H key, using armature layers is more flexible and easy to use. After bones have been hidden, it becomes difficult to select them and to unhide them individually. All hidden bones can be unhidden at once by using Alt+H.

Using armature layers is very straightforward. In the Armature tab immediately under Display Options, you see a row of 16 square buttons. They represent which armature layers are currently set to be visible. By default, only layer 1 is visible. You can make multiple layers visible by holding Shift and selecting layers. Likewise, when you select specific bones, each bone will have a similar row of buttons representing in which armature layers the individual bones are visible. You can select them in the same way.

You'll use three armature layers, as shown in Figure 4.67. The first one shows only deform bones. You'll be mostly looking at this layer when you do the rigging because they are the bones with a direct influence on the mesh. The second armature layer you'll use will have only bones that are pertinent to posing. When you do the posing and animation in later chapters, you'll be mainly looking at this layer. You will put the remaining bones in the third layer. You'll need to look at these bones only when you are editing the armature itself.

Bear in mind that armature layers are independent of ordinary layers used to display objects. Whatever your display options are for your armature, the armature object will remain on the layer it has been placed on in Object mode.

You will begin with the rigging as you did with the simple example at the beginning of the chapter: by adjusting the envelopes. Because you will be weight painting, you can be fairly approximate with the envelopes, but you want to try to adjust the envelopes in a way that will assign each portion of the mesh to the appropriate bone. You can do this by scaling the envelopes in Edit mode by pressing S. You can scale the secondary influence, represented by the white translucent area surrounding the envelope by pressing Alt+S.

Figure 4.67

Displaying groups of bones separately using armature layers

It is a good idea to minimize this secondary area in places where bones are close together, like the fingers, to reduce unwanted influence on verts by neighboring bones. Other than this, you will be mostly relying on weight painting for the weight gradations here, so you don't need to be overly concerned with this secondary influence. Scale the influence of the envelopes to be something similar to Figure 4.68.

You can create vertex groups for all bones with weights based upon the envelope influence. To do this, select all bones in Pose mode by pressing A and then select the mesh. Be careful not to select or deselect bones in the meantime; you want them all selected in Pose mode when you select the mesh. You can do this without switching layers in wireframe view, but it might take several tries to select the mesh instead of a bone. It might be easier to simply make the layer that the armature is on invisible and then select the mesh. With the mesh selected, enter weight paint mode, and be sure to make the armature visible again—if it isn't already. The armature should be fully selected, as shown in Figure 4.69. If multiple bones are not selected upon entering weight paint mode, you have to redo the last few steps because it is not possible to multiply select bones in weight paint mode, only in Pose mode. With all bones selected in weight paint mode, click W and select Apply Bone Envelopes to Vertex Groups. You'll now have a full set of vertex groups. You should deselect Envelopes in the armature modifier tab and make sure Vertex Groups is selected.

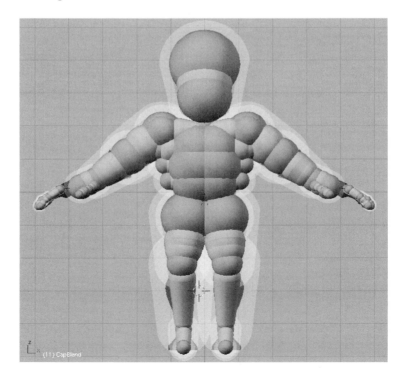

Figure 4.68

Envelopes scaled to enclose the Captain Blender Mesh

Figure 4.69

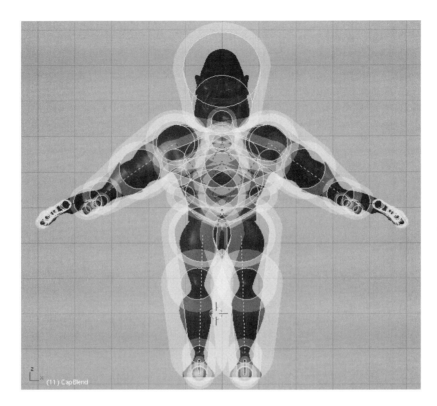

You now begin the task of weight painting. As with the weight painting example in Chapter 3 on the scalp, the zero weights and nonmembers of the active vertex group are represented by dark blue, and the 1 weights are represented by red. For each bone selected, a different pattern of red and blue appears, corresponding with the vertex weights for that bone's vertex group. Essentially, what these colors mean is that when that bone moves, the red vertices move along with the bone, the blue vertices are unaffected, and the vertices between red and blue are affected to varying degrees, depending on their closeness to red. Recall that in the grayscale representation in this book, red appears as light gray, and blue appears as dark gray.

As you select a few bones to get the idea, note that the areas of the mesh that were inside the bones' envelopes are now fully red, whereas the other areas are blue. Areas touched by the envelopes' secondary influence area will fade to yellow and green. The first thing you should do is go through the bones and identify clearly misweighted areas. In the present example, the backs of the calves were not fully enclosed in an envelope, so they are not red when the shin bones are selected, as shown in the illustration in Figure 4.70. They should be, so you can start by painting these red.

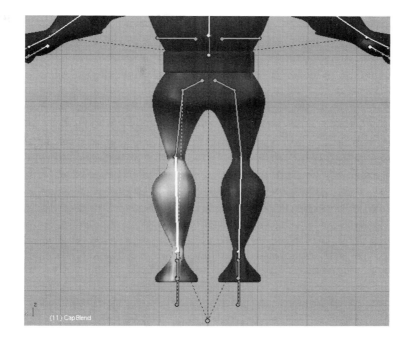

Figure 4.70

A patch of the calf that was not properly weighted by the envelope

I tend to usually use the Mix mode in weight painting and only sometimes adjust the opacity from 1. This way, I am usually applying exactly the weight I want at a given spot. Sometimes I just want to bump the weight at a spot up or down; in this case, I usually just reduce the opacity. It is also possible to do additive, subtractive, or multiplicative painting, and also to restrict the painting to lighten and darken (light meaning higher or redder values; dark meaning lower or bluer values). There are no doubt circumstances in which these finer controls come in handy, but I do not think you need them for this model.

Effective weight painting requires patience and some skill, and experience and practice benefit you more than reading about it, but here are a few pointers you should keep in mind:

- Paint for posing. The whole reason for weight painting is to make sure your meshes deform nicely when posed, so you should pose your model frequently while weight painting, as in Figure 4.71. Areas that deform in unwanted ways will be easy to identify.

- Work with vertex groups directly when you can. There are often cases in which many more vertices belong to a particular vertex group than are necessary. An advantage of weight painting, that it enables subtle weight changes to be applied to verts, is also a disadvantage because it can enable you to inadvertently give verts hard-to-see, near-zero weights that can add up and become problematic. For this reason, it is a good idea to occasionally go into Edit mode with a bone selected and select the vertex group for that bone in the Vertex Groups area. In the present example, if you do this with the neck bone, there are some verts that really don't need to be in that vertex group at all. You could paint these areas blue, but it is more effective to simply remove the verts from that group in Edit mode by selecting the offending verts with the Neck vertex group active and clicking Remove, giving you a selected vertex group for the neck like the one in Figure 4.72. You should definitely check this with the finger bones. You might find verts from one finger grouped with a bone from another finger, which can create annoying problems. Incorrectly assigned verts should be fully and cleanly removed from the vert group in Edit mode. There is a Python script, clean_weights, available to help with this in Weight Paint mode. You'll look at how to run this and other scripts in Chapter 12.

• Be conscious of the possibility of overshooting. If you are painting the pinky red and you are not careful of the position of your mesh, you might inadvertently hit points on other parts of the mesh. You might wind up making the heel green, for example, which would result in messy deformations of the foot every time the hand moves. There are some useful tricks for avoiding this. From Weight Paint mode, go into UV Face Select mode and select the faces that you want to paint. When you return to Weight Paint mode, only the selected faces receive the weight paint. You can hide faces with the H key in UV Face Select mode, and they will remain hidden in Weight Paint mode, enabling you to weight paint hard-to-reach areas. An even more direct method is to simply press the F key while in Weight Paint mode to enter a special mode for face selection. In this mode you can select and deselect faces to receive paint as well as hiding faces with the H key. Hidden faces, like unselected faces, will not receive weight paint.

• Be aware of the effects of unwanted bone influence. If an area of mesh is fully red, but it does not seem to be following the bone it is supposed to follow, it is probably also being influenced by another bone that is not moving. Posing the armature in a drastic way might help to identify the direction that the unwanted deformation is pushing your mesh, and can help narrow down where the offending bone is.

• Make sure that your bones are deform bones. This should be obvious, but it turns out that nondeform bones also can have nonzero weights, even if they don't do anything with them. You might think you're painting a bone's influence, but if the deform button is not selected for that bone, it doesn't move the mesh anywhere. If your mesh is not responding properly to a bone, even if it is properly weighted, this might be the problem.

There are several Python scripts in the standard distribution of Blender that can help clean up vertex weights and reduce problem areas. You can read more about how to use these scripts in Chapter 12.

Figure 4.71

Pose the figure in Weight Paint mode to ensure that the deformations are correct.

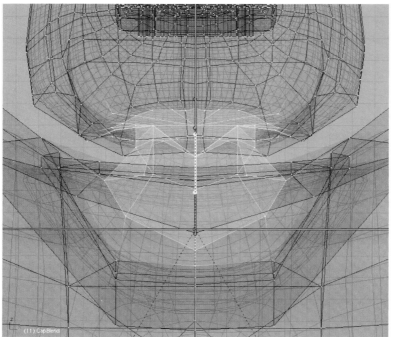

Figure 4.72

These are the verts that should appear when you select the Neck vertex group. Anything else that appears can be removed in Edit mode.

In Figure 4.73 you can see that our hero has begun to come alive! You'll deal with the spaced-out expression on his face in the next chapter when you work on facial rigging.

Figure 4.73

Captain Blender is now almost fully rigged.

CHAPTER 5

Shape Keys and Facial Rigging

Now that you have rigged and skinned the body to an armature so that you can position the limbs, head, and trunk, you'll turn your attention to some important details of rigging characters. In particular, this chapter focuses mainly on setting up a face so that it can be easily posed to express emotion and to make the mouth movements that are necessary for lip syncing. (You'll see how to animate facial expressions and lip syncing in Chapter 8.) There are many ways to go about facial rigging, and this book focuses on an approach that makes heavy use of Blender's powerful shape key system and Ipo (interpolation) curve drivers to associate shapes with armature poses. After introducing shapes and Ipo drivers, and discussing their use for facial rigging, you will also put them to another use: refining the body rig.

- Shape Key Basics
- Building a Shape Key Set for Captain Blender
- Facial Bones and Controls
- Improved Mesh Deformations Using Driven Shape Keys

Shape Key Basics

Blender enables you to create and animate various different shapes for a single mesh using *shape keys*. Shape keys have many uses, but in character animation one of the most important is to create facial expressions. Blender's shape key system is simple to use, but (like many things in Blender) it takes a little getting used to. It's easy to get slightly off-track and find yourself doing something that you didn't really mean to do. Don't worry; I'll point out potential pitfalls.

You'll begin with a very simple example. Start up an instance of Blender; with the default cube selected, go to the Shapes tab in the edit buttons. At present, there are no shape keys defined; you simply have a mesh and it is in the shape you see: a cube. Click the Add Shape Key button to create your first shape key. You'll see a Basis shape key appear as in Figure 5.1.

Figure 5.1

Basis shape key

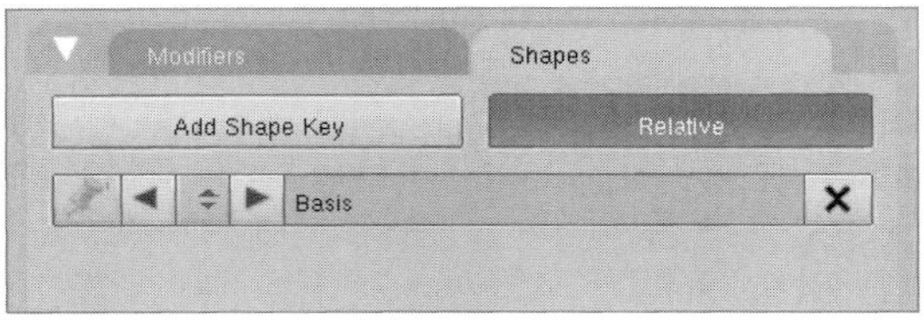

The Basis shape has some unique features, as you'll see shortly. It represents the shape of your mesh in its "rest" position, unaffected by any of the shape keys you will create. In this case, you made the Basis shape on the default cube, which means that now the vertex positions of that cube shape are represented by the Basis shape.

Now that you have the Basis shape, you can use it to build a new shape. The process is simple:

1. Using the right and left arrow buttons in the Shapes tab, make sure that the Basis shape is the currently active key. (In this case, it is because there are no other keys yet.)

2. In Object mode, click the Add Shape Key button. Change the name of the key from the default Key 1 to **Taper 1**. The tab should look like the one in Figure 5.2.

Figure 5.2

Taper 1 shape key

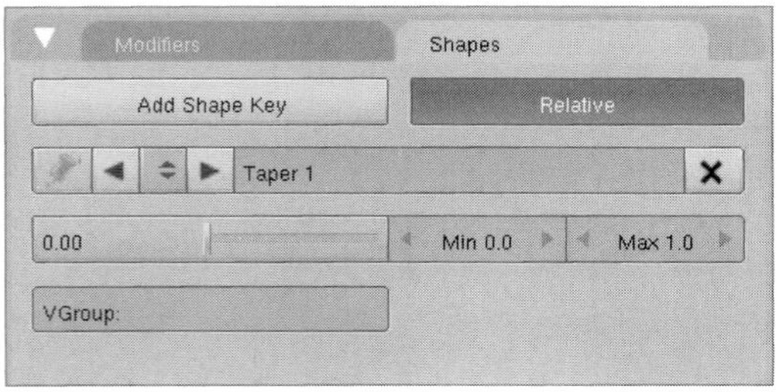

3. Enter Edit mode and edit the shape as you want it by moving vertices (verts). For this first example, select the top four verts and scale the face, using S followed by Shift+Z to constrain the scaling to the X and Y axes. Scale the top of the cube down as in Figure 5.3.

4. Return to Object mode. Now add another key in the same way, but this time name it **Wedge** and edit it to look like the shape in Figure 5.4 by selecting the edge shown and translating it down along the Z axis.

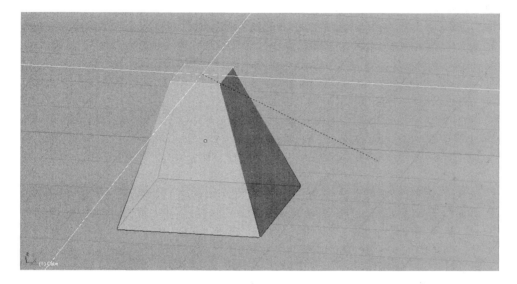

Figure 5.3
Editing the shape

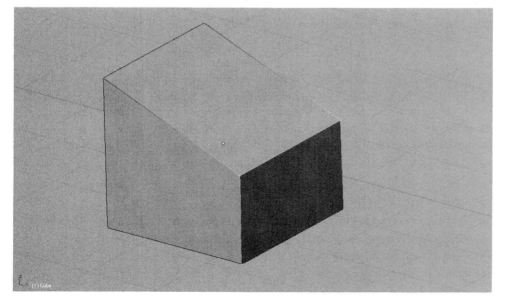

Figure 5.4
Wedge shape

You are allowed to add shape keys in Edit mode, but (in general) you shouldn't. The danger of getting your shape Ipos hopelessly entangled is minimized by doing most adding and deleting of shapes in Object mode. It would be necessary to create a shape key in Edit mode if you inadvertently stumbled upon a useful shape while editing another shape and wanted to register it as a separate shape from the one you were originally editing. However, this should be an exceptional case and should be done with care.

You now have three shapes: the Basis shape and two animatable shape keys called Taper 1 and Wedge. Using the arrow buttons in the Shapes tab, click through your collection a few times. There are a few things you should notice. The first Basis shape is special because it has no slider. Sliders on shape keys represent a gradation from the Basis shape to the shape of the mesh as defined by the shape key. Because the Basis key represents the mesh in its default position, it makes sense for it to have no slider; there's no place for it to slide to.

If you click the arrow to the right to make Taper 1 the active shape key, you will immediately see the Taper 1 shape in the 3D window. This is a special shape preview state and it's important. If you move the slider, you will no longer be in this state.

By default, the slider ranges from 0.0 (no change from the basis mesh) to 1.0 (full effect of the shape key changes on the basis mesh). Position the slider for Taper 1 somewhere between 0.0 and 1.0. You will see the mesh go from the basis cube shape to the fully tapered shape you created in the Taper 1 shape key. You can see how this shape affects the mesh at various levels of influence. But that's not all. What you are actually seeing when you move the slider back and forth is how *all* the shapes are simultaneously influencing the mesh. You are seeing the cumulative effect of all the shapes, depending on where *their* sliders are currently set.

To see how this works, set the slider for Taper 1 to 1.0. Click the right button to make Wedge the active shape key. The moment you switch to Wedge, you will see the full, unmixed Wedge shape in the 3D window, even though the Wedge slider is at 0.0. In this special state, you see what the shape would look like with the slider set to 1.0, even though the slider is actually set to 0.0. This state is particularly special because when you want to make a copy of a shape key later you must be in this state, with the slider set to 0.0. Another reason why this state is special is because it shows you the shape that you will see if you enter Edit mode with this shape active.

The moment you adjust the slider, you are dealing with the actual mesh as it is currently being influenced by the various shape keys. If you now slide the Wedge slider to 1.0, you see the mesh as it is influenced both by Taper 1 and Wedge simultaneously, with both keys exerting full influence over the shape of the mesh. You should be seeing something like the shape in Figure 5.5. If you click the left arrow, you will go back to the shape preview state for Taper 1. However, the slider is still at 1.

The fact that you can go from one shape key to another and set each one's sliders enables you to see how each key is mixing with any and all of the other keys in your shape key set. It also means that you should usually keep your shapes' sliders set at zero while you are creating the shape key set when you are not specifically trying to view them mixed with other shapes to eliminate any possible confusion about what the Basis shape is or what the shape key that you're currently looking at actually looks like. If you forget that one of your shapes is set at something other than zero, you might not see what you expect to see when viewing other shapes.

Blender can extrapolate the movement of vertices in shape keys beyond the range of zero and 1 if you want it to. Zero is always the basis that the key was created on, and 1 is always the form of the shape that you see in Edit mode when you enter Edit mode with that key active. If you make the minimum value in the shape key's range less than zero, you can use the slider to go into the negation of the shape. To see an example, go to your Wedge shape key and set the Min: value to -.25. Now the slider extends down past zero. Move the slider down to see what the shape looks like with the negation of Wedge active. The edge that was pushed down in Wedge is now raised, as in Figure 5.6. Likewise, you can extend the positive change of the shape key by increasing the Max: value beyond 1.

Figure 5.5

The mesh with both Wedge and Taper 1 influencing

Figure 5.6

Wedge shape at a negative slider value

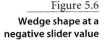

Although you cannot select shape keys in Edit mode, for some reason you *can* delete a shape key with the X button in Edit mode. Be careful not to do this accidentally! If you do, the active key will be deleted, and the next key in the key array will take its place as the active key *with the mesh still in the position it was in before you deleted the key.* This means that the next key down will inherit the currently active vertex position information, just as though you had edited the mesh. The previous shape will be completely lost because there is no way to recover the correct vertex positions for that key. Undo (Ctrl+Z) can work if pressed immediately upon returning to Object mode, but this is a situation that is better avoided.

Additivity

The shape keys you are using work by adding their relative coordinates. This is an important concept to get a handle on if you will use blended shapes.

To see an example of this in action, make sure that all your shape keys are currently set to zero; then use the arrow buttons to select Taper 1. While in the shape preview state, click the Add Shape Key button. By doing this, you have just made a copy of the Taper 1 shape. Rename the shape **Taper 2**. Use the slider to ascertain that it is in fact a copy of Taper 1 and that the default cube shape is visible when the slider is set to zero.

Now, set Taper 2 at 1. Use the arrows to go to Taper 1. Set Taper 1's value to .5. You should see a pyramid very much like Figure 5.7. Don't worry if it's not exact. If you adjust the value of Taper 1, you should be able to get something pretty similar, though. What's more, if you put Taper 1's value higher—at 1, for example—you will see an effect like that in Figure 5.8.

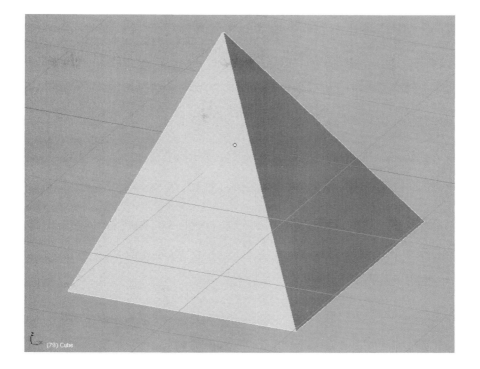

Figure 5.7
**Additive effect of
two Taper shapes at
partial influence**

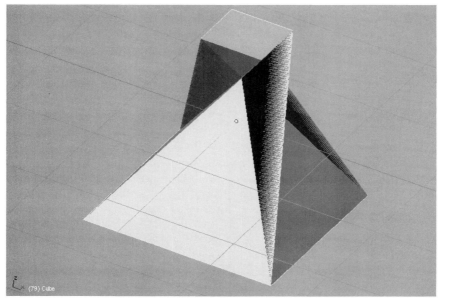

Figure 5.8
**Additive effect of
two Taper shapes at
full influence**

Although Taper 1 and Taper 2 are the same shape, their cumulative effect is not the same because of additivity. It's important to be careful when creating facial shapes that you intend to blend together. If two shapes have a redundant effect, you can wind up with some undesirable additive effects. Additivity is also the reason why the slider should be at zero when you copy a shape key by using Add Shape Key in the shape preview state. I'll leave it as an exercise for you to investigate what happens if you try to duplicate a shape with the slider set at 1. This can be a useful modeling technique, but you should be careful not to do it inadvertently.

Adding and Deleting Verts

Shapes record the positions of verts within a mesh. The verts and the edges that connect them are properties of the mesh itself, so they can be added or deleted in Edit mode. They are not specific to a particular shape, however. If you add verts in a shape, they will also exist in all the other shapes you have defined, but their position will be unchanged from the position in which they were created; you will have to specify their location separately for each shape, in that shape key's Edit mode. In practice, you are better off planning not to do mesh edits involving creating or deleting verts after you have started creating shapes.

Basis Key

The Basis shape is special in some respects and not in others. It is not keyable, so it has no slider. However, in most other respects it is about the same as any other shape key. It can be deleted; if you delete the Basis, the next shape key up in the list of shapes (probably the first one you added on top of the basis) will drop down to the Basis shape key position, and its slider will disappear. Also, if you delete the shape key above the Basis key in Edit mode, your basis will take on that key's mesh configuration. You can change the name of the Basis key, but you will probably never have a reason to do so.

If you change the Basis shape, this change *will not* be automatically reflected in other shape keys. For example, if you make a smile shape key and then later decide to change the eyebrows in the Basis shape, the smile shape will continue to have the original eyebrows. (When you actually run into this situation, you can select the vertices you want to be the same in all shapes, press W, and choose Propagate to All Shapes from the menu. This will position the selected vertices identically in all your shapes. There are other ways to salvage portions of a shape key while discarding others by using vertex groups, which you will see more about later in this chapter). As a general rule, plan not to have to change your Basis shape once you begin making shape keys.

Finally, insofar as the Basis shape key is special at all, it is only special by grace of its being the first shape you create, and therefore the first shape key in your set. In fact, the order of shape keys can be rearranged, and *any* shape key can be the first. In this case, the shape key named Basis will no longer be the true basis key, and it will have acquired a slider. I cannot imagine any circumstance for which this would be desirable, but because keys might become shuffled accidentally, you should know how to put them back in order. To reorder the shape keys, you need to open an Ipo Editor window and set its Ipo Type menu to Shape. The names of the available shapes are listed down the right side of the window, as you saw previously when creating the Ipo drivers. At the top of this list is a special key by the name of "———". Left-click this key name. You now see a special Ipo display that in fact does not display actual Ipos at all; instead it displays a number of blue horizontal lines and a yellow line at the bottom. These lines represent your shape keys, and their order from bottom to top is their order in the shape key array. If you left-click to select one of these lines, you will activate the corresponding shape key and you can move the lines up and down using the G key. You can use it to organize your shape keys however you like, but it is important that the line representing your Basis shape should always be the bottom line. If for whatever reason you notice that your Basis shape key has a slider, this is the place to fix that problem. You can see the shape key Ipo window in Figure 5.9. Don't worry too much if you if you don't fully understand what's going on there; this is a remnant of an older way Blender had of dealing with shape keys, which has been mostly replaced by the much more straightforward methods discussed in this chapter. You will need to deal with this interface only if you want to reorganize the ordering of your shape keys.

Ipo Drivers

As with the action constraints in the previous chapter, Ipo drivers are another case of animation concepts encroaching on the rigging process. Ipo drivers are crucial to the way you want to rig Captain Blender, so it's necessary to introduce them before moving on. However, if you are entirely new to the concept of Ipo curves, you might find it easiest to follow this section after skipping ahead and reading up on Blender Ipo curves in Chapter 6.

In general, an Ipo curve is the representation of some value that changes over time. These changing values, whether they are an object's location, rotation, scale, or any other value—color, specularity, layer… just about any value you can work with in Blender can be made to change over time—form the basis of animation.

However, animation (change over time) is not the only thing you can do with Ipo curves. Instead of making an Ipo a function of time, you can make the curve a function of *any other changing value*. As one value changes (for example, the rotation of a specific bone), another value changes (such as the slider value of a shape key). In this case, you would say the shape key's Ipo is *driven* by the bone's rotation.

Figure 5.9

If you feel the need to reorganize the ordering of your shape keys, do it here.

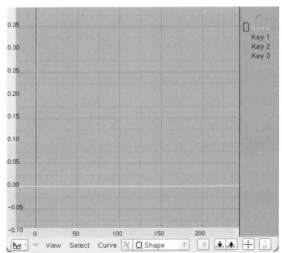

You'll set up a very basic Ipo driver now by using the shapes you have just created.

1. In Object mode, add an armature to the side of the default cube, as in Figure 5.10.

Figure 5.10

Default cube and a single bone armature, front view

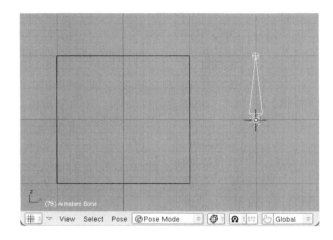

2. Split the 3D viewport in half and open an Ipo Editor window in one half.

3. In Object mode, select the cube. From the drop-down menu in the Ipo Editor, select Shape. You should see a list of shape key names down the right side of the Ipo Editor window. Select Taper 1 by left-clicking the name. A flat line should be visible in the Ipo Editor.

4. Ctrl+click in the Ipo Editor window to add a new vertex to the shape Ipo curve. You now have two control points for the curve. In the Curve menu in the Ipo Editor header, select Interpolation mode → Linear. (If there is a Point menu in the header instead of a Curve menu, press Tab to get out of the curve Edit mode.)

5. Press N to bring up the Transform Properties widget. Click the Add Driver button.

6. Place the control points for the driver curve, as shown in Figure 5.11. Enter **Armature** for the Object, choose Pose for driver type, enter **Bone** for the Bone, and choose Rot Z as the Ipo to use as the driver.

This will make your shape Ipo a function of the local Z rotation of the bone. Notice that the horizontal (X) axis of the Ipo Editor window is now written in degrees. The vertical (Y) axis represents the shape slider. Your curve should extend from 0 to 1 on the vertical axis, and should extend between the angles you want to correspond to the shape's intensity. In this case, you want the shape to be absent when the bone is at zero rotation, and you want it to appear as if the bone rotates to the 90-degree position. To do this, set the X min at zero and the X max at 9, and the Y min at zero and Y max at 1. For obscure reasons, it is sometimes not possible to edit the latter field directly, and you will have to position the control points of the curve in Edit mode. When you work on the Captain Blender mesh later in the chapter, you will see that this is the case there. Note also that in a slight notational quirk, degrees are specified as one-tenth of the value of the actual number of degrees you want to express, so 9 represents 90 degrees in this field (9 degrees would be represented by .9). Note also that keys that are managed by Ipo drivers show a dot in the middle of their selection box, as seen on the Taper 1 and Wedge keys in Figure 5.11.

7. Test the driver by selecting the bone in Pose mode and rotating along its local Z axis (press R, Z, Z). It is a good idea to open up a Transform Properties window (press N) to see the angles displayed, in case the bone's rotation is not what you expect. The rotation should be in the positive direction, which, as you can see in Figure 5.12, is counterclockwise in this case. As the rotation increases to 90, the Taper 1 shape should become more fully realized on the mesh.

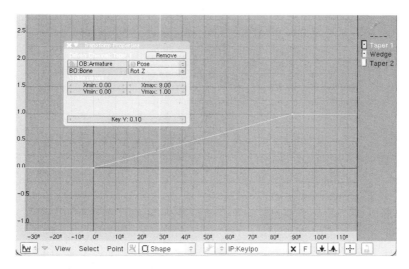

Figure 5.11

The curve describing the Ipo driver for Taper 1

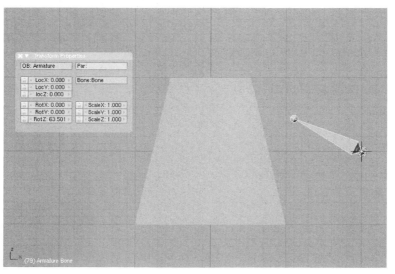

Figure 5.12

The bone rotation drives the shape.

Figure 5.13

Several Ipo drivers operating at once

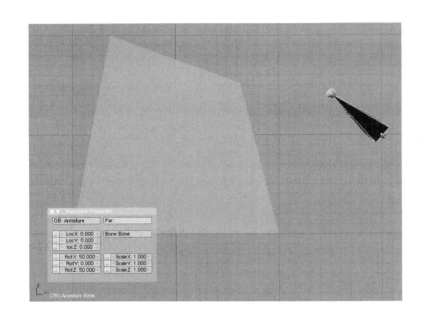

You've now created your first driven shape Ipo. You can drive multiple Ipos with the same Ipo or with separate Ipos on the same object. To see an example and get a little practice, go through the steps you just went through to create another driver (this time driving the Wedge shape) and use the X rotation of the same bone you used to drive the Taper 1 shape. You should wind up with a set of drivers that will allow you to control both shapes with various manipulations of the same bone, as you can see happening in Figure 5.13.

After you set up drivers for the shapes, the driven shapes can no longer be independently controlled with the shape sliders, but if you create a new shape on the basis of a driven shape, the new shape can be controlled independently with its own slider.

Building a Shape Key Set for Captain Blender

Now that you have an understanding of how shapes and Ipo drivers work, you'll turn to putting these tools to work on the character. First, you will use shapes for Captain Blender's facial movements. The eyes and the tongue you will rig up with bones in the next section, but aside from this all the facial expressions and positions will be accomplished by blending various shapes together. This is a common way to create facial movement, but it is by no means the only way. Some people prefer to use bones for certain parts of the face, such as the jaw movement or eyebrows. The Ludwig rig included on the DVD, for example, uses bones to control these features. A more complex approach to facial rigging using bones can be found discussed at `http://blenderartists.org/forum/showthread.php?t=70892`, in which all mouth movements are entirely controlled by bones.

An argument in favor of a bone-oriented setup is that it allows more freedom of movement and posing for the facial expressions, and indeed this might make it more appropriate for heavily toon-styled rigs, in which a lot of exaggeration is the norm in facial expressions. On the other side, for somewhat more realistic facial movements, individual muscle movements are in fact quite simple, and a large amount of freedom in the individual elements is not really necessary, whereas the control afforded by shape keys is more suitable. I chose to model the face movements with shape keys because they are comparatively simple to create. They also offer good examples for discussing the various distinct facial formations that combine to create expressions and lip movements. Regardless of what method of deforming the mesh you use, it is necessary to account for more or less the same set of basic facial shapes. It is worthwhile to experiment with other methods, such as the mouth rig mentioned previously. See Chapter 18 for more suggestions to broaden your understanding of facial animation.

Tweaking the Mesh

As discussed in the previous chapter, adding and deleting verts after you've begun making shapes is not recommended. Now is the last good chance to easily make such changes to the mesh, so it's a good idea to think about whether you have things just the way you want them. In this case, to get a little more expressiveness out of the eyes, I decided to add a few cuts around the eye area, as shown in Figure 5.14. I will do this before creating any shapes to avoid the hassles associated with adding verts to shape keys. Care must be taken to make sure that the UV mapping is still right. The UV map will be automatically updated when I make these cuts, but because there are new vertices in the mesh, there is a possibility that the textures might have become slightly deformed by the change. You should check a render of the texture to make sure that it is still coming out as you want it. If not, you can make subtle adjustments by pinning verts in the position you want them on the texture and unwrapping again.

For presentation reasons, in this book I opted to do modeling, texturing, rigging, and shape keys in that order. This is a common order to do things, but there are also good arguments for saving texturing until later in the process because modeling choices might change in response to rigging and shape requirements. Texture issues that arise because of minor mesh edits can usually be handled retroactively, but there are situations in which more drastic revisions might be necessary. Saving the texturing until last obviates these potential problems.

Figure 5.14

Adding a few more cuts around the forehead and eyes

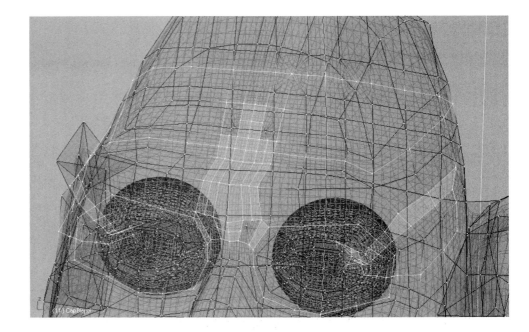

A First Shape: Eyes Closed

If the most basic sign of awareness in the human face is open eyes, then certainly the most basic sign of responsiveness is the blinking of those eyes. Conveniently, closing the eyes is a simple example to start with for shapes and it also affords you a good opportunity to look at the issue of asymmetry and how to incorporate it into Blender shape keys. So you'll begin now by making Captain Blender blink.

First, you want to make your life a little easier by hiding the verts you will not be using so you don't inadvertently select them in Wireframe mode. You do this by selecting the verts you want to hide (which includes most of the back and the sides of the head) and pressing H. The selected verts should disappear, leaving you with the front of the face as seen in Figure 5.15. To unhide all verts, simply press Alt+H.

To create the shape keys, go into Object mode and click Add Shape Key in the Shapes tab as you did in the previous section. This creates the Basis key. Click Add Shape Key again and change the name of the new shape from Key 1 to **EyesClosed**. Now enter Edit mode; select and edit the top eyelid as shown in Figure 5.16, moving the necessary verts downward along the Z axis. For selecting these verts, it is best to use the Circle Select tool (press B, B). Also, to unselect verts, use Circle Select while holding down the Alt key. The middle verts of each eyelid should move down farther than the others. The closed eye-lids should extend just around two-thirds of the way down the eye. Be sure that you have selected the verts of the eyelashes, too, to be sure that the eyelashes move along with the eyelids. You also need to make sure that the eyelids move forward along the Y axis so that the eyeball does not poke through the eyelids. Adjust the eyelids along the Y axis in Solid mode, so that you can see what's happening with the eyeball, as in Figure 5.17.

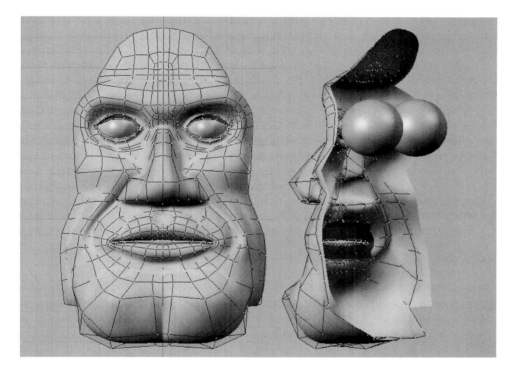

Figure 5.15
The mesh with extraneous vertices hidden

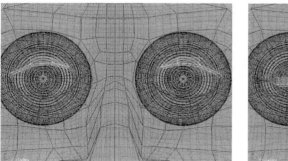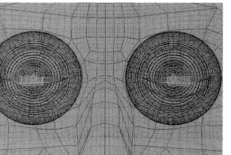

Figure 5.16
Lowering the eyelids

Figure 5.17

Fixing the eyelids along the Y axis

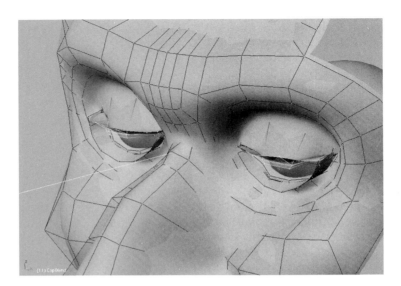

The process is the same for the bottom eyelid. Bring the pertinent verts up to meet the top lid, being sure to also include the eyelash verts.

When you're satisfied with your closed eyes shape, return to Object mode. You should be sure to check the shape at several different points between 0 and 1 to make sure that its full range of motion is clear of problems. In Figure 5.18, you see the EyesClosed shape as it appears with slider values set at 0.25, 0.5, 0.75, and 1. No problems appear. (Characters with protuberant eyes might require a slightly different set of shape keys to take their extreme curvature into account–a basis with the eyes partially closed, one fully closed, and the final one fully open.)

Finally, you'll make use of the shape key's range settings to get a little bit more from this shape. In Object mode, change the Min: value of the EyesClosed shape from zero to –.25. You now have a bit of room on the slider to move in a negative direction, which gives you the wide-eyed shape shown in Figure 5.19 for free.

Asymmetry

It can be convenient to model many shapes symmetrically, whether using X-mirror editing or otherwise. However, humans do not move symmetrically, either in body or in face. To be able to control different halves of the model separately, you must find a way to split the shapes into separate keys. Fortunately, it's not difficult to convert symmetrical shapes to asymmetrical shapes: you can use vertex groups. What you'll do is to create two vertex groups, one representing Captain Blender's left side and one representing his right side. You'll then make copies of the shape keys and apply them to each vertex group separately.

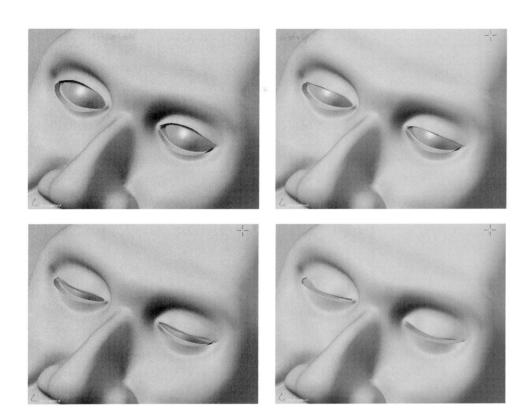

Figure 5.18

The eyes at various stages of closing

Figure 5.19

Eyes closed with a negative slider value

Follow these steps to create the necessary vertex groups:

1. Select the Captain Blender mesh and enter Edit mode. Using the Box Select tool (press B), select all verts along the centerline of the character, as in Figure 5.20. Be sure that you select in Wireframe mode or that you have Limit Selection to Visible turned off, so that you are selecting verts on both the front and the back of the character.

Figure 5.20

Selecting the center verts

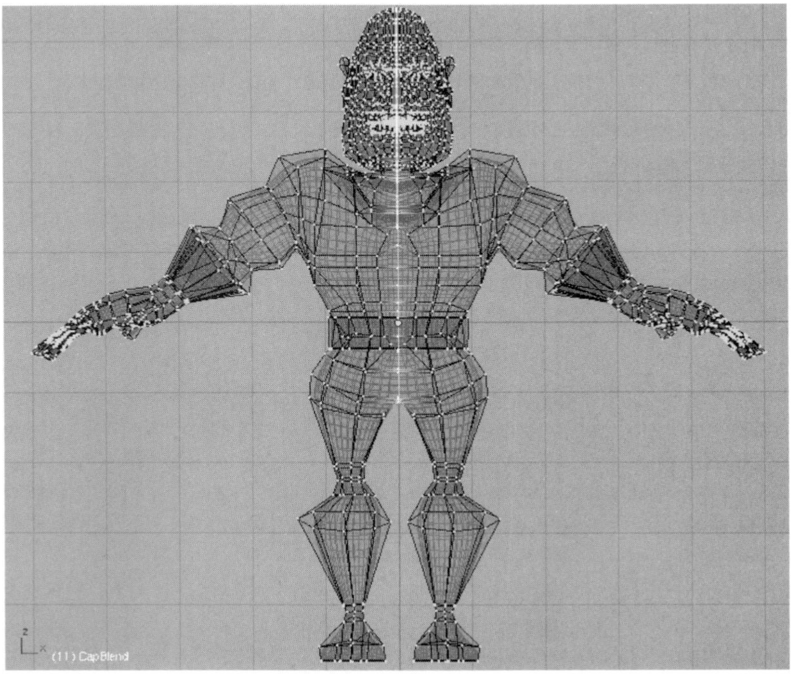

2. In the Links and Materials tab of the Edit Buttons, under Vertex Groups, click New. In the vertex group's name field (which probably says something like Group by default) name the group **CenterLine**. Make sure that the Weight value is 1.000 (this is the default, so it should be) and then click Assign to assign the currently selected verts to this vertex group. You can verify that these are exactly the verts in this vertex group by clicking Desel and Select again.

3. Using the Box Select tool, select all verts on the left side of Captain Blender's body, as in Figure 5.21.

4. In Vertex Groups (with the CenterLine vertex group active), click Desel, which deselects only the verts along the middle of the figure. The selection pattern that results looks like that in Figure 5.22.

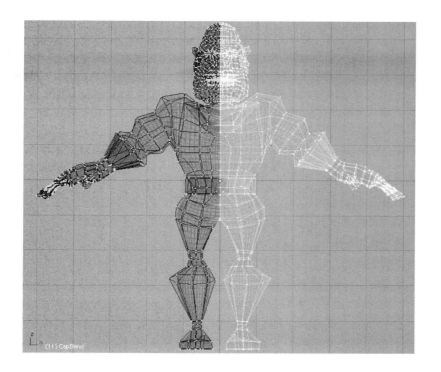

Figure 5.21

The left side (including center verts) selected

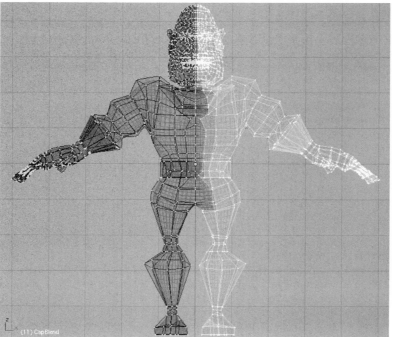

Figure 5.22

The left side verts selected with center verts deselected

5. In Vertex Groups, click New to create a new vertex group. Name it **LeftSide**. Click Assign to assign the currently selected groups to LeftSide.

6. Press A to deselect all and then select Captain Blender's right side.

7. In Vertex Groups, select CenterLine to be the active group and then press the Desel button. This results in the selected right side without the center verts, as in Figure 5.23. Create a new vertex group, name it **RightSide**, and assign these verts to that vertex group.

Figure 5.23

The right side (minus center verts)

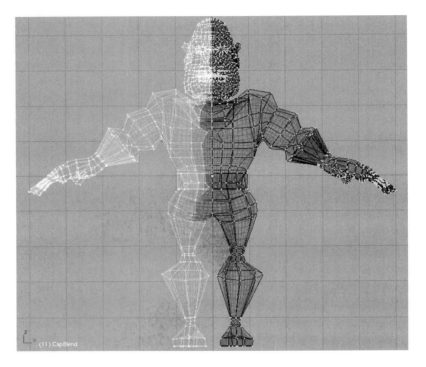

8. Press A to deselect all. In Vertex Groups, select the CenterLine vertex group to be the active group. Click Select. The mesh's center line should appear selected.

9. In Vertex Groups, select LeftSide to be the active group. With the vertex selection still as it was, change the Weight value to .5; then click Assign. You have now assigned the center vertices to the LeftSide vertex group, but only with half weights.

10. Still in Vertex Groups, with the same center verts still selected in the 3D window, select RightSide to be the active group. Ensure that the Weight value is .5; then click Assign. Now the center verts in the mesh are assigned with half weight to the right side and half weight to the left side.

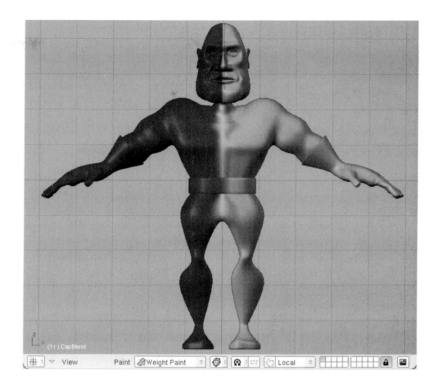

Figure 5.24
**The LeftSide
vertex group as it
appears in Weight
Paint mode**

11. Because different weights are not visible in Edit mode, you need to go into Weight Paint mode to see the effects of the different weighted assignments. Go into Weight Paint mode now. In Vertex Groups, select LeftSide as the active vertex group. You should now see LeftSide's assigned weights shown as weight paint, as in Figure 5.24. The left side of the body should be bright red (shown in the figure as lighter gray), the right side should be dark blue (shown here as dark gray), and the center line should be green. Check the RightSide vertex group's weights in the same way.

Now that you have the RightSide and LeftSide vertex groups defined, you can use them to create asymmetrical shape keys. To create asymmetrical keys for the EyesClosed shape, do the following:

1. In Object mode, with the mesh selected, go to the Shapes tab and select EyesClosed as the active shape. Make sure that you are in the shape preview state. The shape in the 3D view should be displayed with the eyes fully closed, and the slider should be set to zero. If the slider is not set to zero, set the slider to zero (the eyes are now open), click the left arrow, and then click the right arrow to return to this shape and display it in the shape preview state.

2. Click Add Shape Key. You have now created an identical copy of EyesClosed. Name this shape **EyesClosed.L**. In the VGroup field, enter **LeftSide**. The shape is now restricted to the LeftSide vert group.

3. Repeat steps 1 and 2 to create the **EyesClosed.R** shape key applied to the **RightSide** vertex group.

> If you use the Add Shape Key button to copy a key that has an associated vertex group, the new shape key will be a copy of the original key *as applied to the vertex group*, but will not have a vertex group associated with it. For example, if you copy EyesClosed.L, the new key will affect only the left eye, just as with the original, but without the need of a vertex group to limit it. You can use this fact to copy portions of shape keys by creating temporary vertex groups covering the area of the shape key you want to duplicate, applying the vertex group to the shape key you want to duplicate part of, and then copying the shape key with that vertex group applied. The new shape key will differ from the Basis key only in the places covered by the vertex group. This method is also useful for breaking a single facial expression into component shapes. For example, you can create a single "angry" face and then use this method to create separate shapes for different parts of the face, which can then be blended together as you have seen in this chapter. It is also possible to use weight painting to see the different shapes blend in real time, which is a neat trick and a great visual modeling tool.

Shapes for Lip Syncing

The main references for lip syncing in animation are variations on Preston Blair's original phoneme set. In the excellent book *Stop Staring* (Sybex, 2003), Jason Osipa recommends breaking phoneme shapes (and all other expressions) down into more basic component parts, such as vertical stretching of the lips, which are designed specifically not to be used alone, but to form lip positions in conjunction with other shapes. Because the main point here is to illustrate how this all works in Blender, I remain somewhat agnostic with regard to theoretical considerations about optimal shape key sets and cover a middle road between phoneme shapes and component shapes. Still, I cover the main lip positions, which I've described in Table 5.1.

Because you are dealing with blend shapes that can be combined to create phoneme positions, you will not have a one-to-one correspondence between shapes and phonemes. But it should be clear how the shapes you build can be combined to create the phoneme positions listed.

The creation of these shapes itself is straightforward. You can follow the instructions in the previous section for creating, naming, and editing new shape keys. As for the modeling itself, it should, of course, be limited to moving existing vertices around. Some suggestions for facial shape modeling include the following:

- Model symmetrically. Use X-axis mirroring when you can. This can be toggled on and off in the Mesh Tools 1 tab.

- X-axis modeling works only on meshes that are already symmetrical, and it can be sensitive to subtle asymmetries. It might work with some verts in a mesh, but not with others, if the verts do not already perfectly mirror each other. So when using X-axis mirroring, keep a good eye on both sides to make sure that all the verts that you want to move are actually moving.

- For verts that you cannot edit with X-mirror editing, you can approximate mirrored editing by selecting both sides simultaneously and constraining all transforms to specific axes. You can approximate mirrored translating in the X direction by scaling along the X axis to move the verts apart or together.

- You will often select verts in Wireframe mode, and this is much easier to do if you have hidden verts that are not relevant to the shape you're editing. Use the H key to hide verts that you are not working on.

My set of lip shapes is illustrated and described as follows. Note that with lip sync shapes there is no need to make asymmetrical copies because speech is one of the few more or less symmetrical things that human beings actually do. You can always add whatever slight

PHONEME	POSITION	
A, I	Formed with the mouth in a fairly relaxed and open position.	Table 5.1
E	The lips are stretched wider than A and I, but the jaws are much more closed. Teeth are very visible.	**Lip Positions**
O	The mouth is rounded and somewhat open.	
U	The mouth is rounded and is less open than with O, and the lips protrude somewhat.	
C, D, G, K, N, R, S, T, Th, Y, Z	These phonemes are mostly articulated inside the mouth, so the lips do not distinguish them much. The mouth is somewhat more open than with E, and the lips are less wide, but teeth are still quite visible.	
F, V	The bottom lip folds in and connects with the top teeth.	
L, D, T, Th	The mouth is almost as open as A and I, so the articulation of the tongue is visible. This is an option for phonemes that are articulated with the tongue.	
M, B, P	The lips are shut tightly. For plosives such as B and P, they might also curve in slightly before opening suddenly.	
W, Q	This is like U, only more tightly puckered.	
Rest	This is a relaxed position that serves as a pause between phonemes and a transition point from certain phonemes to others.	

asymmetry you might want in the mouth by mixing in shapes from the next section. The set of shapes is as follows (Basis is not shown):

Jaw down Create this shape by selecting the jaw and chin area of the main mesh, also select the tongue and the bottom row of teeth using the L key. In side view, locate the cursor slightly below the ear where the jawbone forms its hinge with the skull; then, using the cursor as the pivot point, rotate the jaw down into an open position.

Lower lip in Select verts on the outside and inside of the lower lip, raise slightly and move inward slightly on the Y axis, and also rotate slightly back around the X axis. Verts below the lip should be moved out and upward slightly to indicate where the teeth would be pushing against the inside of the lip.

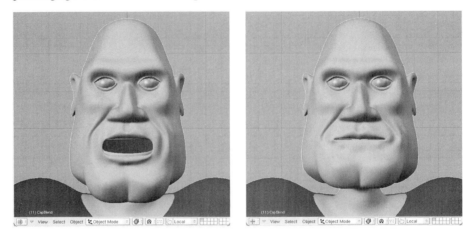

Upper lip in Similar to lower lip in, but rotated downward around the X axis.

Lower lip out Select the same verts as lower lip in, but move them forward and curl the lip slightly downward.

Upper lip out Similar to the previous poses, but the upper lip protrudes and curls upward slightly.

Lips together Similar to the rest pose, but with the lips fully together. Blended with lower and upper lips in, this will give a tightly pursed position.

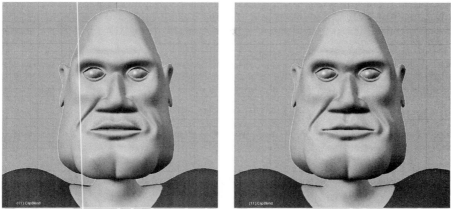

Lips wide Teeth together and lips widely spread, at its maximal point the teeth are fully bared. Simply select and move the verts of the lips to form the shape.

Round Lips are parted vertically and brought together horizontally to form an O shape. Pushed slightly past its maximum and blended with upper and lower lips out, this shape will form a tight pucker. Again, creating this shape is basically a matter of selecting and moving the lip verts until you are happy with the shape.

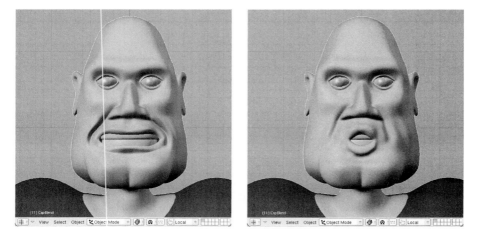

This collection of shapes and the various blended positions you can get with them, in conjunction with the tongue rigging you will see later in the chapter, provide you with all you need for basic lip syncing.

Shapes for Expressing Emotion

There is no hard and fast rule about what shapes are necessary to give a character a full range of emotional expressiveness. The most expressive parts of the face are the areas surrounding the eyes, so it is necessary to have a range of shapes to control eyelid movement, eyebrow movement, and some upper cheek movement. The mouth is, of course, important for smiling and frowning, but it is worth emphasizing that the sincerity of smiles and frowns usually comes from the eye areas, not the mouth. Also, with mouth movement, the crease running down from the flap of the nose to the edge of the mouth is important to emphasize the smile. A smile that does not affect the cheek and the area around the nose appears unnatural.

The modeling suggestions for lips hold for these shapes, too. I modeled them all symmetrically first; I then made asymmetrical copies where necessary using the RightSide and LeftSide vertex groups.

It is certainly important to have separate discrete shapes for different parts of the face that can be blended together to create expressions. However, there is a lot of flexibility in how you create these shapes. One common approach is to model full expressions in advance and then isolate small component shapes using the vertex group technique referred to previously. This ensures that the component shapes work well together to create complete expressions and reduces the chance that their additive properties will conflict with each other. For the sake of expediency, I did not take the extra step of creating full expressions in advance; I modeled component facial movements directly.

The shapes are described in the following sections.

Brows Together This shape is actually formed less by the eyebrows coming together (although they do, slightly) than by the wrinkles forming between the brows. You form the wrinkles by bringing neighboring edges forward and back along the Y axis, and emphasize the depth of the wrinkles by moving the edges closer together. This shape is usually used in conjunction with other shapes to create a range of eyebrow movements, often indicating concentration, anger, or fear. It is not possible to knit only one brow, so there is no need to make right and left copies for this shape.

Nose crinkle (left and right) Raise the flap of the nostril while pushing the crease around the nostril deeper and bringing the cheek slightly forward, further emphasizing the crease. The wrinkle at the bridge of the nose can also be included in this shape. This shape occurs in a variety of expressions; it is very pronounced in expressions of disgust and some angry expressions, but it also will have an effect in a big smile.

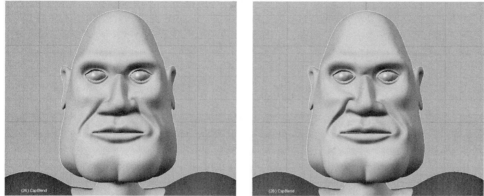

Smile (left and right) The edges of the mouth are raised and rotated slightly. The crease from the nose is deepened, and the cheek is brought forward slightly. This mouth shape is an important component of a smiling expression, but it is not the only one. It must be mixed with appropriate movements of the cheeks, nose, and the area around the eyes to convey the desired emotion.

Frown (left and right) Edges of the mouth are brought down and rotated slightly. This shape is often used with expressions of dismay, sadness, or anger.

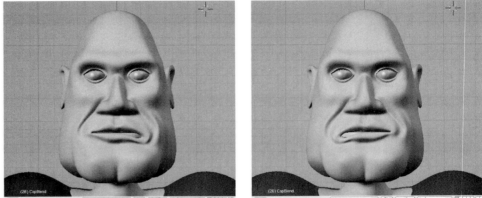

Squint (left and right) The crease at the edge of the eye is emphasized, and the cheek is raised. In addition to being used to indicate concentration (or of course physical difficulty seeing something), a squint is also a component in a big smile.

Brow middle up (left and right) The portion of the brow over the nose is raised, and forehead wrinkles are emphasized. This shape is often used in expressions of worry or fear.

Brow outside up (left and right) The portion of the brow furthest from the nose is raised, and forehead wrinkles are emphasized. This shape is often used in expressions of delight, surprise, or disbelief.

Brow down (left and right) The entire brow is brought downward. It is often used in conjunction with the brows together shape and can indicate anger, concentration, and (when applied asymmetrically) can suggest suspicion.

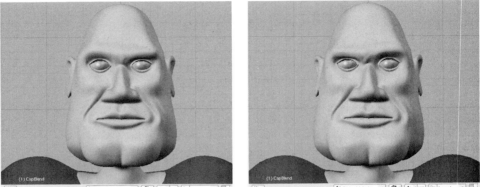

Jaw left/jaw right The same jaw area that drops in jaw down is moved slightly from side to side. It is an emotionally very neutral shape that can be applied to add variation to a lot of different expressions and often is part of a thoughtful expression.

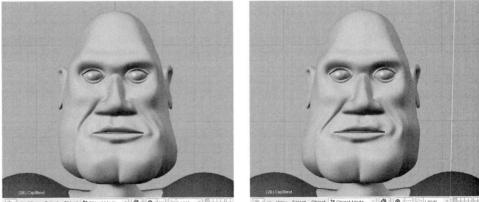

You now have a pretty complete set of facial poses to create facial animations with. In the next section you will see how to associate these various shapes with driver bones, so that when you get to animating, you can control everything by using a well-organized set of armature controls.

Facial Bones and Controls

As mentioned earlier, there are lots of possibilities for how to rig a face. In fact, almost all of them make use of some combination of shapes and bones. Bone-oriented methods usually incorporate some driven shapes to gain a little more control over certain deformations because facial movements can often be complex in subtle ways that are difficult to mimic using only bones. Likewise, the approach here—which leans heavily on shapes—uses bones for several things. First, you will use them to control the eyes because they are simply the most straightforward way to control eye rotations. You will also use bones to rig the tongue. Depending on your style of lip syncing and the degree of realism you are after, the tongue might be important for certain phonemes. However, its exact movement should usually be independent of other mouth shapes, which makes it difficult to do a good job of animating the tongue using only blend shapes. For example, if you want the tongue to tap the teeth, encoding it with a blend shape works only if you assume that all the other connected shapes are held to a particular position. The additive nature of shapes means that the position of the tongue depends on the degree of openness of the mouth, so tapping the teeth with the mouth open wide requires an entirely different shape than tapping the teeth with the mouth only slightly open. For this reason, you'll go with bones for the tongue for more control and freedom.

Finally, you will be using bones as Ipo drivers for all the facial shapes. This will simplify posing, enabling you to have complete control of the character through the single armature.

Rigging Eyes and Eyelids

The character's eyeballs are rotated by the use of bones. Furthermore, you will set up bones to raise and lower the bottom and top eyelids to follow the vertical motion of the iris, which will create a much more realistic eye-movement effect. To set these bones up, take the following steps:

1. In Object mode, select the left eyeball object. Press Shift+S and select the option Snap Cursor to Selection.

2. Select the armature and enter Edit mode. Press the 3 key to go into side view and add a bone with the space bar. The bone should appear with the base at the center of the eyeball—where the cursor is. With the cursor selected as the pivot point, rotate the bone -90 degrees, so that it is pointing straight forward with its base still in the center of the eyeball.

3. Repeat these steps for the right eyeball. The bone setup should be as in Figure 5.25. Parent both eye bones to the HeadDeform bone. Name them **Eye.L** and **Eye.R**.

Figure 5.25

Eye bones

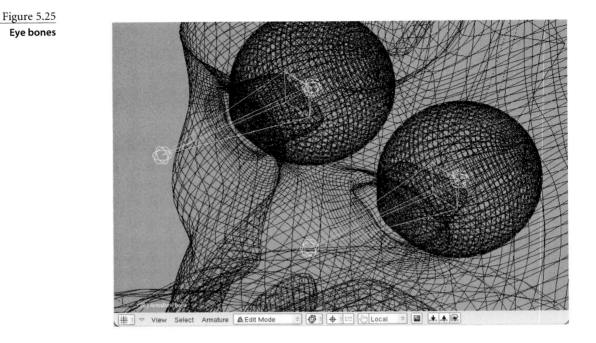

4. Extrude a bone from the Head bone. Select this new bone and press Alt+P to disconnect the bone from its parent. Move the new bone some distance out ahead of the face along the Y axis, and rotate it 90 degrees around the X axis, as in Figure 5.26. Name this bone **Gaze**.

Figure 5.26

Gaze bone

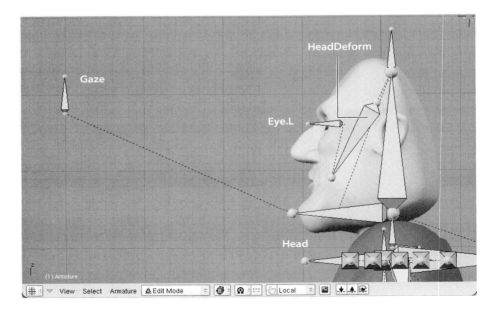

5. With the armature still in Edit mode, snap the cursor to the base of the left eye bone. In side view, copy the bone by pressing Shift+D and rotate the new bone up about 30 degrees (the cursor should still be selected as pivot point). Name this bone **UpperLid.L**. Copy the eye bone again and rotate it downward about 30 degrees. Name this bone **LowerLid.L**. Now copy the eye bone one more time and scale down to about 50 percent of the size of the eye bone without rotating or changing the location at all. This should be called **LidMove.L**. Parent UpperLid.L and LowerLid.L both to LidMove.L, making them both unconnected children of that bone. Parent LidMove.L to HeadDeform. You should now have a setup like the one in Figure 5.27. Do the same on the right side.

6. In Pose mode, you need to set up two types of constraints on each eye. First, set up an IK constraint on the Eye.L/R bones, with the target the Gaze bone. (You could use a Track-to constraint, but doing so might introduce some unwanted incidental rotations, so for this case I find IK the simpler option. The intention is the same.) Make sure to set the IK chain length to 1. Your eye bones should now follow the movement of the Gaze bone.

7. The second constraint you will set up is a copy rotation constraint on LidMove.L/R with the target as Eye.L/R, respectively. However, you do not want to copy the rotation on all axes. You want the eyelids to move up when the eye rolls upward, and you want the eyelids to move down when the eye rolls downward, but you do not want the eyelids to move from side to side when the eyeball swivels to the side. So you must make sure that the local X axis button only is selected, and toggle the other axis buttons off in the copy rotation constraint panel. You should now be able to move the Gaze bone around and have the Eye.L/R bones follow its movement, whereas the eyelid constructions go up and down in response to vertical movement of the Eye.L/R bones, as in Figure 5.28.

The eye armature is now complete; what remains is to rig the mesh to it. There are several things to keep in mind:

- Make LidMove.L/R non-deform.

- Attach the eyballs to the eye bones by selecting an eyeball; then Shift+select the corresponding eye bone in Pose mode, press Ctrl+P for Parent, and select Bone from the popup menu. This process makes the eyeball object the child of the eye bone, and only the eye bone. Generally speaking, it is the preferred method of attaching mechanical joints in Blender, of which ball-in-socket is an example.

- Weight paint the upper eyelids to UpperLid.L/R and the lower eyelids to LowerLid.L/R. As with any weight painting, test how this looks in several poses to make sure the weights are distributed as well as they can be.

Figure 5.27

Eye bone, eyelid bones, and eyelid motion bone

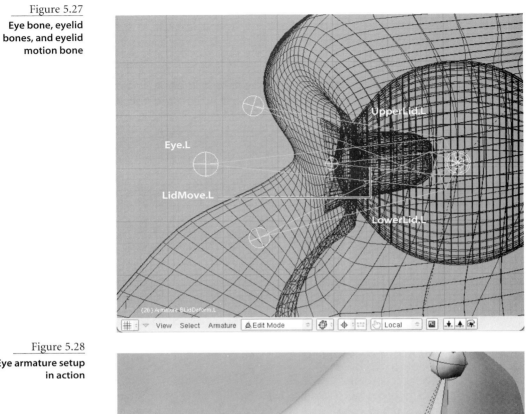

Figure 5.28

Eye armature setup in action

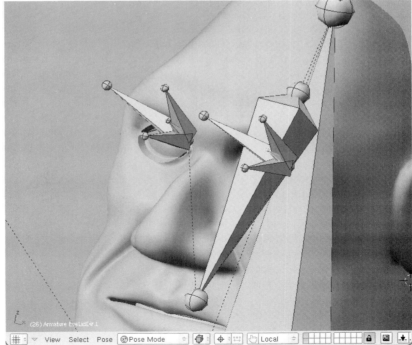

Custom Bone Shapes

For bones that have special uses (especially facial bones, which are often clustered together and can be difficult to distinguish), it is a good idea to create recognizable shapes for them to take. To do this for the Gaze bone, create a new mesh object in Object mode. I began with a 32-section circle and used some very simple modeling to create the form in Figure 5.29 to represent the Gaze bone. Give the object a recognizable name such as **Gaze**. Because Blender keeps track of objects based on their type (Armature, Mesh, Ipo), having both a bone and a Mesh object with the name Gaze is not a problem.

In Pose mode, select the Gaze bone and find the OB field in the Selected Bones panel. Enter **Gaze** as the name of this object. You will now see the Gaze bone represented by this mesh object, as in Figure 5.30. You can control the rest size, rotation, and location of this representation by adjusting the size, rotation, and location of the bone itself in Edit mode.

Rigging the Tongue

You'll rig the tongue as a three-bone-long IK chain with stretch constraints very much in the style in which you rigged the spine. First, extrude and disconnect a bone from the tip of HeadDeform. Place this bone at the root of the tongue and extrude three bones forward in the Y direction, as shown in Figure 5.31. Name the bones (back to front) **Tongue1**, **Tongue2**, **Tongue3**, and **Tongue.IK**. Reparent Tongue.IK to the HeadDeform bone. In Pose mode, set up a length 3 IK chain targeted to Tongue.IK. Make sure that the Rot option is selected. Give each bone a Stretch value of 0.300.

Figure 5.29

A custom bone shape for Gaze

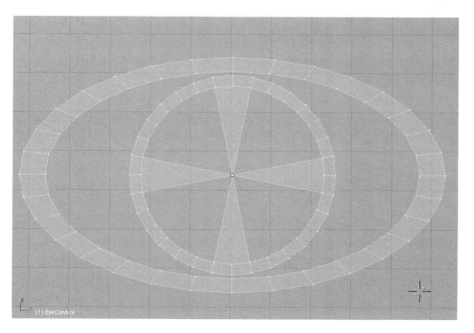

(f) EyeControl

Figure 5.30

**The custom-shaped
Gaze bone**

Figure 5.30

**The custom-shaped
Gaze bone**

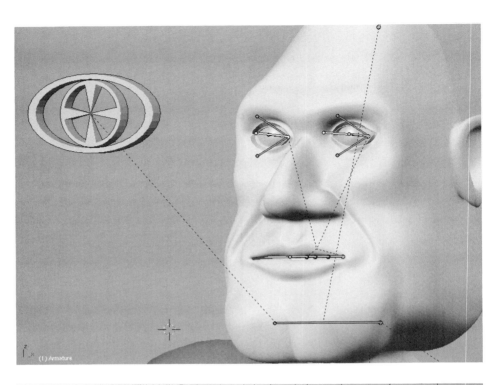

Figure 5.31

Tongue bones

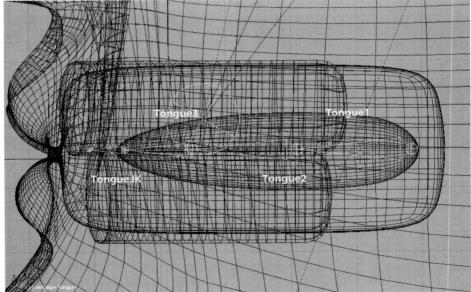

Now make copies of the three bones in the tongue armature, leaving them in place, so that they overlap with the currently existing bones, as you did with the spine. Name these bones **TongueStretch1**, **TongueStretch2**, and **TongueStretch3**. Reparent each of these bones to HeadDeform. Set up copy location and copy rotation constraints on each of these bones, targeted at the corresponding tongue bone. TongueStretch1 should copy the location and rotation of Tongue1, and so on. Finally, add the stretch-to constraints to each bone. TongueStretch.1 should stretch to Tongue2. TongueStretch2 should stretch to Tongue3. TongueStretch3 should stretch to Tongue.IK.

Tongue1, Tongue2, Tongue3 and Tongue.IK should all be non-deform bones. The bones that should deform the tongue mesh are TongueStretch1, TongueStretch2, and TongueStretch3. Again, you can add these bones to the vertex groups list by hand and assign the tongue verts to the appropriate bones by hand in Edit mode.

This setup will give you a very flexible and poseable tongue rig, as shown in Figure 5.32.

Shape Key Controls

At the beginning of this chapter, you saw that it's possible to use bones to drive shape keys. You now return to that topic. You're going to put this technique to use to make the face poseable with the armature.

A Controller for Lowering the Jaw

You'll start with the bone to control the movement of the jaw. This bone will drive both the jaw down shape and the jaw left and jaw right shapes, but you'll focus on jaw down first. Extrude and disconnect a new bone from HeadDeform and place it in front of the face as in Figure 5.33. Rotate it 90 degrees to make the bone's local Y axis point up and down. This bone will be called JawControl.

Figure 5.32

Tongue armature in action

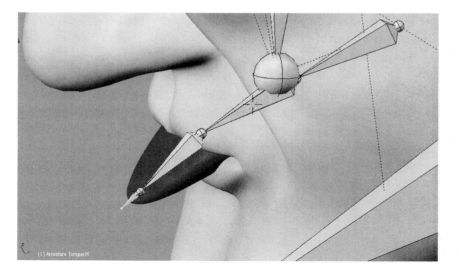

(1) Armature TongueIK

Figure 5.33
JawControl bone

Figure 5.33
JawControl bone

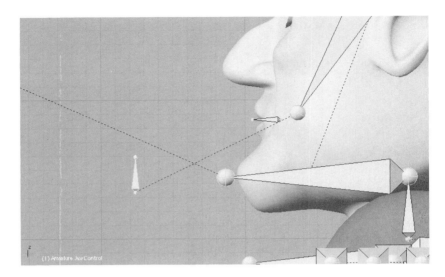

The facial controls all have custom forms associated with them, and you might as well design them as you go. For JawControl, I modeled a mesh object to represent Captain Blender's chin, as shown in Figure 5.34. To be able to organize things at a glance, I use the same material for all of the placeholder shapes, which is simply the default material in pure green. Putting the custom bone shape in place as you did with the Gaze bone gives you a JawControl as in Figure 5.35.

Figure 5.34
**Custom bone shape
for JawControl**

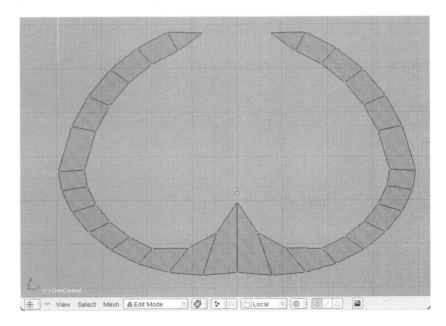

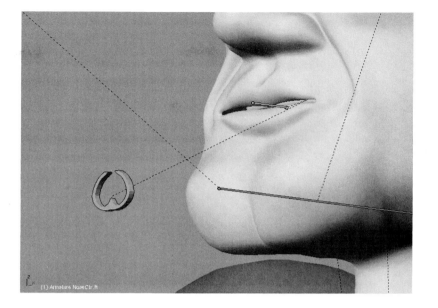

Figure 5.35

JawControl custom bone

Now you must set up the Ipo driver. The driver you will set up first will drive the jaw down shape. Because the bone's original position will correspond to zero on the shape, you already know that the X and Y axis values on the driver curve will meet at zero. The maximal value of the shape will be something just over 1, maybe 1.5 or so. What bone value should this correspond to? To avoid a lot of guesswork, you can check on that in advance by pressing N in the 3D viewport to bring up the Transform Properties window. Move the JawControl bone downward in the local Y direction to the place you want to represent the fully open mouth. About -0.5 looks like a good location to have the mouth fully open in my model. Bear in mind, your model might be constructed at a different scale, so this value might be different. Set it in a way that makes sense to you, and, if need be, refer to the fully rigged Captain Blender model on the accompanying DVD to see how the drivers should look in action. It does not need to be precise, but it's good to get an approximate idea of where the curve should go.

To set up the driver, follow these steps:

1. With the mesh selected in Object mode, open an Ipo Editor window and select Shape from the drop-down menu in the header. Left-click the jaw down shape in the list of shapes along the right. The colored rectangles to the left of the names indicate the presence of keyed Ipo curves for these shapes. You probably did some keying as you were creating the shapes because moving the slider automatically creates keys. So most of these shapes will have colored rectangles next to them. It doesn't really matter

right now. If you want to see the currently set keys, you can look at them in the Action Editor. You can delete them all if you like. Either way, you will be editing the location of the keys in the Ipo Editor window.

2. In the Ipo Editor window, press N to bring up the Transform Properties window. Press the Add Driver button.

3. Create an Ipo Curve with two key points. If there is already an Ipo curve with two points, you don't need to change anything. If there is an Ipo curve with more than two points, delete one point by tabbing into Edit mode, selecting the point to delete, and deleting it with the X key. If there is no Ipo curve, create one with Ctrl+LMB. To create a second key point, click Ctrl+LMB again (please see the following note for further details). Make sure that the curve's Interpolation mode is Bezier and its Extend mode is constant. Both of them can be selected in the Curve menu in the header (it becomes the Point menu when in Edit mode).

4. Set the points of the curve to the appropriate values. The X axis of the Ipo curve graph represents the value of the driver. The Y axis of the Ipo curve graph represents the value of the driven Ipo; in this case, the shape. Because you want the -0.5 position of the bone to correspond with the 1 value of the shape (and also want to extend the curve a bit farther to allow for possible further stretching), set the curve values as in Figure 5.36. There are several ways to move the points of the curve. In Edit mode, you can select a control point on the curve and move it manually. You can also input the coordinates of the selected control point in the Transform Properties window. The JawControl bone will now control the opening of the mouth when moved downward along the local Y axis.

Figure 5.36

Curve values for the jaw control driver

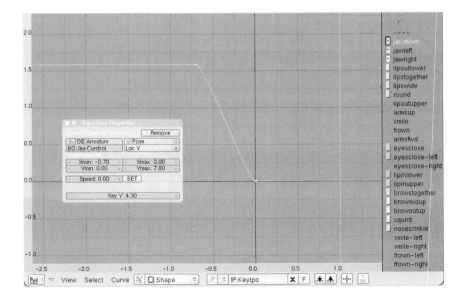

If there is no curve at all currently active for the shape (or other value), Ctrl+left-clicking will add a new curve with one key point at the position you clicked. You can add key points to a curve in the Ipo Editor window by Ctrl+left-clicking at the location where you want the new key point, and the Ipo curve will be updated to pass through that point. However, this short-cut will create a new key point only if you click sufficiently far (more than one frame) away from the already extant point. If you click within one frame of an existing point, that point will simply move. If it is the only point, the Ipo line will remain flat and move vertically. Because Ipo drivers often work on distances of less than one, you might need to position a new key-point within one frame of another. To do this with Ctrl+LMB, you must create the new point farther away than one; then select and reposition it.

In the example, you can see that the Ymax field's value is 7.80. This value is automatically generated and not pertinent to what you want to do here. Depending upon the exact steps you took in building your shapes and shape keys, you might have a similar value in this field, and you might not be able to edit this field. You should ignore this value and set the values of the driver curve's points directly.

Smile and Frown Controls

To control the smile and frown shapes, you'll use two custom control bones, one for each edge of the mouth, as in Figure 5.37. Create these bones by copying the JawControl bone in Edit mode twice and using the mirror editing to place the bones in a symmetrical way. Call the bones **MouthEdgeControl.L/R**. Create an appropriate mesh shape for each controller. Frown and smile are mutually exclusive, so you can control the smile by moving the controller bone up and frown by moving the controller bone down, having both shapes' values at zero when the controller bone's Y location is zero. Again, you will be driving the shapes' Ipos with the Y loc value of the bones.

When making custom bone shapes with mesh objects, be sure to recalculate all normals outside when you have finished modeling each object. Normals issues can sometimes be visible in the custom bone display, which are not visible in the mesh itself.

To create the four drivers necessary for the full smile and frown controls, begin with the smile-left driver. Set this driver up in the same way that you set the JawDown driver up in the previous section. In this case, you want the full smile shape to be in effect with the bone raised to about 0.2. Again, your distances might vary slightly, depending on the size of your object in relation to the background grid. Your shape key driver should look like the one in Figure 5.38. Test it and make sure that raising the bone activates smile-left. When you have this working, select the entire curve and send the curve to the Blender

Clipboard by using the down arrow button in the window header. Buttons like these should be familiar from when you used them to copy and paste poses and also to copy textures. By clicking this button now, you are making a copy of that curve on the Clipboard, which you can now make available to other drivers.

Figure 5.37

Custom bone controls for the mouth edges

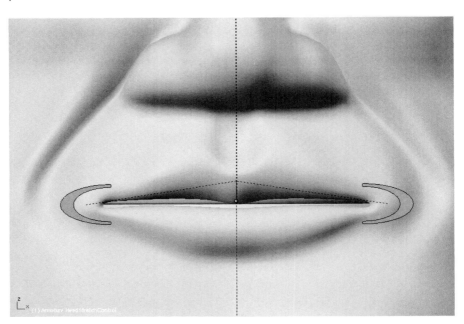

Figure 5.38

Driver curve for smile-left

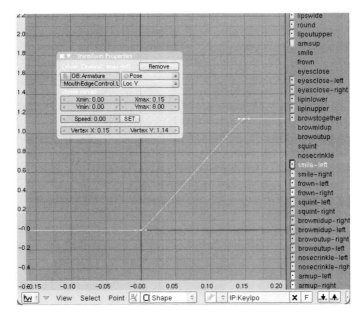

Select smile-right and press the up arrow button to take the curve from the Clipboard and paste it into the window. Now all you have to do is change the bone driver name from MouthEdgeControl.L to **MouthEdgeControl.R** (because this is the right side), as you can see in Figure 5.39, and you're done. Again, click the downward-pointing arrow with the curve selected to put the curve onto the clipboard.

Now select frown-right and paste the curve from the Clipboard with the up arrow button. In this case, you have the right bone driver (MouthEdgeControl.R), but you have it driving the shape key as it moves in a positive direction along the Y axis. You want it to drive the key in the negative direction. Simply select the top vertex by right-clicking the center point on the Bezier control point. In the Vertex: field in Transform properties simply put a minus (–) sign in front of the current value. Instead of 0.15, change the value to -.15. The result will be a reverse of the smile curve, as you see in Figure 5.40. Once again, send the curve to the Clipboard, switch to frown-left, bring the curve up from the Clipboard, and change the driver bone from MouthEdgeControl.R to MouthEdgeControl.L, as in Figure 5.41.

You should now be able to control the smile and the frown shapes by moving the controls up and down. Test this and make sure it's working, as in Figure 5.42.

It is a good idea to lock these controls to moving only along the necessary axis. Do this by selecting the bone and pressing N in the 3D viewport to call up the Transform Properties window. In the case of the mouth edge controllers, you should toggle the lock button on for all rotations and location transforms except for the Y location transform. This way, the bone can move only along the axis you want it to move along. You should do this for all your controls.

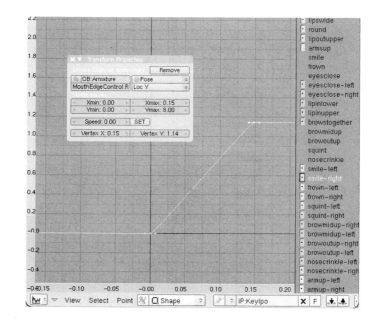

Figure 5.39

Driver curve for smile-right

Figure 5.40

Driver for frown-right

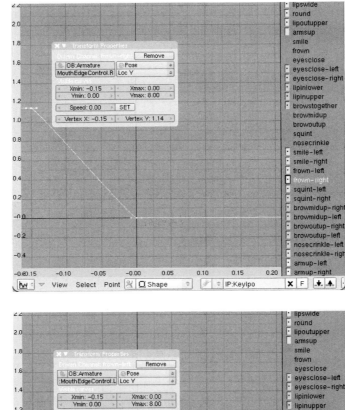

Figure 5.41

Driver for frown-left

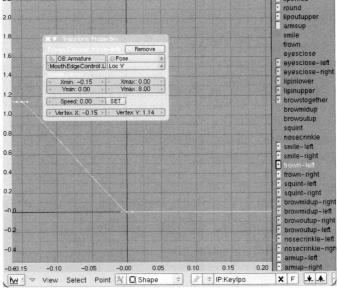

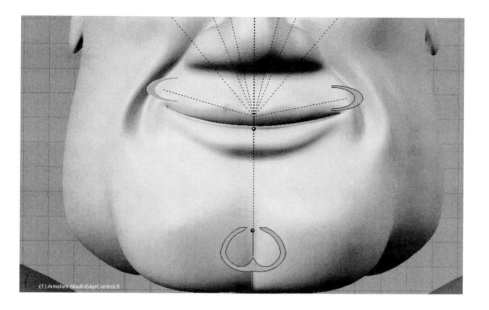

Figure 5.42

Smile drivers in action

In Figure 5.43, you can see the set of meshes I use for my controls, and in Figure 5.44 you can see the placement of these controls at rest in front of the character's face.

Figure 5.43

A collection of facial controls

Figure 5.44

Facial controls in position

The controls are as follows:

Eyebrow controls Vertical motion (Y axis) controls the mid brow raise for the respective eye. Rotation (Z axis) controls the outer brow raise. Locked to Y loc and Z rot transforms.

Squint controls At the edge of the eyes, the squint controllers activate the squint for their respective eye by moving toward the eye along the X axis. These are locked on all transforms except X loc.

Eyelid controls The eye-shaped controls directly in front of the eyes close the eyes when lowered along the local Y axis and widen the eyes slightly when raised. Locked on all transforms except the Y loc.

Brow knit control The single control at the bridge of the nose knits the brow when lowered slightly. Locked on all transforms except Y loc.

Nose crinkle controls When raised along the local Y axis, these controls raise and crinkle their respective nostril flap and cheek. Locked on all transforms except Y loc.

Upper lip control When raised slightly, this control activates upper lip out. When lowered, it activates upper lip in. Locked on all transforms except Y loc.

Mouth edge control Smile and frown controls. Locked on all transforms except Y loc.

Lip part control Placed directly in front of the lips, this controller activates the round lip shape when raised and activates the wide lip shape when lowered. When rotated along the local Z axis, this control activates the lips-together shape, tightening the lips. Locked on all transforms except Y loc and Z rot.

Lower lip control When raised, this control activates lower lip in. When lowered, it activates lower lip out. Locked on all transforms except Y loc.

Jaw control When lowered along the local Y axis, this control activates the jaw down shape, opening the mouth. When moved slightly to the right along the X axis, it activates jaw right, which moves the jaw slightly to the right. When moved to the left, it activates jaw left, moving the jaw slightly to the left. This control is locked on all transforms except Y loc and X loc.

Storing Custom Control Shapes

The shapes you create for custom bone controls have to be meshes, so they need to be placed somewhere. To minimize the risk of confusion or of them popping into view during final rendering, you can parent them all to a single empty, scale the empty down very small, and hide the objects on a rarely used layer. To tuck them away even more securely, you can hide them inside the Captain Blender mesh, as in Figure 5.45. Be sure to vertex or bone parent the empty so that it stays inside the chest area even when the character is moving around.

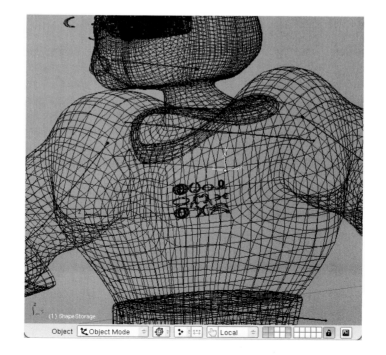

Figure 5.45

Hiding the shapes somewhere safe

Improved Mesh Deformations Using Driven Shape Keys

You've seen how bones can be used as controls for facial shape keys. Shape keys can also be used to augment ordinary armature mesh deformations. If you have played around with posing the Captain Blender rig, you know that there are certain positions in which the rig, currently weight painted, does not deform very well. In general, meshes deform most nicely when the mesh is close to the bone, so skinny characters tend to be a bit easier to rig. With Captain Blender, the beefy shoulders and biceps are likely to cause a problem when the arm is raised. Figure 5.46 shows the unnatural deformation that results. You might think this problem can be solved by clever weight painting, but because of the angle of the bone and the location of the vertices, this is not always the case. In cases such as this shoulder, there is no way to paint the vertices that can result in a good looking deformation for the entire shoulder and upper arm.

However, as you know now, armature deformation isn't the only way to get bones to influence the shape of the mesh. Driven shapes are a tool that you can use here. Basically, you want to create a shape that will force the vertices into a more natural-looking configuration when the arm is raised. This means that the shape will be applied when the arm is raised, but not when it is lowered. You can do this by driving the shape with the Z rotation of the bicep bone. As the bicep bone is raised over Captain Blender's head, the appropriate shape of the shoulders and upper arm is applied. In Object mode, add a new shape key based on Basis. Name this shape **arms-up**.

Figure 5.46

A muscle-bound Captain Blender with poor mesh deformations

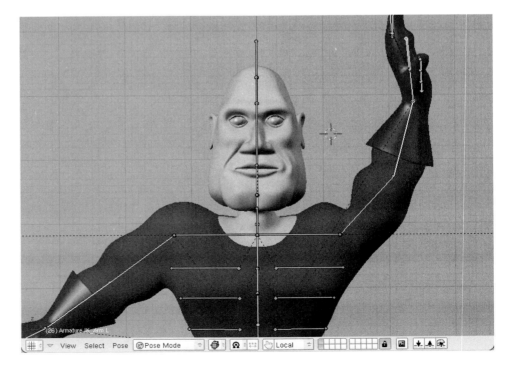

So how do you model this shape so that you can be sure it looks good in the specific pose you want to use it for? This is where Blender's modifier display options can be very useful. As you saw in Chapter 2, each modifier enables you to choose when its results are displayed. You can choose to display or not to display the modified mesh in renders, in the 3D window, or in Edit mode. By default, an armature modifier's results are not displayed in Edit mode, so when you toggle between Object mode and Edit mode with a deformed mesh, the mesh will pop back into its nondeformed position in Edit mode. However, you can select to see the deformed mesh in Edit mode simply by toggling the rightmost button next to the modifier's name on the Modifier Tab. The icon on the button is a small square of edge connected vertices. Furthermore, by toggling the circular button to the right of these options, you can apply the modifier to the edit cage itself.

When you select these display options and go into Edit mode, your deformed mesh will still be visible, and the edit cage will also be posed, as in Figure 5.47. You can toggle between Wireframe mode and Solid mode using the Z key, as usual.

Now, make sure that X-mirror editing is turned on and begin to model. As you did with the facial expressions, you will be modeling this shape symmetrically and then later you will split it into a right and a left shape. Because the left arm is raised, focus on making the left arm look good in this position. The right arm, which is not raised, will look funny, but this is okay because the shape will not be applied to the mesh when the arm is not

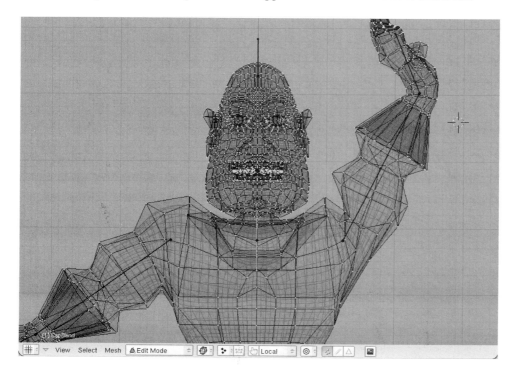

Figure 5.47

The mesh in Edit mode with the armature modifier set to display in Edit mode and to affect the edit cage

raised. Because the editing is mirrored, you can freely edit either side directly, and the edit should apply to both sides. Sometimes it will be helpful in this case to do some of the editing directly on the right shoulder and see how the left shoulder responds.

Finally, you should wind up with a shape that looks something like the one in Figure 5.48. The right arm is distorted and swollen looking, but the left arm looks pretty good. Next, use the rightside and leftside vertex groups to create arm-up-left and arm-up-right shape keys.

Creating the shape key drivers is the same process as has been described in this chapter previously with one slight complication. The driver bone for this shape should be Bicep.L/R, of course, because this is the bone whose Z rotation you want the shape influenced by. However, because the bicep bones are part of an IK chain, their local rotations are not displayed in the Transform Properties window. This is nothing other than a quirk in Blender's transform display interface; the rotations are calculated and accessible to drivers in the same way any other bones' rotations are, but it's not straightforward to *see* them. This means that when you set up your Ipo driver curve for these shapes, driven by the Z rotation of the Bicep.L/R bones, you will need to do some guessing and some trial and error. Put the curve's key points where you think they make sense and test out raising the arm. Move the key points until you have the shape's zero and 1 values corresponding to the correct angles of the arm. The good news is that thanks to the Clipboard option, you need to do this guessing and fiddling only once. You can copy the curve for the opposite arm and you will only have to invert the driver angles.

Figure 5.48

Arms-up shape

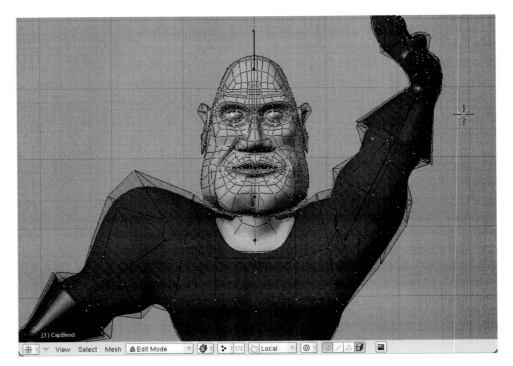

With the drivers in place, your arm should look like the one in Figure 5.49 as it goes through its range of motion.

Congratulations! If you've followed the steps in this book so far, you should have a pretty solid character modeled, rigged, and ready for its starring role in your animation. It's highly likely that you'll be revisiting many of the modeling steps again as you progress because a lot of problems with modeling can come to light during the animation stages. You might find that in certain poses, your weight painting isn't doing the job it should, or that some of the geometry or texturing isn't working with the deformations as you would like it to. Later in the book, you'll look at the best ways to apply your revisions while in the middle of working on animations. There are really very few true points of no return in Blender, and almost anything can be tweaked and fixed at any stage. But it can't hurt to play around with your rig a bit now, posing it and doing some renders, to test it out and make sure it's ready for the big time.

Figure 5.49

Raising the arm with the driven shape applied

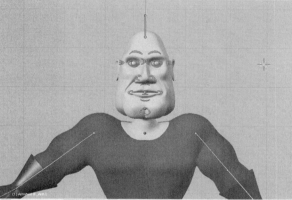
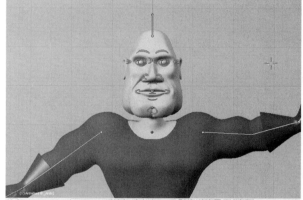

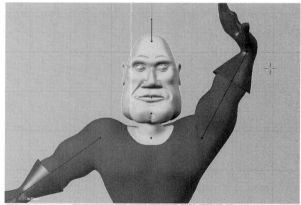

Bringing It to Life: Animation

In Part II, *you move into actual animation using the character created in Part I. In this part, you will be introduced to all the basic functionality of Blender as it relates to character animation. You will learn how to work with keyframes and interpolation (Ipo) curves, and how to pose and animate with armatures. Nonlinear animation, lip syncing, interacting with props, and a variety of other issues will be covered. Ideas of general relevance to character animation are woven in among concrete descriptions of how to accomplish practical animation tasks.*

CHAPTER 6

Basics of Animation

In this chapter, you'll set aside your rig briefly to take a general look at how animation happens in Blender. I'll be introducing a few terms that anybody familiar with CG animation will know and presenting them in the context of Blender's animation system. If you are new to CG animation, you'll want to pay close attention because although the details are Blender-specific, the ideas are universal, and the functionality is essentially the same as you will find in any other 3D software.

- **Keyframes and Ipos**

- **Using the Ipo Editor: Bouncing a Ball**

- **Interpolation and Extend Types**

Keyframes and Ipos

Animation involves creating a series of slightly altered still pictures that, when viewed in rapid sequence, create the illusion of motion. In this respect, it hasn't changed since Winsor McCay essentially invented the art form by painstakingly drawing out tens of thousands of individual frames for his early animated short films. In most other respects, it's gotten a heck of a lot easier.

In the so-called golden age of hand drawn animation—after Walt Disney came up with a few improvements on McCay's workflow to speed up the process—an animator would draw a series of pictures, several frames apart, representing main points in the character's motion. These points would usually be the "extreme" poses, which were the ones most crucial to conveying the illusion of physical substance and motion. Although I'm slightly simplifying some of the jargon, generally speaking these drawings were termed *keyframes* (a term that's still in use). After the animator finished the task of drawing the keyframes, an assistant would come around, empty the animator's ashtray, and draw the *in-betweens* (another term that survives as *tweening*). A skilled assistant would make the transitions between the animator's drawings as smooth and unobtrusive as possible. A tendency toward stricter workplace smoking laws has made the first part of the job of the animator's assistant redundant. The second part has been made redundant by *Ipo curves,* which are the topic of this section and will be playing a major part through much of the rest of this book.

In Blender, as in other 3D software, the concept of keyframing survives in a different form. You set keys at specific frames for the values you want to animate from one extreme of a range to the other. Blender automatically calculates a curve between the keys over time by *interpolating* between the keyed values. This curve is called an Ipo, or interpolation curve. Keyable values in Blender include angles and location coordinates. They also include a wide variety of other values, such as scale, color, parameter values for many effects and properties, influence values for constraints such as the IK constraint, display layers, and slider values for shapes. In short, any value that can change over time in an animation can be keyed, and Blender fills in the transitional values between the values you key.

Keys and automatically generated Ipos aren't the end of the story, though. To paraphrase a comment I heard once by an experienced animator, you're responsible for what goes on between the keyframes, too. Ipo curves are like a diligent and precise assistant, but not a terribly bright one. Unless you want all your motion to look like a series of unbroken sine waves (or like CG animation from 1985), you need to work with Ipo curves directly, making decisions about their modes of interpolation and editing the shapes of the curves themselves as appropriate. Blender gives you plenty of tools to do this, and you'll be looking at these tools.

The Timeline

There are a couple of windows you'll use when doing animation. One is the Timeline window (see Figure 6.1). This window does not require much vertical screen space, so I often split my Buttons window vertically and put the Timeline between the Buttons window and the 3D viewport. You can also select the Animation screen from the screen drop-down menu in the Information window header, which organizes your windows in this way by default (see Figure 6.2).

The Timeline's basic functionality is self-explanatory. When the play button 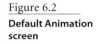 is pressed, the animation is played from the Start frame to the End frame on continuous repeat. The current frame is displayed in the field to the right of the Start and End fields, and you can input a desired frame number here directly. You can also use the left and right arrow keys on your keyboard to advance forward and backward by single frames, and use the Up and Down arrow keys to advance forward and backward by ten frames at a time.

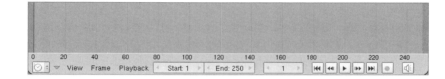

Figure 6.1
The Timeline

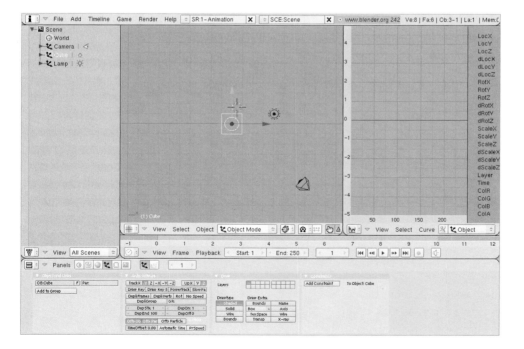

Figure 6.2
Default Animation screen

In addition to the play button in the Timeline, you can also play back animation by pressing **Alt+A** in the specific window in which you want the playback displayed, such as the 3D viewport. Pressing **Alt+Shift+A** plays back the animation in all windows.

You'll also want to look at an Ipo Editor window, so you should split the 3D viewport horizontally and bring up an Ipo Editor in one of those windows. If you have selected the Animation screen layout, your Ipo Editor will already be displayed to the right of the 3D window. This screen setup contains all the windows you'll need for this section. You'll look more closely at the Ipo Editor in the next section.

Using the Ipo Editor: Bouncing a Ball

I'll introduce the basics with a classic piece of beginning animation: the bouncing ball. Start up Blender, and without leaving top view, delete the default cube and add two mesh objects—a plane and a UV sphere with eight segments and eight rings. I put a subsurf modifier on and set the sphere to smooth, just to make it look nice (see the result shown in Figure 6.3).

Move to front view (numeric 1 key). Make sure the plane object is lined up with zero on the Z axis. Move the sphere object to 10 Blender Units (BUs) above zero along the Z axis.

The first thing you'll do is key the ball's vertical motion. In Blender, the I key is used to insert a key. You want to key the ball at frame one at the high point of its bounce. On the Timeline, make sure that you are in frame 1. Press **I** to insert a key, and choose Loc, as shown in Figure 6.4. You'll see some horizontal lines appear in the Ipo window, which represent the X, Y, and Z coordinates of the ball. The X and Y coordinates are both 0, so these two lines lie on top of each other at the zero point.

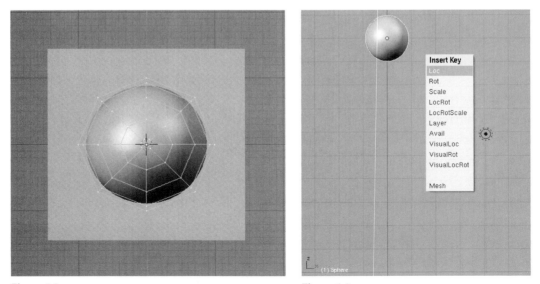

Figure 6.3
Adding a plane and a ball

Figure 6.4
Keying the ball's location

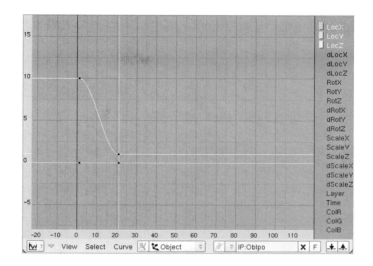

Figure 6.5
Ipo Editor window

As in the Timeline, you can move back and forth one frame at a time in the Ipo Editor using the left and right arrow keys and 10 frames at a time using the Up and Down arrow keys. Press the up arrow key twice to move 20 frames forward. The default frames per second setting is 25 fps (this setting can be changed under the Playback menu of the Timeline), so moving 20 frames forward moves you just less than a second forward in time. This is about right for the amount of time it will take for the ball to hit the ground, so move the ball down along the Z axis until it is touching the ground you created. Key this position in the same way you keyed the previous one. Note the curve shown in the Ipo Editor in Figure 6.5. The LocZ curve now dips from 10 to about 1.

You have now added Ipo curves to three *channels*, which are listed down the right side of the Ipo Editor. The channels that are available for Ipo curve creation depend upon which type of Ipo datablock you are working with. It is selectable using the drop-down menu in the Ipo Editor header. Currently you are working with an Object Ipo datablock. You may recall from Chapter 5 that when you created driven shape keys you dealt with the Shape Ipo datablock. To look at the curve for specific channels, left-click the channel name and hold down Shift to select more than one. You can also toggle the visibility of all curves by using the A key with your mouse over the channel list.

Key Mode

In the Ipo Editor, you can toggle into and out of Key mode using the K key. In Key mode, you can copy and move the values that you keyed forward and backward in time. Keys are represented by vertical yellow lines that appear brighter when selected. They can be selected by right-clicking, copied with Shift+D, and moved around with the G key. They can be translated only horizontally, along the Timeline, so you cannot change the actual values of the keys, only their position in time. As you move the keys, the Ipo curve is automatically recalculated to pass through the appropriate points. Holding down Ctrl while you move the keys constrains the translation to full frame distances.

Figure 6.6 shows the curve for the ball in Key mode. Select the first key with the right mouse button, click **Shift+D**, and move the new key 40 frames forward, holding the **Ctrl** key as you go. As you can see in Figure 6.7, the curve follows this key upward when you move the new key past the second (low) key.

You now have a single up-down motion for the ball, which ends in the same place it begins. You can make a cycle out of it by setting the Start and End frame on the Timeline to 1 and 40. Note that the duplicate of the first key is actually at frame 41, so frames 1 and 41 are identical. This means that cycling from 1 to 40 gives you unbroken repetitions of up and down movement.

Figure 6.6

Ipo Editor in Key mode

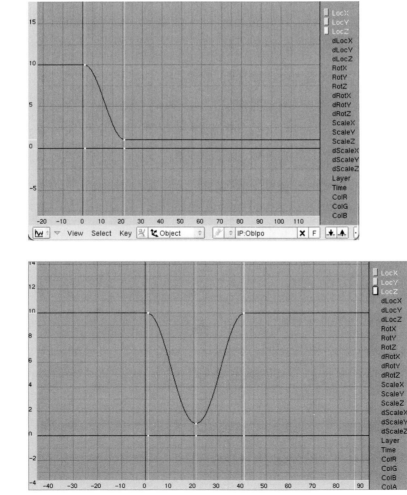

Figure 6.7

The full down and up cycle

Press play on the Timeline to watch the ball move. You should be seeing the ball rise and fall in smooth repetitions. (If there is any jerking movement, you need to check your keys and make sure that they are the right values and placed correctly.) However, the motion is clearly not the motion of a bouncing ball. Bouncing balls do not drift smoothly up and down like this. You need to adjust the motion between keyframes. To do this, you need to edit the curves themselves.

Edit Mode

In the Ipo Editor, with one or more curves selected, you can enter Edit mode using the Tab key. In Bezier Interpolation mode, which is the default, Edit mode enables you to edit the curves as Bezier curves, using control points with handles you can manipulate. Selecting the center point of the control point enables you to move the entire control point, handles and all. Selecting either of the handles enables you to control the shape of the curve. With a control point selected, you can change the handle type under the Point menu in the header. The options for handle type are as follows:

Auto Blender automatically calculates the length and direction of the handles to create the smoothest curve. This is the default.

Aligned A straight line between the two handles is maintained, so if one handle is moved, the other one is also moved.

Free Either handle's endpoint can be moved independently of the other's.

Vector Both handles are adjusted to point directly to the previous and next control points.

The main problem with the bounce curve is that the low point of the bounce is slowing down gradually and then speeding up when the ball returns upward. In a real fall, the object would continue to accelerate due to the force of gravity, so the curve would get steeper and steeper on the way down, before the ball is suddenly stopped by the unyielding ground. The ball retains most of its kinetic energy after this collision, but its direction is reversed back upward, which means that it starts back upward with almost the same velocity it had when it struck the ground. For this example, you'll ignore the loss of energy and assume that the ball can keep bouncing forever, in which case the kinetic energy going upward out of the bounce is the same as that coming into the bounce. This energy, in countering the resistance of gravity, diminishes until the top of the cycle, when once again gravity takes over as the strongest force acting on the ball, and the ball comes down again.

In practice, this all means that you want two parabolic curves angling downward to meet at a point. You need to adjust the lowest point on the LocX curve. Select that vertex by clicking on the midpoint of the control point, as shown in Figure 6.8.

A quick way to create a sharp vertex is to use the V key to change the handle type to vectors. Try this, and you will see that the handles now point in the direction of the preceding and following vertices. This is an improvement, as you see if you run the animation now. But the curves straighten out too soon, and the acceleration of the ball is not maintained all the way down. To adjust this, you can bring these handles' controls closer together, making for a steeper curve. Editing a vertex-type handle automatically changes it to a free type, so you can go ahead and select one of the handle points and press the **G** key to move it slightly toward the middle of the curve, as shown in Figure 6.9. Play your animation and see the improvement in the bouncing motion.

Figure 6.8

Ipo Editor in Edit mode

Figure 6.9

Sharpening the Ipo at the bounce

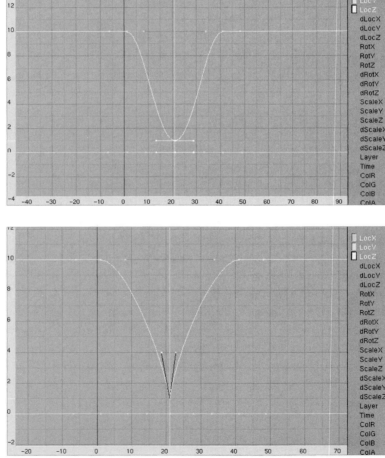

Keying Scale: a Simple Squash/Stretch Effect

Now that the ball's bouncing motion looks more or less right, you'll add a little squash and stretch to add some more dynamism to the motion. The use of squash and stretch effects in this way dates back to early drawn animation, and the style at that time was inevitably cartoony. Squash and stretch are real physical phenomena, but the exaggerated degree to which they are often used in animation is not realistic. Real squash and stretch depends upon the material of the object and the forces it is subjected to. A steel ball and a water balloon, obviously, have different degrees of squash when bounced against a surface and different degrees of stretch when dropped from a height. Something like a baseball, for example, would have an imperceptibly slight squash and stretch in real life. Anyone who has seen photographs of a baseball contacting a bat knows that although the bat makes a deep instantaneous impression on the ball, the impression is quite local and does not alter the roundness of the ball very much. However, in a cartoon-styled animation, the squash and stretch for a baseball would be highly exaggerated to emphasize the dynamism of the ball.

You will take a very simple (and not very flexible) approach to animating squash and stretch here, simply keying values for scale. To do this, follow these steps:

1. Go to frame 1. With the ball selected in the 3D viewport, press **I** and select Scale. You should have keys appear, as in Figure 6.10.

Figure 6.10

The original scale

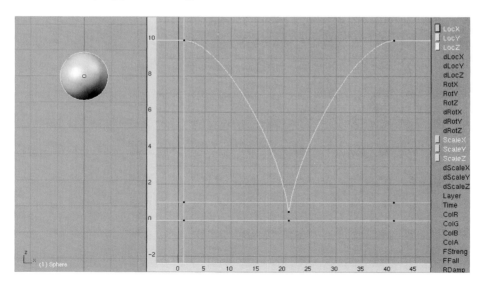

2. Go to Key mode in the Ipo Editor, select this first key and copy it with **Shift+D**. Move the new key 40 frames to the right, holding down the **Ctrl** key.

3. Skip forward 20 frames (press the up arrow key twice) and scale the ball to a squash shape. To do this, scale the ball down along the Z axis to .5. Then scale again; this time use **S** followed by **Shift+Z** to scale up in the other two directions to 1.5. Be sure not to change frames without keying this new scaling, or you will lose it (it will go back to whatever is keyed for the frame you go to; in this case, the first keyed value). Key the new scaling, as shown in Figure 6.11.

4. Because the ball is now scaled down vertically, you need to lower the low point on the LocZ curve so that the ball comes in contact with the ground instead of bouncing back just short of it. Do this by selecting the center control point on the LocZ Ipo curve and lowering it with the **G** key and the down button. Adjust it until your squashed ball is properly set on the ground. Note that this should be done by editing the curves directly; if you were to simply move the ball onto the ground in the 3D view and then reset the key with I, you would lose your special edits to the handles of the Ipo curve at that key.

5. The stretch effect is a result of gravity and should be at its maximal point at the same time that the gravitational acceleration is highest. This is, of course, the frame immediately before the ball makes contact with the ground. Go to this frame and press **Alt+S** on the ball to clear all scaling. Then scale up along the Z axis to 1.25 and scale down along the X,Y plane to .75. Key the scaling as shown in Figure 6.12.

Figure 6.11

Scaled to a squash shape

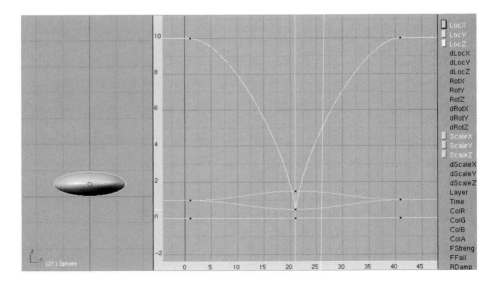

6. Because the kinetic energy of the ball is still high on the recoil, it should spring back into the stretched position quickly, but because it is not influenced by hitting a solid surface, it does not have to spring back within the space of a single frame. Duplicate the stretched key from frame 20 and place it on frame 24, for example, which is three frames after the actual contact frame (see Figure 6.13). The animation looks smoother with these intermediate frames in-between the full squash and the full stretch.

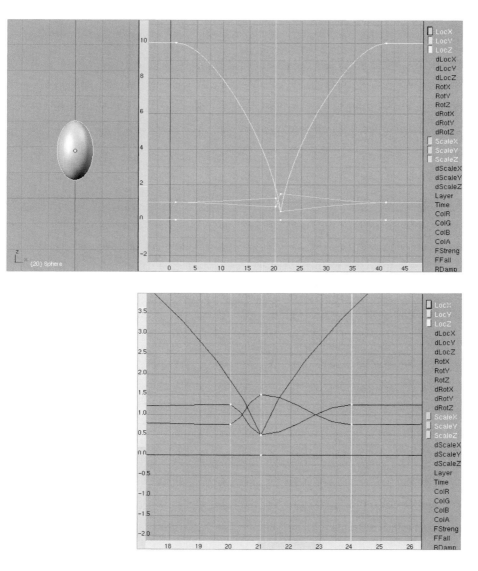

Figure 6.12
Scaled to a stretch

Figure 6.13
Placing the stretch keys

Interpolation and Extend Types

Blender generates an Ipo curve that passes through a set of keyed values. You can determine the kind of curve by selecting the interpolation and extend types of the curve. *Interpolation* refers to the algorithm Blender uses to calculate the shape of the curve between keyed values. *Extend* refers to the algorithms used to calculate the shape of the curve forward and backward in time beyond the first and last keyed value.

Interpolation

There are three types of interpolation available in Blender: Bezier, linear, and constant. Each of these types has a markedly different effect on the motion of the object it is applied to, and each offers different possibilities for editing.

Bezier Interpolation

The default interpolation type is Bezier, which creates a smooth, rounded curve between the keyed values. When in Edit mode, the key points become Bezier control points with two handles, and the curve's shape can be edited manually, as you saw in the previous section. Taking the two initial Z location keys you created for the ball as an example, this default interpolation results in the curve shown in Figure 6.14.

This curve type creates the most naturalistic movement of any of the three types, although this does not mean that unadjusted Bezier curves will always produce convincing movement. It is important to consider the physical forces being applied to the object.

An equally important quality of Bezier interpolation is that it is the only interpolation type that allows editing of the shape of the curve itself.

Figure 6.14

Bezier interpolation

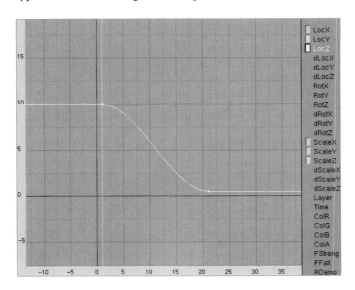

Linear Interpolation

Linear interpolation creates a straight line between keyed values. This can be useful for mechanical movements, but it is also useful for animating properties other than movement, which might change in a linear fashion or for use in Ipo drivers. Linear interpolation is not a convincing way to model organic movement. In Edit mode, you can move vertices around freely, but you cannot change anything else about the shape of the curve. A linear interpolation between the points in the example can be seen in Figure 6.15.

Constant Interpolation

Constant interpolation holds each keyed value constant until the next value is keyed, as in Figure 6.16. It should be obvious that this does not model motion at all, but rather sudden, discrete changes in position or value. This is the interpolation mode to use for instantaneous changes. In fact, when keying an object's layer, this is the only interpolation mode possible. For animation, this interpolation mode might seem useless to novices, but it can be very effective at blocking out the key poses of an animation sequence, making sure the gross timing is correct before going on to further refine the animation.

Extend Types

There are four extend types: constant, extrapolation, cyclic, and cyclic extrapolation. All of these types can be used in conjunction with any of the interpolation types. In the following examples, they are shown with a curve using Bezier interpolation. I have included two examples for each—one with two key values and one with three—to emphasize cases in which this makes a difference to the behavior of the curve.

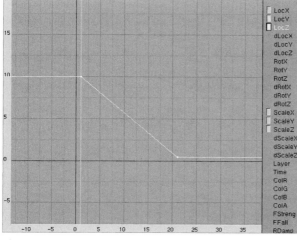

Figure 6.15

Linear interpolation

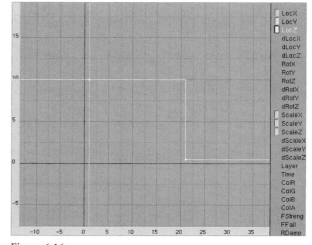

Figure 6.16

Constant interpolation

Constant

Constant extend holds the values of the first and last keyed values constant in the positive and negative direction on the Timeline. Constant extended curves can be seen in Figure 6.17. This is the default extend value.

Extrapolation

Where the constant extend type holds the value constant, extrapolation holds the *angle* at which the curve passes through the first and last keyframes constant and calculates the continuation of the curve as an extension of the line at that angle (see Figure 6.18). Two

Figure 6.17

Constant extend

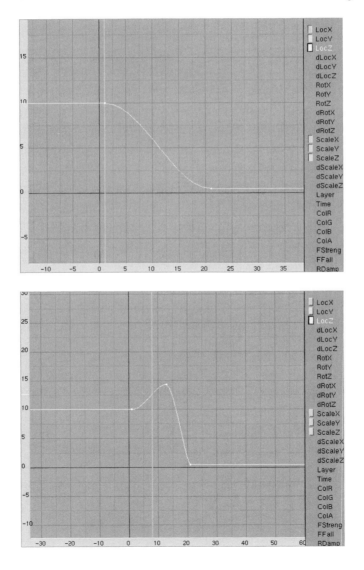

points can be used to create a straight Ipo curve at any angle. This can be used, for example, to continue certain transforms indefinitely, such as rotation. An extrapolated extend with two defining values on the rotation curve is a good way to animate a spinning wheel.

In the case of three or more points, the extrapolation extend appears as in Figure 6.19. This is a much less common use of extrapolation.

Cyclic

Cyclic extend repeats the same segment of Ipo exactly over and over again, as in the cases shown in Figure 6.20. Cyclic extend, clearly, is most used for repetitive movement.

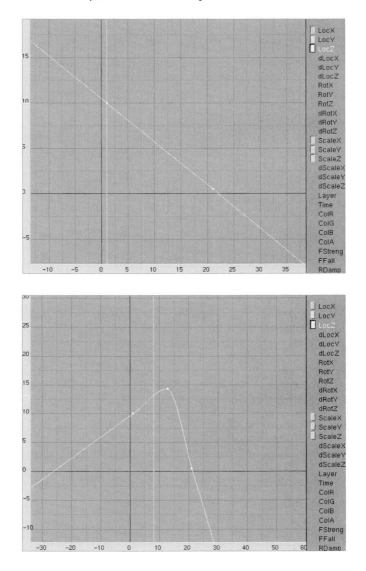

Figure 6.18
Extrapolation extend defining a straight line

Figure 6.19
Extrapolation extend with more than two key points and Bezier interpolation

Cyclic Extrapolation

Cyclic extrapolation, as the name implies, is a combination of cyclic extend and extrapolation extend. It basically creates a cyclic repetition of the Ipo, but beginning each successive repetition at the point where the previous repetition left off. In the case of a straight line

Figure 6.20

Cyclic extend

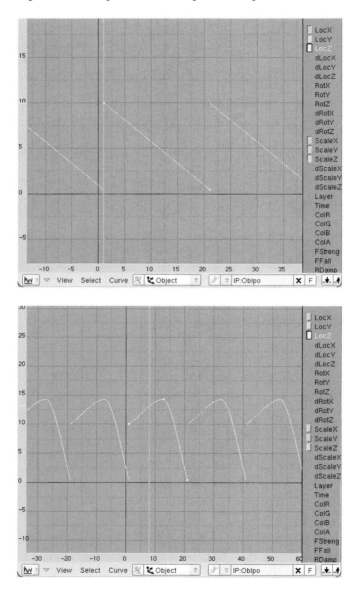

defined by two key points, as shown in Figure 6.21, it is identical to the ordinary extrapolation. In the case in which the first and last key points are the same, the effect is identical to the ordinary cyclic case. In the case of multiple, nonstraight Ipos with different start and end points, the effect is shown in Figure 6.22.

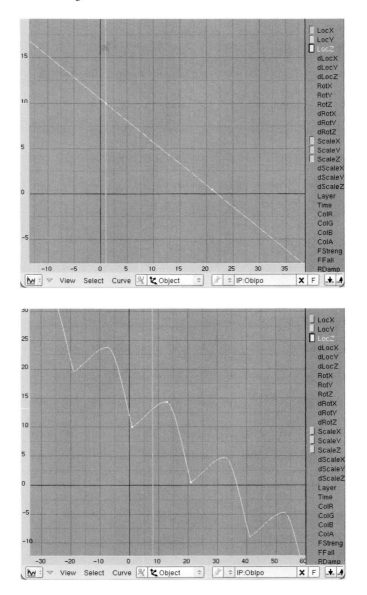

Figure 6.21
Cyclic extrapolation extend of a straight line defined by two points

Figure 6.22
Cyclic extrapolation extend of a curve defined by three points

The Incredible, General Ipo

Ipo curves are the basis of all animation in Blender. Any time a value changes, there is an Ipo guiding its change. In the next few chapters, you will see a number of different ways and places in which keys can be created and manipulated; some values are keyable in the buttons area, some values are keyed by using sliders, and much of the armature-based work you will be doing will take place in the Action Editor window and the Non-Linear Animation Editor. Nevertheless, all these contexts are fundamentally interfaces laid over the basis of Ipo curves and key values. It is important to remember that when problems arise in these other areas, you can always find the Ipo curve that's giving you trouble in the Ipo Editor and find out what's going on with it directly.

CHAPTER 7

Armature Animation

In this chapter, you finally get down to the business of full-fledged character animation in Blender. You rigged the character, had a look at the underlying mechanisms of how animation works, and hopefully have become pretty comfortable with the interface. It's time to see what you can make Captain Blender *do.*

Although this book is not intended as a substitute for in-depth study of the art of animation, this chapter touches on some basic principles of creating convincing motion that have stood the test of time from the early days of Disney to the present. Animation is a descendent art form of cartooning, which used simple drawings to express a wide range of emotions and ideas, and as such exaggeration is a crucial aspect. Although CG can enable you to work with very realistic images, the exaggerated, cartoon-influenced aspect remains significant, as anybody familiar with such "live action" films as *The Mask* or *The Matrix* is aware. In hyper-realistic CG, use of motion capture and related technologies can move out of the realm of proper animation and into something else entirely. In films such as *King Kong* and *Lord of the Rings*, for example, the character models for Kong and Gollum essentially amount to digital costumes applied to a human actor.

This book is mainly concerned with animation in the traditional sense, which almost inevitably assumes a certain degree of exaggeration. For this reason, I will point out places and ways in which tools such as squash and stretch and other forms of exaggeration can be used to make motion more vivid and convincing.

- **Posing and Keyframing with the Action Editor**
- **Walk and Run Cycles**
- **Pose-To-Pose Animation**

Posing and Keyframing with the Action Editor

The starting point for armature animation is the Action Editor, which you can access by selecting the little running (or drowning?) man icon in the Window Type drop-down menu, as shown in Figure 7.1. The Action Editor is essentially an interface for keying and organizing collections of Ipo (interpolation) curve keys. Keys created in the Action Editor represent actual key points in the underlying Ipos and can be edited as such, but the Action Editor makes it much easier to see the arrangement of keys for all the bones in an armature at once instead of having to deal with a huge number of Ipo curves and keys. For example, the location and rotation of a single bone at a particular point in time actually involves seven different Ipo curves. You don't want to have to see all those curves just to know that the bone has been keyed for location and rotation. The Action Editor enables you to see pertinent information about where keys are without giving you too much information.

The Action Editor enables you to create and edit separate actions independently of each other. As you saw in Chapter 4, this is useful when creating action constraints. The action constraints you applied to the feet and hands of your rig were examples of independent actions at work. As you will see in the next few chapters, there are other ways in which individual actions can be used and combined. This chapter will focus on creating and working with individual actions.

Bouncing Captain Blender

You'll begin by creating a basic jump action. First, place the character so that he's standing on the ground, which you'll make at the zero point on the Z axis. Move the armature in Object mode upward along the Z axis. Note that the mesh should be object-parented to the armature so that when the armature is moved in Object mode, the mesh follows it. Also, add a plane at the zero point, as shown in Figure 7.2, and scale it up along the Y and X axes. This will be the ground.

Figure 7.1

Action Editor

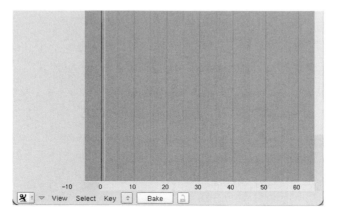

Figure 7.2

Positioning the character on the floor

Now you'll really start animating. You'll want a 3D viewport window and an Action Editor window open here, as well as a Timeline. One option is to select the Animation Screen from the Screen drop-down menu at the top of your work area to create a display like that shown in Figure 7.3. This gives you a setup that includes the necessary windows. The default animation length is 250 frames, which corresponds to a 10-second animation.

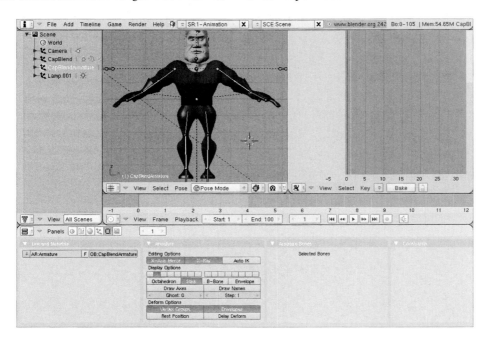

Figure 7.3

Animation screen

There are several ways to create a new action. All currently existing actions can be found under the drop-down menu in the Action Editor header (to the left of the Bake button). The initial setup you see in the figure is what the Action Editor looks like with no active action (in fact, there are no actions at all yet). In this situation, selecting Add New from that drop-down menu creates a new action called Action. Subsequent new actions will be called Action.001, Action.002, and so on, and you can rename them simply by typing a new name into the field. If there is an action currently active in the Action Editor, Add New creates a new duplicate of that action.

When there is no active action, as in the present case, you can simply start keying. Make sure that your Timeline says you are on frame 1, select the Torso bone, and key its location and rotation by pressing the **I** key in the 3D viewport and choosing LocRot from the menu that pops up. A new action is automatically created with the name Action. (In my examples, the name is Action.001 because I have another action created that I'm not showing you right now. You can rename this action jump later.) In the area on the left side of the Action Editor, the action's *channels* are listed; in this case, only Torso. A yellow, diamond-shaped key indicator will also appear at frame 1 in the Torso channel, indicating that the Torso bone has been keyed there. Recall that this key is in fact shorthand for seven different Ipo keys that have all been created on that frame. Do the same with UpperBody, Head, and the Ball_Heel_Rotation.L/R bones. The channels will be automatically added to the action, as you can see in Figure 7.4. These are the main bones you're concerned with for the jumping motion. Other bones will also be involved to enhance the effect, but the main motion will depend on these bones. You'll create a cycle that begins and ends with the armature's rest pose, so you'll key the relevant bones now.

> You can rearrange the order of channels in the Action Editor as you like by selecting a channel and moving it up or down with the Up arrow and Down arrow keys on your keyboard.

You'll incorporate a little exaggeration right off the bat, here in terms of the timing. Because you want to emphasize the motion and the height that Captain Blender is jumping to, you'll make the whole motion slightly slower than it would be in real life. The whole action will take 50 frames, or 2 seconds. This is not slow enough to appear to the viewer as actual slow motion, but it will highlight the sense of mass and energy in the motion.

There are three main parts to this motion, aside from the rest positions at the beginning and end. There is the initial crouch as the character gets ready to launch upward. Next is the apex of the jump, where the character is at his most extended point, and then is the recoil point after pressing the ground on the way down, which forces the character down into a position not much different from the initial crouch.

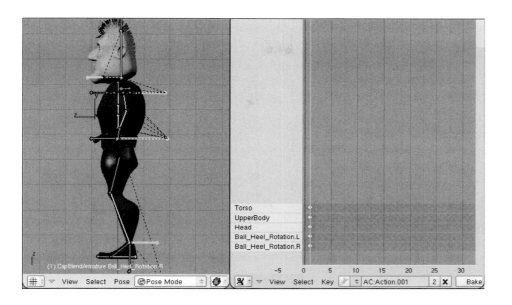

Figure 7.4

Keying bone positions automatically creates Action Editor channels for the bones.

The timing of the up and down motion needs to be symmetrical because, like the ball bouncing, the rise and fall of an object with gravity create a parabolic shape. So you want the figure's movement into and out of the crouching position at the beginning and the end of the jump to be considerably slower than the leap and landing, which you want to be explosive and jolting, respectively.

Figure 7.5

Crouch pose

To complete the keyframing for the jump, follow these steps:

1. Ensure that Torso, UpperBody, Head, and the Ball_Heel_ Rotation.L/R bones are keyed in the rest position in frame 1, as described previously.

2. Go to frame 16 by entering the frame number in the Timeline field. Position and key Torso, UpperBody, Head, and the Ball_ Heel_Rotation.L/R bones at frame 16, as shown in Figure 7.5. This gives the figure a bit longer than one-half second to get down into the crouching position.

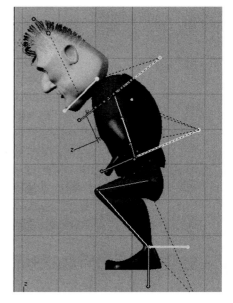

3. Go to frame 26, select all bones with the A key and then press Alt+R and Alt+G to clear all location and rotation transformations on the bones. Pose the character as shown in Figure 7.6, which will be the apex of the leap. Notice that the chest is somewhat stretched and curved back. Key these bone positions.

4. In the Action Editor, select all the keys in frame 16 with the box select tool (B key). Selected keys will be yellow. Selecting keys with the box tool does not automatically unselect other keys, so double-check that only the keys in frame 16 are selected. Press Shift+D to copy the keys. Then while holding down Ctrl, move the copied keys to frame 36. Holding down Ctrl while moving keys constrains their placement to full frames. The UpperBody bone here can be lowered slightly to add to the squash effect.

5. You'll make a few small modifications here to improve the effect. One will be to key the rotation of the FootRoot.L/R bones. They should be in rest position before and after the jump, and rotated as shown in Figure 7.7 at the apex of the jump.

6. The second modification you make is to incorporate an unrealistic touch to exaggerate the strain of the leap and the impact of the landing, adding a slight squash and stretch effect to his head. To do this, key the HeadStretch bone in its rest position in the first and last frames. During the initial crouch, the HeadStretch bone should also be in rest position. At the apex of the leap, it should be raised slightly, as shown in Figure 7.7. At the recoil point, the second crouched position, the HeadStretch bone should be at its lowest squashed position, as shown in Figure 7.8. However, this is not sufficient because you now have a smooth transition from the stretch of the apex to the squash of the recoil. The change should be abrupt, not smooth. You want the

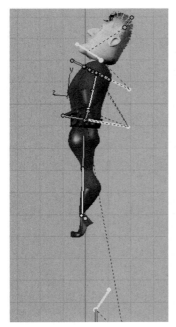

Figure 7.6

Apex of the leap

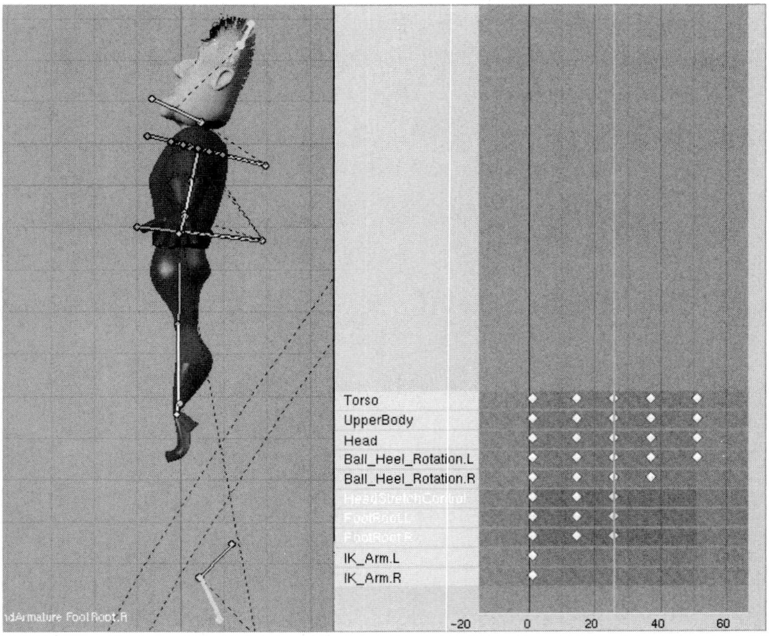

Figure 7.7

Modifications to improve the effect

stretched position of the apex to remain constant as the character is following, and to begin to change exactly at the point of contact with the ground. To do this, select the HeadStretch bone's key at frame 26 (maximally stretched point) and copy it by pressing Shift+D; then move this key to frame 33, three frames ahead of the maximally squashed position, and coinciding with the contact point of the feet with the ground.

7. Position and key the arms as shown in Figures 7.9, 7.10, and 7.11.

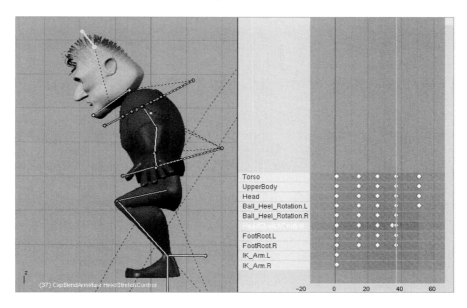

Figure 7.8

Head squash to emphasize impact

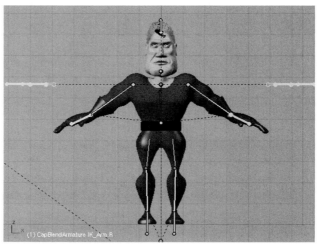

Figure 7.9

Rest arm position (frames 1 and 51)

Figure 7.10

**Crouched arm
position (frames
16 and 36)**

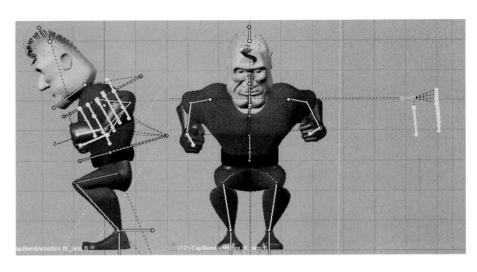

Figure 7.11

**Apex arm position
(frame 26)**

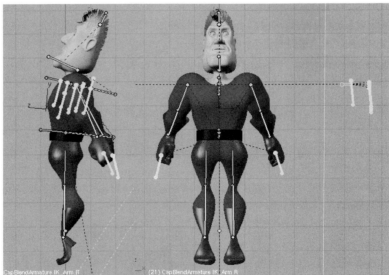

Previewing Your Animation

Now that you have finished the basic keyframing of your jump action, you'll want to see
how it looks. There are several ways to do this. One way is to press the play button on
the Timeline to activate the animation. The animation can also be animated by pressing
Alt+A over the window in which you want the animation to be activated or by pressing
Shift+Alt+A to activate the animation in all windows.

The problem with simply watching the animation in this way is that, depending on the speed of your computer's processor and the complexity of your character mesh, the delay caused by calculating the figure's position for each frame means that the animation might play back either much too quickly or too slowly to give you an accurate portrayal of the motion. With a fairly high-poly mesh like Captain Blender, including particle hair, this calculation is likely to be unusually slow and certainly does not give you a realistic idea of what your animation really looks like at the proper frame rate. A quick-and-dirty solution is to select only the layer with your armature object and watch the animation run with only the armature. This will still be slowed down from the correct frame rate, but it will probably be watchable as movement. For certain troubleshooting tasks, this is a useful method. However, it is still important to see the full mesh figure deforming at full speed to see what your animation really looks like.

The other extreme is to properly render out an animation, as I'll show how to do in Chapter 11. However, this process is impractical at this project's early stage of development, because it takes up large amounts of time and resources calculating light and surface effects for each frame that you do not need to see right now.

The most accurate way to play back an animation in real time without fully rendering the images is to use the 3D viewport's own render button, which you can find on the header of the 3D viewport (it is the rightmost button displaying a scene icon). Clicking this button gives you a render of the 3D window exactly as it is currently shown, and holding down Ctrl while pressing this button renders the full animation as it appears in the 3D window. After it has been rendered, the animation can be played back at full speed, using either the Play button in the render buttons, the Play Back Rendered Animation option under the Render Menu, or Ctrl+F11. Because it is your 3D viewport that's getting rendered here, you can use numeric 0 to go into Camera View mode to get a render of the animation from the camera's point of view. So you can render your animation from a few different perspectives and see how it looks. If you run into problems with this part, you might want to skip ahead to Chapter 11 to read up more fully on rendering animations.

There is still another option for playback, which is probably the most suitable for our purposes here. In the Anim/Playback Buttons window, whose icon is the curving line right next to the Render Buttons icon, there is toggle button labeled Sync (see Figure 7.12). Enabling Sync tells Blender to attempt to play back animations triggered by the Play button or Alt+A in real time. If necessary, Blender skips frames to show you the proper timing of your animation. Before going to the trouble of doing the OpenGL render suggested previously, using the Sync option is definitely worth a try. It gives acceptable results, even under demanding circumstances. Also, one advantage of keeping your animation preview live (nonrendered) is

Figure 7.12

Sync option for animation playback

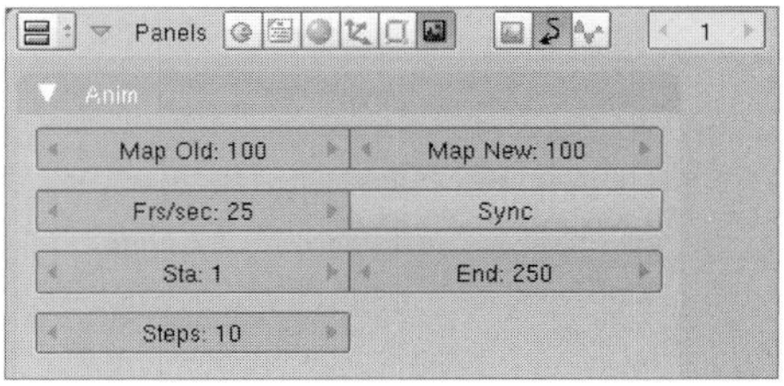

that Blender enables you to transform the view, even while it is playing your animation in real time. Try using the scroll wheel, Shift+MMB drag, and MMB drag in a third window while your animation loops in real time!

Tweaking Ipos

When I rendered the jumping animation, it turned out pretty well, but the jump was happening awfully quickly. Quick may be realistic for a jump like this, but to get the motion effect I was after, I wanted to exaggerate the length of time spent at the apex slightly. This would help to emphasize the character's physical strain at the apex and give more of a sense of height, power, and mass.

To do this, you need to work directly on the curve responsible for holding Captain Blender in the air—namely, the LocZ Pose Ipo on the Torso bone. With your Torso bone selected in the 3D viewport, switch your Action Editor to the IPO Editor, select Pose from the Ipo type drop-down menu, and select LocZ from the Ipo list. Enter Edit mode by pressing Tab. In Figure 7.13, you can see that the curve is too sharp right now. The character is returning to the ground too abruptly, so you'll want to round off this curve. You can do that by simply selecting the two Bezier handles and scaling up with the S key. The result is the rounder curve shown in Figure 7.14.

Check the new motion with Alt+A. Never mind whether it's more realistic; it's definitely better looking and more evocative.

You can see an overview of each keyframe and its poses and keys for the complete action in Figure 7.15. The fully rendered video of the action is in the file jump.avi on the accompanying DVD.

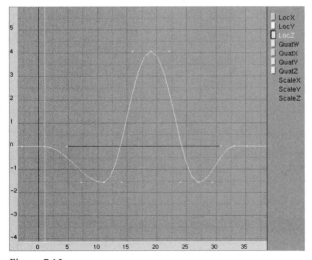

Figure 7.13
Z axis Ipo as calculated

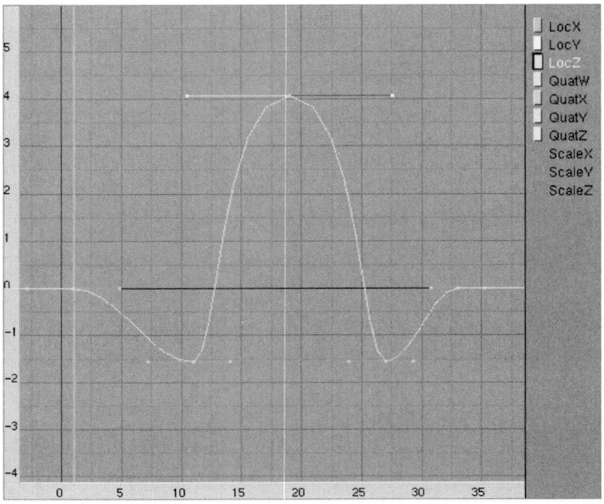

Figure 7.14
Rounded off to exaggerate

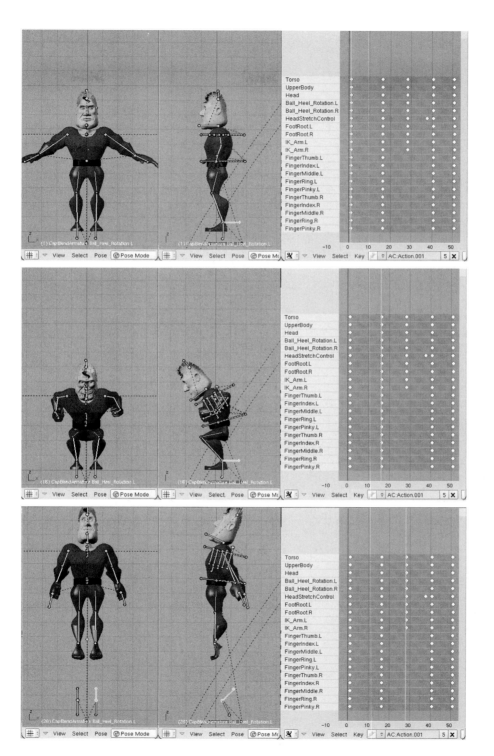

Figure 7.15

Jump action

Figure 7.15 cont.

Jump action

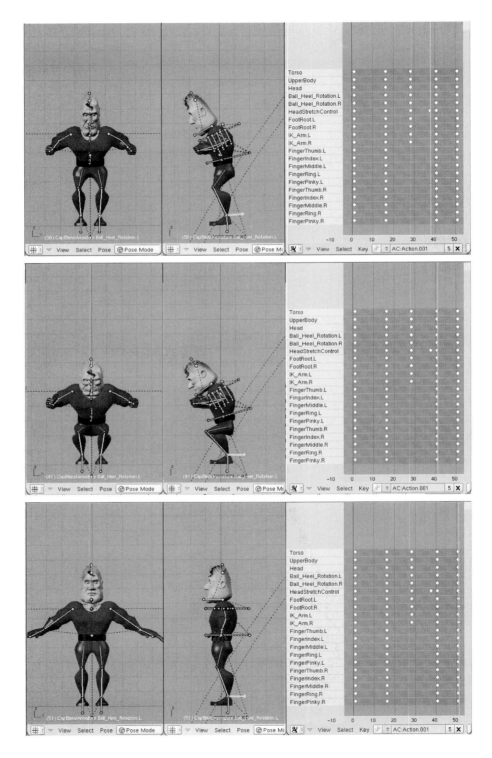

Ipos make the task of animation much easier by automating a lot of the most painstaking work. However, it is important to remember that a balance must be struck between doing things by hand and using automated tools. Getting a sense of how much to tinker with Ipos requires experience and skill. Overkeying and overediting curves can result in choppy, erratic movement, whereas simply letting the Ipos do all the work yields unconvincingly smooth motions.

Line of Action

"In animation the line of action is the basis for rhythm, simplicity and directness!"
—Preston Blair, Animation

An important aspect of animation, as with cartooning, is boiling down complex visual information to its simplest, most basic elements. This is related to the exaggeration discussed earlier. You know that you need to exaggerate certain aspects of form and pose to get the motion effects you want. The question is this: what to exaggerate? A big nose, for example, is a form of exaggeration, but enlarging Captain Blender's nose at the apex of his jump obviously does not contribute to the effectiveness of the animation. The answer to how to use exaggeration effectively can be found in an awareness of *lines of action*.

The line of action for a pose is a single smooth line that can be drawn through the pose, which conforms to the pose in terms of energy and direction. It is more basic to the pose than any specific portion of the figure or armature's position. Effective animation can be seen as an interplay between lines of action, and one important trait of a good animator is some intuitive feeling for these lines. They do not have any explicit manifestation in your software, but you should try to cultivate an awareness of them in your mind.

I drew lines of action through the extreme poses in the jump animation in Figures 7.16 and 7.17. As you can see, these lines capture the curled, hunched quality of the crouch position and the stretched, arcing quality of the apex pose. They also give you an insight into what needs to be exaggerated to make the pose more effective. The squash of the head agrees with the line of action in the crouch pose, as do the stretch of the head and the exaggerated rotation of the feet in the apex pose.

Not all poses have such immediately obvious lines of action, but it is a good idea to think in these terms when creating your poses. If you can envision a single line that expresses the energy and motion of each pose, and work to make your exaggerations and secondary movements complement and support this line, your animation will be much more effective.

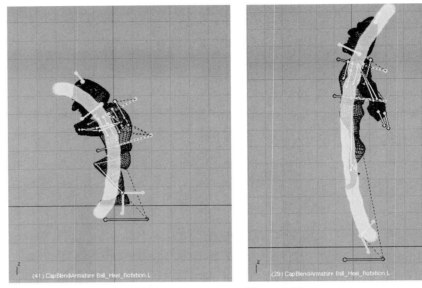

Figure 7.16

Line of action for the crouch pose

Figure 7.17

Line of action for the apex pose

Manual vs. Auto Keyframing

Keying a value such as a bone position fixes that value for subsequent frames in the animation. You can pose a bone in a particular frame and it will hold that pose (pressing Alt+G and Alt+R to clear position and rotation is the same as posing to the rest position) as long as you are on that frame. However, if you do not key the positions, they will jump back to their previously keyed positions as soon as you move to another frame (this will also happen if you change visible layers).

It is possible to set Blender to use automatic keyframing in the User Preferences by selecting the button shown in Figure 7.18. Selecting this option inserts a keyframe every time you change the pose of your armature or transform an object, eliminating the need to use the I key. Using this is entirely a matter of personal preference. Some people find that it speeds their workflow, whereas other people prefer to set up their pose first and then key the positions when they have them as they like them. In both cases, it is important to make sure that you are on the correct frame before you begin keying, so that you don't delete any keys unintentionally. The danger of doing this is slightly higher when using auto keying.

Figure 7.18

User Preference for auto keying

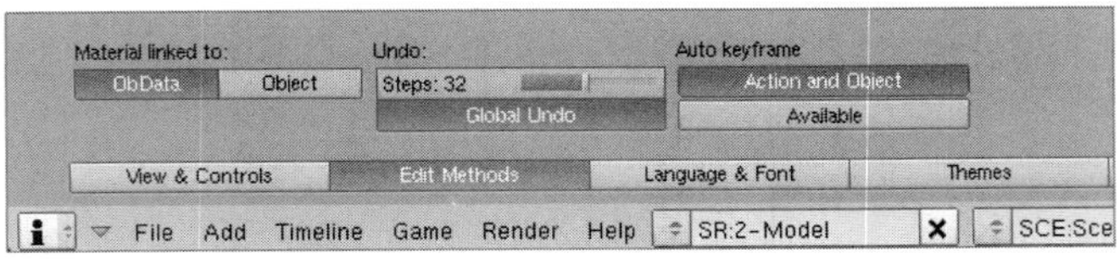

Walk and Run Cycles

Walking and running are two of the most basic actions for most characters. Because these movements are by nature repetitive, you want to create the action so they can be easily repeated. In this section, you'll set up simple bipedal walk and run cycles for your character.

Setting up a Basic Walk Cycle

With actions that are designed to repeat cyclically, it is necessary to consider the best pose to use as start and end points. In the previous example, each jump was entirely self-contained, beginning and ending with the rest pose. In the case of walking, however, the action is cyclical and does not break and return to the rest pose at any point. A good place to start in such cases is at an *extreme* pose. The term sounds a bit more exciting than it actually is. In fact, an extreme pose simply means the point at which the action has hit its limit in some respect. The rest of the motion typically consists of moving from one extreme pose to another. In the case of walking, the extreme poses are the ones in which each foot is extended the farthest, one with the right foot forward and the left foot back, and the other with feet reversed. You'll start with the left foot forward extreme. Because the foot movements are the most basic part of a walk cycle you'll start with the bones relevant to the feet—namely, the FootRoot.L/R bones and the Ball_Heel_Rotation.L/R bones. Key the four of them in frame 1, as shown in Figure 7.19.

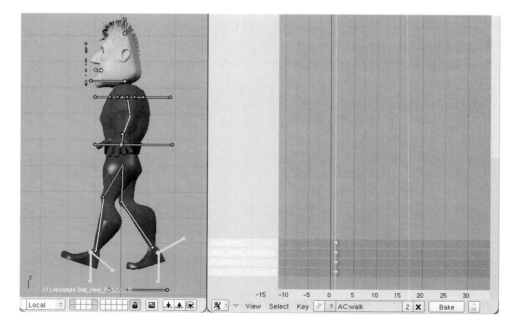

Figure 7.19

Keying the first extreme pose for a walk cycle

A single step in a leisurely walk can be expected to take about a second, so you will put the right foot forward extreme 25 frames later, at frame 26. To place this second extreme keyframe, follow these steps:

1. With the current frame at 1, select these four keyed bones: FootRoot.L, FootRoot.R, Ball_Heel_Rotation.L, and Ball_Heel_Rotation.R. Make sure that these bones have had their positions correctly keyed as described previously.

2. Copy the pose of the bones to the Clipboard using the ⬇ button in the 3D viewport window's header.

3. Go to frame 26, either by moving the green frame marker line with the arrow keys or by typing **26** into the current frame field on the Timeline.

4. Paste the mirror image of the copied pose in reverse using the ⬆ button. This function requires that the bones all be named correctly, with matching bones on the left and right having the same base name followed by .R and .L. If you have problems with this working, go back and double-check that your bones are properly named.

5. In this case, the four bones you're concerned with should already be selected. However, in cases in which the mirrored pose uses different bones than the original pose, the relevant bones are *not* automatically selected. The original bone selection remains unchanged. So before keying the new pose, be sure that all the bones you want to key are selected. Then key the pose as shown in Figure 7.20.

To complete the walk cycle, in the Action Editor window, select the four keys in frame 1. Make sure that only these keys are selected. Press Shift+D to copy the keys and move them to frame 51, holding Ctrl down as you move the keys. Set the end frame in the Timeline to 50. Preview the animation. You should have a smooth (albeit very slidey) start to a walk cycle.

Figure 7.20
Keying the mirrored extreme pose

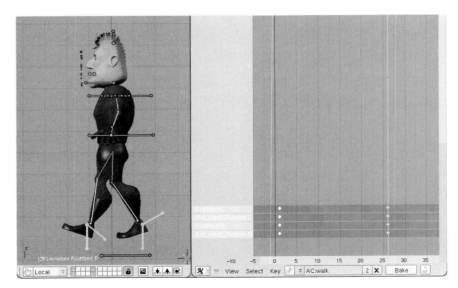

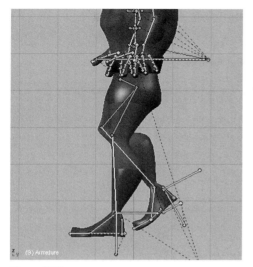

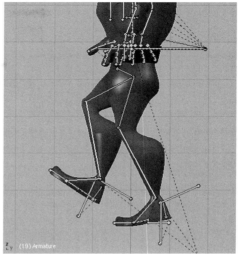

Figure 7.21
Keying the first in-between pose for the feet

Figure 7.22
Keying the second in-between pose

When people walk, their feet come off the ground during the forward motion, and you need to reflect that. Following the same steps as the extreme poses, key the pose in Figure 7.21 at frame 9 and key its mirror image (using Copy and Paste Mirrored) at frame 34. Then key the pose shown in Figure 7.22 at frame 18 and key its mirror image at frame 42. Again, preview the animation. It should look more like an actual walk.

The last thing you need to do with the lower body is key the vertical motion of the Torso bone. At frames 14 and 38, key the Torso at its rest position (remember, you can always select the bone and hit Alt+G to make sure that it is in its rest position). During the extremes, the body is slightly lowered because the legs are extended. Go to frame 1 and move the Torso bone down slightly along the Z axis until you have a natural-looking pose. Key this position, and copy this key to the other extreme frames: frame 26 and frame 51. Preview the animation again to make sure it looks natural.

Why Start with the Extremes?

Traditionally, the extreme poses are arranged first because they hold most of the interesting information about the form and mood of the movement. The in-between poses, although very important, can be thought of as functioning largely to fill in the space between extreme poses.

In CG, there is another reason to give some thought to the placement of extremes, particularly if you want to create a cycling action. In this case, it is important that the curves leading out of the action match up seamlessly with the curves leading into the action, both in value and in angle; otherwise, the repetition will be jumpy. The easiest place to make curves match is at the point where they are both at zero angles, which means that the apex of a curve whose value is reversing is a very good spot for this. As mentioned earlier, the pose extremes tend to be the places where values are reversing, which make them good candidates for cycle points.

To get a clearer idea of this, compare the curves in Figures 7.23 and 7.24. Both curves represent a 10-frame-long segment of a cyclic curve rising to five Blender Units (BUs) above zero and falling to -5 BUs below zero. In Figure 7.23, the point at which one segment meets the next is flat—the nadir of the curve. This is very easy to match; you need to ensure only that the value in frame 11 is identical to the value in frame 1. However, in Figure 7.24 the segments meet in the middle of a slope.

This gives you several additional challenges. First, you need to ensure that the angle is correct. In the previous case, Blender calculates the zero angle automatically. In this case, you have no such automatic assistance; you have to match the angles by hand, and if the keyframes are moved relative to each other, the angles have to be edited again to match. Second, as can be seen in the figures, more key frames are required to create the same cycle.

Upper Body Movement in the Walk Cycle

You now have the lower body moving the way you want it. But the human walk involves more than just the legs and feet. The whole body is involved in walking, and this section looks at the movements of the head, shoulders, and arms.

A basic principle of character animation is that the character's movements say as much or more about the character as the visual aspect of the character itself. Most animators practice their skills on extremely simple models to focus their energies on expressing emotion through motion. At all points of creating actions, you should be considering what the pose says about the character's mood and personality.

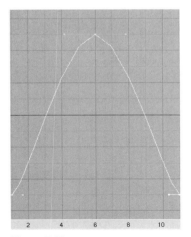

Figure 7.23

A cyclic curve that repeats on an extreme

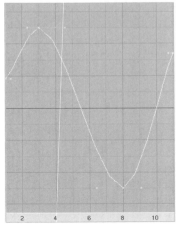

Figure 7.24

A cyclic curve that repeats on a slope

Captain Blender's walk is a confident, deliberate walk as befits a superhero of his stature. You'll give him a pronounced swing to the shoulders to emphasize this. This is a simple, smooth motion that needs to be keyed only on the extremes. The upper body moves in opposition to the legs in a normal walk, so in frame 1, rotate the UpperBody bone along the Z axis to bring the right shoulder forward, as shown in Figure 7.25. Use the Clipboard copy pose mirroring to put the reverse pose at frame 26, as shown in Figure 7.26. Of course, the key from frame 1 should also be copied to frame 51.

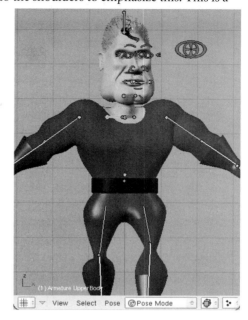

Figure 7.25

First keyed shoulder position

He is now swiveling a lot, but this is not quite enough to give you the confident, determined aspect you're looking for because his head is moving back and forth as well. To fix this problem, you should key the head to be in a forward position at frame 1 and frame 26, as shown in Figure 7.27. I recommend doing the poses for both frames by hand, without using the copy function or being overly precise, to enable a slight amount of variation into the movement. So far, you've been using a lot of copying and mirroring tools, which can lead to robotic movements. Of course, frame 51 needs to be identical to frame 1 to keep the cycle smooth, so it needs to be copied directly.

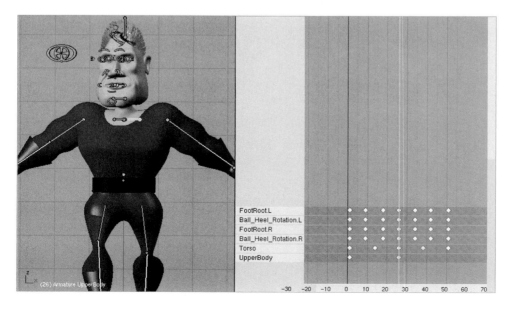

Figure 7.26

Keying the mirrored shoulder position

Figure 7.27

Keeping the head pointed forward

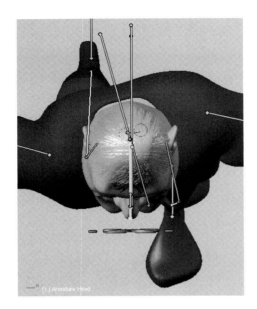

Constraint Influence

The shoulders and head should be moving nicely now. You want to finish things off by getting some nice poses for the arms. However, the arms are currently set to use IK posing, which uses the endpoint of the IK chain to pose the chain. So, for example, if you key the arm IK target at two positions, the Ipo created moves the target in a straight line from the first position to the second position and poses the arm appropriately along the way, as shown in Figure 7.28. This is appropriate for certain kinds of motions, such as reaching to grab an object, but it is not how an arm swings freely. To get the kind of arcing movement you see in a free swinging object, you are better off using forward kinetic (FK) posing. If you turn off the IK constraint and create a similar arm movement using FK posing (in this case, I have simply rotated the bicep bone), you see a much more natural swinging motion, as shown in Figure 7.29. Note that in both cases only the first and last positions shown are keyed. Blender has interpolated the middle position. Also note that in the second case, the *rotation* of the hand itself is still dependent upon the Ik_Arm Bone because you also have a copy rotation constraint that you are leaving in place.

To use FK posing, set the IK constraint influence on the forearms to zero in the Constraints tab, as shown in Figure 7.30. You might wonder why this is controlled by a slider, given that it would be fairly rare to want to use both FK posing and IK posing at the same time. Sliders enable IK and other constraint influences to be keyed to change gradually over several frames, so that there is no sudden jolt when the target influence is turned on and off. You can create a keyframe for this value by clicking the Key button that you see to the right of the influence slider. Because you do not plan to animate this value during the walk cycle, it is not necessary to key it.

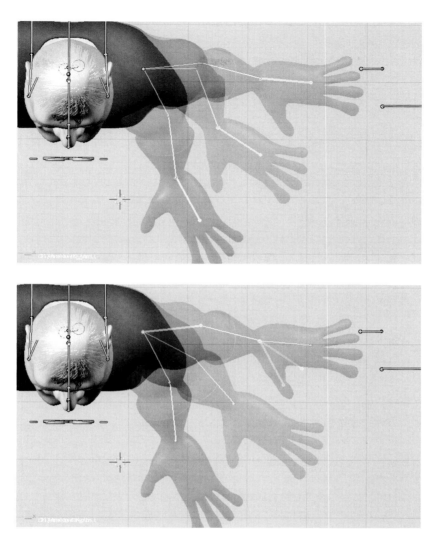

Figure 7.28

IK posing (IK influence set to 1)

Figure 7.29

FK posing (IK influence set to 0)

Figure 7.30

Turning off IK influence

Arms and Hands

Using FK posing, you can now pose the bicep, forearm, and hand (the hand's angle is still controlled by IK_Arm) to swing naturally along with the walk. It is enough to pose the arms to coincide with the extreme frames. First, pose the left arm for frames 1 and 26, as shown in Figure 7.31, and then use the Clipboard and pose mirroring to duplicate the motion on the right side, as in Figure 7.32. Making some very slight modifications in the right- and left-side arm and hand movements can help to loosen things up, but do not make them too uneven or else the walk will look strange.

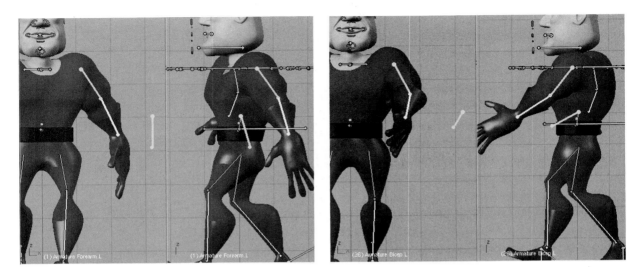

Figure 7.31

Backward and forward movement of the left arm

Figure 7.32

**Mirroring the
arm poses**

The last thing I did was put each hand in a fist when fully forward using the action drivers for the fingers. To do this, rotate the action drivers along the local Z axis so that the hand closes, as shown in Figure 7.33. I keyed the drivers to release slightly as the arm moves back to give some movement to the hands. Do not overdo this because there is no natural reason for the hand to open and close regularly as it swings.

Figure 7.34 gives a complete overview of keys and poses for the walk cycle. The video file, which is called walk.avi, can be found on the DVD.

A Run Cycle

This book doesn't walk you through the run cycle because the process of creating the run cycle is more or less identical to the walk cycle. The main difference between running and walking is that in a walk, at least one foot is always in contact with the ground, whereas in a run, the body spends a fair amount of time completely aloft. The extreme poses, in particular, feature both feet fully off the ground. The other difference, of course, is that running tends to be faster on a strides-per-second basis. Instead of a 50-frame cycle, as in the case of the walk, the present run cycle is 38 frames long.

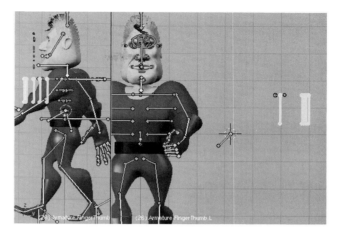

Figure 7.33
Closing the hands into a fist

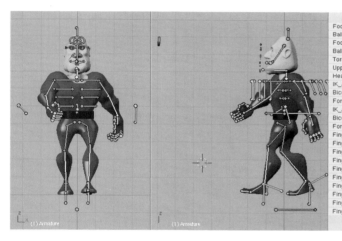

Figure 7.34
Walk cycle keys and poses

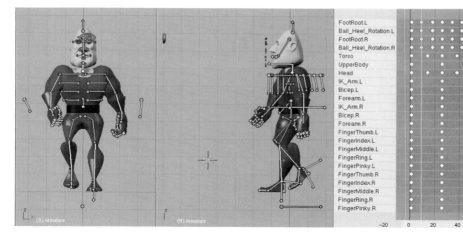

Figure 7.34 cont.

Walk cycle keys and poses

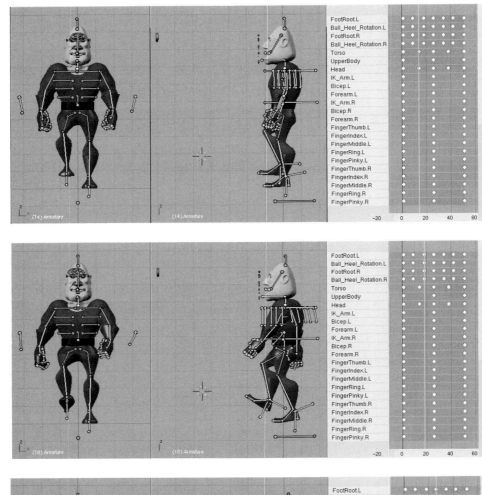

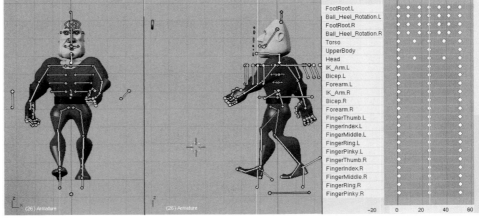

Figure 7.34 cont.

Walk cycle keys and poses

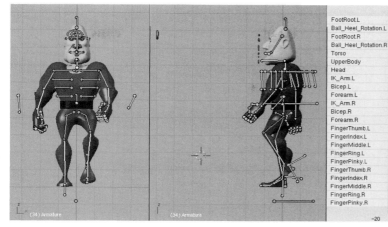

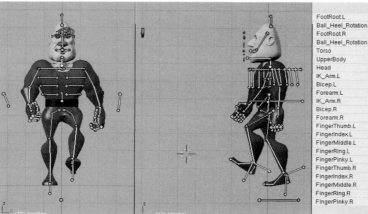

Figure 7.34 cont.

**Walk cycle keys
and poses**

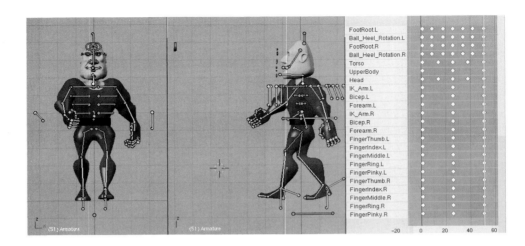

Figure 7.35 is an overview of the run cycle poses' keyframes. You should be able to figure out the details of their placement yourself. Pay special attention to the posing of the upper body; notice that the figure strains forward on the extremes. Also because there is a considerable amount of up and down movement, make sure that you key the head to point approximately in the same direction throughout the action. Use the Gaze bone's position to gauge this as you pose the Head bone. Do this by hand, and not too precisely, because it will not be realistic if the head's direction is robotically fixed while the character is running at full speed.

The animated run cycle can be seen in the file run.avi on the DVD.

To speed up or slow down the cycle, you can select all the keys and scale them by pressing the S key. This process scales them toward or away from the vertical green line, so it's a good idea to put this at frame 1 to keep all the values positive. Also be sure to adjust your animation's end frame accordingly. If you choose to scale your action to adjust the timing, you can, after you're done, snap the keys onto whole numbered frames by pressing Shift+S and replying OK to the prompt.

Expressing Weight

Certain points in a run cycle can exhibit evidence of mass that are not visible at the slower speeds of the walk cycle. Specifically, with a fairly massive character such as Captain Blender, you should emphasize the force of his impact, which you can do similarly to the way you did it in the jump animation. You can see this illustrated in Figure 7.36, in which the head stretch and upper body bones are keyed just before the impact frame, after which a slight squash is applied, which relaxes again over the course of the next several frames.

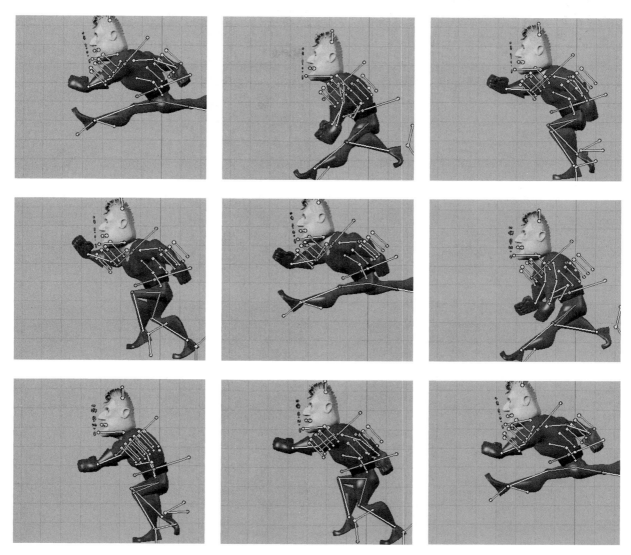

Figure 7.35

Keyed poses for a run cycle

Making Adjustments

While working with the Action Editor, it is possible for Ipos to get a little bit tangled. It is a good idea to try to keep your keys directly on full frames instead of between frames. You can snap keys to the nearest frame in the Action Editor by selecting the key and pressing Shift+S, as mentioned previously.

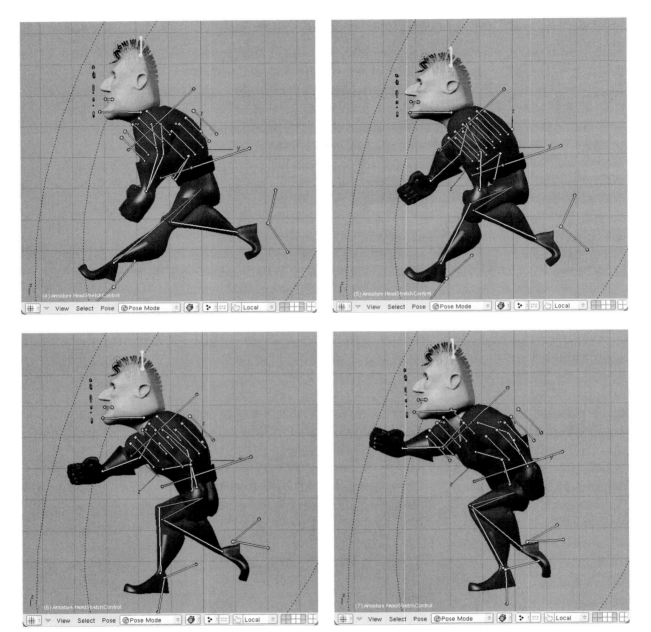

Figure 7.36

A slight head squash applied to emphasize impact

If any place in your animation exhibits a quick "pop" or a jerk, it is likely that several keys have been placed very close to each other (this can be difficult to see in the Action Editor). Action Editor keys are replaced if values are rekeyed directly on the frame of a previous key, but if either key is slightly offset, you can get multiple keys that cannot be easily discerned.

In this case, it is a good idea to look at the offending Ipo. Identify the bone that is jerking, select it, and look at its Ipo curves in the IPO Editor. Figure 7.37 shows an example of the Ipo block for a bone that is exhibiting jerky movement. Clearly there is a problem in the neighborhood of frame 34. In such cases, you want to edit the curves directly to get rid of the jerky points. You can delete a key point on an Ipo curve by going into Edit mode with Tab, selecting the offending point, and pressing the X key.

Remember that with character animation, perfect stillness is the kiss of death. Living things are never perfectly still. A single perfectly motionless limb on a character can be enough to remind viewers that they are not truly seeing a living being and jerk them out of the animation experience. The key is to combine a variety of smooth movements with complementary directions and timing to create an overall feeling of movement that is irregular, but not choppy or inconsistent. Whenever you work with armatures, keep all these things in mind so that you can work toward convincing, natural-looking movement for your characters.

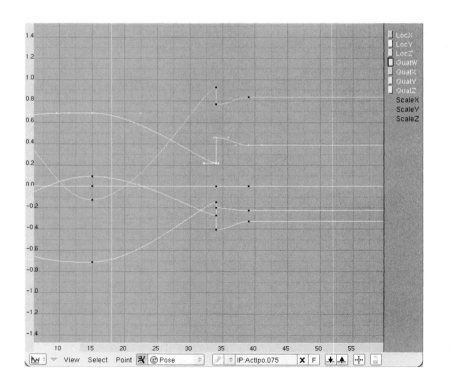

Figure 7.37
Jerky Ipos

Pose-to-Pose Animation

In traditional animation, two methods of animation are often distinguished: *straight-ahead* animation and *pose-to-pose* animation. Straight-ahead animation, in its purest sense, consists of starting at the beginning of an animation and progressing forward, creating each new frame as the motion unfolds. Pose-to-pose animation, on the other hand, consists of placing specific desired poses at carefully considered places along the Timeline and then filling the spaces in-between with intermediate poses.

The straight-ahead approach is typically thought of as being freer and potentially yielding more flowing and spontaneous animation. Pose-to-pose animation, on the other hand, enables much more control over precise timing and positioning. In fact, even in traditional animation, it is generally recognized that the best way to work is with some combination of the two of these approaches. This hybrid approach blocks out complex motion with the pose-to-pose approach, but it fills the intermediary positions with the straight-ahead method.

In CG, the medium is much more forgiving than traditional animation, so the distinction is blurred even more. It is perfectly possible to key certain body parts, for example, in a pose-to-pose manner, whereas other body parts can be posed completely straight ahead in the same animation, allowing for the best of both worlds. Furthermore, with the amount of control over key positions and Ipos that CG allows, it is possible to finesse the timing of straight-ahead animation and to loosen up the feel of pose-to-pose animation, making the distinction often more a matter of how the animator chooses to think about a task than an actual practical choice to be made. Nevertheless, it can be helpful to bear the difference in mind and to think in terms of taking advantage of both straight-ahead and pose-to-pose approaches.

Changing Location

Walk and run cycles such as the ones you looked at so far are well and good, but the real reason why characters walk and run is to get someplace. There are several ways to make this happen. In Chapter 9, I will describe how to make the armature follow a curve path while using a bone called a *stride bone* to keep the feet positioned properly. Although it is the "official" way of producing walking animation in Blender, I am not a big fan of this method, and I prefer the control of moving the armature and positioning the feet manually. The approach I take here is an example of the hybrid pose-to-pose/straight-ahead method mentioned previously. The basic walk cycle is the same pose-to-pose walk cycle you looked at earlier in the chapter, whereas the forward movement is accomplished in a straight-ahead way.

The first thing to recall is that the Torso bone governs the position of most of the other bones through direct or indirect parent relationships. It does not govern the Root bone, but you don't have to worry about the Root bone here.; it remains where it is. Also, the Torso does not govern the FootRoot.L/R bones, which are the IK solvers for the legs. This means that the Torso (and by extension, the rest of the body) can be moved independently of the feet.

To change the in-place walk cycle to an actual mobile walk, what you want to do is make sure that for each step the contact foot remains motionless and then replace its backward motion (in the in-place case) with forward motion of the rest of the body (the Torso bone and the noncontact foot's FootRoot bone). So after you have a clear idea of what you want to do, you can do it simply by deleting some keys and moving or rekeying some other keys along the Y axis. You don't need to touch any other bones besides the FootRoot.L/R bones and the Torso bone.

1. In frame 1, select the FootRoot.L bone. This is the contact foot for the next few frames, so it needs to be held in place until the next extreme. To do this, simply delete the next two keys, copy this key by pressing Shift+D, and place the copied key on frame 26, where it will replace the previous key there, as shown in Figure 7.38. Be sure to hold Ctrl down when you move the key, so that it will be placed exactly on frame 26. It does not replace the previous key if it is not placed exactly.

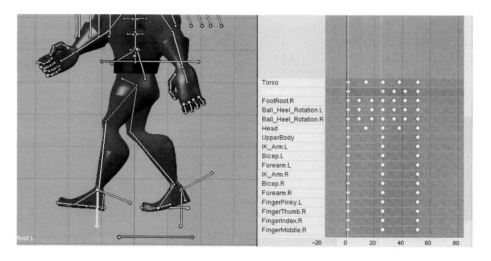

Figure 7.38
Keying the contact foot in place

2. Move to frame 14. The figure appears to be leaned back awkwardly because that left foot is no longer moving back under him. Fix this by moving the Torso bone (only) forward, constrained to the global Y axis. Position the Torso so that the body is directly above the left leg, as though supported on the left leg, as shown in Figure 7.39.

Figure 7.39

**Moving the Torso
bone forward**

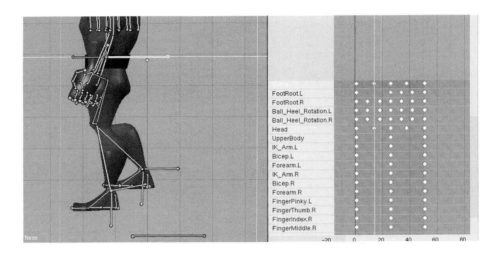

3. Move to frame 26. Again, the character is leaning back awkwardly. This time, however, you need to move both the Torso and the right foot forward. Select Torso and
   FootRoot.R, and move both of them along the global Y axis to position them in a natural right foot forward extreme, as shown in Figure 7.40.

Figure 7.40

**Moving both Torso
and FootRoot.R
forward**

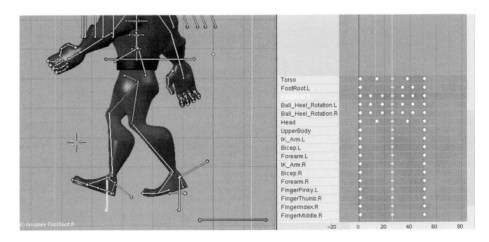

4. You're progressing nicely, but you need to back up a moment. The right foot is not in
   the right position in frame 18. Go to frame 18 now and move the FootRoot.R bone
   only forward to match the position in Figure 7.41.

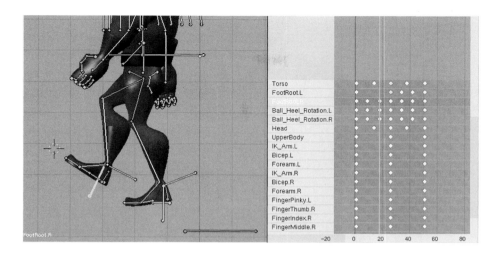

5. In frame 26, the right foot takes its place as the contact foot. Delete the subsequent two keys on FootRoot.R and copy the key from frame 26 to frame 51, just as you did with the left foot in step 1.

6. Go to frame 38. The figure is in an awkward, jerked-back position. Select the Torso bone only and move it forward so that the body is directly over the right leg. Key the Torso bone in this position, as shown in Figure 7.42. Note that the left leg is still pulled back. You do not want to change that here because it would involve adding a brand new key, which you do not want to do. You can take care of this in the next step.

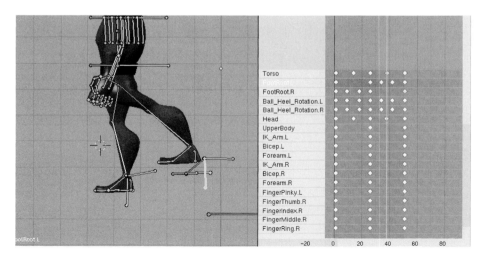

Figure 7.42
Moving the Torso bone forward

7. Go to frame 34 and move the FootRoot.L forward along the Y axis to the more natural position shown in Figure 7.43.

Figure 7.43

Going back to the last FootRoot.L key; moving the Foot-Root.L forward

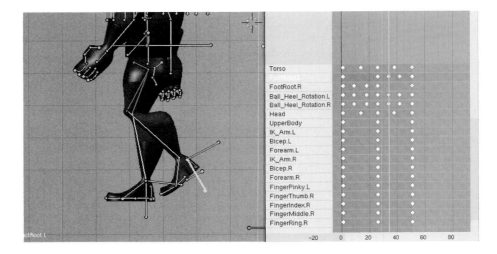

8. Go to frame 51. Select both FootRoot.L and Torso, and move them forward into the next extreme position, as shown in Figure 7.44.

Figure 7.44

Moving both Torso and FootRoot.L

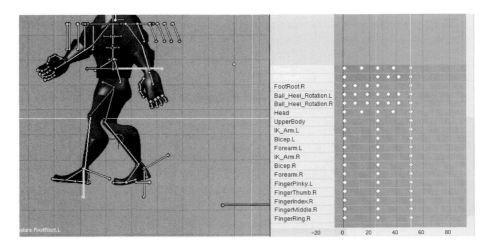

9. Go back to back to frame 42, and move FootRoot.L forward, as shown in Figure 7.45.

10. Select all the keys except for those on frame 1. Copy by pressing Shift+D and move the entire block of keys up 50 frames while holding the Ctrl key, resulting in the block of keys shown in Figure 7.46.

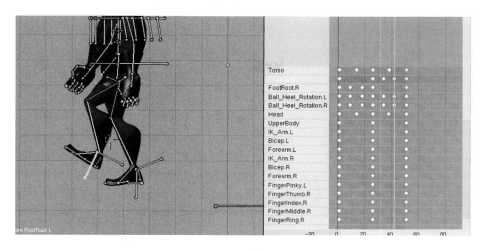

Figure 7.45

Going back to the last FootRoot.L key; moving the Foot-Root.L forward

11. Follow these steps to create subsequent strides:

    1. Clear and copy contact foot keys.

    2. Bring forward the Torso at the point between extremes.

    3. Move back several frames to update the noncontact foot's first in-between key.

    4. Bring forward the Torso *and* the noncontact foot on the next extreme.

    5. Move back several frames to update the noncontact foot's second in-between key.

    6. Repeat.

Figure 7.46

Copying the entire block of keys (except the first frame) and moving the copied frames 50 frames forward

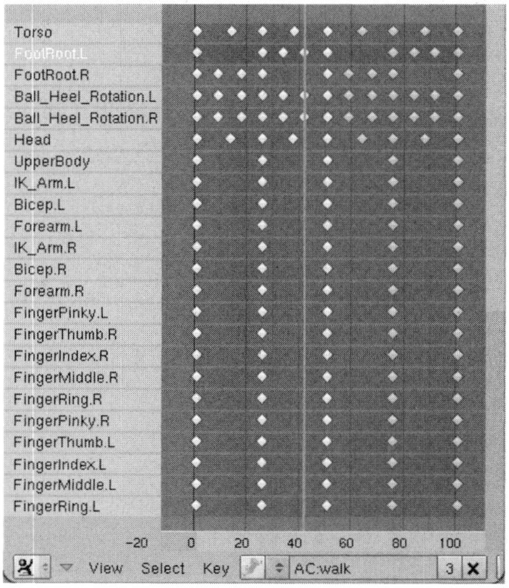

Weighty Words from Captain Blender

Timing movements to coincide with sounds is a good example of a situation that might call for a more pose-to-pose–oriented approach. In this example you look at animating Captain Blender's basic movements while uttering a very simple pronouncement. In the next chapter, you'll combine these movements with lip sync and facial movements; in Chapter 9, you'll look at combining the action you have created with the walk cycle by using the nonlinear animation editor.

To get started, you must first load and position the sound file you'll be using for syncing. Find the sound file on this book's accompanying DVD; it is called every-era-has-its.wav. Place this file in a convenient location on your hard drive.

In Blender, you'll start by looking at two important windows for this. Open an instance of the Audio window; in the Buttons window, go to the Scene buttons and select the Audio subcontext. In the Sound tab, select Open New from the Blender Soundblock drop-down menu, which opens up a File Browser window, in which you can find and select the .wav file. Now that the soundblock is loaded, you can access it in the Audio Window, through the drop-down menu in the Audio Window header. After you have loaded and selected this audio file in both places, your work area should look something like the one shown in Figure 7.47. Select Sync and Scrub in the Sequencer tab.

You can listen to the audio now by pressing Play in the Sound tab. The sentence is "It has been said that every era has its visionary."

Sequence Editor

You'll now take your first look at a very important tool in Blender: the Sequence Editor. This tool works much like a nonlinear video editor, and in many respects that's what it is. In Blender, it has several important uses. It is used to collect frames or segments of an animation and render them together as single video clips, as you will see in Chapter 11. It can be used to do compositing, and its powers as a compositing tool have been improving drastically with each version released. Finally, it is used as a tool to sync video with sound.

At present, although the soundblock for the .wav file has been imported, you have no way to place this soundblock on the Timeline. You use the Sequence Editor to do this.

Importing files into the Sequence Editor is simple. Simply open a Sequence Editor window and press Shift+A over the window to add a sequence strip. You are given a choice between several types of sequence strips. Select Audio(Wav). In the File Browser, find the every-era-has-its.wav file. You should see a strip appear like the one shown in Figure 7.48. Place this strip so that it starts at frame 1.

Figure 7.47

Audio window and Audio buttons area

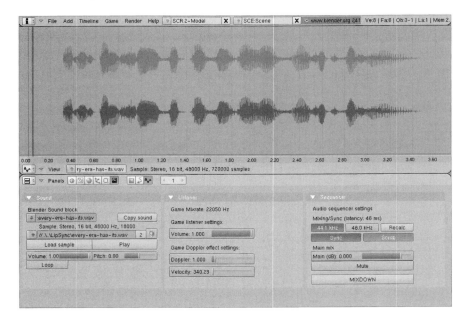

At the time of this writing, Blender can export separate synced video and sound files, but it cannot be used to mix sound and video for export as a single file on Windows or Macintosh (support for this functionality is further along for Linux). This remains a glaring limitation in terms of its use as a basic video editor, but remedying it is high on the list of developer priorities, so future versions should not have this limitation. In the meantime, there are a number of free tools that can put sound and video together, such as the very useful program Virtual-Dub by Avery Lee (included on this book's DVD).

Posing with Speech

Note that when you move from one frame to another, you now hear the snippet of sound that corresponds to the .wav file at that specific frame. Likewise, dragging the frame indicator within the Sequence Editor plays the audio as the indicator passes over it. This technique is called "scrubbing," which is why you turned on the "scrub" button earlier. It is the basis upon which you sync all action with sound.

For Captain Blender's gesticulations, you can do a very simple pose-to-pose animation. As he utters "It has been said that every era has its visionary," you have him raise one hand grandly to coincide with "said" and then gesture widely with both hands as he says "every era." And then, as he says the word "visionary," you have him bring his hands inward in a slight clutching motion while lifting his head hopefully.

The start frame is 1, and the end frame you use is 85. You should determine the placement of the poses based upon listening to the sounds at each frame. You can key the three poses described and also a more naturalistic "rest" pose than the actual rest pose (which, of course, has the character's arms out at a strange and not very restful angle).

You can see the poses and their associated keys in Figure 7.49.

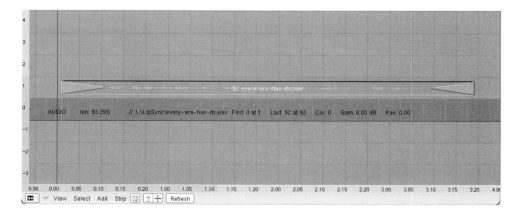

Figure 7.48

Sequence Editor

Figure 7.49

**Poses to accompany
the phrase "It has
been said that every
era has its visionary"**

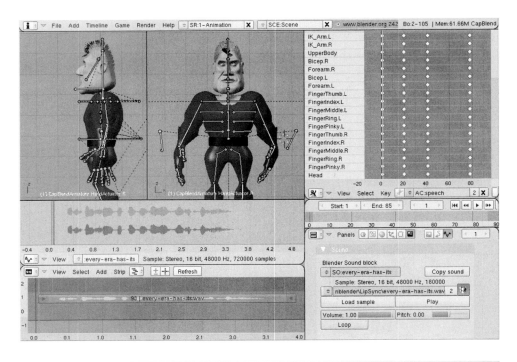

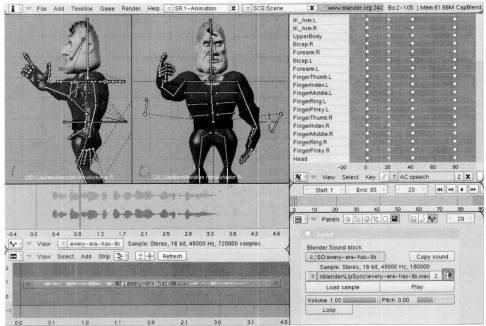

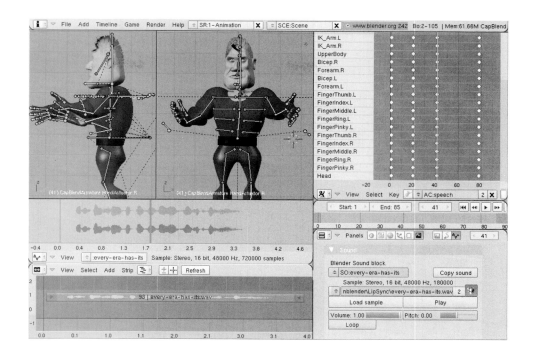

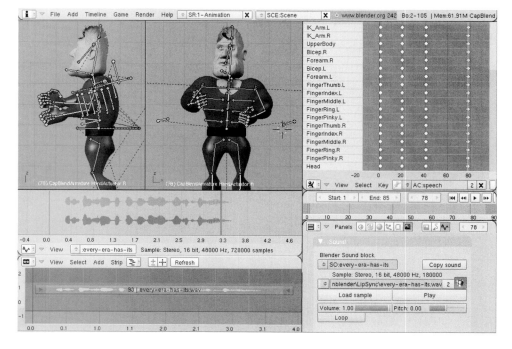

Figure 7.49 cont.

Poses to accompany the phrase "It has been said that every era has its visionary"

This is all you need for the time being. Name the action **speech**. You can now move on to adding facial animation to sync up with the sound. In the next chapter, you will use the facial rig that you created in Chapter 5 to add lip sync and expressions to go with the movement you have created here.

CHAPTER 8

Facial Animation and Lip Sync

This chapter builds on the pose-to-pose example from the previous chapter, adding facial movements and lip sync to go with the gesticulations you have already put into place.

Lip syncing and facial animation are sophisticated arts that can take years to become proficient in. The goal here is just to get you started with this kind of work in Blender, so be prepared to spend time practicing before your results are exactly how you want them. Furthermore, as with almost everything in Blender, there are a variety of ways to go about doing lip sync and facial animation. As I mentioned in Chapter 5, I have chosen to use shape keys driven by bones. I find this to be an easy way to work, and it is a good fit with nonlinear animation, as you will see in more detail in the next chapter.

In Chapter 18, I suggest several tutorials to look at for different approaches, including one approach based entirely on shape keys, without bone drivers, and another approach based almost entirely on using a sophisticated facial armature to do mesh deformations. Your own work will certainly benefit from trying a variety of approaches to see which suits your personal animation style best.

- **Facial Posing**
- **Lip Sync**
- **Playback**

Facial Posing

The approach I'm taking to facial posing will use the controller bones exclusively to pose the face. Aside from the tongue, none of these controls deforms the mesh; the controls all act as drivers for shape keys. This driver setup enables you to treat facial posing as if it were armature posing (more or less the same as the armature posing you did in Chapter 7). The bones are keyed in the same way they were keyed previously, and you have to keep many of the same issues with the Ipo (interpolation) curves and key placement in mind to avoid facial movements becoming robotic.

One difference is that you won't be using much mirroring here. For one thing, it's not necessary. Unlike something like a walk cycle, facial posing doesn't involve complex, repetitive movements that need to be nearly identical on right and left. In fact, even in cases in which you have fairly symmetrical facial expressions, such as a smile, your facial posing will benefit by some asymmetry. Whereas asymmetry in a walk can wind up looking like a limp, properly used asymmetry in facial animation creates more convincingly human expressions.

The trick in facial animation is to understand the way shapes combine to form expressions. In Figure 8.1, you see several full facial expressions for Captain Blender. These expressions represent the emotions of pleasure, trepidation, satisfaction, rage, terror, and suspicion. Compare these expressions with the sequence of face shapes described in Chapter 5. A few fairly simple shapes can yield a broad palette of emotional expression when combined properly. In the figure, you can see how the bones controllers are positioned to yield each facial expression. Note that the Gaze bone is not shown, and other armature bone positions other than the shape drivers (for example, the head bone) are not shown.

In the first expression (a), pleasure, a slight (and slightly asymmetrical) curlup of the nose emphasizes the smile. The smile itself is not simply the smile shape, either, but also involves widening the lips and lowering the jaw slightly. The eyes are slightly squinted and the eyebrows are raised; in particular, the left outer brow is raised.

In the second expression (b), trepidation, the mouth gets its shape from a combination of rounding and frown to bring the edges down slightly. The brows are knit and raised in the middle.

In the third expression (c), satisfaction, the brows are raised very slightly. The mouth is closed, and the edges of the mouth are raised in a smile. Furthermore, in this expression the eyelids are lowered slightly, giving an example of how the eyelids also play an important role in expressing emotions (other than drowsiness).

In the fourth expression (d), rage, the eyebrows are down with the outer portion slightly raised, angling them downwards even more sharply. The mouth is closed with a hint of frown, and the lips are pursed inward slightly. The nose is crinkled asymmetrically. Perhaps the most important thing to note about this expression is the importance of the angle of the head. Head, neck, and even shoulder positioning is a sometimes overlooked but crucial aspect of facial posing.

The fifth expression (e), terror, combines wide lips, a very slight frown, and a slightly dropped jaw for the mouth position. Eyebrows are up in the center and knitted. Again the nose is asymmetrically crinkled. Again, the eyelids play a part; they are considerably widened beyond the rest position.

The last expression (f), suspicion, also demonstrates the importance of head positioning, and in this case the importance of head position in relation to gaze; the sidelong glance here is an important component of this expression. The eyebrows are down, and the right outer eyebrow is raised. There is a slight squint to both eyes, and the mouth is fully closed with just the hint of a frown.

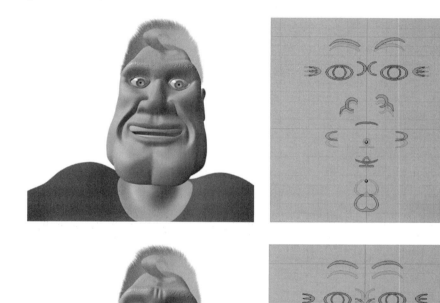

(a)

(b)

Figure 8.1

Expressions of (a) pleasure, (b) trepidation, along with their bone positions

Figure 8.1 cont.

Expressions of (c) satisfaction, and (d) rage, and (e) terror, along with their bone positions

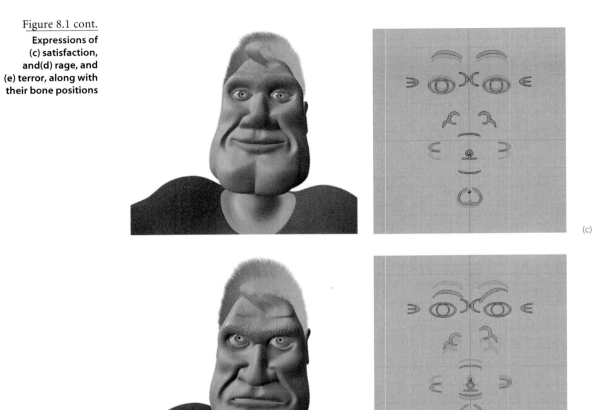

(c)

(d)

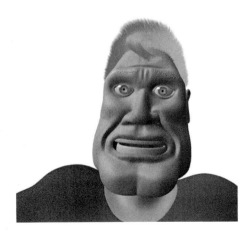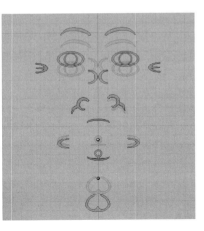

(e)

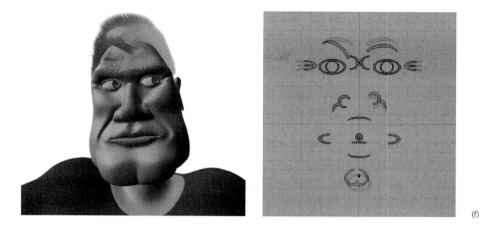

Figure 8.1 cont.
Expression of (f) suspicion, along with its bone positions

(f)

To get started posing the face, go into the Action Editor as you did previously to pose the body. Select all face bones in the rest position and key their location and rotation in frame 1 with the I key in the 3D viewport, as you did with other bones. Once keyed, channels will be created for the bones in the Action Editor, as shown in Figure 8.2.

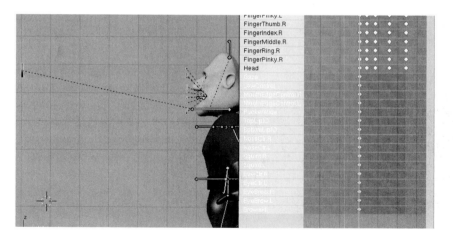

Figure 8.2
Keying face bone rest positions

Pose-to-Pose vs. Straight-Ahead Revisited

Facial animation presents a special case of the choice to be made between a pose-to-pose approach and a straight ahead–oriented approach, introduced in Chapter 7. The importance of timing might suggest that a pose-to-pose approach would be appropriate, but flow is equally important. Simply moving from one face shape to another does not yield convincing facial animations. Another challenge here is that the timing is particularly demanding in the case of lip sync. If timing is slightly off, it can be quite noticeable, and it can be difficult to get the timing precisely right the first time without seeing a real-time playback of the animation.

When you don't have to worry about lip sync, facial posing for expressiveness is much less demanding. You can do something like the pose-to-pose animation you did at the end of the last chapter for that here. You don't touch the mouth or the lower face right now; simply pose the eyes in a way that makes sense with the utterance. You can always go back and adjust it if there are problems with the timing or the interaction with the lip sync.

To time your animation to a specific sound file, it is necessary to load the sound file and position it where you want it on the Timeline. For this, you'll use the file every-era-has-its.wav, which you can find on the accompanying DVD, in the /Tutorials/samples directory. To place the sample where you want it on the Timeline, you will take your first look at Blender's Sequence Editor. Open up a Sequence Editor window now. In the Sequence Editor, press Shift+A to load media, and select Audio(Wav) from the available options. Find the sound file from the DVD and select it. The file now appears as a block in the Sequence Editor. Place this block so that it is flush against the zero point in the Timeline, as shown in Figure 8.3.

Figure 8.3

The sound file as it appears in the Sequence Editor

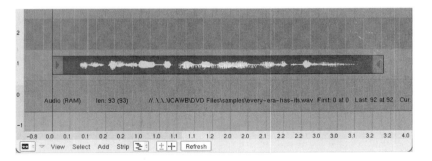

Look now at the Sound Block buttons shown in Figure 8.4. This is a subcontext of the Render buttons. Notice that the sound file you loaded in the Sequence Editor is now listed as a sound block. Finally, select Scrub in the Sequencer buttons to allow the sample to play incrementally frame by frame as you advance frames, and select Sync to time the video playback to the audio. You should be able to play back the sound file by pressing Play in the Sound panel, and you should also hear it play when you press Alt+A in the 3D window.

In Figure 8.5, you can see a selection of the main key points in the animation of the area around the eyes. Note the frame number parentheses at the bottom of each screenshot. The first frame is the rest position. Frame 35 occurs approximately at the end of "It has been said," which marks the beginning of the pronouncement. The expression is dispassionate here. In frames 48 and 86, as the main portion of the utterance is being spoken, the character emotes more strongly. The last two screenshots show the expression going back to approximately the rest pose. Note that you will not be making this action cyclic, so there is no need for it to end as it began. It is no problem that Captain Blender's brows remain slightly knitted.

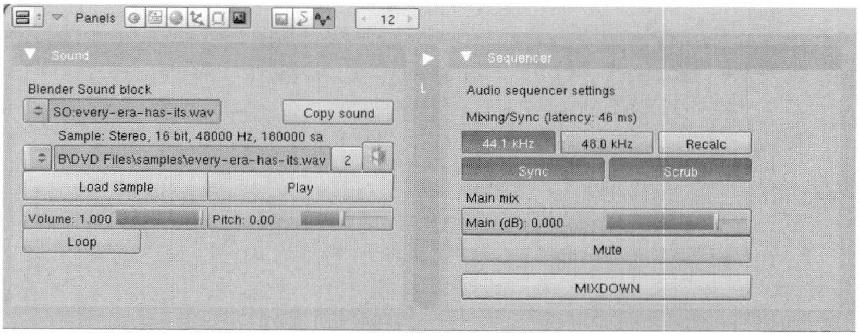

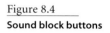

Figure 8.4
Sound block buttons

The second-to-last screenshot catches the character in midblink. Be sure not to forget to make your characters blink. People ordinarily blink more than once every 10 seconds or so, and it will become noticeable if your character does not blink occasionally. A total of six frames—three frames to shut; three frames to open—is a good length for a blink. If you can place a blink for dramatic effect, it is a bonus, but you should have blinks in any case. It makes for a nice realistic effect to have a character blink when changing the direction of its gaze, but do not do this all the time. One hard and fast rule about placement of blinks, which holds for any film medium, is that shots should not be cut on blinks. No shot should begin or end with the character's eyes closed, no matter how briefly. For this reason, don't place blinks too close to the beginning or the end of an animation because it could restrict your options for editing the shot later.

Figure 8.5

Animating the expressions of the eyes

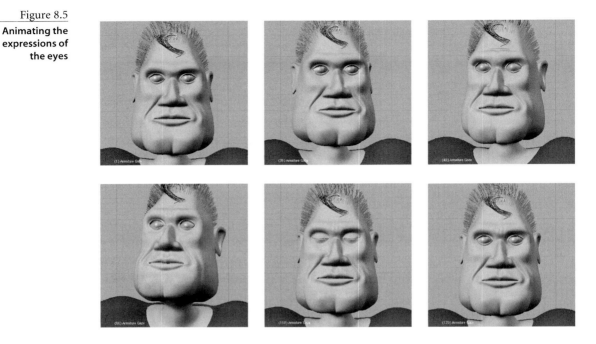

I mentioned the importance of not having facial movements coincide too much with one another. As you can see by looking at the keys in Figure 8.6, even in this simple series of movements around the eyes, I tried to mix things up. The eyebrows do not move in sync with the squint movements, but instead they begin to move first and then the squints follow. The first blink begins in between the starting point for the eyebrow raise and the

Figure 8.6

Keyframes for eye shapes

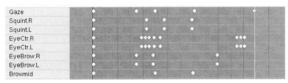

starting point for the squint, and the blink is followed by a widening of the eyes that, again, does not sync directly with any other movement. Several movements beginning and ending in an overlapping manner help to conceal the essentially linear nature of shape keys.

Lip Sync

My approach to lip syncing is really neither pose-to-pose nor straight ahead, although it probably bears more in common with straight ahead. I go from one segment of speech to another, and in each local segment I key in a straight ahead fashion while scrubbing through the sound frame by frame. It might seem painstaking, but there is really no easy way to do lip syncing, and this is really not too bad. I do a fairly rough runthrough first and then modify the placement of my keys and controllers based upon how things look. It's better to do a rough run through the whole animation, or at least a reasonably long chunk of it, because real-time playback requires a few steps and isn't something you want to be doing every time you key a frame.

The best way to get a sense of lip syncing using shapes and drivers is to do it, and the best reference for what kind of mouth pose is best suited to a specific sound is your own face. Have a mirror on hand while you do lip syncing and check it as you go.

Figure 8.7 shows the poses and keys for several frames throughout the utterance. Jaw movement is, unsurprisingly, important. The movement of the jaw makes a difference to the roundness of the mouth, which enables you to express the difference between sounds such as "ee," located high in the mouth and spoken with a wide mouth and "ah," located lower in the mouth and spoken with a less-wide mouth.

The first four images cover the portion of the utterance "It has been." The concern here is simply on the shape of the open mouth until you hit the "b," which requires a closed, slightly pursed mouth that will open in a rapid burst, after which the jaw remains high and the lips round slightly.

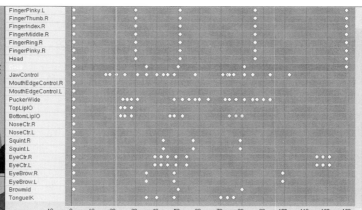

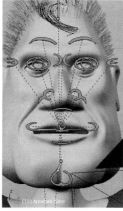
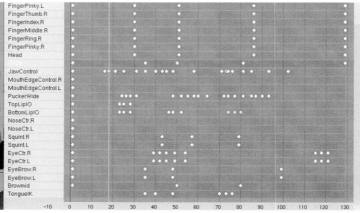

Figure 8.7
Animating the first part of the utterance "It has been said that every era has its visionary."

Figure 8.7 cont.

Animating the first part of the utterance "It has been said that every era has its visionary."

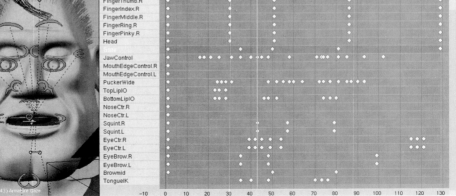

In the last image, the portion of the utterance in frame 43 between the words "said that" seemed to call for some tongue movement. Not all sounds that use the tongue necessarily demand that the tongue be animated. If you can't see it, don't animate it. But between the "d" and the "th," it seemed conspicuous when I omitted tongue movement on my first pass through this animation.

In Figure 8.8 the focus is on the word "visionary." The frames shown represent every other frame for the lip sync of that word. The "v" is created by putting the lips together, mainly by raising the jaw, and rolling the lower lip in by raising its control bone. This shape releases and moves into a widening of the mouth as the PuckerWide bone is lowered. The jaw remains fairly high. The rest of the movements are fairly subtle. The "zh" sound in "visionary" is enunciated entirely within the mouth, out of view, so you don't deal with this. Also, although "visionary" ends with an "ee" sound, the actual pronunciation in the recording is sufficiently deemphasized that an exaggeratedly wide "ee" position would not fit the sound well.

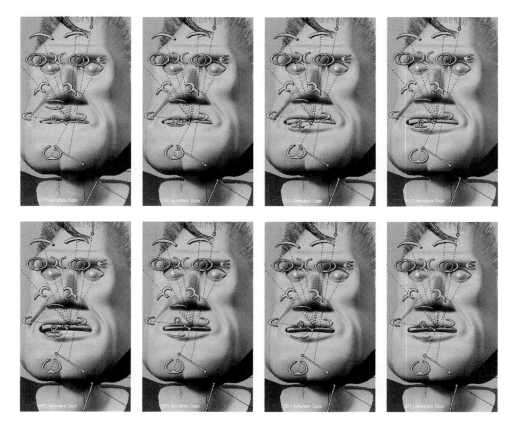

Figure 8.8
A closer look at "visionary."

Another approach that works more quickly is to create shapes for each of the phoneme sets mentioned in Chapter 5. Instead of manipulating a number of individual controls to form the long "e" sound, you simple activate the single "e" shape controller. Depending on what system you choose to use, you can make anywhere from 10 different shapes that will pretty much cover all human speech, down to just a few. Of course, the fewer shapes you create and use, the less convincing your lip sync will be. The advantage of this system is that you can name each shape by its associated sound (for example, "ee"), making it easy to identify the proper controller and set keys while scrubbing through the audio. This quicker approach can be combined and refined by using the individual controllers mentioned previously, really tweaking the facial shapes as each case demands. If you don't need camera closeup hero animation, a shortcut like this can save a lot of time. Obviously, the level of detail and nuance you need in your shape set also depends a lot on the degree of realism you're going for in your animation.

Keying Shapes Directly

The Action Editor can also be used to key shape values directly by using its shape sliders. A simple example of this can be seen in Figure 8.9. When a mesh is selected in Object mode,

Figure 8.9

A shape key keyed directly in the Action Editor

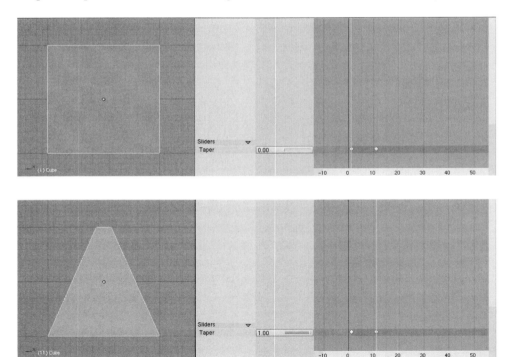

the channels displayed in theAction Editor correspond to available shape keys. In this simple example, there is a single shape key, Taper, defined for the cube, with no drivers associated with it. The single channel in the Action Editor corresponds to this shape. To the right of the channels is an area for shape sliders, which is hidden by default. Clicking on the triangle icon next to the word Sliders displays the sliders as in the figure.

New keyframes can be placed by clicking the slider. If you click the slider only, a key with the current slider value is created; if you slide the slider, a key with the new value is created, as in the lower image. This keying is automatic and does not require the I key.

Direct keying of shape sliders becomes more complicated (and less advisable) when the shapes are also driven by bones. The key points from the driver Ipos themselves are displayed as keys in the Action Editor, as you can see in Figure 8.10, which shows the Action Editor display of the shapes you have been working with in this chapter (note that the mesh, not the armature, is selected). This way of displaying keys might be slightly confusing and it is best ignored. You should not attempt to edit these keys in the Action Editor.

If for any reason you want to key shapes directly in addition to having them driven, it is possible to do this, but the results might not be what you expect. In this case, the shapes will have an additive influence, which can lead to the kind of additivity issues you saw in Chapter 5.

Although I cannot think of any good reason to mix direct keying of shapes with driven shapes, there are certainly people who prefer to work with direct keying. It is easier in this case to have a visual representation of exactly where a shape key's influence begins and ends, and to know the value of the shape's influence at any point on the Timeline. When working with bone drivers, this information is less directly accessible.

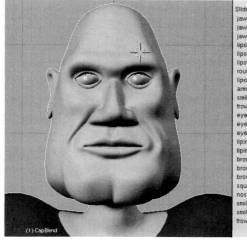

Figure 8.10
The Action Editor display of driven keys

On the other hand, the bone posing approach is intuitive and direct in terms of working with visual representations of the shapes. Furthermore, posing bones enables you to incorporate facial movements into the same action as other bone movements, as you have done in the example in this chapter. This is not possible to do with the current Action Editor. Finally, only actions associated with armatures can be used to create nonlinear animation strips, which you will be looking at in the next chapter. This is likely to change in future versions of Blender, but for now it is a limitation on a direct-keying approach to shape-based facial animation.

Regardless of how you choose to key your shapes, the task of creating lip synced animation remains essentially the same. It involves working with a few basic shapes, frequent reference to a mirror, and a healthy dose of trial and error. To find out how your keys are looking, you need to know how to play back your animation at full speed with your sound synced.

Playback

Depending on your hardware, Blender might very well be capable of displaying your animation with sound for an acceptable real-time preview without rendering. Make sure that Sync is enabled in the Audio buttons and that the audio file is positioned properly in the Sequence Editor Timeline. This will keep the video timed with the audio, dropping frames when necessary if the video cannot be drawn fast enough to keep up with the audio. With this selected, pressing Alt+A in the 3D window plays back your animation with sound. It is likely, however, that with slower computers there will be a considerable delay with this mode of playback. As you saw in Chapter 7, simply playing back the animation in the 3D viewport might not be really adequate to get a good idea of the timing. This is doubly true if you are dealing with sound sync. As the need for precision is greater, so is the delay in playback. So, as in the previous case, you have to render out a rough of the animation to see it played back at full speed. There's an added complication here, though: Blender's render playback simply plays back rendered animations. There is no facility for it to play back sound simultaneously when dealing directly with rendered images.

To get the sync sound playback you want, you have to turn once again to the Sequence Editor. You also need to look a little bit more closely at what actually happens when you render your animation.

Sequencing Rendered Frames

Chapter 11 deals in considerably more depth with the issues surrounding rendering animation, so I will not send much time on this here. If you run into any trouble following the steps here, you might want to skip ahead and read that chapter to get a clearer understanding of what's going on. For now, I will stick to the necessary points and assume that everything is set to defaults. To prepare the render output, read the renders into the Sequence Editor, and view your real-time playback, follow these steps:

1. The frames you output when you render an animation are, by default, stored in the `/tmp/` directory. If you render a variety of different animations, their frames will all be stored in the same directory, which can lead to confusion in managing and playing back the files. For this reason, you'll add a subdirectory in which to store this particular animation. You can edit it in the top field in the Output tab in the Render Buttons area. You can type the name of the directory into the field directly, as shown in Figure 8.11. Note that in these fields, Blender considers both slash and backslash to indicate a directory. So the slash at the end of `speech` has the same meaning as the backslash at the end of `tmp`, and means that `speech` is a subdirectory of `tmp`.

2. Now, when you render, your frames appear, by default, as a collection of numbered JPEG files in this directory. Render the contents of the 3D viewport now by clicking the Render button on the header of the 3D viewport while holding down Ctrl. Remember to go into Camera View mode to get the best idea of how your animation is looking. You can zoom the whole 3D view forward and backward for better framing by using the + and - keys or by rolling your mouse wheel, if you have one.

3. After your animation has fully rendered, open a Sequence Editor window. You actually want two Sequence Editors open, so split this window. In one of the two Sequence Editor windows, select Image Preview from the header drop-down menu shown here.

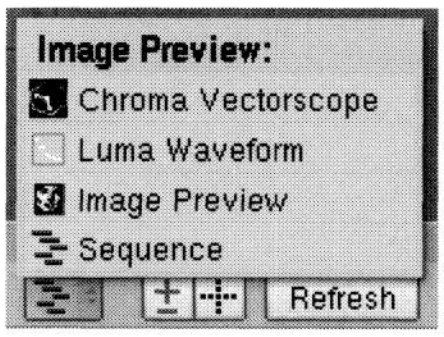

4. In the Sequence View window, you should already be seeing the audio strip that you imported previously. You want to bring in the images now, so, press Shift+A to add a sequence strip and select Images from the available options. In the File Browser, go to the `/tmp/speech/` directory where the frames are. Select the entire contents of this directory with the A key and click Select Images. You are returned to the Sequence Editor.

5. You can move Sequence Editor strips around using the G key in much the same way that you move other things in Blender. Place the new strip so that the first frame of the strip is at frame 1.

6. Play back the sequence using Shift+Alt+A, or by pressing the play button in the Timeline. This process ensures that the animation is played back in all windows, as shown in Figure 8.12. After maybe one or two slow runs through, your animation should play back at full speed with the sound. If the sound is not synched with the video, first try to adjust the relative placement of the audio strip in the Sequence Editor to get the best possible match.

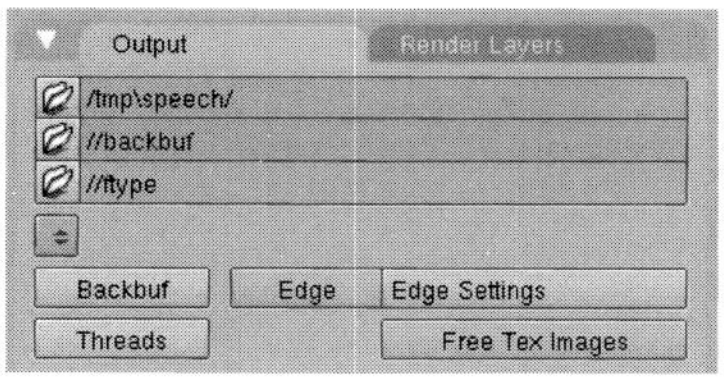

Figure 8.11

Setting the render output directory

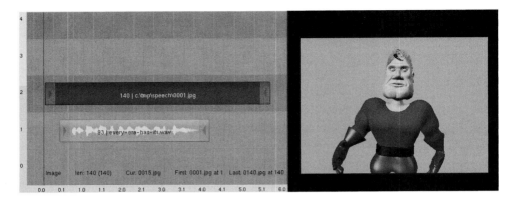

Take note of the places where the facial and mouth movements are unconvincing or seem out of sync. Then go back to the Action Editor and fix the positions and timing. When you've got this working to your satisfaction, it is time to move on to see what else can be done with the actions you created so far.

In this chapter and in previous chapters, you have worked a fair amount with actions. You have seen how the Action Editor works as a convenient front end for the more complicated and involved Ipo curves, and how multiple separate actions can be created to serve a number of purposes: to keep movements grouped together in meaningful ways, or to put together combinations of movements that can be controlled by simple bone movements in action constraints. But this is not all you can do with actions. The next chapter discusses the Non-Linear Animation (NLA) Editor, and you will see the rest of the story on actions.

CHAPTER 9

Nonlinear Animation

The Blender Non-Linear Animation (NLA) Editor is a powerful tool that enables you to build large, complex animation sequences by layering, repeating, and blending the actions you have already created.

The relationship between individual actions and the animation generated by the NLA Editor is sometimes a source of confusion for beginning users. In this chapter, I will describe how to use the NLA Editor and point out some of the common points of confusion. You'll see several examples of the main uses of NLA, including control over cycling actions, using curve paths and the stride bone to control walks, and combining multiple actions to create a complex nonlinear animation.

■ **Using the NLA Editor**

■ **NLA in Action**

■ **Mixing Actions: Walking and Talking**

Using the NLA Editor

At first glance, the NLA Editor appears very similar to the Action Editor, as you can see in Figure 9.1. It shows a representation of the Timeline and has an area at the left in which its channels are displayed. Both editor views serve the similar functions of arranging a set of underlying Ipo (interpolation) curves to output an animation. Although the Action Editor is a simplification of many Ipo views, each Action key representing up to seven different Ipo keys, the NLA Editor is a simplification of the many Action views. The main type of element in the NLA Editor is called a *strip*, and each strip represents one of your already-created actions. In this way, you can use the NLA Editor to place many different actions on the Timeline as strips, layering them, repeating them, and applying other parameters to them to generate a final animation.

Linking Actions to the NLA

To understand the relationship between individual actions and the animation created by the NLA Editor, you'll take a look at a very simple example. Start up a new blend, delete the default cube, and add an armature object with a single bone. Make sure that you have your workspace set up so that you can see a 3D viewport, an Action Editor, and an NLA Editor simultaneously, as shown in Figure 9.2. (You will probably also want a Timeline visible.)

You'll create two actions. The first action will have the bone swing gently from side to side. Rotate the bone slightly to the right and key the rotation at frame 1. The key will appear in the Action Editor as you expect. In the NLA Editor, a channel will be automatically created for the armature object. Under this channel, slightly indented, is a channel representing the current action, as you can see in Figure 9.3.

Press the Up arrow key on your keyboard to advance 10 frames to frame 11. Rotate the bone to the left extreme and key the pose, as shown in Figure 9.4. Copy the key from frame 1 and move the duplicate to frame 21. Rename the action **SideToSide**, as shown in Figure 9.5, and notice that the name of the action channel has changed to reflect this in the NLA Editor. Also, set the end frame in your Timeline to 20 to make this animation repeat smoothly.

Figure 9.1

NLA Editor

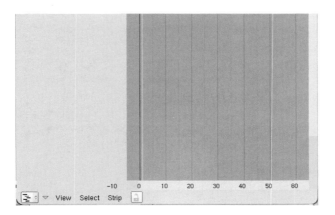

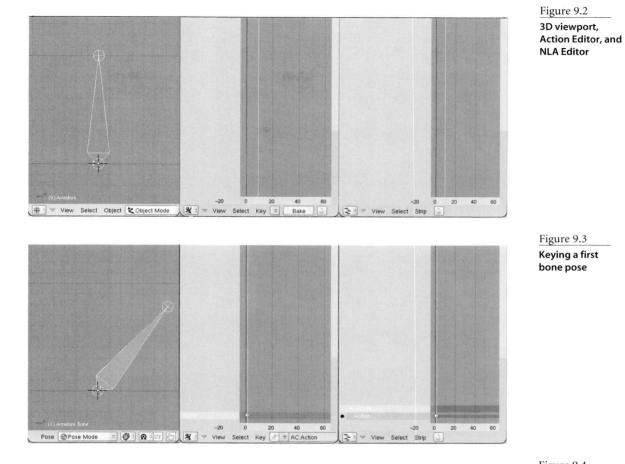

Figure 9.2

3D viewport, Action Editor, and NLA Editor

Figure 9.3

Keying a first bone pose

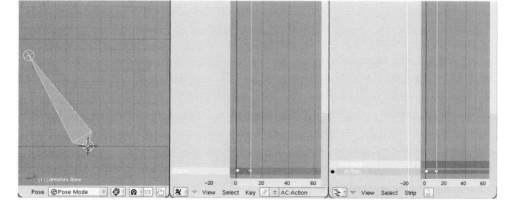

Figure 9.4

Second bone pose

Figure 9.5

SideToSide action

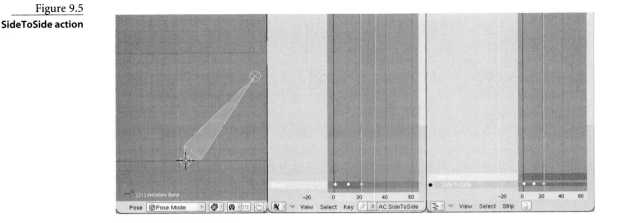

Now that you've finished creating the SideToSide action, you'll create a new action called FrontToBack. To do this, you *could* simply select Add New from the Actions drop-down menu, which would duplicate the SideToSide action and give you a new action called SideToSide.001. In this case, however, you start fresh with a brand new blank action. To do this, click the X to the right of the action drop-down menu, which unlinks the SideToSide action from the armature. Note that this does *not* delete the action from your blend file.

> When actions are created, they are given a fake user by default. For this reason, actions remain part of your blend file, even when they are not in use by any object. (Recall the discussion of fake users in Chapter 1.) To fully delete a created action from your blend file, find the action in the Data Browser and remove the fake user by selecting the action and toggling the fake user off with the F key. After this is done, assuming that no objects are using the action, the action will not be persisted the next time the file is closed.

For now, rest assured that you're not likely to accidentally delete actions. All this does is remove the action's association with the armature and thus removes it from the NLA Editor. Select the bone and press Alt+R to clear any rotations on the bone so you can truly start fresh with the new action, as shown in Figure 9.6. Although you have unlinked the action from the armature and removed it from the NLA Editor, notice that the bone stays in whatever position it was in when you unlinked the action. If you want to start from a completely clean slate, be sure to select the bone and press Alt+G and Alt+R to clear any translations or rotations.

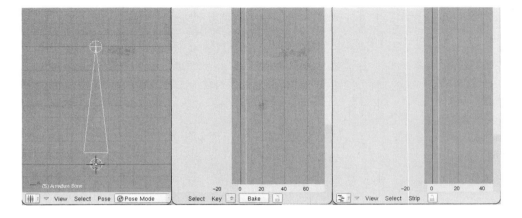

Figure 9.6

Starting fresh with a clear Action Editor

To create the second action, simply rotate the bone forward a bit around the X axis and key the pose in frame 1. Again, this will automatically create an action called "action," which you will rename **FrontToBack**. As you can see in Figure 9.7, FrontToBack is now the active action; as such, it is represented in the NLA Editor under the Armature channel.

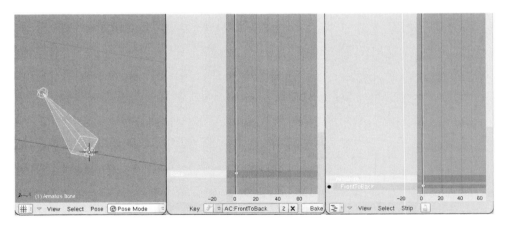

Figure 9.7

Creating FrontToBack

Finish creating a back-and-forth swinging motion around the X axis by keying a back frame and duplicating frame 1 to frame 21, as shown in Figure 9.8.

You now have two actions created. Currently, the active action is FrontToBack because that is the last action you worked on. If you select SideToSide from the Actions drop-down menu in the Action Editor, it becomes the active action, and it will be the action represented in the NLA Editor. Your windows will return to the state they were previously (refer to Figure 9.5).

Figure 9.8

Completing the FrontToBack action

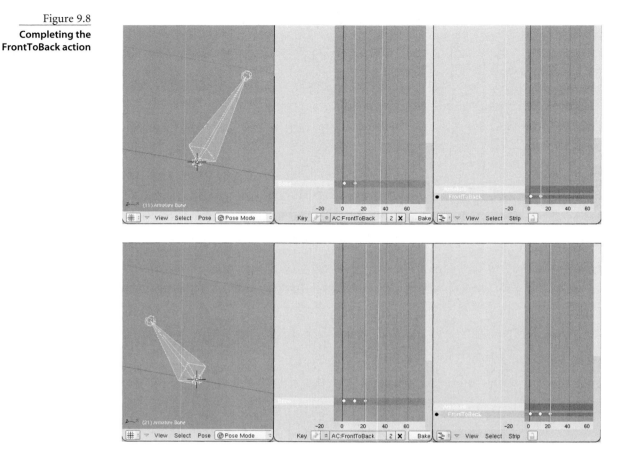

Working with NLA Strips

The NLA Editor wouldn't be much use if all it did was display the currently active action; as you can guess, it does considerably more than this. To insert an action into the NLA Editor so that the action can be incorporated into the final animation, it is necessary to create an *NLA strip* from the action. As should become clear, the NLA strip for an action is separate from the action itself; instead, it is a representation of an action that can be processed in various ways by the NLA Editor.

To create an NLA strip for the action SideToSide, position the mouse anywhere over the armature's channel in the NLA Editor, press Shift+A, and select SideToSide from the menu.

The resulting NLA strip appears as shown in Figure 9.9. Note that it has its own channel, slightly further indented than the active action channel. The name of this strip is the same as the name of its corresponding action.

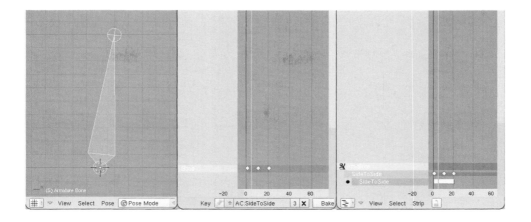

Figure 9.9
NLA strip for the SideToSide action

Now, in the Action Editor, select the FrontToBack action from the drop-down menu and make it the active action. Note what happens (see Figure 9.10): the active action channel in the NLA Editor now contains FrontToBack, but the SideToSide NLA strip remains in place. After an NLA strip has been created for an action, the strip remains in the NLA Editor regardless of what happens in the Action Editor. NLA strips can be deleted like anything else in Blender with the X key, but don't do that now. Instead, position the mouse over any of the NLA elements or channels for the armature, press Shift+A, and select FrontToBack to create an NLA strip for FrontToBack, which will appear as shown in Figure 9.11. Notice on your monitor that selected strips appear in yellow, whereas unselected strips appear in pink. You can select strips in the same way as you select other objects in Blender, by right-clicking or by selecting all strips and keys with the A key. You can also select a strip to be active by clicking on it. The active strip is indicated by the black circle to the left of the strip. When you select a strip to be active, it automatically becomes the currently active action. However, selecting an action in the Action Editor does not affect which strip is active.

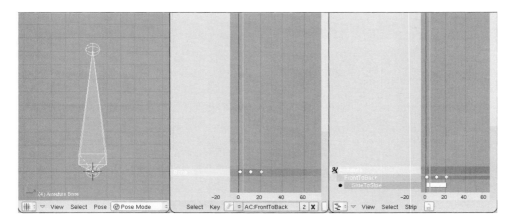

Figure 9.10
FrontToBack as active action

Figure 9.11

**NLA strip for Front-
ToBack**

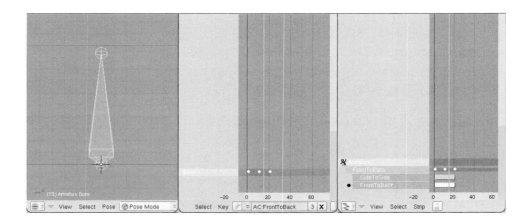

Action Output and NLA Output

Animation generated from the NLA Editor is based upon the interaction of NLA strips.
The animation generated by selecting an action in the Action Editor is clearly different
from this. You can toggle the method Blender will use (NLA or Action Editor) by clicking
the icon to the left of the Armature's name in the NLA Editor channels area. If the Action
icon (identical to the Action Editor icon, featuring a running man) is displayed, clicking
the play button (or pressing Alt+A, or Shift+Alt+A, or rendering the animation) will play
the currently active action, which is called Action mode. Clicking this icon toggles NLA
playback mode, displaying the NLA icon (identical to the NLE Editor icon, which looks
like a series of stacked indented bars). When this icon is displayed, Blender plays back an
animation based on the strips in the NLA Editor, which is called NLA mode.

If the actions in overlapping strips in the NLA Editor deal with separate bones or
separate Ipos, they are played back simultaneously while in NLA mode. In the present
case, however, the two NLA strips are the same length, and both represent location
and rotation keys on the same bone, so, by default, they are mutually exclusive (it is
possible to make their Ipos additive, as you will see shortly, but the default is strict
precedence, not additivity). In cases like this, Blender plays back the *bottommost* strip.
You can move a selected strip up or down in the channels with the Page Up and Page
Down keys. Note that the animation played back in both cases (see Figure 9.12) are
identical. In the first case, the NLA Editor is in Action playback mode, and SideToSide
is the active action. In the second case, the NLA Editor is in NLA playback mode, and
the SideToSide strip has been moved to the bottom channel, so it takes precedence
over the FrontToBack strip.

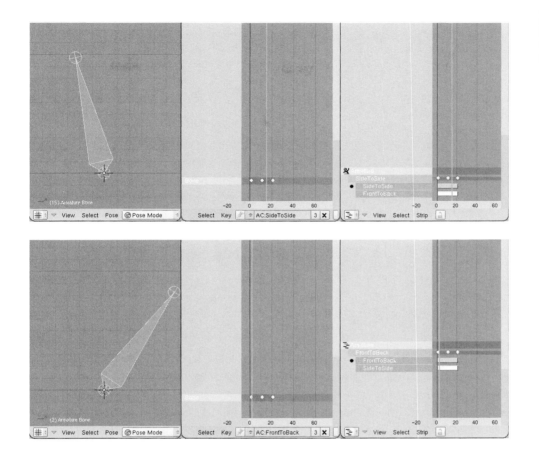

Figure 9.12
Both cases play back the SideToSide motion

More Fun with NLA Strips

As mentioned previously, NLA strips are more than simply instances of actions. They also have a number of properties of their own that determine their behavior and how the action they contain interacts with the whole animation. To see the properties of the SideToSide NLA strip, select the strip by right-clicking it; then press N to display the Transform Properties floating window.

Among other things, the strip's transform properties determine the starting and ending point of the strip and the number of repetitions of the action the strip represents. When first created, the number of repetitions is 1 and the length of the strip is identical to the length of the action itself. To see what happens when these parameters are changed, bump the repetitions up to 2 by changing the value in the Repeat field, as shown in Figure 9.13.

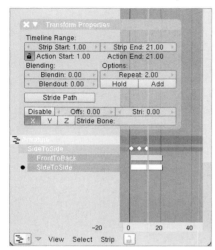

Figure 9.13
NLA strip transform
properties

As you can see, a line appears in the middle of the strip, indicating that it is now separated into two repetitions. Furthermore, because the starting frame and ending frame for the full strip have not been changed, the action is now played back in the strip at double speed. This adjustment is also reflected in the Action Editor.

You can now see the difference between playback modes very clearly. In Figure 9.14, in NLA animation playback mode, the bone swings back and forth at double speed, per the repeating strip. If you toggle into action playback mode, as shown in Figure 9.15, you no longer get the double repetition; *however, the speed remains doubled*, just as it was in NLA mode. The bone now swings back and forth quickly within the first 10 frames and remains still during the second 10 frames of the animation. You are seeing the action isolated, but you are seeing it as it has been processed by the NLA Editor because the NLA strip is the active channel in the NLA Editor, identified by the black circle. When the black circle indicates the NLA strip, the action in both Action playback mode and the Action Editor corresponds to the NLA-processed version of the action. To see the raw action with its original timing, click the active action channel in the NLA Editor, as shown in Figure 9.16.

Additive NLA Strips

As I mentioned earlier, it is possible to make an NLA strip's effect additive instead of precedence-based. In this case, the values of the strip's Ipo curves do not override those of lower-priority strips; instead, they add to them. To make SideToSide additive, simply select the Add button in the Transform Properties window. This takes effect in NLA animation playback mode, of course. When Add is selected in this case, the motion of the FrontToBack strip is also visible during the animation.

Figure 9.14
NLA playback mode

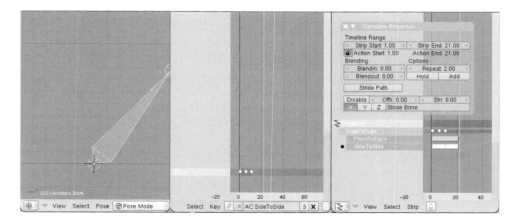

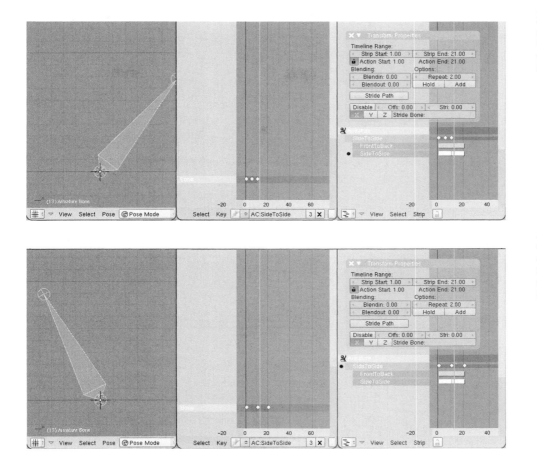

Figure 9.15

Action playback mode with the NLA strip active in the NLA Editor

Figure 9.16

Action playback mode with the raw action active in the NLA Editor

NLA in Action

This section takes a look at a few basic uses of nonlinear animation. In the first example, you'll see how to use an NLA strip to sync two unrelated cyclical motions to cycle nicely together. In the second example, you'll see how to use the NLA Editor to enable a walking figure to follow a path using a stride bone to prevent foot slippage.

Syncing Cyclical Motions: a Walk Cycle with Camera Rotation

If you looked at the walk cycle video in the walk.avi file on the DVD, you probably noticed that it wasn't exactly what you were rendering at the end of Chapter 7. To present the animation in a more appealing way, I gave it some nice lighting, a background color, and a material for the ground he walks on. Furthermore, I added a slow rotation on the camera to show the walk cycle from all angles. If you play the video file with auto-repeat turned on in your media player, you'll see that the walk cycle and the camera rotation are timed to repeat at the same point, creating a fluid cycling of both movements as the video repeats.

This is simple to do using NLA strips. To set this up, open up the blend file in which you created the original walk cycle in Chapter 7. You should have a 50-frame-long cyclic walk cycle like the one shown in Figure 9.17.

Setting Up the Camera Motion

Before you deal with the walk cycle itself, you'll create a smoothly rotating camera motion. Applying a track-to constraint to a camera targeted at an empty is a very useful and general-purpose method of aiming the camera. To set up the camera rotation, follow these steps:

1. In top view, add an empty on the same layer that the camera is on. It is a good idea to have these two objects on their own layer, so that they can be accessed independently of the other objects in the scene. Place the empty at the center of the subject of the shot (in this case, the Captain Blender figure). In this case, because you haven't moved the Captain Blender figure from the origin point, you should be able to place the empty directly at the origin point for the X and Y axes. Position the camera directly in front of the empty, some distance away, as shown in Figure 9.18.

2. Select the camera first and then choose the empty second (making sure no other objects are selected). Having them on their own layer should be helpful for this. Press Ctrl+T and select the TrackTo constraint, which causes the camera to point directly at the empty at all times. Next, with the same objects selected in the same way, press Ctrl+P to create a parent relationship. This parents the camera to the empty so that when the empty moves, the camera also moves

Figure 9.17
Walk cycle from Chapter 7

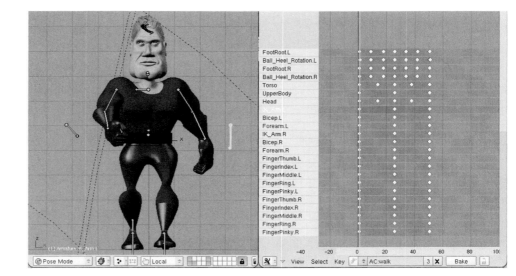

3. Press numeric 0 to go into Camera View mode. In this mode, you can select the camera object by clicking on the rectangular line around your view. Move both the camera and the empty to create a nicely framed view of your subject. Remember that to move the empty or the camera up or down, you can select the object and translate along the global Z axis. To zoom the camera in and out, select the camera and translate along the local Z axis. Press G and then press Z twice. Your shot should wind up looking something like the example in Figure 9.19.

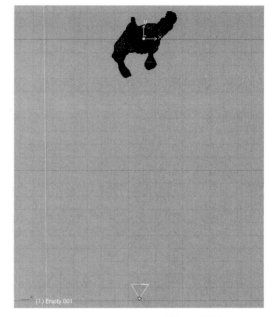

4. Press numeric 7 to get back into top view and select the empty. Key its rotation. Move forward 10 frames, rotate the empty slightly counterclockwise, and key its rotation again.

5. With the empty selected, open an Ipo Editor window. Make sure that the Object Ipos are displayed. Select the RotZ Ipo. This should be the only Ipo that is not flat. With this curve selected, find the Extend Mode option in the Curve drop-down menu and select Extrapolation. Your curve should now appear as a straight, sloped line.

Figure 9.18

Initial camera and empty positions

6. Press N to display the transform properties for the curve. Tab into Edit mode and manually enter the position for each of the two key points. To do this, select the points one at a time (be sure to select the midpoint of the key point instead of one of the handles) and enter the point's Vertex X and Vertex Y value into the appropriate fields. You want the time of the rotation to extend from frame 1 to frame 401, so these are what will be entered into the Vertex X fields of the first and second points, respectively. The Vertex Y field should reflect a 360-degree rotation, so the first point should be 0 and the second point, recalling the quirk in the numerical display here, should be 36.0. Fill these values in as shown in Figure 9.20. Remember that you can scale the view of the grid in the Ipo editor with Ctrl+MMB, just as in other windows. You can also move this view around with Shift+MMB, as in other windows.

One shortcut that is handy when working with Ipo windows is the Home key, which rescales and translates the view to show all objects. If your Ipo view becomes unwieldy, pressing Home can help you get your bearings.

You should now have a smooth camera rotation that cycles after 400 frames. Set your Timeline end frame to 400, go into Camera View mode with numeric 0, and press play to watch the rotation from the camera's point of view.

Using NLA Strips to Sync the Walk Cycle Repetitions

Getting the walk cycle to sync up with the camera rotation is simple. In the NLA Editor, create an NLA strip for the walk action by pressing Shift+A over the armature channel in the NLA Editor and choosing Walk, as described in the previous section.

After you have created a strip, call up the Transform Properties window with the N key and edit the transform properties as shown in Figure 9.21. The Strip End value should be 401 because you want the final animation to loop smoothly when it is played back. Because

Figure 9.19

The shot from the camera view

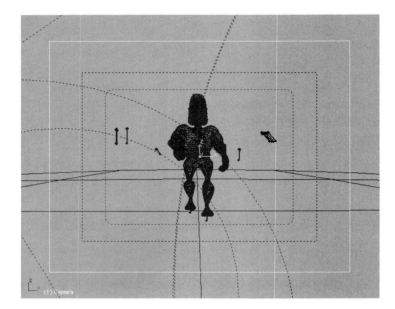

Figure 9.20

The empty's rotation Ipo

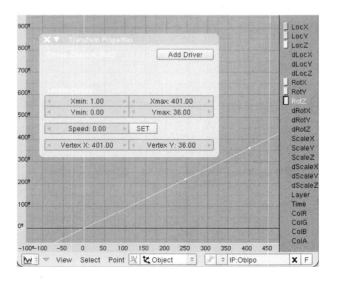

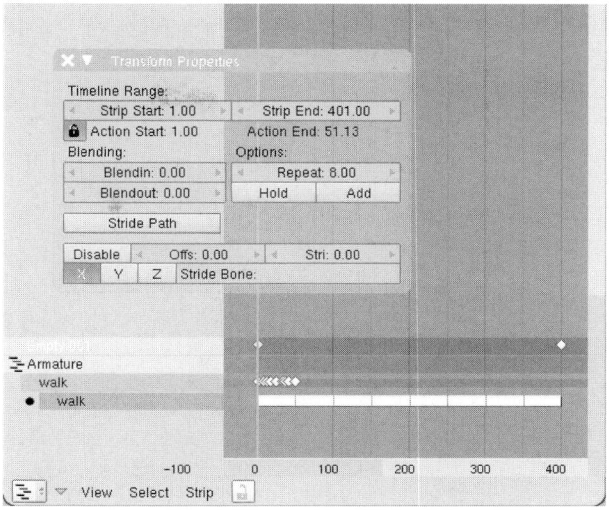

Figure 9.21

Walk action strip to match the camera rotation

the walk cycle is naturally 50 frames long, 8 repetitions fit into a 400-frame animation without alteration of the speed. (If you choose more or fewer repetitions here, the speed of the action will be automatically adjusted to fit, as you saw in the previous section).

For a quick preview, play the animation with only the armature layer and the camera layer visible, which plays back much faster than including the mesh in the view and shows how smoothly the cycle point turned out. Be sure that the NLA mode playback is toggled on in the NLA Editor, or else playback will occur in Action mode, and the walk cycle will play only a single time.

Another Application of NLA: Following a Curve with the Stride Bone

One method of making an object move from one place to another in Blender is to use a Follow Path constraint, which causes the object to move along a curve object at a speed determined by an Ipo. The problem with using this method on its own with characters is that the perfectly smooth motion of path animation can lead to slippage of the feet, sometimes called skating. As you saw in Chapter 7, during a walk or run cycle, each foot spends some time in contact with the ground, and as you have keyed it, the contact foot slides across the ground while the whole armature remains relatively in place.

Using a stride bone is a method of ensuring that the backward motion of the contact feet in the walk cycle action sync up properly with the forward motion along the path to produce the illusion of the feet staying in place. As such, it presents an alternative to the manual approach to moving characters from place to place (which I presented in Chapter 7).

Many people find the stride bone approach useful, and since it is not self-explanatory it is worth a bit of explanation here. However, this approach has a number of limitations. Compared with manually moving your characters, it is much more restrictive. The characters are constrained to the curve and not much variation can be incorporated into the walk itself because it is simply a repeating walk cycle. It also requires some nontrivial setup, which if not done properly can lead to foot slippage or completely nonsensical results. If you have cases where you want a character to walk fairly long distances (more than a few strides) with a perfectly uniform gait, this may be the best approach. However, it is more usual in animations to have multiple shots of fairly short and varied periods of movement. If your character is moving only a few paces, interacting with obstacles or props, or moving in an expressive or varied way, you will probably be better off keying the walk manually.

Setting Up the Stride Bone

The stride bone is a new bone that needs to be added to your armature. Add the bone between and below the feet in the location shown in Figure 9.22 and name the bone **stride**. Parent the stride bone to the Root bone. Make sure that the pointy end, the tip, is pointing forward. Note that because the local Y axis of the bone runs from the tip to the root, the character is facing negatively along the bone's local Y axis. When you have the bone created, make sure that it is selected in Pose mode and click the Stride Root button in the Armature Bones palette of the Edit buttons.

Figure 9.22

Stride bone

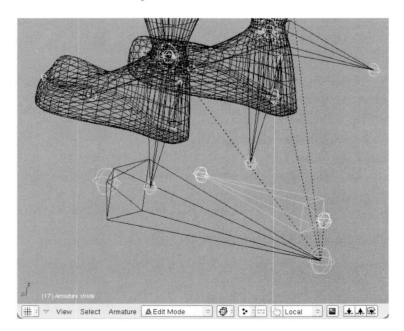

You can think of the stride bone in several ways. Most intuitively, it is a point in space past which the figure is moving, like a brick on the sidewalk that the character is walking past. Basically, you will key the relative location of this "brick" as precisely as you can, and Blender will calculate the correct forward motion of the armature object along the path for each repetition of the walk action based upon this information.

To key the stride bone's motion, you'll take advantage of another fact: the position of the "brick" on the sidewalk is motionless with respect to the contact point between the figure and the ground. For this reason, you can begin by simply keying the stride bone to be horizontally flush with the contact foot.

Before starting to key the motion of the stride bone, make sure that you are in Action playback mode, and that the black dot in your NLA Editor is selecting the action itself, not an NLA strip. You want to focus on the action here, not on anything from the NLA Editor.

For a reference point, I am using the joint at the ball of the foot. In frame 1, position the stride bone along the Y axis so that its root is directly flush with the joint at the ball of the left (contact) foot, as marked in Figure 9.23. Between this frame and frame 26, you want to keep the stride bone as close to flush with the left foot as you can. Because the horizontal speed of the foot can vary slightly (which is the whole reason you need the stride bone), it is necessary to key the stride bone's position at several points. I keyed the position at frames 11, 21, and 26, as you can see in Figure 9.24. If your stride bone seems to be pulling away from being flush with the contact foot at some point, key it into place to make it flush.

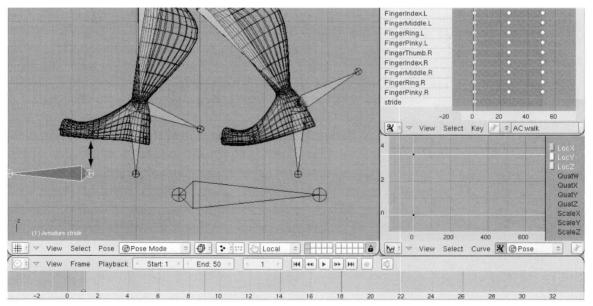

Figure 9.23

Keying the stride bone for frame 1

Figure 9.24

Keying the stride bone for frames 11, 21, and 26

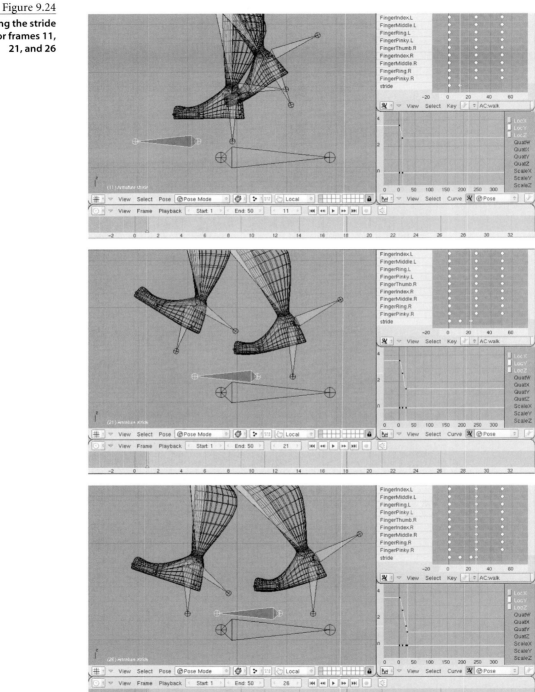

After frame 26, the method of keying changes. Think back to the brick on the sidewalk. The figure has now passed the brick, and the brick should be behind the figure, moving off into the distance. But the brick—the stride bone—is still moving at the same speed, and it is still motionless with respect to the contact foot, which is now the right foot. So you want to key it in the same way you keyed it before, relative to the contact foot, but now with one stride-distance offset.

To accomplish this, you add two empties temporarily to help key the positions; they will function as a yardstick. Position the first empty flush with the ball joint of the contact (right foot). Position the second empty flush with the stride bone's root, as shown in Figure 9.25. Now parent the second empty to the first, so that when the first empty is moved, the second empty also moves. Now you have a one-stride-length yardstick to use to key the stride bone to the movement of the contact foot. Key the current stride bone position at frame 27.

Move forward 10 frames to frame 37. Slide the "yardstick" of empties back along the global Y axis, so that the front empty is lined up with the contact foot, as shown in Figure 9.26. Then move the stride bone back along the Y axis so that it is flush with the rearmost empty and key the location, as shown in Figure 9.27.

Go forward another 10 frames to frame 47. Once again, slide the empties back so that the front empty is flush with the contact foot and key the stride bone to be lined up with the rear empty, as shown in Figure 9.28. Repeat this process once more for frame 50. When you have done this, go through the action frame by frame and make sure that the stride bone lines up well with the contact foot for the first part of the action (through frame 26) and that it lines up with the contact foot, separated by the distance between the two empties, from frames 27 to 50. The closer the stride bone is to lining up with these positions, the less risk of slippage in the walk cycle.

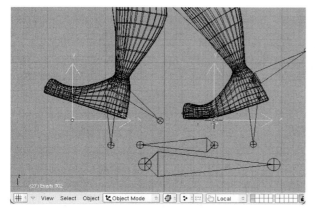

Figure 9.25

Positioning empties to act as a yardstick

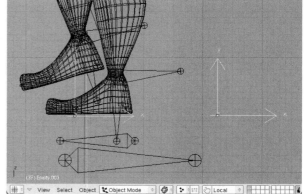

Figure 9.26

Bringing the front empty flush with the contact foot for frame 37

Figure 9.27

Keying the stride bone for frame 37

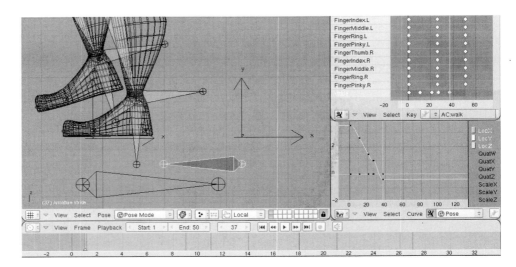

Figure 9.28

Keying the stride bone for frame 47

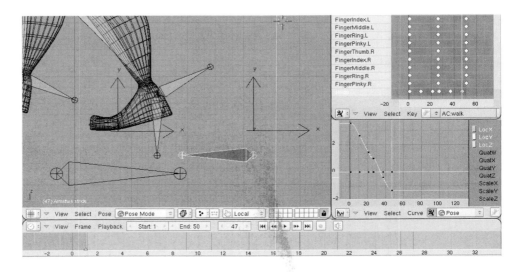

Following a Path

Now that you have created the stride bone and defined its Ipo, you can set the armature to follow a curve. To do this, first add a path by pressing the spacebar and selecting Add → Curve → Path. Place your path in front of the armature, with its tip as close as possible to the armature's center point, as shown in Figure 9.29. In Object mode, select the armature and, holding Shift, the path. Parent the armature to the path with Ctrl+P and select Normal Parent.

Figure 9.29
Positioning the path

You can now define the Stride Path in the NLA Editor Transform Properties window. Make sure that you have created an NLA strip for the walk action. With this NLA strip selected, press N to open the Transform Properties window. Select Stride Path, select Y for the axis of the stride bone from which the motion will be calculated, and enter **stride** in the Stride Bone field. The only other thing to note is that the length of the strip must be sufficient to account for all frames of the path animation. You should set Strip End at 500 to make sure that there is plenty of strip length to work with. Because you are working with a Stride Path, the Repeat value is not used here. Figure 9.30 shows the properties you set. Any values set here will be ignored.

Finally, define the speed with which the figure traverses the path by selecting the path and editing its Speed curve. The X value of this curve is the frame of the animation and the Y value is the portion of path traversed. A Y value of 1 represents the end of the path. The steeper the slope the faster the armature will progress along the path. You'll have the object complete the path at frame 400, so you should place the points of the Speed curve as shown in Figure 9.31.

Preview your animation now. Be sure that you are in NLA playback mode to do this. If the character's feet seem to be slipping, check again that the stride bone's motion is properly lined up with the motion of the feet in Action mode. If the walk seems to be too fast or too slow, adjust the path's Speed curve.

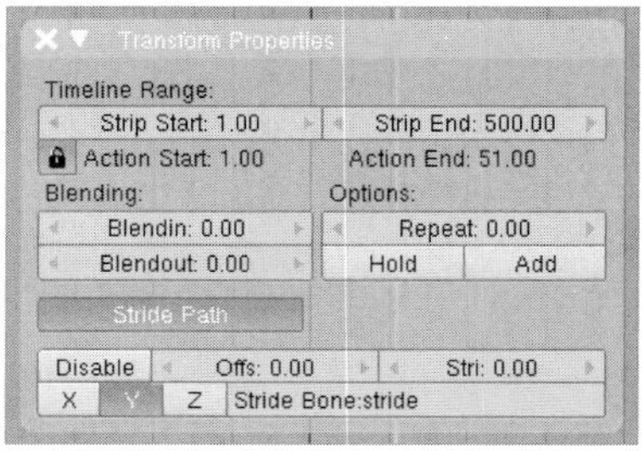

Figure 9.30
Transform properties for the NLA strip with Stride Path defined

Figure 9.31

The path's Speed curve

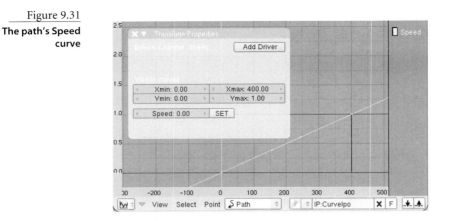

Actions for Nonarmature Animations

Actions were originally developed as a way to organize armature movements. For this reason, they were not initially designed to accommodate nonarmature object animations. If you try to key location and rotation of the default cube into the Action Editor, you will see that you can't do this. However, the functionality of the NLA Editor can be useful for objects other than armatures: This requires a slightly different approach. You must do your keying in the Ipo window, as you normally do when dealing with object Ipos. To the left of the Ipo type drop-down menu, you will see the familiar Action icon, as shown in Figure 9.32. If you click this, these Ipo curves will be made available in the form of an action.

Figure 9.32

Setting object Ipos as an action

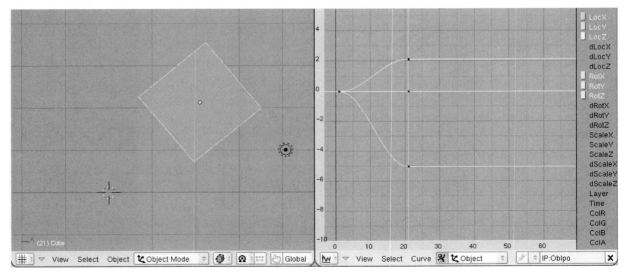

The action created in this example with the default cube will show up as shown in Figure 9.33. This action can be brought into the NLA Editor like any other, and an NLA strip can be created from it.

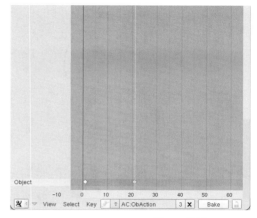

Mixing Actions: Walking and Talking

The real power of the NLA Editor lies in its capability to combine multiple actions into a single animation. When several animations overlap, Blender decides whether there are any Ipo curves that overlap each other, and if so, it assigns a precedence to the curves (or, if you chose additivity, it adds them). In cases where curves do not conflict, such as when separate Ipo channels are involved or when the Ipos belong to different bones, the motion from all Ipos is played simultaneously.

Figure 9.33

The resulting object action

In this example, I assume that you have a blend file set up with a walk action and the speech action you created before. If necessary, append the actions you need from a separate file. There is no camera rotation in this example, so if you have that keyed in, delete the rotation keys for the time being.

Your speech action should look like the one shown in Figure 9.34.

To set up a nonlinear animation using the two actions walk and speech, follow these steps:

1. In the NLA Editor, press Shift+A over the armature's channel and then select the walk action to add the strip.

2. In the Transform Properties window (press N) set Strip End to 300 and Repeat to 6, as shown in Figure 9.35.

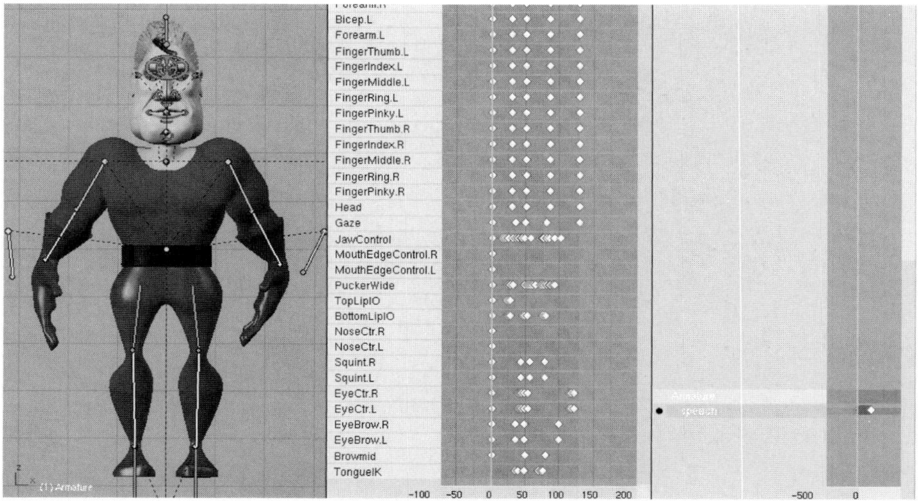

Figure 9.34

Speech action from Chapter 8

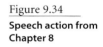

3. Press Shift+A over the armature in the NLA Editor and select the speech action.

4. Move the speech NLA strip to approximately the middle of the animation by selecting it and moving it with the G key. Give it a Blendin value of 30 and a Blendout value of 30. These values refer to the number of frames over which the action's Ipo values gradually increase and decrease their influence. If these values are 0, the arms will jump suddenly from their positions in the walk action to their positions in the speech action. Thirty frames give them about a second to transition from one action's pose to the other. Your NLA Editor window should look like Figure 9.37.

Preview your animation and watch Captain Blender walking and talking at the same time. Be sure that the NLA Editor is in NLA playback mode, as shown in Figure 9.38. You can see a render of this animation on the DVD in the file walkandtalk.avi.

Figure 9.35

Creating an NLA strip for walk

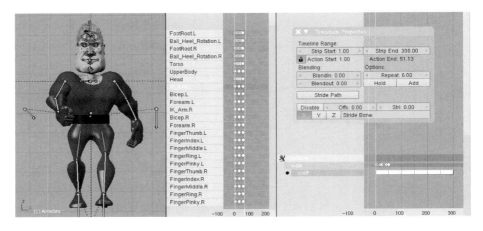

Figure 9.36

Creating an NLA strip for speech

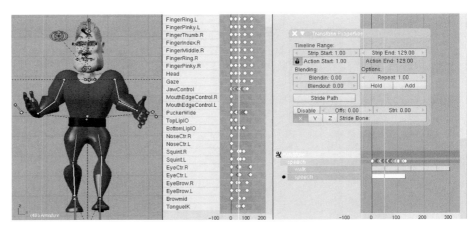

You've covered quite a bit of ground at this point, and by now you should have a pretty solid basic understanding of how to do character animation in Blender. You know how to build and animate a character using armature deformations and shape keys, and you know how to combine basic animations to create more-sophisticated ones in the form of actions in the NLA Editor. There are still a few topics left to cover, though, before you'll be ready to produce your own animated shorts to completion. In the next chapter, I'll go over a few more tips and techniques related to character animation that I haven't had the chance to discuss so far.

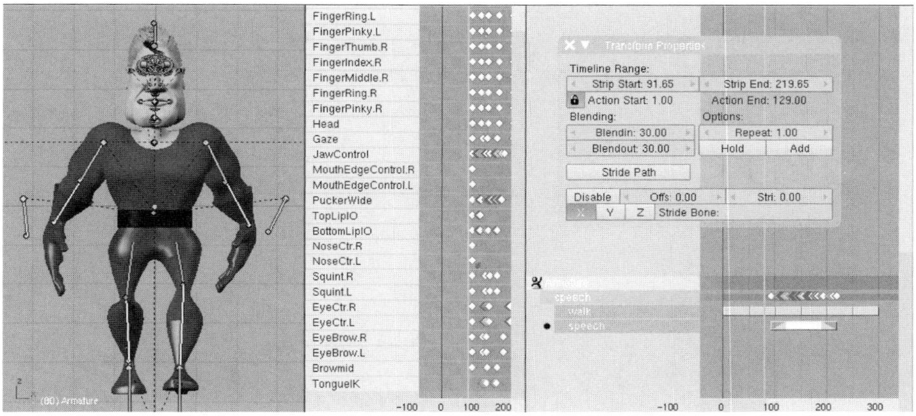

Figure 9.37

Positioning and setting blend in and blend out parameters for the speech strip

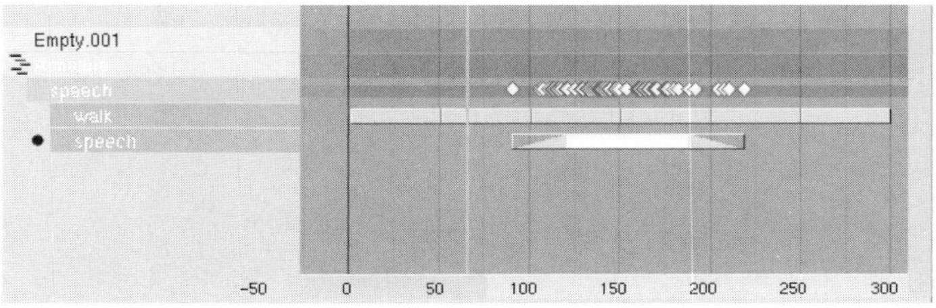

Figure 9.38

The finished NLA animation set to NLA playback mode

CHAPTER 10

Further Issues in Character Animation

Before going on to the issues of lighting, rendering, and editing, there are a few more topics I want to cover here. In the first part of this chapter, I'll give you an idea of how you can use constraints to incorporate props smoothly into your character animations. The rest of the chapter is concerned with various ways to represent particular physical effects: lattices enable you to deform your meshes in ways that would not be possible using only bones, the softbody system simulates realistic soft object behavior, and metaballs can be used to create interesting effects that are not possible with meshes.

- Interacting with Props
- Deformation with Lattices
- Softbodies and Metaballs

Interacting with Props

Almost all character animation involves the use of props at some point. The challenge with props is that they influence or are influenced by the character's movement, but are not part of the character itself.

In some cases, the interaction between the character and the prop is too complex to allow automatic solutions, and the best approach is to key the action by hand. In other cases, tools exist to make the job much easier than it would be if you needed to key everything directly.

Furniture

With props such as chairs and tables, the interaction typically involves the character's whole body and might even involve other props. It is more often than not simplest to do most animation by hand in this case. If the armature is sufficiently versatile, then interactions with furniture should not be difficult to key manually. Seating the character on a chair, for example, can be done by simply keying the location of the Torso bone.

In a case such as that shown in Figure 10.1, you want the figure's hands to stay fixed to the table, in spite of other motion of the rest of the body. The character should be able to stand and sit or lean forward or to the side, without the hands moving from their position on the surface of the table. To do this with the Captain Blender armature, there is one modification to be made. At present, the Arm_IK bones are parented to the Torso bone, which makes sense generally. (Normally, when the upper body moves, the hands would be expected to move along with it.) In this case, the IK bones of the hand need to be independent of the Torso movement. Once keyed into place, they should not move just because the Torso bone moves. This is simply a matter of unparenting the Arm_IK.L/R bones from the Torso. Do this in Edit mode. If you are using the .blend file from the previous chapters, you have to select the forearm bones (Forearm.L/R) and set the influence of their IK constraints back to 1.

Aside from that, the design of the Captain Blender armature, based on the Ludwig armature by Jason Pierce, is well-suited to this kind of pose because the rotation of the hand bones is constrained to the rotation of the IK solvers. If this were not the case, the location would remain fixed, but the hands' angles would change to conform to the changing angle of the forearm. As it is, unparenting and keying the IK bones into place is sufficient. The Torso, UpperBody, and Head bones can all be moved independently of the hands on the tabletop, as shown in Figure 10.2. Don't be afraid to set up a "special" version of your rig like this for a specific shot. Small edits to a rig for a narrow purpose, instead of trying to use one grand, all-purpose rig, can often save you time and grief as an animator.

Figure 10.1

"What do you mean my account's empty?"

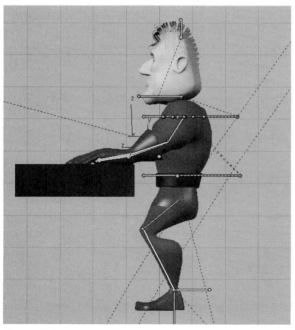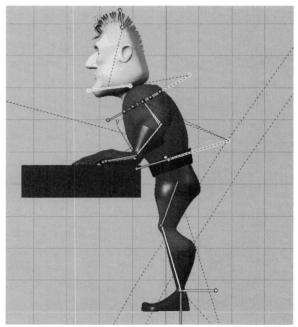

Figure 10.2

Moving the body with the hands planted

Grabbing and Holding Objects

Most props, however, are more than just obstacles, and for this reason they require a different approach. In many cases, the character needs to hold and manipulate the prop. This is not as simple as the case of furniture because in this case you want the prop to behave as an extension of the character itself when being held, but to behave as an independent entity when not being held. In the case of a sword or a stick, for example, you want the prop to be posable in the same way that the character is posable if the character is using the weapon to fight. It would be far too complicated and inflexible to key the object entirely independently. Nevertheless, if the character drops or throws the prop, it should no longer depend on the character's movements.

This is simple to do by using copy location (and in some cases copy rotation) constraints, as you will see in the simple example of Captain Blender picking up and throwing a ball.

Picking Up and Throwing a Ball

This example focuses on the use of constraints to enable good prop interaction. I'm not going to go into the various bone poses that compose the action. Figure 10.3 gives an overview of the full animation. The animation shows Captain Blender crouching forward, grasping the ball, pulling back for a pitch, and throwing the ball. The main concern is the motion of the ball. Of course, with an object Ipo (interpolation) curve, you can control the movement of the ball for every frame in the animation if you want to. You could simply key the ball's position to follow Captain Blender's hand. But it is not a good solution. If you do this, you might need a large number of keys to make the ball follow the motion of the hand, even if the motion itself is determined by only a few bone movements. Furthermore, if you edit the throwing action at all, which is very likely with a movement like this, you have to adjust or even rekey many location keys for the ball. Clearly, what you want to do is to have the ball follow the hand's motion automatically.

To make this possible, you will create a new bone by extruding and detaching a new bone from Hand.R, called hold.R, as shown in Figure 10.4. This bone is located in the middle of the space just below the palm of the hand, in approximately the spot where you would like a held object to be. It is not connected to any other bone, but, as mentioned, it is parented to Hand.R.

> Remember that when extruding the hold.R bone from the Hand.R bone, the same extrusion happens on the left side if you have X axis mirror editing turned on. However, when you detach the bone with Alt+P, this operation is not mirrored.

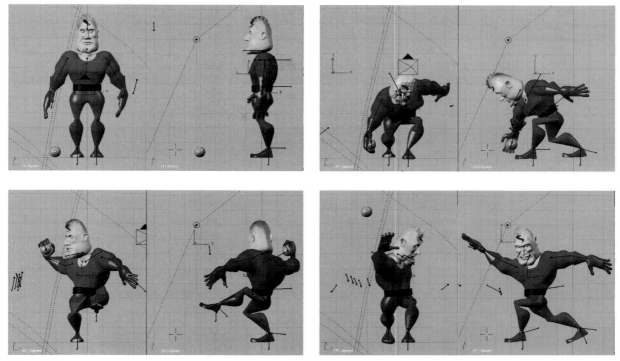

Figure 10.3

Overview of the pick-up-and-throw action

After you create and place the ball (a subsurfed UV sphere with 12 segments and 12 rings), the next thing to do is to set up a copy location constraint on the ball, as shown in Figure 10.5. In the OB field, put the armature's name, in this case simply **Armature**. When an armature's name is input in this field, a second field appears for the bone name. Put the name of the **hold.R** bone here.

The influence slider determines which portion of the ball's location is determined by the constraint. If the slider is set to 1, the ball is fixed to the hold.R bone's location. If the slider is set to 0, the ball will return to its original position and be completely independent of the bone or armature's movement. Intuitively, a value of .5 places the ball halfway between its own original (or keyed) location and the location of the hold. R bone.

Most importantly, the influence of the constraint can be keyed to an Ipo curve by pressing the Key button to the right of the influence slider. You begin by keying the constraint influence to 0, and keying the ball's location to the place you want it to be at the beginning of the animation.

Figure 10.4

**Adding the hold
bone in wireframe
and solid views**

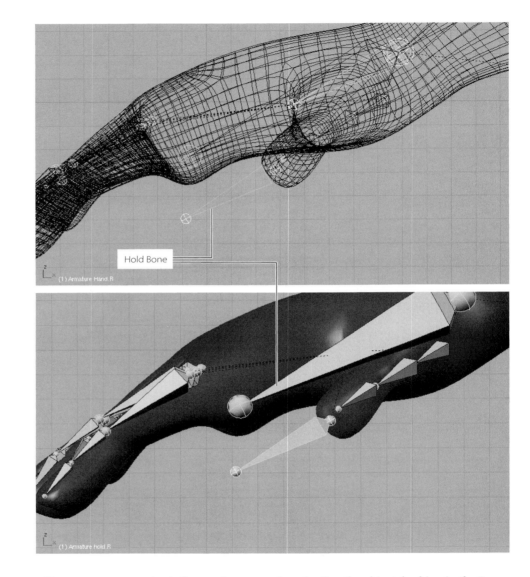

Hold Bone

You can see constraint influence Ipo curves by selecting the object, looking in the Ipo
Editor, and selecting Constraint in the IPO type drop-down menu. Figure 10.6 follows the
copy location constraint's influence curve from 0 to 1 as Captain Blender picks up the ball.
Figure 10.7 follows the more sudden release of the ball when he throws it. Note that the
Ipo Editor is scaled slightly differently in Figure 10.7, so it is important to pay attention to
the values themselves.

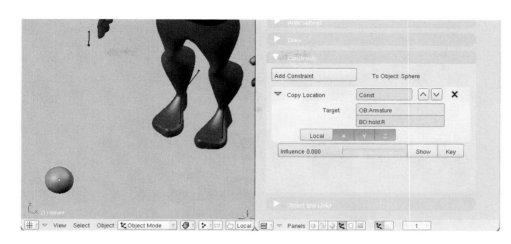

Figure 10.5

Setting the copy location constraint on the ball

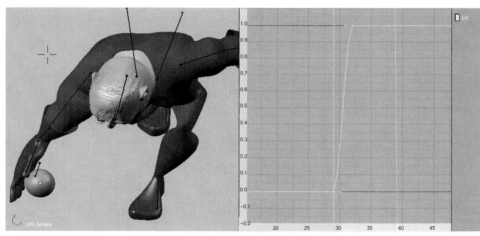

Figure 10.6

The shift in constraint influence as the character picks up the ball

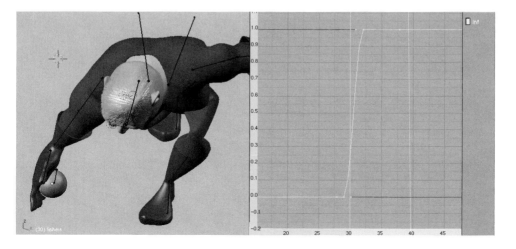

Figure 10.6 cont.

The shift in constraint influence as the character picks up the ball

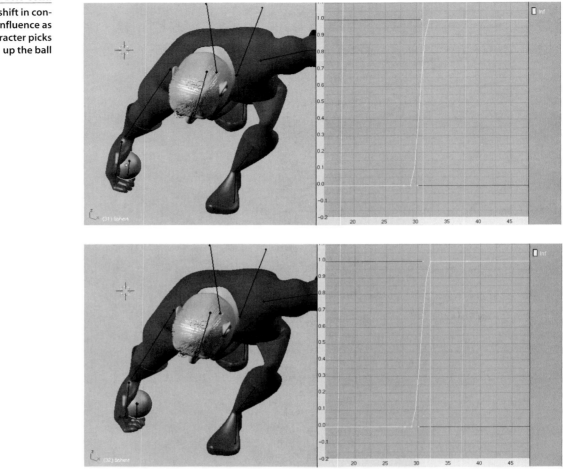

The ball's location needs to be keyed so that when the constraint influence is turned off, it will spring to the appropriate location. It is necessary to take the actual location Ipos of the ball into account, even during the period when the constraint is active. For example, if you keyed the ball's location to the ground in frame 1 and made no more location keys until the point after the ball is thrown, you would see the ball begin to float toward that destination even before the character picked it up. For this reason, you will need at least one duplicate key of the ground position, located after the ball has been picked up, to keep the Ipo flat up until that point.

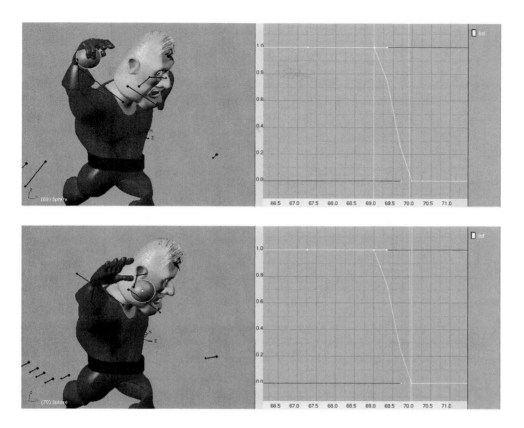

Figure 10.7
Releasing the ball

Floor Constraint

Another constraint that can be used to interact with "props" such as walls or the floor is the floor constraint. When applied to a bone, this constraint prevents the bone from being moved below the target object's center point. (This is by default. You can change the axis and polarity of this constraint.) This constraint works only on bones that would otherwise be freely moveable. If a bone is controlled by an IK constraint, and the IK target goes below the floor, the bone is not subject to the floor constraint. Likewise, a connected bone that is posed by FK posing is not subject to the floor constraint if its parent's motion pushes it below the floor.

Like the stride bone, the floor constraint might appear to inexperienced users to be more of a general solution than it really is. The floor constraint has a number of limitations. It uses the floor object's center only, so if the floor is in any way uneven, it is not taken into consideration. The next version of Blender will partially address this deficiency because it will allow you to rotate the target object to simulate sloped floors, but even so, the method remains restrictive.

Furthermore, because the floor constraint is a relationship between bones and a point in space, it does not consider the shape of the mesh around the bone. Because what you really care about is not the bone's relationship to the floor but that of the mesh, it is necessary to correct for any difference in position between the foot bone and the bottom of the foot mesh. It is possible to define an offset on the floor constraint, but this requires some effort to get right and still does not address the potential problem of an uneven floor. I have generally found it easier and more flexible to key this kind of thing by hand.

Deformation with Lattices

Lattices are an important tool for creating certain kinds of uniform deformations on meshes that would be much more difficult to do by editing the mesh directly or by using bones. Unfortunately, development in Blender lattices has lagged somewhat behind advances made in mesh deformation, so although mesh shapes are now handled very easily using shape keys, as discussed in Chapter 5, lattices can still be animated only by using the older and more difficult vertex keying method. I expect this to change in the near future, yielding a more intuitive and easy-to-use interface for lattice animation, but for now you still have to do it the hard(er) way.

Lattice Modifier

A lattice is a three-dimensional, right-angled grid of vertices. Like an armature, it is intended solely as a modifier of other object types. And like an armature, it never shows up at render time. Its default form is a simple eight-vertex cube, but it can be subdivided into more compartments by changing its width (in vertices) along each dimension. When a mesh is modified by the lattice, moving the vertices of the lattice results in a proportional distortion of the shape of the mesh. For example, if you modify a figure with a rectangular lattice and then edit the lattice to fatten the middle, the figure is fattened around the middle.

As an example, you will create a lattice to animate a deformation of Captain Blender's eyeball. The classic cartoon bugging eye is a good example of a deformation that is comparatively easy to do with lattices, although it can also be done by using shape keys. (Unfortunately, at present it is not possible to use lattice deformations to create shape keys, so a combination approach is currently not an option.)

To deform the left eyeball with a lattice, follow these steps:

1. Select the left eyeball object. Snap the cursor to the object using Shift+S. In front view, use the spacebar popup menu to add a lattice object, as shown in Figure 10.8. Resize the object to fit around the eyeball, as shown in Figure 10.9. Make sure that you do not do this resize in Edit mode; otherwise, your eyeball will shrink as soon as you apply the lattice.

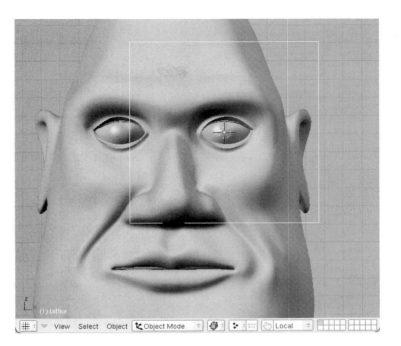

Figure 10.8
Adding a lattice

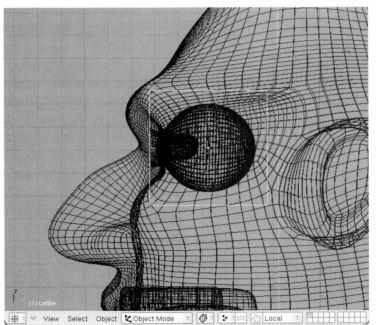

Figure 10.9
Resize the lattice to fit the eyeball

2. In the Lattice tab (see Figure 10.10) set the lattice resolution to be three deep along all dimensions U, V, and W, resulting in the lattice shown in Figure 10.11.

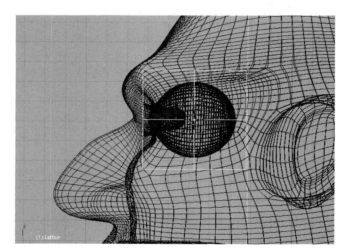

3. Select the left eyeball object and add a Lattice modifier in the modifiers tab. In the Ob field put the name of the lattice, **Lattice**, as shown in Figure 10.12. Take care to select the correct eyeball, which might require reorienting the view slightly to double-check.

Figure 10.11

A 3x3 lattice on the eyeball

Figure 10.12

Adding the lattice modifier

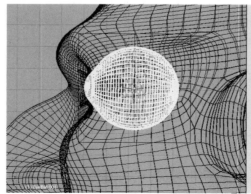

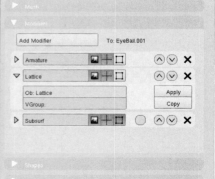

4. With the lattice selected, open an Ipo Editor window and make sure that Shape is selected in the IPO type drop-down menu. Key the lattice shape by using the I key in the 3D viewport and selecting Lattice from the Insert Key drop-down menu as shown in Figure 10.13. When you set this key, the curves shown in Figure 10.14 appear. This means you have set your basis shape. The horizontal yellow line represents this basis shape. Disregard the red curve for the moment; its meaning will become clearer soon.

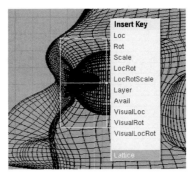

Figure 10.13
Keying the basis lattice shape key

5. Skip forward about 20 frames. With the lattice selected, tab into Edit mode. Edit the shape of the lattice so that the eyeball is distorted into a cartoony, bugged-out shape, as shown in Figure 10.15.

6. Once again, using the I key, key the Lattice value. You now see a blue horizontal line appear, intersecting the curve at the current frame, as shown in Figure 10.16. This line represents the shape you just made. Furthermore, the red curve now represents the change between the basis shape key and the new shape. The point where the horizontal line intersects with the curve is the point in time at which the shape represented by the horizontal line is fully realized. Skip through frame by frame to see what's happening here. At frame 1, the red line is even with the basis shape key, so the basis shape is fully realized. Moving forward to frame 20, the bugged-out shape gradually becomes fully realized. You can move these horizontal lines up and down to adjust the timing of the animation; however, it is a good idea not to put them out of order.

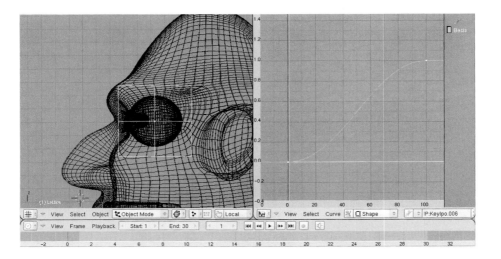

Figure 10.14
The basis key and curve

Figure 10.15

Bugging out the eye

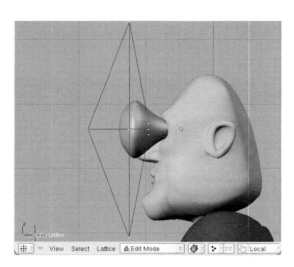

Figure 10.16

Bugged-out shape key

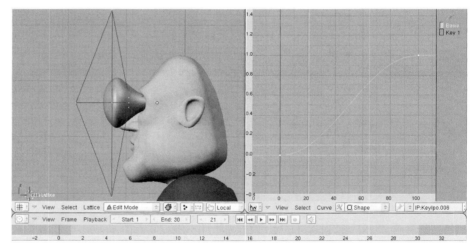

7. Go back to frame 1. The lattice should return to its basis shape of a small cube around the eyeball. Once more, press the I key and select Lattice. Another blue horizontal line will appear; this time directly over the yellow line at the zero point. In the Ipo Editor, right click on this horizontal blue line and use the G key to move it up. The line you are moving should be blue or green, not yellow or orange. Move this line to a position above the previous blue line. This shape represents, once again, the undeformed shape of the lattice. Placing it above the deformed key animates the lattice's return to the basis shape. Looking at Figure 10.17, you can see that at frame 40 or so, where the last key intersects with the curve, the shape of the lattice is back to normal.

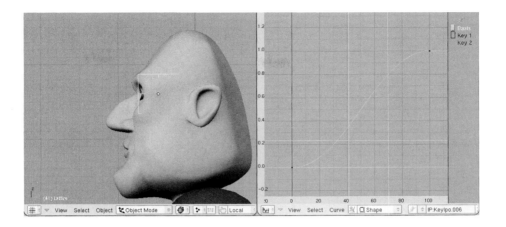

Figure 10.17
Returning to the original shape

8. You now have three horizontal lines that represent (from the bottom up) the undeformed shape, the deformed shape, and the undeformed shape again. By editing the red curve and positioning these three horizontal lines to intersect with it at the appropriate points on the Timeline (maintaining their ordering), you can time the lattice deformation however you like.

9. Follow the same steps to animate a lattice modifier for the right eye.

After you complete these steps, you're ready to incorporate this effect into a full facial animation, as shown in Figure 10.18. Remember what I said before about exaggeration?

Figure 10.18
Example of the kind of subtle and nuanced performance you can get with lattice deformations

Softbodies and Metaballs

If lattices enable you to deform your meshes like Silly Putty, softbodies and metaballs enable you to create Jello and Slime, respectively. So moving along in order of liquefaction, you'll look at those two tools in this section.

In fact, the two tools play very different roles in character animation. As you'll see, I included metaballs more as an amusing side note than as any crucial character animation tool. Softbodies, on the other hand, can be very useful for adding realism to a variety of character types.

Using Softbodies

The softbody simulation system is one of several impressive physics simulation systems built into Blender, but it is the only one you will be looking at in this book. As its name implies, it is a way of simulating softness, bounce, and elasticity in objects. There are a number of ways to use the softbody simulator, including as a rudimentary cloth simulation (this use is slated to be replaced by a fully developed cloth simulator in future versions of Blender), but it is usually used to create a bouncy, gelatinous effect for the softer portions of solid objects.

Captain Blender Puts on Some Pounds

For an ideal showcase of softbodies, you'll return to the jump action you created in Chapter 7—but with a slight modification. It seems that during a recent vacation from do-gooding, Captain Blender gained a little bit of weight, and, typical for guys his age, it all went straight to the belly. In fact, he gained so much weight he couldn't even fit into his trusty utility belt, as you can see in Figure 10.19.

Figure 10.19
Captain Blender's spare tire

I'm not going to go into any depth on the modeling of Captain Blender's new physique, as it was simply a matter of pushing a few verts around, as you can see in Figure 10.20. (When you make this modification to the model, be sure to do a Save As to not ruin your original file.) What you're concerned with is how to apply a softbody simulator to Captain Blender's new belly to give it some real jiggle as he strives to get back into shape with a grueling regimen of jumping in place.

To apply softbody behavior to Captain Blender's belly, follow these steps:

1. Because you want part of the mesh to be soft and part of the mesh to retain its form completely, you need to use a vertex group. With the Captain Blender mesh selected tab into Edit Mode and in the Links and Materials tab, under Vertex Groups, click New. Name the new vertex group **Softgoal**. Select all vertices in the mesh and assign them all to the vertex group, making sure that the weight is set to 1.

2. You don't really want all the weights set to 1. In fact, for the portion of the mesh that you want soft, namely the belly, you want the weights set to 0. Enter Weight Paint mode and select the Softgoal vertex group from the Vertex Groups drop-down menu. Using the Weight Paint tool with weight set to 0 and opacity set to 1, paint the belly as shown in Figure 10.21. It will work best to use X axis mirroring. Furthermore, I found that the top-middle portion of the belly works best if painted at 0.5 weight. Most of the belly should be at 0, though. The whole mesh should be red in Weight Paint mode, except for the belly, which should be dark blue. The area just below the sternum should be green. When you finish weight painting, switch back into Object mode.

Figure 10.20

Captain Blender's weight gain in Edit mode

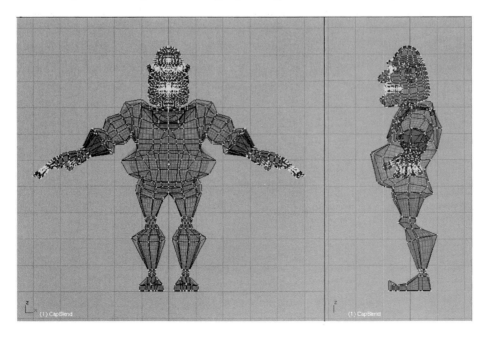

Figure 10.21

Weight painting the soft belly

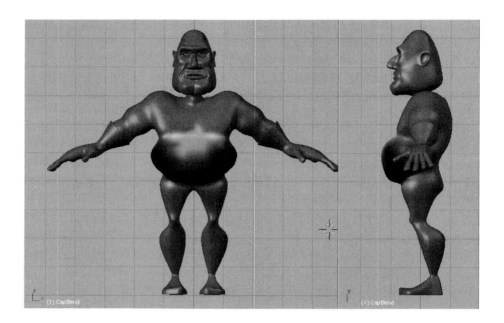

3. In the Object Buttons context, in the Physics Buttons subcontext, find the Soft Body tab, and with the Captain Blender mesh selected, click the Enable Soft Body button. Set the settings as shown in Figure 10.22. For information on what the various fields actually do, hover your mouse over the field and read the ToolTip that pops up. However, even with this information, finding the correct settings for a specific use often involves some trial and error, and you should expect to do a lot of experimenting before you have an innate sense of how these parameters affect the outcome.

4. Now you've got the softbody simulator set up. Check on your modifier stack. You'll see that a modifier has appeared called Softbody. However, you want the Softbody modifier to be sensitive to the movement of the character's body. To have that information, it must have access to the movements created by the Armature modifier. If you think back to Chapter 2, recall that the ordering of mesh modifiers is closely bound up with what kind of information is available to each one. In this case, the Softbody does not react to Armature motion as-is. You need to bump the Softbody modifier down a notch using the Down arrow button on the modifier itself, so that the Softbody modifier *follows* the Armature modifier. After you do this, you're good to go. Preview your animation to see the effect of the Softbody simulator. A side view wireframe representation of several frames from this simulation can be seen in Figure 10.23.

Figure 10.22

Settings for the soft-body simulator

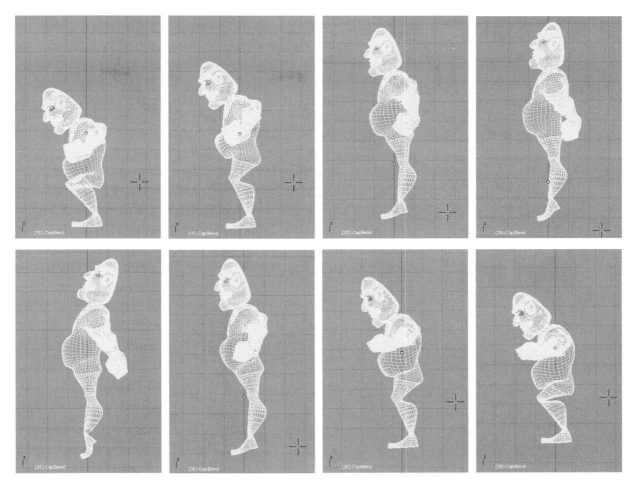

Figure 10.23
**Wireframe shots
from the softbody
animation**

Metaballs

Metaballs are spherical mathematical constructs that merge or cling together when placed within a set proximity of each other, as shown in Figure 10.24. They are a very limited tool for modeling, but their liquid-like properties are very difficult to mimic in any other way. Perhaps the best-known Hollywood examples of what metaballs can be used for are the liquid metal character in Terminator 2 and the animated green goop from Flubber. Metaballs are the basis for the Meta object type in Blender, and the various meta objects are all essentially built from the basic metaball.

Although metaballs cannot take an armature modifier, it is possible to use bone parenting to control the movements of metaballs with an armature if the metaball model is built of separate metaball objects that can be parented independently, as shown in Figure 10.25.

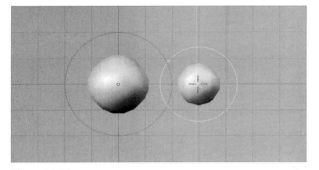 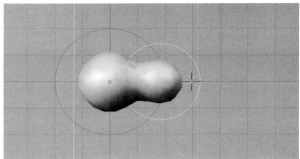

Figure 10.24
Behavior of metaballs

To parent a metaball to a bone, make sure that the armature is in Pose mode, select the metaball object (Blender reverts to Object mode automatically), select the armature again (Blender reverts to Pose mode) and, with the desired bone selected, press Ctrl+P. Select the option to parent to a bone.

In this way, it is possible to create a poseable character with metaballs that also retains the liquid qualities special to metaballs, as you can see in Figure 10.26.

In this chapter, I tried to give you a hint of some of the possibilities for animation in Blender. Unfortunately, there are many useful and interesting tools and tricks that I do not have space to cover. Using dupliverts, duplipaths, and dupligroups; using curve deform; and using modifiers such as array, build, and wave are all topics that warrant extensive discussion, but are outside the scope of this book. In Chapter 18, I point out where to look to find out more about these and other useful functions.

Figure 10.25

**Applying an arma-
ture to a metaball
figure using bone
parenting**

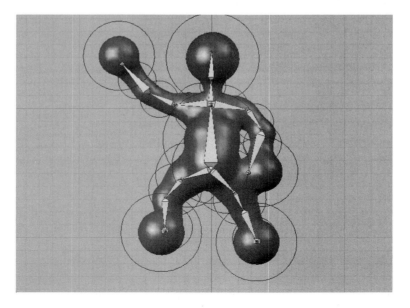

Indeed, there is really no end to the possibilities for both modeling and animation by using Blender's various tools. I hope that what you read so far has begun to whet your appetite. It is far from the end of the story. In Chapter 11, you'll look at the basics of how to light and render your scenes to create good-looking, fully realized images. You'll also see how to use the Blender Sequence Editor to combine sequences of rendered images to create completed animations.

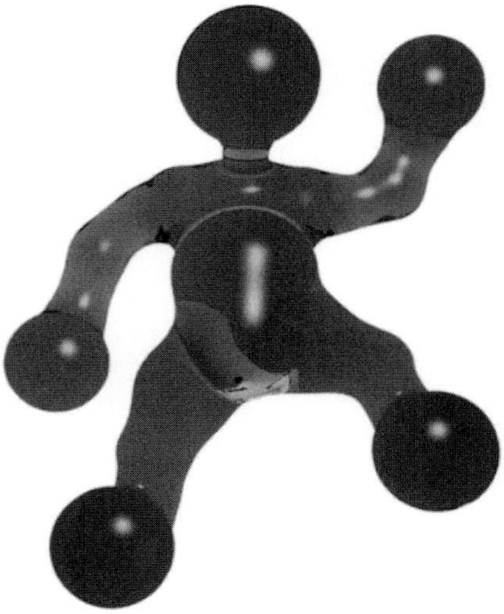

Figure 10.26

Animated grape jelly man

CHAPTER 11

Lighting, Rendering, and Editing Your Animation

At this point, you've learned the basics of creating and animating characters in Blender. However, before you can see your animations the way you envision them, it is necessary to go over some fundamentals of presenting and outputting your work. In this chapter, I'll give you a brief overview of Blender's lamps and lighting system and then tell you a little bit about how to light your scenes and characters. I'll also describe the process of rendering and talk about your options there. Finally, I'll give you a little bit more information about the Sequence Editor and tell you how to output finished animated sequences in the format you want.

Lighting, rendering, and editing are all topics that deserve a great deal more attention than what I'll give you here. This chapter will get you started, but will only scratch the surface of what there is to know about these aspects of CG animation and of Blender's capabilities in particular. See Chapter 18 for references and further information on these topics.

- **Lighting Basics**
- **Rendering Your Animation**
- **Editing in the Sequence Editor**

Lighting Basics

Perhaps the area in which CG animation is most similar to traditional cinematography is in lighting. The methods used in CG lighting mirror the methods used in traditional film very closely. Lighting is a matter of selecting and placing lights, and adjusting their values.

You can preview lighting setups in a number of ways, short of a full render. View modes can be selected using the drop-down menu to the right of the Mode Select drop-down menu in the 3D viewport header, with the cube-like icon. In Solid view, as shown in Figure 11.1, although the object appears "shaded," this is default shading, intended only to give you a sense of the object's shape. It does not reflect any influence of the lighting of the scene, as you can see in that figure, where the light on the figure appears to come from the viewer's left, when in fact there is a spotlight on the right. This is the default view mode, and on most ordinary computers it is much faster to work with than any other view (except, of course, wireframe).

To get a sense of the shading based on the actual lighting of the scene, you can use the Shaded View mode, as shown in Figure 11.2. This view mode enables you to see the effect of your lighting on the object to a degree. You can see the intensity and direction of the light, but shadows are not calculated, and surface effects of the light are only hinted at. This view will update in real time as you move the lamp, but it is computationally expensive, so many processors will experience a significant lag.

Finally, there is the Shift+P preview window, as shown in Figure 11.3. This gives you the most accurate preview of what you will see when you render. Still, as you can see in the figure, it is just an approximation of the behavior of the light on the subject. Moreover,

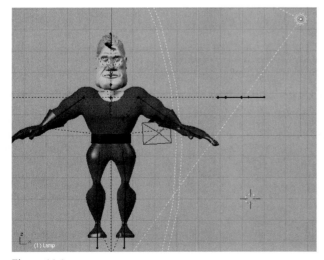

Figure 11.1
Solid view mode

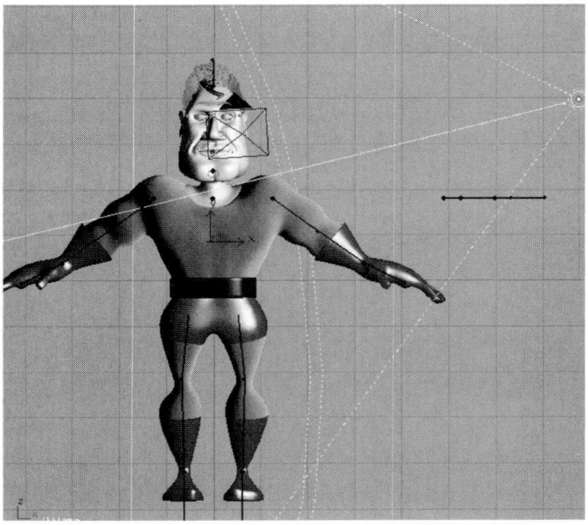

Figure 11.2
Shaded view mode

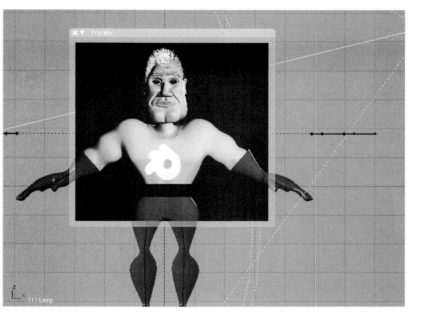

Figure 11.3

Solid view with the preview window

because the orbs around Captain Blender's eyeballs are transparent, they require ray tracing to render properly. In the preview, the zero alpha value yields empty holes in the place of eyeballs.

These various tools can be useful in placing lights, but I find that for assessing lighting, nothing beats a proper render. I rarely use the Shaded View mode.

Cheats

A "cheat" in film lighting terms is an unnatural or unlikely use of light to give a desired effect. Because a film audience views a scene with fixed borders and from limited angles, it is possible to take many liberties even with real lights (adding light sources that would not exist in nature, moving light sources from their "true" positions, and so on). Cheats are the norm in traditional lighting and even more so in CG lighting, in which moving lights costs nothing and adding lights costs only additional render time. Nevertheless, it is a good idea to have a sense of when you are using cheats and to consider what the ultimate effect of your lighting will be on the viewer. Always have an idea in mind of what the actual lighting situation in the 3D scene *should* be and where the viewer should perceive the light as coming from. Because they are by definition unnatural, cheats should never be obvious to the viewer.

Lamps

Lights are represented by the object type Lamp, which has the following subtypes:

- Lamp
- Spot
- Hemispheric Lamp
- Area
- Sun

The Lamp buttons area is a subcontext of the Shading buttons area, as you can see in Figure 11.4. This figure shows a typical example of the buttons and parameter values for a spotlight. In the left panel, the lamp's type is selected. In the middle panel, parameters such as the lamp's Distance, Energy, and RGB color values are accessed. In the right panel, in the case of spotlights, you can adjust the size and sharpness of the spot and shadow properties.

Control over shadow properties is one of the areas in which CG lighting differs most drastically from traditional cinematographic lighting. Unlike reality, you can switch the shadows cast by a lamp on and off completely independently of the lamp itself. Furthermore, you have the choice between several different methods of calculating the shadows. You can use either buffer shadows, which are relatively quick to calculate and approximate, or ray shadows, which more accurately reflect the shapes of the objects casting the shadows. You will see a concrete practical example of the difference below.

The graphic representation of the light in the 3D viewport tells you what shadow options are active on the light. In Figure 11.5, you can see the three options active for a spotlight, in order of appearance: no shadow, buffer shadow, and ray shadow. Ray shadow and buffer shadow are mutually exclusive, so the middle graphic is unambiguously buffer shadow only.

Each of the different lamp types has specific properties and options that can be associated with it, and each has its own uses in practice. In this section, you'll look briefly at the different lamps and their effects.

Figure 11.4

Lamp buttons

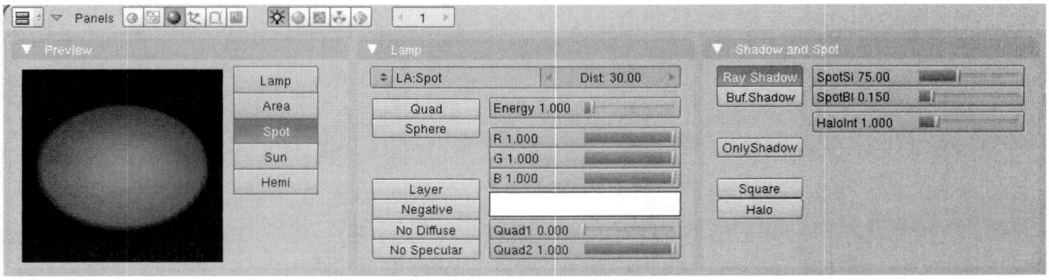

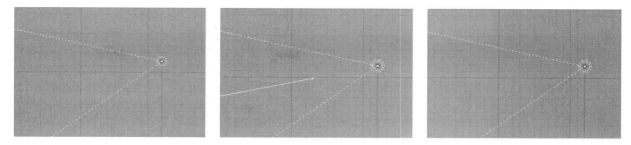

Figure 11.5

No shadow, buffer shadow, and ray shadow options for lights

Lamp

The default lamp is an omnidirectional lamp that can cast ray shadows or have shadows completely disabled, but does not have an option for buffered shadows. The default lamp offers no control over the direction and throw of the light beam. An example of the light provided by the default lamp can be seen in Figure 11.6. (This render used the ray shadow option.)

Although something approximately like omnidirectional lights are common for household lamps and streetlights, there are not a lot of omnidirectional lights on movie sets or theatrical stages. But there *are* a lot of spotlights. The reason is simple: lighting requires

Figure 11.6

Lighting by a single lamp

control over where the light goes. Spotlights give this control; omnidirectional lamps don't. In the present example, with a single lamp illuminating a single subject, the difference is negligible. However, when you have more than one subject and are concerned with lighting various parts of a scene convincingly with shadows, highlighting, and fill lights, you very quickly run into situations in which you cannot do without the control you get with spotlights. Furthermore, because the default lamp casts light from a single point, it is inappropriate to use on its own for ambient light and is not especially suited for soft fill light. So, in spite of its apparent generality, the default lamp is actually quite limited in its practical applicability. It is useful as a prop light, for example when you have a lamp in your scene that needs to cast omnidirectional shadows. But for actual lighting, I rarely if ever use the default lamp.

Spot

The spotlight is the most frequently used type of light in most lighting situations. The light itself has the same qualities as that of the default lamp, but the beam can be controlled. The direction, distance, width, and sharpness of the beam are all parameters that can be set in the lamp buttons area.

Figure 11.7 shows the spotlight setup for the renders that you'll see in Figures 11.8, 11.9, and 11.10. Notice that the throw of the spotlight is clearly represented in the 3D viewport.

Unlike the default lamp, spot lamps have three options for shadows. These options have different applications, and there are some potential quirks to be aware of.

Figure 11.7

Spotlight setup in the 3D viewport

NO SHADOW

Using lamps with the shadow turned off is a classic CG cheat. In Figure 11.8, you see a render with shadow off. Note that the render still has places that are *in shadow*. They are simply the places where the light does not reach. In CG (although not in the physical world) this is completely different from cast shadows. Shadows thrown from one object onto another are calculated separately from the increase in energy on surfaces that are facing the light source.

Being able to turn off cast shadows can be very convenient because unwanted shadows are the bane of complex lighting setups in traditional lighting. However, there are issues to be aware of. Like any cheat, it is noticeable if used in an obvious way. If your character is walking through the desert under a hot sun, turning off cast shadows is unnatural and distracting. In general, the light source that your audience perceives as the main light source (which might or might not truly be the main light source) should appear to cast shadows. Nonshadow lights are very good for fill lights, however, because they eliminate the real-world problem of double shadows that occurs when using fill lights that cast shadows.

When cast shadows are turned off, light affects individual objects naturally, but does not calculate the shadows they cast onto other objects. In effect, objects become transparent in relation to each other. Note how it affects Captain Blender's hair in Figure 11.8. You

Figure 11.8
Spotlight with no shadows

would not expect the hair on the right side of his head to be illuminated so brightly. But because no shadow is being cast by Captain Blender's head mesh, these particles are behaving exactly as if the light were shone on them directly. Worse, they are behaving as though light were shone directly from the wrong side of the head, as indeed it is.

The effect is relatively subtle in this case because Captain Blender's hair is only a small feature of him. But for hairier characters, this effect can lead to serious problems, making the character's hair seem to glow in a very unnatural way. For this reason, it is necessary to take extra care when using lights without shadows when particle hair is being used.

BUFFER SHADOW

Buffer shadows work by making a small, grayscale render of the occluding objects from the light's point of view and then mapping that image onto surfaces behind the object. The shadow cast by the character's head onto his right shoulder in Figure 11.9 is a buffer shadow. Contrast this with the unnatural highlight in Figure 11.8, in which no shadows are cast. Buffer shadows can be relatively quick to compute and are often very efficient to use. However, in certain cases the limitations of buffer shadows become apparent. The sharpness and darkness of buffer shadows are not entirely dependent on lighting conditions, as would naturally occur, and denser mesh areas tend to produce darker buffer shadows, which can be obvious in cases in which the shadow is clearly visible. Furthermore, buffer shadows of insufficient resolution do not affect particles, leading to the same problem with the hair in Figure 11.9 that you saw previously in Figure 11.8.

Figure 11.9

Spotlight with buffer shadows

Figure 11.10
Spotlight with ray shadows

RAY SHADOW

Ray shadows are calculated by tracing the light beams emitted from the lamp, in a way most closely approximating the way that actual shadows fall in nature. This yields the most realistic shadows; the qualities of the shadows are entirely dependent on the lighting conditions.

The shadows in Figure 11.10 were generated using ray shadows. Because there is only one light source, they are dark and sharply defined, as would be the case in nature. Furthermore, they correctly interact with the particles of the hair to result in accurate shadow patterns on Captain Blender's head.

Hemi Lights

Hemi lights provide a very diffuse light source, meaning that the rays of light are scattered and moving in many different directions. This is typical of light in many real-world conditions, in which much of the light you see is reflected. In this respect, hemi lights are both more "naturalistic" than spots and much less naturalistic because no lamp exists in nature that is capable of producing the kind of illumination that hemi lights produce. In Figure 11.11, you can see the figure lit by a single hemi lamp, positioned in exactly the same place as the spot from the previous renders. Note that although there is a tendency for the highlights to be on the left side of the figure and the shadows to be on the right side, there are actually no completely unlit areas anywhere on the figure.

Figure 11.11

Hemi lamp

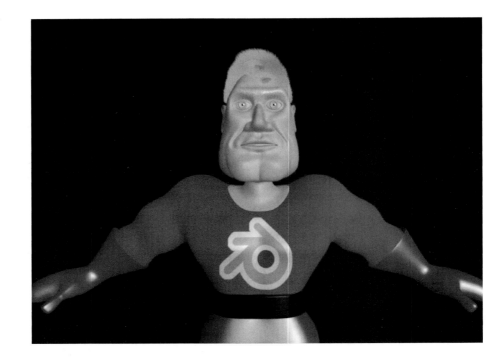

Hemis are useful for nondescript, utilitarian lighting purposes. Putting a hemi into a file with a model results in inoffensive and fully visible renders of your model, and it is a good choice for a default light for a model when the model itself is the emphasis of the render. It is not a very good choice for serious lighting, however, because it will result in a flat and lifeless appearance, as in the render here. It is not generally very good for showcasing objects or for lighting complex scenes. When working with animation, however, in which you try to reduce your render times per frame as much as possible, the hemi light can be useful as a fast, though not very accurate, outdoor fill light. When kept at low intensities and paired with a good key light for the sun, it can help you produce passable renders faster than with other methods. A hemi placed in the 3D space illuminates the whole rendered area. It does not matter where the hemi lamp actually is. The hemi is sensitive only to the angle at which it is placed. All the subjects of the scene will be lit from exactly the same angle, regardless of their position with respect to the hemi. In Figure 11.12, you can see a hemi placed pointing directly downward. Although the light is not positioned directly above the Captain Blender character, the illumination of the character is straight down, as can be seen in Figure 11.13.

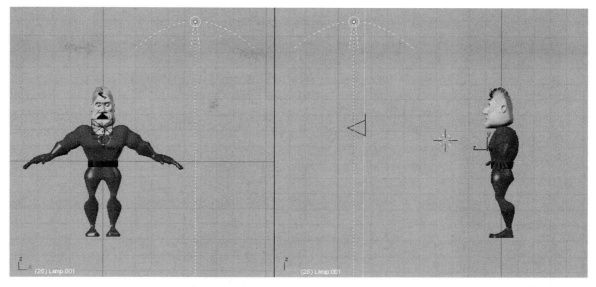

Figure 11.12

A hemi lamp set up to cast light vertically

Figure 11.13

Captain Blender lit by a vertical hemi

Sun

The sun lamp has the same uniform directional properties as the hemi lamp. Like the hemi, it will result in a uniform angle of lighting for all subjects in a scene, regardless of the lamp's position in the 3D space. All that matters is the angle of the lamp. This resembles the sun in that sunlight, because of the distance of its origin, behaves as a uniformly directed light source. The differences between sun and hemi lamps are that the sun lights only from a single direction, and that you can enable ray shadows with a sun lamp. As you can see in Figure 11.14, the lighting is much starker than that of the hemi.

In spite of its name, the sun lamp should not be mistaken for the actual sun. You will probably need more than a single sun lamp to light a sunny outdoor scene convincingly. The main thing the sun lamp provides is a way to light multiple objects from a uniform direction, for example casting parallel shadows with only one light source.

Area

Area lamps represent light that emanates from a large area and can be used in certain circumstances to represent the kind of light that comes from the sun, the moon, or an explosion. These lights are also often used in architectural rendering to show light from windows or banks of fluorescent lights, and in product shots or any situation in which a real-life photographer or cinematographer would use diffusers.

Figure 11.14

Sun lamp

Figure 11.15
Area light

As you can see in Figure 11.15, an area light can be useful to illuminate somebody peering into a fridge or being abducted by aliens, but it is unlikely to become your first-choice lamp for lighting characters in most situations.

Lighting Setups

In most cases, it is advisable to use more than one lamp for lighting subjects. With more-complex scenes, it is almost a necessity. For the simplest lighting possible, a hemi lamp is tough to beat, but it will not result in the most attractive render.

Three-Point Lighting

Three-point lighting involves using three lamps, typically spots, with the main illumination provided by the *key* light, shadows softened by a low energy *fill* light, and highlights provided around the shaded portions of the form by backlighting, as shown in Figure 11.16.

Any introductory textbook on lighting for film, photography, or CG will inevitably cover three-point lighting. It is such a ubiquitous and widely recognized approach to lighting that hit has become almost a cliché. This, combined with the fact that it almost never occurs in nature and has fallen out of favor with filmmakers working in naturalistic styles, has led to something of a backlash against it among some CG practitioners.

Figure 11.16

Three-point lighting setup

Three-point lighting isn't naturalistic. But then, neither are bugging eyes, slow motion bullets, or stretchy human heads. They are all cases of artistic license taken with realism to achieve a visual effect. As such, three-point lighting can have very effective uses. It was developed as a means to use light to highlight and define shape, which was a basic goal in early cinema and remains a basic goal in most of 3D animation. It should be regarded as an important tool, but you should also keep in mind that using stark three-point lighting can give a "studio portraiture" look to your work, so it should be used judiciously.

The three images shown in Figure 11.17 demonstrate the purpose served by each of the three lamps in the three-point lighting setup shown here. In the first render, only the key light is on. This mostly illuminates the subject, but leaves the far side of the subject completely in the dark and undefined. The second image adds a low-energy fill light to the character's right side. This reduces the intensity of the shadows and brings the rest of the face into view. Note that even with two spots, the contrast is considerably starker than with a single hemi lamp, as you saw previously. Also, note that the fill light is set not to cast shadows. You don't want double shadows. The third render adds the backlight, which brings out the definition of areas that are in relative shadow and adds a dramatic aspect to the scene that is lacking with only the key and fill light.

Figure 11.19

Captain Blender lit with a spot and a hemi

Rendering Your Animation

Rendering involves calculating all the various information Blender knows about the lighting and materials of a scene and producing a fully realized, detailed visual representation of the scene. When you are working in the 3D viewport, the scene is necessarily very much simplified. Rendering gives you the real deal. Depending on the complexity of the scene, the vertex count, and the light effects that you want to emulate, the process of rendering can take a long time and use a lot of computing resources. In this book, you will be using the default Blender internal renderer to do the rendering. Blender also has native support for YafRay, an open source ray tracer, and export scripts are available for a number of other renderers. Native support for several commercial renderers is currently under development. Although other rendering engines have many features that the Blender internal renderer lacks, the Blender internal renderer is relatively fast and is a good choice for animation.

Render Buttons

The render buttons area enables you to set the various parameters and options for rendering your scene. In the Output tab, you identify the location on your hard drive in which the finished animation renders will be sent. The default for this is the /tmp/ directory, which is created automatically if it does not already exist. This is fine for very casual renders, but if you are rendering work that you want to do more with, for example rendering a sequence of stills with the intention of later sequencing them in the Sequence Editor, it is a good idea to set a specific directory for the project. You can do this by simply putting the name of the desired output directory in the top field on the Output tab. Note that the directory's name must end with either a slash or a backslash (Blender considers both the same here) to specify that is a directory, as you can see in Figure 11.20. Without this, the name will be treated as a simple filename prefix and the files will be placed in the directory above.

The Render tab, shown in Figure 11.21, enables you to select options related to the quality and size of the render. It enables you to toggle features such as ray tracing and radiosity and to select between Blender's internal renderer and the YafRay ray tracer, which is also directly compatible with Blender. OSA (oversampling) determines the degree of antialiasing Blender will apply to the render (broadly speaking, the higher this value the better the image will look, but the render time will increase greatly). For very quick renders, this should be turned off or set to 5, and a smaller than full size render can be made by selecting the 75%, 50%, or 25% buttons. The Render button on this tab will make a full render of the current frame according to your specifications. If you render a single frame in this way, the render will not be saved automatically. You will need to press Ctrl+F3 to save the render to a file.

The Format tab shown in Figure 11.22 gives various options for the size and aspect ratio of the render. In addition, it enables you to specify the output file format. I discuss the pros and cons of some of these options in the next section.

The Anim tab, shown in Figure 11.23, enables you to render and play back rendered animations. If you are outputting a sequence from the Sequence Editor, you must select Do Sequence; otherwise, the render will be based upon the camera view in the 3D space.

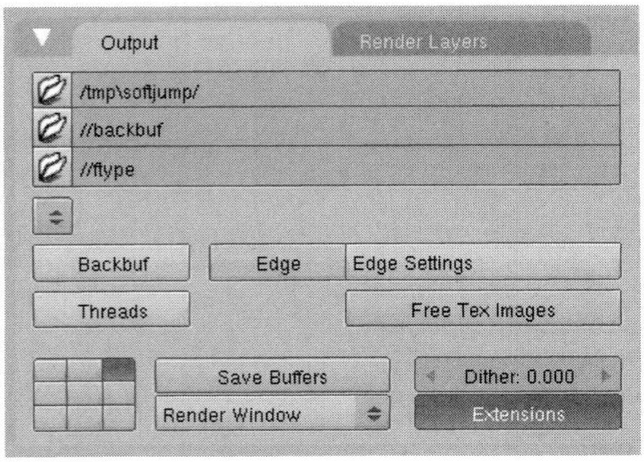

Figure 11.20
Render buttons Output tab

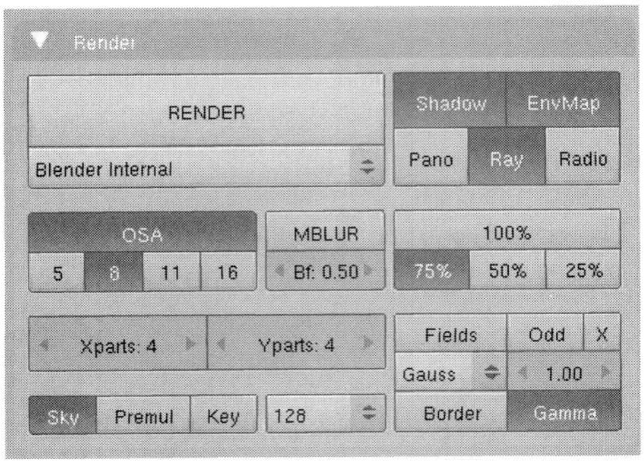

Figure 11.21
Render tab

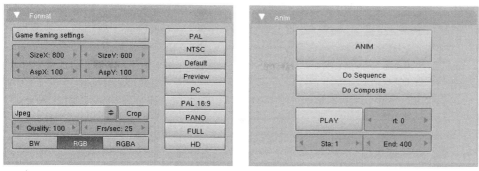

Figure 11.22
Format tab

Figure 11.23
Anim tab

Output Formats

The Format tab offers a variety of choices for the type of file to which you output your rendered animation. The choice you make can make a big difference, so make sure to select the appropriate output format for what you're trying to do.

Movies and Stills

The first choice you need to make is whether to output the file to a movie or a still format. Most people eventually want their animation to be in some kind of movie format, but this does not necessarily mean that you should select a movie format here. Still formats have the advantage of being easy to stop and start rendering in the middle for whatever reason (you simply pick back up rendering the next still from the last still you rendered), which cannot be done with most movie formats. If, for whatever reason you must kill a render midway, you will probably lose the whole output if it was a movie file. Remember also that rendering animation is likely to take hours, even days (actually, the sky's the limit) on an ordinary computer. If you have a power outage three days into a week-long render, you might want to have those three days worth of stills. Working with still sequences is very easy in the Blender Sequence Editor. You can do your initial renders to still frames and then render the sequence to a movie file in the Sequence Editor.

When you do finally render to a movie format, select a format with the appropriate degree of compression. Uncompressed file formats such as AVI Raw will create extremely large files. Unless you know for sure that you want an AVI Raw file, I would not recommend selecting this option. If you are rendering a movie for display on the Internet, a good option is AVI Codec, with an appropriate codec selected. MPEG4 is a compact and common codec for this kind of file.

Alpha Channel

One advantage that certain formats have over others is the presence of alpha channel information. In addition to RGB values, certain formats, such as Targa and PNG (but not JPEG or TIFF), allow a value to determine the transparency of portions of the image. By default, the background, which appears blue in renders, has a zero alpha value when rendered to these formats using the RGBA option on the Format tab of the render buttons. As you will see in the next section, this is often necessary for compositing tasks.

Off-Site Rendering

As mentioned previously, the rendering process is very demanding of computer resources. Although you can do a lot on an ordinary personal computer, certain things greatly increase the memory and time required to render your scenes. High vertex counts, large numbers of particles, lighting effects such as ambient occlusion and radiosity, high OSA values, some motion blur effects, and other factors can create a scene that takes ages to render and brings most personal computers to their knees. Even fairly simple scenes can easily become computationally expensive if these kinds of effects are present.

Rendering remains one of the prohibitive areas of animation; however, the available options are increasing. ResPower at `www.respower.com` offers rendering services for Blender users, currently for the very reasonable price of $20 per month, with the option to quit at any time. This price is exclusive to Blender users, and users of other 3D software packages can pay up to 100 times this for comparable services. The $20-per-month package for Blender users limits renders to a maximum of 15 minutes per frame, but their compute nodes are powerful enough that the service is very useful even given this restriction. Other inexpensive options are also available to Blender users who require more render time per frame, up to an hour per frame for $60. I used ResPower's service for most of the rendering of the animations used for this book. Check their website for up-to-date pricing and offers.

Another promising possibility for off-site rendering is a project just getting under way to create distributed rendering networks, which make use of many different users' idle processor time. The Big and Ugly Rendering Project (BURP) is based upon the Berkeley Open Infrastructure for Network Computing (BOINC), which is software that enables computation-intensive tasks to be shared across a large network of computers, using the free processor time of many different machines to complete the tasks more efficiently than if a single machine were working on it. Members of the BURP project would allow network rendering to be done on their computers at a low priority when the computers are not being used and collect points toward rendering their own work at a higher priority on the network. Membership and use of BURP would be free, and if a large number of users were participating, rendering could be done very quickly. At present, BURP is in a pre-Alpha development stage, however, and it is often unstable or not accepting job submissions at all. Still, it is worth keeping an eye on. You can see the project at `http://burp.boinc.dk/`.

Editing in the Sequence Editor

It is often desirable to render animation frames to individual image files and to concatenate them into sequences in a separate step by using the Sequence Editor. It might be desirable to break things down even further than single frames, rendering certain portions of a single image separately from other portions and putting them together later, before doing a final sequence render. This is called compositing, and Blender has a very powerful node-based compositing system that can be used for advanced compositing tasks. The node system is beyond the scope of this book, but simple compositing tasks can be accomplished without using nodes, and I will look at one such simple example here to give you an example of how the Sequence Editor works.

Before beginning the Sequence Editor, I rendered the animation in the file `run.blend` and sent its output files to the directory `/tmp/run/`, as described in the previous section. I also rendered the file `background.blend` to the directory `/tmp/background/`. I rendered both to PNG files, and for the walk animation I used the RGBA option to make sure that the foreground image had alpha information encoded. You can find the rendered stills on the DVD accompanying the book, which will save you from having to do these renders yourself.

Adding Media

To use the Sequence Editor, you will want two instances of the Sequence Editor window open in your workspace. One of the windows should be set to the Sequence View in the output preview drop-down menu in the header, and the other should be set to Image Preview.

In the Sequence View window, press Shift+A to add a sequence strip. As you can see from the options here, there are a number of possibilities for the kind of media you can add. Select Images from the Add Sequence Strip menu and go to the `/tmp/run` directory in the File Browser (or wherever the rendered frames of your foreground are located). Select all the files in the directory with the A key and press Enter. This will take you back to the Sequence view, with a new sequence strip in tow representing the files you just selected, in order. Drag them so that the first frame lines up with frame 1 on the Timeline. With the arrow keys, you can now move through the Timeline and see the animation in the Image Preview window, as shown in Figure 11.24.

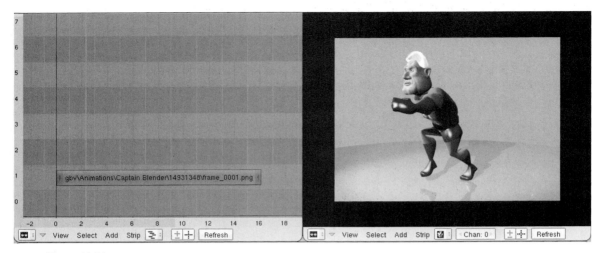

Figure 11.24

Run animation sequence in the Sequence Editor

This is all you need to do to prepare to render to a movie file. You can now go to the render buttons and select your output format just as you would for an ordinary render. Select the start and end frame and the size of the picture, and press Anim, making sure that the Do Sequence button is selected.

Basic Compositing

You can now use a simple compositing feature of the Sequence Editor to drop a new background into the animation. As I mentioned, the background was created and rendered in advance to /tmp/background/.

> This background animation was created with a very simple use of the array modifier, by the way, which you can find out more about in the references listed in Chapter 18.

Add the background animation images as you added the foreground images: press Shift+A and select all the images in the appropriate directory. Drag this strip to be flush with the previous strip. The channels are displayed bottom to top, and alpha information is not calculated by default. So when you put the new strip in channel 2, you do not see any difference in the display. Channel 1, our Captain Blender animation, is still displayed. You can try moving the strips around to see how this changes when the strips are positioned differently. Placing the foreground animation above the background animation will display only the background animation.

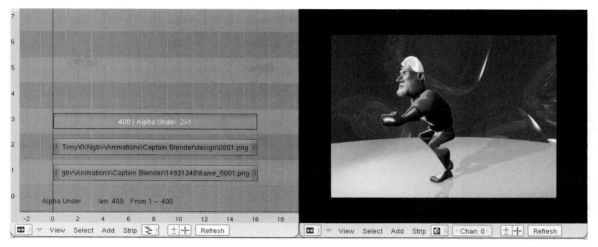

Figure 11.25

A simple composite using Alpha Under

What you want to do is to create a metastrip that combines the two strips in certain ways. Select the foreground strip; then, holding Shift, select the background strip (the order matters here). To add the metastrip, press Shift+A as you would to add any other media. Select Alpha Under.

The resulting metastrip replaces its component strips in the display and causes the background to show through the zero alpha areas of the foreground. Blender's default background has an alpha value of zero, regardless of what its RGB values are. The resulting composite looks like the image previewed in Figure 11.25.

You can now render the sequence exactly as it appears in the Image Preview.

Sound

As you saw in Chapter 8, it is possible to add .wav files to the Sequence Editor for syncing. It is also possible to create a mixdown from sound files in the Sequence Editor and output this as a single sound file. However, at present it is not possible in the official release (2.42) to output video and sound to a single, complete video file in Windows and Macintosh. The Linux build of Blender does have this capability, however, with full ffmpeg support. Full integration of this feature into all official Blender builds is an eagerly awaited development. There are some alternative software packages available to create files with both video and audio. I describe these options in Chapter 17.

In the next chapter, you will take a brief look at Blender's powerful Python scripting capability, and learn how to use currently existing Python scripts to make your job as an animator easier.

COMPOSITE NODES

In addition to enabling you to create node-based materials, Blender's Nodes system also allows you to apply advanced image compositing techniques that are tightly integrated with the render pipeline. One of the basic sources of input for the Composite Nodes system is Render Layers. In the Render Layers tab in the Render buttons area, you can separate elements of your image so that they render to different render layers and in that way can be used as separate inputs into the composite nodes. When you select Do Composite in the render buttons and start a render, the output will be the final result of the network of composite nodes.

To use nodes for compositing, open a Nodes Editor window, toggle the Composite Notes icon button (the Materials icon button is on by default), and select Use Nodes. When you do this, a render layer input node for render layer 1 and a composite node will appear. You can add new nodes by pressing the spacebar and selecting the node you want from the menu. Here is a very simple nodes setup with two render layers.

Render layer 1 includes the foreground with the monkey, and render layer 2 includes a plane upon which the monkey rests. These are rendered separately. The output from layer 2 is then used as input for a blur filter node, and the blurred output of this node is used as the backdrop in an Alpha Over node, which lays the monkey render over the background. The output of this node is sent to the composite node, which becomes the final output. The viewer node can be attached at any point to allow a better look at the composite at that point. Both the viewer's output and the composite image can also be viewed in the UV/Image Editor window.

More detail on using composite nodes is beyond the scope of this book. Check Chapter 18 for pointers on where to go to learn more.

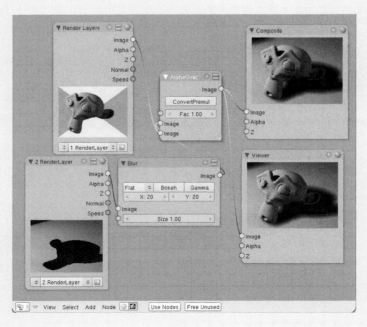

CHAPTER 12

Using Python Scripts

Python is a high-level, object-oriented scripting language. Powerful and relatively easy to learn, it is an obvious choice as a standard scripting language for an open source 3D application such as Blender. With Python scripts, you can automate a great deal of interaction with your 3D objects and scenes, and add functionality without needing to touch actual Blender code. It also has shown itself to be a good way to try out new functionality that can later be incorporated into Blender's C/C++ source.

Experienced programmers will find Python fairly easy to pick up and will quickly see its usefulness as a tool for tweaking 3D objects. Writing scripts in Python, however, is beyond the scope of the book. From the user's standpoint, Blender's Python scripting capability means access to numerous useful utilities and plug-ins, and this chapter will show you what some of them are and how you can use them. You will learn how to install and execute Python scripts, survey some pertinent scripts bundled with the standard Blender distribution, and focus on some particularly interesting and useful scripts for character animation tasks that are not included with the standard distribution.

- Installing and Executing Python Scripts
- Standard Scripts
- Extended Functionality with Scripts

Installing and Executing Python Scripts

Installing Python scripts so that they can be accessed through menus is very simple. Any Python script placed in your Blender installation's script directory is installed and will be recognized and placed into appropriate menus when Blender is started up next. The location of the script directory depends on your OS. For Windows, it is under your main installation directory in `.blender/scripts`. In OSX, you'll find it in the installation directory under `blender.app/Contents/MacOS/.blender/scripts`. To access it on a Mac, you will need to navigate to the scripts folder through a terminal window, as the Mac OS X Finder will not allow you to access the `.blender` folder directly. In Linux, you will probably find the scripts directory under `~/.blender/scripts`.

Information in the script's own header determines where the script can be accessed from the Blender desktop. In Listing 12.1, you can see an example of a standard Blender Python script header.

Listing 12.1

Standard Blender Python Script Header

```
#!BPY
"""
Name: 'Clean Meshes'
Blender: 242
Group: 'Mesh'
Tooltip: 'Clean unused data from all selected mesh objects.'
"""
__author__ = ["Campbell Barton"]
__url__ = ("blender", "elysiun",
"http://members.iinet.net.au/~cpbarton/ideasman/")
__version__ = "0.1"
__bpydoc__ = """\
Clean Meshes
Cleans unused data from selected meshes
"""
```

The Name field, obviously, contains the script's name. The Blender field contains the version number of Blender for which the script has been tested. The Group field tells Blender where to make the script accessible. In this case, the script belongs to the "Mesh" group. This means that it can be accessed through the Scripts → Mesh menu in the Script window, shown in Figure 12.1. More directly, it can be accessed through the Mesh → Scripts menu in the 3D viewport header when in Edit mode, as shown in Figure 12.2. Most script groups are accessible through the Scripts window, and many are available through appropriate context-sensitive menus in the 3D viewport, UV window, and elsewhere. Scripts in the Help group are available through Blender's Help menu.

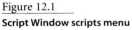

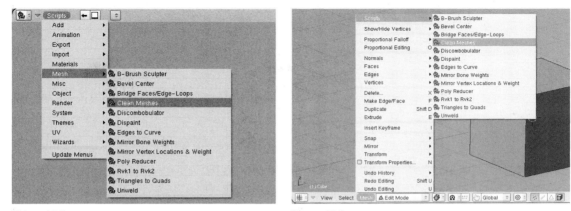

Figure 12.1
Script Window scripts menu

Figure 12.2
Another place to find Mesh scripts

When Python scripts appear as menu items, executing them is simply a matter of selecting the script in the menu. However, it is possible to run any Python script from any location by opening the text file of the script up in Blender's text editor, as shown in Figure 12.3. To execute the open script, press Alt+P or select Run Python Script from the File menu.

Standard Scripts

The standard distribution of Blender comes with a variety of scripts included. This section takes a brief look at a selection of some of the standard scripts that are most likely to be of

Figure 12.3
Opening a script in the text window

use in character modeling and animation with the current version of Blender. In most cases, using the scripts is self-explanatory when the script is run. This section is intended to give you an idea of some of the kinds of things you can do with scripts.

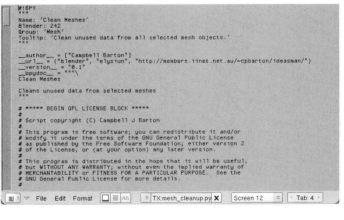

If you don't see a script that does what you want here, there is still a good chance that the script you're looking for has been written and is available on the Web somewhere. Check the resources listed in Chapter 18 for some suggestions on where to start looking.

Object Scripts

Scripts in Blender are contributed by users, and the decision about their grouping depends on the writer of the scripts. In general, the scripts are grouped intuitively. Scripts that function within Edit mode that alter the mesh or its characteristics are found in the Mesh Script menu, whereas ones that function on object-level data or use two or more objects to generate an effect usually reside in the Object Script menu.

Figure 12.4

**Using Apply Defor-
mation on an arma-
ture-deformed
NURBS tube**

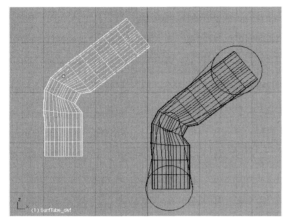

Apply Deformation When executed with a modified object selected, this script makes a copy of the object with modifier deformations applied, without applying the modifier to the original object. This enables you to use modifiers such as armatures and subsurf as modeling tools where you apply your modifications to obtain a static, finished mesh. But it can also be used with other object types, such as in the case of the armature-modified NURBS tube shown in Figure 12.4.

Axis Orientation Copy When more than one object is selected, this script sets the current axis orientation of the selected objects to be the same as the last selected (active) object. In Figure 12.5, the axes of the right cube are copied to the left cube. The left cube does not change its orientation, but its local axis is now set identically to the one from the right cube.

Figure 12.5

**Copying the axis ori-
entation from one
object to another**

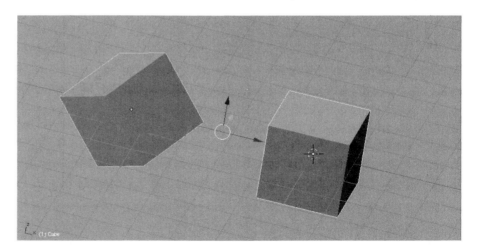

Batch Object Name Edit When this script is executed with a group of objects selected, the menu shown in Figure 12.6 appears, giving a number of options for edits to be made on all object names. When you select the kind of edit you want to make, a dialog box will appear with the appropriate fields, along with an option to apply the name change to associated object data as well.

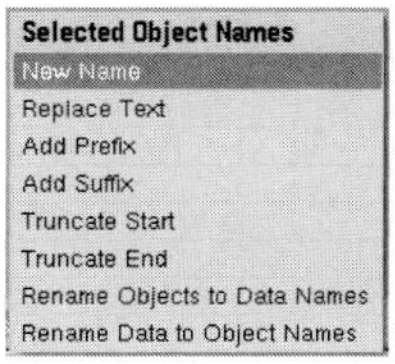

Object Name Editor This script provides another interface for naming multiple objects at once, which enables you to select the objects to be named from within the interface, as shown in Figure 12.7.

UV Copy This script enables you to copy the UV values from one mesh object to another mesh that shares the geometry of the first. This script does not require that the second object have the same seam pattern, or indeed any seam pattern at all because no unwrapping is involved. UV information, including mapped images, is copied as-is onto the second mesh. This enables you to do the UV mapping only once and to apply the resulting UV coordinate information to multiple objects.

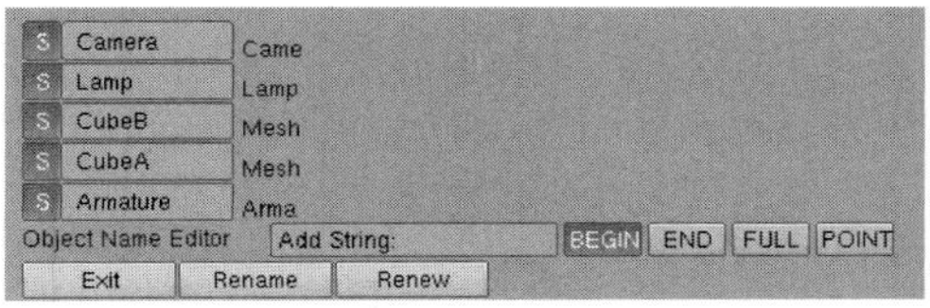

Figure 12.6

The batch naming menu

Figure 12.7

Object Name Editor interface

Mesh Scripts

These scripts usually alter the mesh data itself, but the distinction between them and many of the object scripts is sometimes arbitrary, and the main difference is simply that these scripts are accessible under a different menu.

B-Brush Sculpter This script provides an alternative mesh modeling method to the box and extrusion modeling methods you have used since Chapter 2 in which vertices can be displaced directly by the mouse. This results in a very easy way to make organic-looking modifications to the surface of a mesh, as shown in the example in Figure 12.8. This script provides several options for editing including options for displacement types and mirroring. Note that this functionality will soon be replaced by a fully integrated Sculpt mode, which will be coded directly into Blender. At the time of this writing, CVS test builds are available with this feature, but it remains to be seen whether it will be incorporated into a full release by the time this book goes to print.

Bevel Center This tool allows sharp edges to be beveled, as shown in Figure 12.9. Selecting the optional recursive bevel will create a more finished look, as can be seen on the cube at the right. The difference between this and Blender's built-in Bevel function is that this script will bevel selected edges, whereas the built-in tool works only on the entire mesh.

Figure 12.8

Sculpting on a sub-
divided, subsurfed
cube with the B-
Brush Sculpt tool

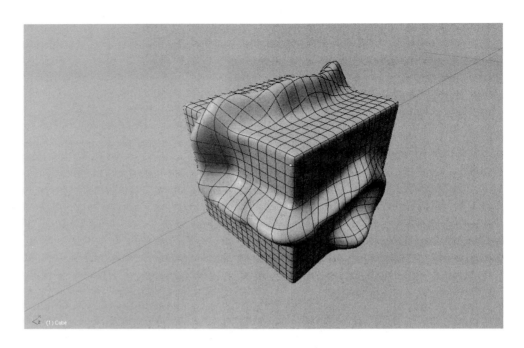

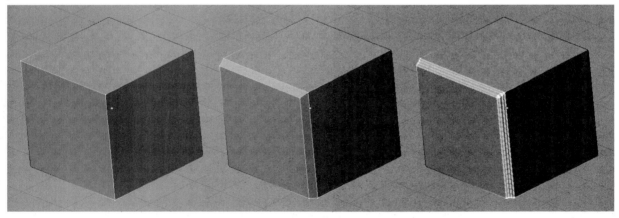

Figure 12.9

A cube with selected edges beveled by the Bevel Center script and with a recursive bevel applied

Bridge Faces/Edge Loops This script takes two edge loops and bridges them with faces, as shown in Figure 12.10. It is not necessary that both edge loops have the same number of vertices, although mismatches are likely to result in triangles being used in the bridge. Several options for calculating the bridge are available in the event of vert count mismatches. This can be a quick-and-dirty way to attach an ear to a head.

Mirror Vertex Locations and Weight This script enables you to make a mesh perfectly symmetrical across the X axis. It functions best if the vertex counts and edge geometry on the right and left are the same, and if the two sides are already fairly close to each other. However, it will attempt to make any mesh symmetrical, even meshes that do not have symmetrical geometry.

In addition to mirroring vertex locations, this script also creates mirrored weight painting for bone weights in a way that is sensitive to the standard Blender right and left bone-naming conventions.

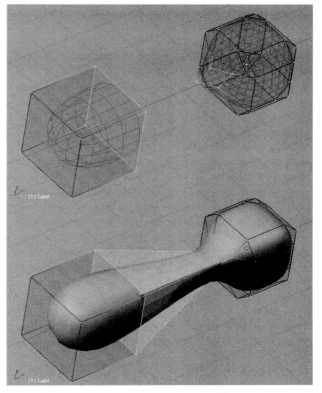

Figure 12.10

Creating a bridge between two edge loops

Poly Reducer This script reduces the polygon count of a mesh in an intelligent way. The resultant mesh is simpler and less detailed than the original mesh. When the script is run, a dialog box appears with a variety of options for the reduction, including how much to reduce by and how faithful to remain to the original mesh. The quality of the reduction can also be varied over a single mesh by using vertex weighting.

This script is excellent for creating low-resolution versions of your character meshes for long-distance shots and for crowd situations, because it attempts to retain quads when reducing the poly count.

Triangles to Quads This script converts triangles in a mesh to quads where possible.

Animation Scripts

The scripts in the Animation group have no particular object they work on. They may work on armatures, Ipos, or other objects.

Armature Symmetry When applied to an armature, this script will symmetrize an asymmetrical armature in an analogous way to the way the Mirror Vertex Locations and Weights script works on meshes.

BlenderLipSynchro This script allows a certain amount of automation of the lip sync process by importing phoneme sequences exported from specialized lip sync software such as JLipSync, which is described in slightly more detail in Chapter 17. Phonemes in the imported sequences can be associated with shapes, which can then be automatically keyed according to the location of the phoneme on the Timeline.

I can't comment on the quality of the results of these automated lip syncing methods because I have not seen any examples of completed lip synced animations using them, but there a number of areas in which I can foresee they may run into challenges. The first crucial factor is the quality of the exported phoneme file, and its accuracy with respect to the original sound file if it is automatically generated. Also, if realistic lip syncing is desired, some coarticulation must be factored into the lip syncing, and this might involve more than simply blending from one phoneme to the next. It seems likely that a considerable amount of manual tweaking might be necessary to yield good results, and given the ease with which lip sync movements can be keyed manually to begin with, it is not clear that the automation would greatly reduce the work involved. Still, the script definitely seems to be worth experimenting on.

Shape Widget Wizard This script enables you to create handy 3D slider controls for shape keys, which can be useful in cases in which your shapes are not already driven by bones. There are a number of options for settings for the sliders; you can determine the range the slider represents. You can also activate up to four shapes at once on the same slider, with several options for how the shapes interact as the slider's value changes. In Figure 12.11, you see an example of the simplest shape key widget: a slider ranging from the -1 value to the 1 value on a single shape on the default cube, a tapered, pyramid-like shape called Taper. The diamond shape in the slider is constrained to moving up and down; its top value corresponds with the 1 value of the shape, and its bottom value corresponds with -1.

Trajectory When the Trajectory script is activated, it turns on a graphical display of the trajectory, followed by a selected object as it moves through 3D space, as in Figure 12.12. Keyframes show up along the trajectory as yellow squares. The distance that the highlighted trajectory extends before and behind the object can be adjusted.

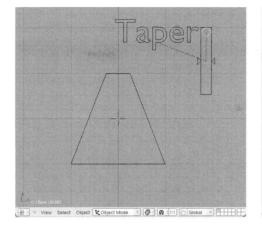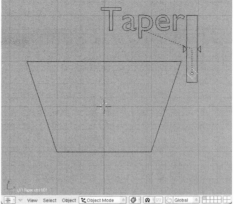

Figure 12.11

A widget generated by the Shape Widget Wizard script

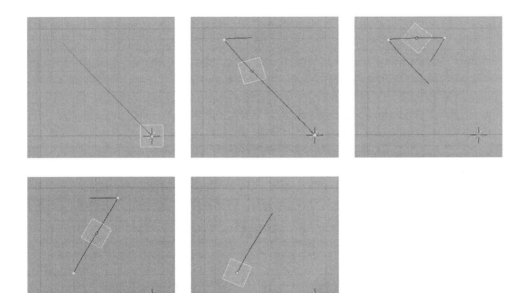

Figure 12.12

Drawing an animated object's trajectory

Extended Functionality with Scripts

There are several potentially useful script-based tools currently under development outside of the standard Blender distribution. You should be aware that any time you move outside of the realm of the standard distribution with Blender or any other open-source software you are more likely to run into bugs or incompatibilities than if you stick with the standard releases. (A file you create in an unofficial build of Blender might not be loadable in an official version, and thus on any render farms you might choose to use.) This includes using CVS development builds (which are often available) and Python scripts. It is worth proceeding with care. Always back up your work, particularly when working with software whose effects you are unsure of.

BlenderPeople

Roland Hess' BlenderPeople is a suite of Python scripts that enables you to create convincing crowd scenes of an arbitrarily large scale (within the limits of your computing resources, of course). Using a single armature (or small set of armatures), a single mesh character (or a small set of mesh characters) and a collection of pertinent actions that are combined using nonlinear animation, BlenderPeople can automate crowd movement over the ground and simulate a variety of crowd behaviors, from fighting, to marching, to milling around an object. An example of a melee generated by BlenderPeople can be seen in Figure 12.13.

Figure 12.13

A still from a battle scene generated by the BlenderPeople script

Actors' movements over the ground are controlled by weight painting of the ground object; the actors tend to move toward higher-weighted areas and will completely avoid zero-weighted vertices. The actors' movements are also influenced by parameters set for each individual actor. Actors can be set to vary in their speed, the degree to which they stick with others on their own team, their strength in attack or defense, their degree of cowardice, and even their intellect. Hierarchies can also be set up so that some actors are subordinate to others and follow their leaders.

BlenderPeople's character animation capabilities are a recent development, and the system remains highly experimental, but it has a great deal of potential, and I encourage you to give it a try. Be aware that getting up to speed with it is not trivial. The BlenderPeople software, a sample crowd animation created with BlenderPeople, and the necessary BlenderPeople user documentation in PDF format can be found on the DVD accompanying this book. You certainly need to read the documentation.

In addition to a recent Python installation, you need a MySQL database server on your machine and the appropriate Python modules to interface with it. These components are all freely available online, but you have to check the appropriate documentation for installing and using them.

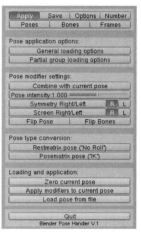

Figure 12.14

The Pose Handler top panel

Library Tools

For any serious project, it is important to be able to save and reuse objects and datablocks. The library scripts provide tools to make this easier.

Pose Handler

The Blender Pose handler by Basil_Fawlty is a tool that enables poses to be stored and imported from file to file. It is a powerful and versatile script with a lot of options. Figure 12.14 shows the top panel of the script's interface, with the options for applying a loaded pose to the currently selected armature. Figure 12.15 shows the bone selection interface, which enables you to choose which bones' information will be stored. The script can be found on the DVD.

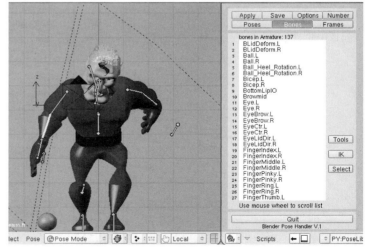

Figure 12.15

Selecting bones to include in the saved pose

Blender Library

The Blender Library is a script by Mariano Hidalgo that enables you to save any type of object to an organized library, with multiple levels of categorization and preview images. It looks to be a potentially very useful tool, but unfortunately as of this writing it does not seem to be up to date with Blender version 2.42, and there appear to be some problems in exporting objects to the library and handling materials. Nevertheless, it is worth mentioning, and several users have reported success in using it. Keep an eye on that project here: `http://uselessdreamer.byethost32.com/blender_library_intro.html`.

Part III of this book takes a look at how Blender has been used in large-scale projects, requiring the reuse and sharing of 3D data. Looking at how the *Elephants Dream* and *Plumiferos* teams handle these tasks will yield even more insight into how to use Blender's tools to create first-rate animation projects.

These characters, created by Zoltan Miklosi, demonstrate some of the incredible power and flexibility Blender provides for realistic character modeling.

These scenes are from the open-source movie *Elephants Dream,* the result of the Blender Foundation's Orange Project. It was intended to showcase Blender's power as an animation tool and also to spur the development of needed production functionality.

The Orange Project consisted of a core team of eight people who created the film with the help of actors, a scriptwriter, and volunteers to contribute such things as texture photography and additional artwork. Coders from the Blender developer community worked on software to meet the needs of the production. The film and all its production files are included on the accompanying DVD and also freely available for download from www.elephantsdream.org.

By Sacha Goedegebure (Sago). Sago is known for his humorous and some-times grotesque images and animations. His short animation *Man in Man*, winner of the Blender Foundation's Suzanna Award for best animation in 2006, can be seen on the accompanying DVD.

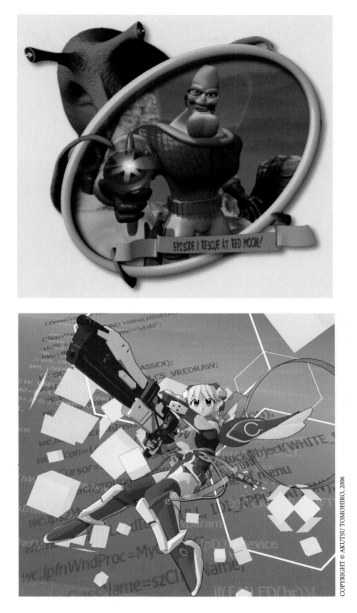

Top, by Trevor Jacobs; bottom, by Akutsu Tomohiro. Here are couple of examples of less realistic styles possible with Blender. Jacobs' animation can be seen on the accompanying DVD. Akutsu's image here is an excellent example of toon-style shading.

This collection of characters is from the upcoming feature-length animated film *Plumíferos*.

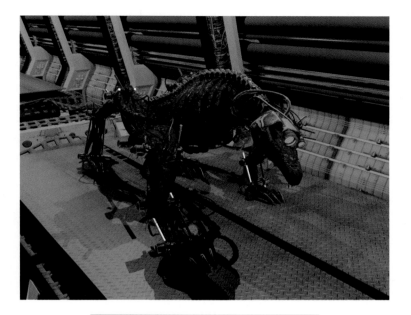

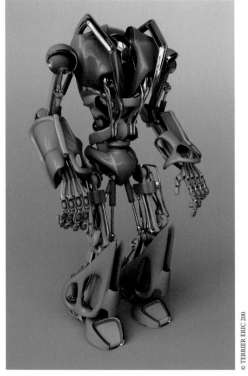

Eric Terrier's realistic science fiction characters are also featured in an
animation sample on the accompanying DVD.

"to the competition"   Bu||[X]2006

Top: by Mauro Bonecchi; bottom: "Super WuMan," from a concept and design by Sacha Goedegebure (Sago), was modeled and animated by Andy Dolphin (AndyD). These further demonstrate the variety of stylistic options available, and how textures and materials can help to make an image more realistic or cartoony.

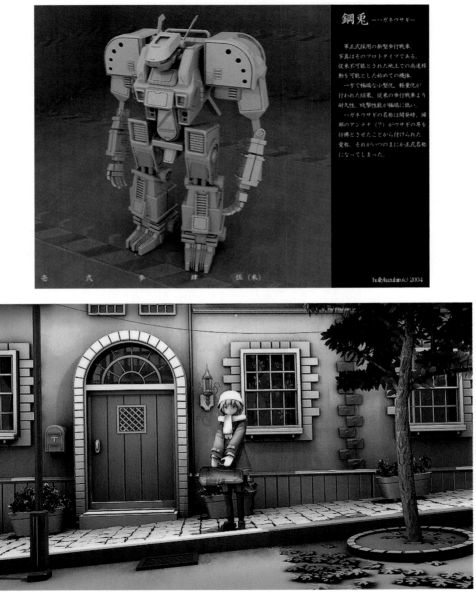

As different as they are from each other, Yuichi Miura's images both show the unmistakeable influence of the Japanese anime style.

Top: Scott Wilkinson's "Ex Nihilo" is an example of highly realistic portraiture. Bottom: Jonathan Williamson's "Pilot" focuses on full-figure modeling and posing.

David Revoy's animated short "The Little Fairy," as well as a `.blend` file containing the rigged model of the main character, can be found on the accompanying DVD.

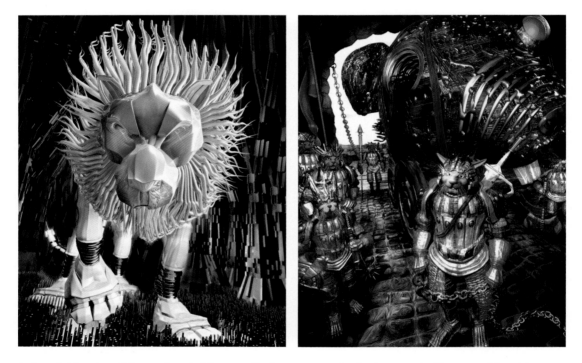

Robert J. Tiess's striking and varied images display a range of techniques and effects possible with Blender.

Left: by Robert J. Tiess; right: by Derek Marsh.

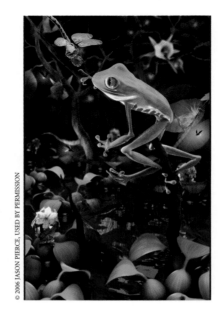

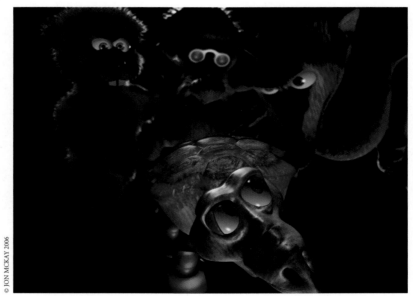

These images by Jason Pierce and Jon McKay make use of lighting, color, texture, and contrast to create vivid animal character images.

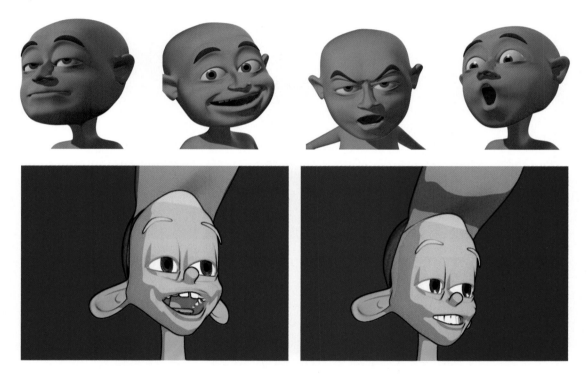

The top character was created by Andy Dolphin (AndyD), who has produced several highly recommended tutorials for Blender users. His tutorial on lip sync and facial animation is part of the official online documentation, and can be found at http://en.wikibooks.org/wiki/Blender_3D:_Noob_to_Pro/
Advanced_Tutorials/Advanced_Animation/Guided_tour/Mesh/Shape/Sync
The bottom character, "Zhar," is copyright 2006 Andersen Publishing; character modelling and rigging was done by Norm Dwyer.

These images are from a short titled "Suburban Plight," by Colin Levy which makes use of motion tracking software and Blender's compositing functionality to incorporate animated CG images into live action video footage. You can find some excellent tutorials on doing this on Colin's website at www.peerlessproductions.com.

Blender in Production

Blender is a *comparatively new contender in the world of professional quality CG animation, and it is worthwhile to take a look at some of the major animation projects that have used Blender as their primary tool. In this part, you look at the short "open movie" Elephants Dream and the feature length commercial film Plumiferos, which is currently in production. There is a lot to learn from each of these productions, both in how Blender was incorporated into the workflow and also in the details of how the animators used Blender to rig and animate expressive and engaging characters. The rigs you'll look at from those productions will provide you with a lot of interesting ideas and approaches to add to what you learned in Parts I and II about creating and animating characters. Seeing how Blender can be used in this environment might even inspire you to think bigger when planning your own projects.*

CHAPTER 13

Full-Scale Productions: *Elephants Dream* and *Plumiferos*

As Blender's capabilities improve, it has become an increasingly attractive alternative for use in creating full-scale, professional-quality 3D animation projects. This chapter introduces two recent projects that mark Blender's transition into the world of professional animated film production. The first is the Blender Foundation's own *Elephants Dream*, an ambitious short film that has received a great deal of attention not only for the content and quality of the film itself but also for the unprecedented manner in which it was released—with both the film and the files used to create it licensed to be freely available to the public to copy and modify. The second project you will look at is the currently in-production Argentinean feature film *Plumiferos,* a full-scale production intended for traditional box office release.

You'll also take a brief look at some of the questions related to using free software in professional production. There are sometimes misunderstandings about the implications of using open-source software on for-profit projects, and talk about releasing content under a Creative Commons license can sometimes obscure the issue even further. This chapter begins by clarifying what these various licenses are and what they might mean to you and your project.

- GPL, Creative Commons, and the Blender Artistic License

- *Elephants Dream,* the World's First "Open Movie"

- A Preview of *Plumiferos*

GPL, Creative Commons, and the Blender Artistic License

Any discussion I attempt of licenses or copyright-related topics needs to be prefaced with the standard disclaimer: I am not a lawyer, and if you have any questions about how you should proceed with licensing or handling of copyrights, you should seek qualified legal advice. Anything I say on the subject is accurate to the best of my knowledge, but I might be insufficiently informed, out of date, or just plain wrong about details. I'll include links to refer to the source documents where pertinent, but nevertheless, if you have legal questions, you should not rely on this book solely for your answers.

The license under which you release your work codifies the permissions that you are granting the public with regard to your work. Regardless of which license you choose to release the work under, you are the owner of the copyright for what you create. Individuals, companies, and organizations can feel fully at ease using open-source software in their creative pipelines, knowing that their own rights with regard to their work will not be affected.

With that said, let's have a look at these licenses.

GNU Public License (GPL)

The GPL is one of the best known and most widely used licenses for what is referred to as free software or open-source software. Blender's code is released under the GPL. You can read the full text of the GPL here: `http://www.gnu.org/copyleft/gpl.html`. The license was created by Richard Stallman, who is known for his advocacy of freely distributable, freely modifiable code. The GPL states, in essence, that the licensed code can be copied, modified, and redistributed without restriction by anybody, provided that modifications are clearly identified as such and that the subsequent derived code is also released under the GPL and according to the guidelines set out in the GPL.

The GPL is fairly strict in its insistence that free code interact primarily with other free code, although explicit exceptions are made for operating systems. Issues can arise with the use of nonopen libraries or APIs, so proprietary plugins for GPL software or GPL-derived plugins written for proprietary software can potentially infringe on the GPL. Other licenses exist, such as the Limited GPL and the Berkeley Software Distribution (BSD) license, which allow more freedom of interaction between free and proprietary code. You can learn more about the BSD license here: `http://en.wikipedia.org/wiki/BSD_license`.

The writer of the code always retains the copyright to the code, and although that person can release non-GPL'd copies of their code at any time, any code already released under the GPL will remain so. Furthermore, with a code base as broad as Blender's, there are numerous contributing coders and therefore many copyright holders, all of whom would have to agree to change the GPL status of future releases of their code if such a thing were to be considered (it isn't).

The GPL deals with software. Specifically, it deals with publicly distributed software. You can do whatever you want with GPL code within the confines of your own project, and licensing of derived code need never become an issue until you decide to release your code to the world. In-house plugins or alterations are not a problem and do not need to follow any special criteria. Furthermore, the GPL bears *no relation at all* to content created with the software. Content you create with Blender or any other GPL'd software is copyrighted to you in exactly the same way as content created in any other kind of software.

Creative Commons License

The Creative Commons license does cover content and is an option for licensing your artistic creations. The decision to license your work under the Creative Commons license is entirely unrelated to the tools you used to create the work. Using open-source software does not obligate you to release your work under a Creative Commons license.

There are several alternatives for Creative Commons licenses. You can license your work to be freely copiable, but require that the work be attributed to you and that copies of your work be restricted to noncommercial uses. You can allow commercial uses but require attribution, or you can relax the requirement for attribution.

If you want people to be able to freely copy, show, and distribute your work on the Web without fear of copyright repercussions, releasing your work under a noncommercial Creative Commons license might be a good choice. You remain the copyright holder, and you can revoke the license at any time. Your own use of the work (for example, if you sell it or license it for broadcast) might have an impact on whether you can continue to release it under the Creative Commons license if the buyer or broadcaster objects.

Blender Artistic License

The Blender Artistic license is a variation on the Creative Commons license, which applies to images, `.blend` files, and animations. It allows copying and modification of files with some restrictions to ensure attribution. Material hosted on the `www.blender.org` website is required to be released under this license or the more permissive Open Content License. As in the case of the Creative Commons license, releasing work under this license is voluntary on the part of the creator, and is not implied by use of Blender to make the work.

Elephants Dream, the World's First "Open Movie"

Although the Creative Commons license and the GPL are unrelated legally, they are closely aligned in spirit. Both of them acknowledge the importance of sharing ideas and building upon previous work as essential aspects of the creative process, while protecting the right of creators to receive credit for their work and to maintain some control over potential uses. So it was only natural that the first film created by the nonprofit Blender

Foundation, intended primarily to showcase the abilities of the free software package Blender, would be released under the Creative Commons license, with not only the film itself but all the production files relating to the film also freely released. And so it was that *Elephants Dream* became the world's first "open movie."

Elephants Dream (see Figure 13.1) was produced by Ton Roosendaal, founder of the Blender Foundation and chief developer of Blender. The film was directed by Bassam Kurdali, and the rest of the core team included Art Director Andreas Goralczyk, Technical Director Toni Alatalo, and Lead Artists Matt Ebb, Bastian Salmela, and Lee Salvemini. Music and sound effects were composed and recorded by Jan Morgenstern.

The film was intended as a vehicle to demonstrate the potential of Blender in a large-scale production and also to spur development of Blender in areas in which weaknesses became apparent. Production of the film was further constrained to using only open-source software for all visual aspects of the film (the music was not subject to this constraint), which meant that functionality that could not be adequately found in other open-source software, such as professional-quality video compositing, had to be built in to Blender.

The film itself is a dark and enigmatic piece of surrealist art. The story follows the journey of two strange men through the bowels of a bizarre and dangerous mechanical world, exploring the drastically (and eventually fatally) different ways in which the two men perceive their surroundings. To be sure, the story is not everyone's cup of tea. The creators of *Elephants Dream* took the freedom afforded by the software and the Creative Commons release very much to heart, eschewing any pretense of trying to make the film marketable or broadly accessible. Instead, they gave themselves complete creative freedom and created

Figure 13.1

Proog in *Elephants Dream*

a short film that is both visually stunning and thematically provocative. In spite of the abstruseness of its subject matter, the film garnered a considerable amount of press attention for the way it was created and released, including a feature article in *The Wall Street Journal.*

As a demonstration of Blender's capabilities, *Elephants Dream* holds up very well. Using advanced character modeling and animation tools, and specially developed compositing functionality, *Elephants Dream* more than demonstrates that Blender is ready for prime time, visually speaking. Given the time and budgetary restrictions on the production, and considering that many members of the team were relatively inexperienced in working in a production environment, the results are impressive. It's also apparent from the freely available "making of" interviews that the team produced progressively better work as members became accustomed to working together.

The film is freely available in multiple formats: both as ordinary downloads and as BitTorrent files on the film's official website: `www.elephantsdream.org`. The "making of" interviews and all the source `.blend` files can also be found at that website. You can also purchase the DVD, which has all these features as well as both NTSC and PAL versions of the film. The DVD that accompanies this book includes a high-resolution video of the film as well as all the source `.blend` files.

A Preview of *Plumiferos*

With a budget of $700,000 USD, the feature-length family film *Plumiferos,* produced by the Argentine studio Manos Digitales, is without a doubt the largest-scale all-Blender CG production to date and promises to represent another important step in the evolution of Blender into a top-level CG production package.

The goals of *Plumiferos* (see Figure 13.2) are different from those of *Elephants Dream.* Unlike *Elephants Dream, Plumiferos* is not intended primarily as a showcase of Blender's capabilities, nor is it an open movie. *Plumiferos* is an independently produced commercial film intended for wide theatrical and DVD release. Blender and other free software were chosen for the project for very practical reasons: because *Plumiferos* is an independent film, it was necessary for Manos Digitales to produce enough high-quality material to woo investors and financial backers to the project. Lacking the cash up front to devote to expensive software packages, Manos Digitales saw the obvious appeal of free alternatives. After financial backing was secured, using free software enabled the money to be spent on salaries for the production team. As any independent filmmaker is all too painfully aware, a few thousand dollars here and there can make or break a production, and with an alternative like Blender available, it made little sense to consider expensive proprietary options. The Blender developer community itself proved to be an unexpected additional asset to the project, being very responsive and eager to help with needed developments on the software.

Figure 13.2

The birds of
Plumiferos

Plumiferos differs greatly from *Elephants Dream* in subject matter, content, and style. Although *Elephants Dream* threw notions of accessibility to the wind, and in so doing may have helped pioneer the use of CG animation in the "art film" genre, *Plumiferos* is clearly aiming to be widely accessible family entertainment. This is, of course, reminiscent of the very successful approach taken by CG juggernaut Pixar, and *Plumiferos'* success in finding a wide audience would represent an exciting and ambitious development for Blender and the Blender community.

Over the next few chapters you'll look a little bit more closely at both of these productions to learn from the techniques used in them. *Elephants Dream,* with its freely available .blend files, represents a great opportunity for this, and you will only scratch the surface of what can be learned from studying these files. I very much encourage you to dive in to study them on your own. In the case of *Plumiferos,* you will be taking a very special peek at one of the main character rigs used in the film. This material is *not* freely available, but has been provided to me courtesy of Claudio "malefico" Andaur, one of the main creators of the film, for which I am very grateful.

CHAPTER 14

A Look Into *Elephants Dream*

It's hard to overstate the benefits to Blender and the Blender community that have arisen from the Blender Foundation's Orange Project and its flagship short film production, *Elephants Dream*. Not the least of these benefits have been the opportunities for learning about animated filmmaking in Blender afforded by the free release of the original "source" files—the blend files used to produce the movie—to the public.

The full film's `.blend` files occupy nearly eight gigabytes and can be found on this book's companion DVD, compressed in two separate `.rar` files. Each archive contains a top-level directory called ORANGE, and all subdirectories from both archives should be placed together under a single ORANGE directory to maintain internal file dependencies. Given the sheer volume and complexity of these files, within the scope of this book I can only scratch the surface in looking at them. I decided to focus on a few interesting details that help to illustrate or add to some of the material already covered in this book, which I hope whets your appetite for investigating these files in more detail.

- **Proog and Emo Rigs**
- **Texturing Proog**
- **Ways of Walking: Following a Path vs. a Manually Keyed Walk**
- **Tips on Studying the *Elephants Dream* Files**

Proog and Emo Rigs

The two protagonists of *Elephants Dream* (see Figure 14.1) are anything but your typical cuddly animated film stars. The characters are unsettling and off-putting; Proog is an irritable, domineering, and very likely insane old man, whereas Emo is a sniveling, somewhat diseased looking man-child. Both of them are awkward, edgy, incongruous people, and these characteristics are expressed in the way the characters are modeled. You can find both blend files under /ORANGE/production/lib in the directories with each character's name.

As you can see in the wireframe depictions of the two characters shown in Figure 14.2, the mesh structure of each character's bodies is deliberately jagged and shaky-looking. The mesh structure of the character's clothing, in particular, stretches and bunches and tugs in a way that suggests that the material is about to break apart. Proog's trousers are tired and slack, bunching up slightly around his ankles and shins, whereas Emo's jacket appears to be so ill-fitting and constricting as to call to mind a straightjacket.

The circles you are seeing all over these blend files indicate forces. In particular, you see many curve guides used to guide the character's hair. With the Captain Blender rig, you only scratched the surface of what can be done with particle hair and curve guides, using a few guides to create a very simple hairstyle. Curve guides are a powerful but painstaking tool. When slightly more complicated or realistic hair effects are desired, such as in these blends, you will quickly find that a large number of curve guides are required. To learn about how the *Elephants Dream* hair effects are accomplished, I suggest you spend some time with these files, editing and adjusting the various curve guides.

Figure 14.1

Proog and Emo in
Elephants Dream

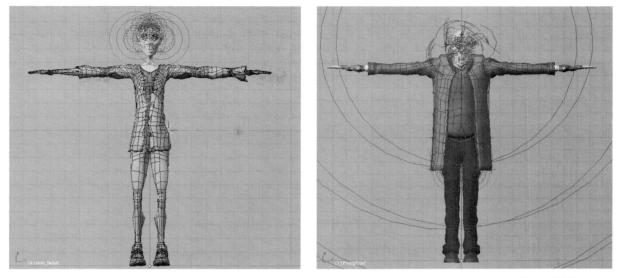

Figure 14.2
**Emo and Proog
meshes**

Figure 14.3 shows a few examples of shape keys on Emo. (It also provides a very clear view of the curve guides influencing Emo's hairstyle. Although his hairstyle appears fairly simple, getting a realistic effect is not trivial, as you can see.) The approach to facial animation taken by the *Elephants Dream* character modelers is analogous to the approach I described in Chapter 8 (which is no coincidence because I borrowed many of the approaches I described directly or indirectly from work by the same people who created *Elephants Dream*; both Captain Blender and the rig he was based on—Jason Pierce's Ludwig—owe a great deal to Bassam Kurdali's Mancandy rig, also included on the companion DVD).

Emo's armature can be seen in Figure 14.4. The first image shows only the bones needed to do basic full-body posing; the second image shows the full armature with all bone layers displayed. An animator never needs to touch or see many of these bones. They are used for a variety of functions. Some of them are used as "fan bones," which move based on the movements of other bones to help to give more control over joint deformations; other bones are used for other functional purposes within the armature.

Note the use of custom bone shapes here. In the Captain Blender example, you used custom bone shapes only for the facial controls, but there is no reason why you cannot use them for other bones. The bone to control the swivel of Emo's hips, for example, is shaped like a flattened box around his hips. The root bone of the armature appears as a compass-like circular base to the character, and the foot controls are shaped like the parts of the feet which they control.

Figure 14.3

Some facial shape keys on Emo

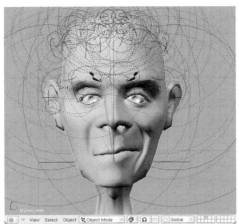
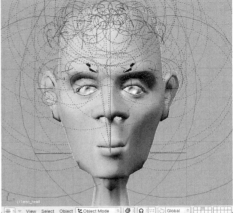

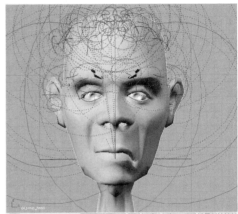

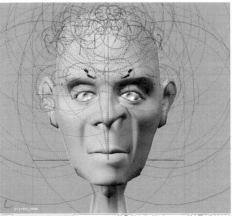
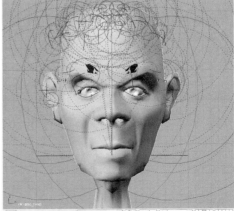

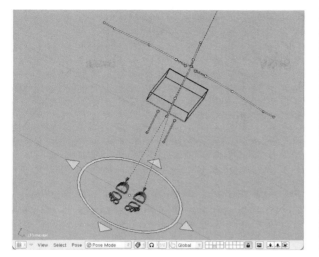
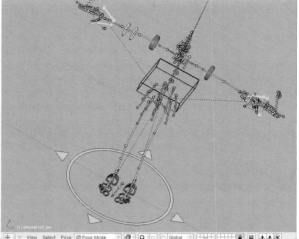

Figure 14.4

Emo's armature

Another Approach to Hand and Foot Rigging

In the Captain Blender rig, you followed the lead of Jason Pierce's Ludwig rig in implementing hand and foot controls with action constraints. The hand and foot rigs in *Elephants Dream* follow a different approach, which is very simple and affords a high degree of control and ease of posing.

Hands

In Figure 14.5, you can see the basic deform bones of the fingers. The three bones of each finger each make up an inverse kinematic (IK) chain, with the fingertip bone as the IK solver (indicated by the dotted line extending from the highlighted bone to the base of the index finger—in Figure 14.5, the IK targets are not shown). Note that the smaller bones you see branching off at the knuckles are fan bones used to correct mesh deformations. I'll talk about fan bones shortly, but for now you can disregard them.

Using IK chains for fingers is not a bad idea, but it can make it difficult to get the fingers to bend consistently in the correct manner. What makes the *Elephants Dream* hand rig interesting is how the IK target is used. In Figure 14.6, you see the IK target. The fingertip IK solver is IK constrained to the finger-length highlighted bone, which in turn is connected/ parented to the same hand bone to which the root of the finger IK chain is parented. With this setup in place, it is possible to simply rotate this finger controller to have the entire finger follow the rotation. What's more, *scaling* this bone in pose mode with the S key results in bending or extending the finger, as you can see in Figure 14.7. Figure 14.8 shows a hand pose with the deforming bones hidden—only the bones that are necessarily to pose the hand are shown. This is a very nice solution to finger posing.

Figure 14.5

Finger deform bones form an IK chain

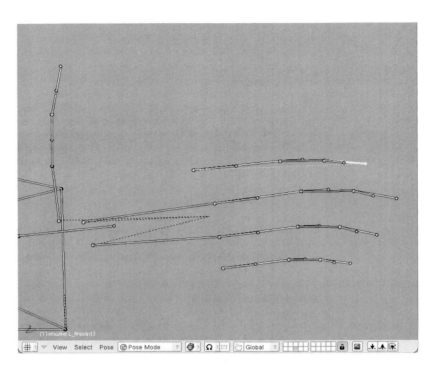

Figure 14.6

IK target bones are connected to the base of the fingers

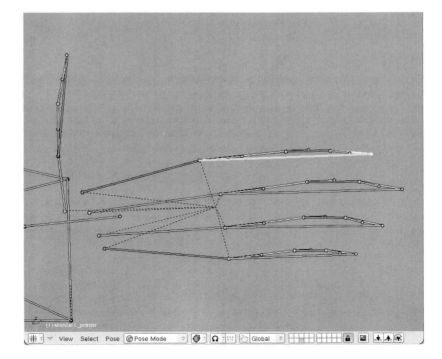

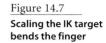

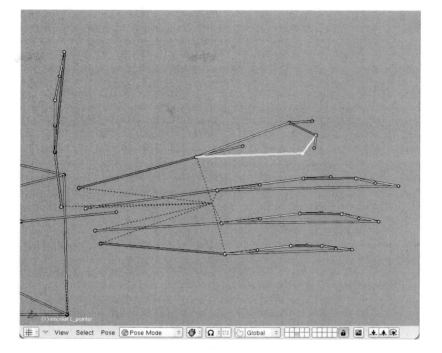

Figure 14.7
Scaling the IK target bends the finger

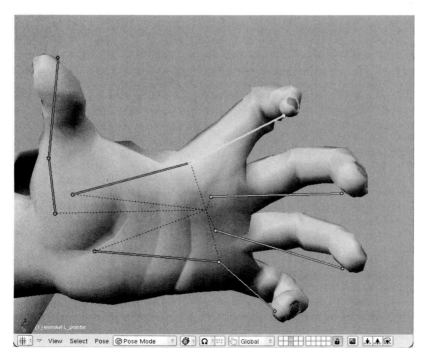

Figure 14.8
Posing is simple with this IK setup

Figure 14.9

Foot rigs for Proog

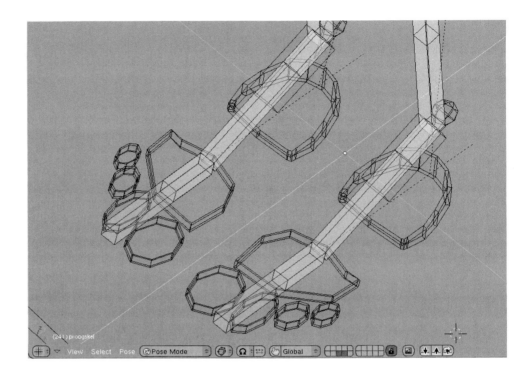

Feet

As with the hand rig, the foot rig for the *Elephants Dream* characters accomplishes a lot with a relatively simple setup—without using Action constraints. Figure 14.9 shows the full bone structure of the feet in B-bones view. The most immediately notable aspect of the feet is the use of custom bone shapes to identify the toes bone, the foot bones repre- sented by the heel portion, and the ankle bones, represented by the small, roundish custom bones to the rear of the ankle joint. (I am dropping the preceding L_ and R_ from the names of the bones here.) These custom bones are the only bones that the animator needs to touch.

In Figure 14.10, you can see a view of the foot rig from the side and in octahedron view: a) shows the foot rig as it actually is; b) shows it exploded and labeled to clarify the place- ment and relationships of the bones. Arrows show where the exploded bones fit in the rig, and the dotted lines indicate nonconnected parenting. Connected bones are shown in their correct positions, attached by joints to their parent bones. The principle parent rela- tionships here are between the foot bone and its nonconnected children. These include the toes bone and the ankle bone. Note the placement and position of the ankle bone. Its actual location is somewhat different from where the custom bone shape appears. Parenting the toes bone to the foot bone enables the tip of the foot to follow the overall movement of the foot and also enables the tip of the foot to be raised and lowered by rotating the foot bone. The ankle bone controls the angle of the foottop bone through a Copy Rotation constraint on the foottop bone, targeted to ankle. The foottop bone is also constrained to point to the ankle by an IK constraint. The ankle bone is also the connected parent of the legIK bone; in this way raising or lowering the foot bone controls the position of the IK target for the leg, enabling the foot to be moved around.

Figure 14.10
Bones of the foot

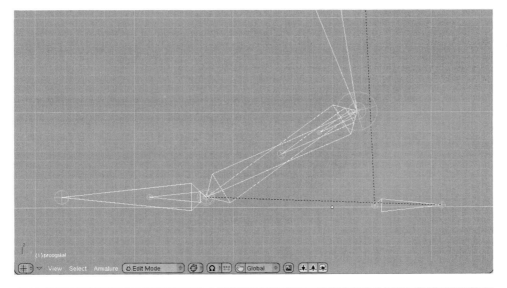

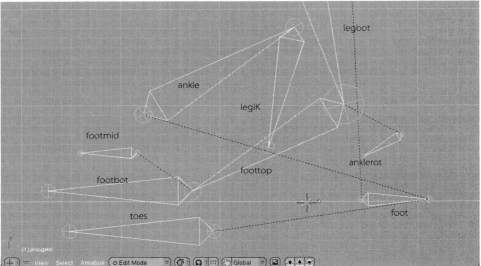

The ankle bone, being a child of foot, can also be rotated independently, as you can see in Figure 14.11. In a) and b) you can see the rest pose and the heel up pose of this bone; c) shows the actual position of the bone (because custom bones can be arbitrary shapes, it is not always possible to see where the pivot and influence of a bone is without looking at the bone in its original shape). Note that in the Transform Properties window all transforms are locked on this bone except for X rotation. Rotating this bone has two main effects: it raises the upper end of the bone, thus raising legIK and bending the leg to accommodate the raised ankle; and it rotates foottop, which is constrained to follow ankle's rotation. In this illustration, you can also see the behavior of the fan bones of the foot, which I'll discuss shortly.

Figure 14.11

Ankle rotation a) no rotation, b) in a heel up pose, c) displayed without custom bone shape

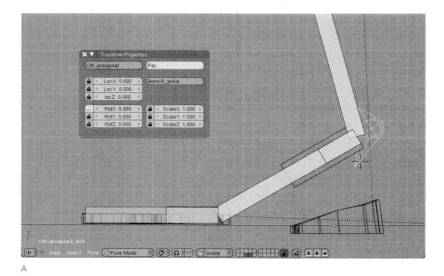

A

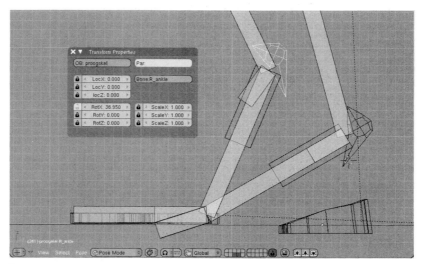

B

Figure 14.11
(continued)

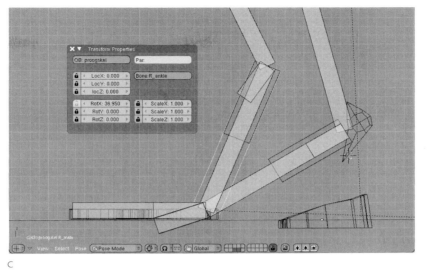

Figure 14.12 shows a few simple leg poses that involve moving the foot with the foot bone, raising the heel with the ankle bone, and raising the toe by rotating the foot bone. Recall that these last two are the same motions for which you used Action constraints in the Captain Blender rig created in Chapter 4.

Fan Bones

Fan bones are bones used to improve deformations by mitigating the localized effect of a sharply angled joint in an armature. In some cases, they can be used in place of or in addition to the bone-driven shape key approach to improving joint deformations discussed in

Figure 14.12

Leg poses involving the foot bone

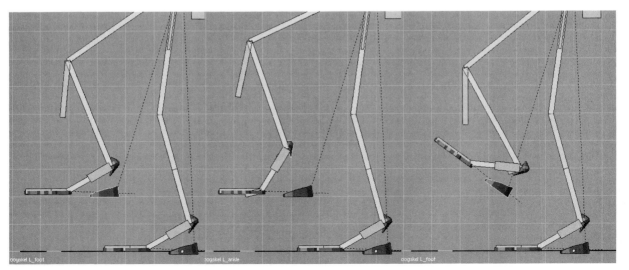

Chapter 5. In the leg poses shown in Figure 14.13, visible fan bones are indicated with arrows. The fan bone in the right (rearmost in the figure) ankle is not visible because the bone it is constrained to is not rotated. The most obvious fan bones in this image are the ones extending down from the knees; fan bones are also visible at the left (raised) ankle and slightly visible at the balls of the feet where the toe bends. The two fan bones of the foot are named footmid and anklerot, which can both be seen in Figure 14.10. Although these bones are constrained to copy the rotation of footbot and foottop, respectively, the influence of the Copy Rotation constraint is set at 0.5 instead of 1.0. The same is true of the fan bone extending from the knee, which is aligned to the lower leg bone in rest pose and set to copy the lower leg's rotation with a 0.5 influence. This provides an intermediate level of rotation, as you can see in the figure. These bones must be deform bones, of course, because their purpose is to soften the effect of the joint on the mesh.

Proog's Jacket

Living characters aren't the only things that often need armatures. In *Elephants Dream*, Proog's jacket has something of a life of its own. In addition to being modified by the Proog armature to follow the movements of Proog's body, the jacket has its own armature to govern the way the cloth hangs and responds to movement, as you can see in Figure 14.14.

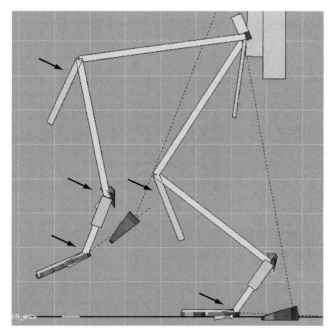

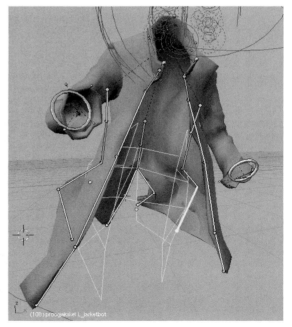

Figure 14.13

Fan bones

Figure 14.14

Proog's jacket in action

One of the most interesting things about this setup is how the jacket incorporates a softbody modifier to assist in its cloth simulation. In Blender, cloth simulation is not yet fully implemented (although work is under way). Ordinary Blender softbodies currently lack the capability to calculate for self-collision, and are furthermore slow to compute with large numbers of vertices.

Proog's jacket's rig works around these problems by doing the softbody calculations on an invisible, low-poly "lining" for the jacket, which is shown selected in Figure 14.15. It has very few vertices to compute, so you can do softbody calculations very quickly with it, but it is placed in relation to the coat so that it mimics the way the actual jacket should hang if it were soft.

To allow the drape of this low-poly lining to control the drape of the actual jacket, empties are vertex-parented to verts in the lining, as shown in Figure 14.16. The highlighted empty is vertex-parented to the coattail vertex. Finally, this empty is assigned as an IK target for the highlighted IK solver bone shown in Figure 14.17. This armature controls the movement of the actual jacket mesh. By using this method of vert parenting IK target empties to the softbody jacket liner in several key places, a softbody effect can be approximated for the jacket without dealing with the various problems that would come with putting a softbody modifier onto the jacket directly.

In future versions of Blender, it is likely that the roundabout approach of parenting IK solvers to empties to vertices will no longer be necessary to achieve a similar effect because the coders are currently working on a system that will allow one mesh, such as the low-poly liner, to directly deform another mesh, such as the high-poly coat in this example. This would be a practical improvement and make this approach even more attractive.

Figure 14.15
Low-poly soft body "lining" for the jacket

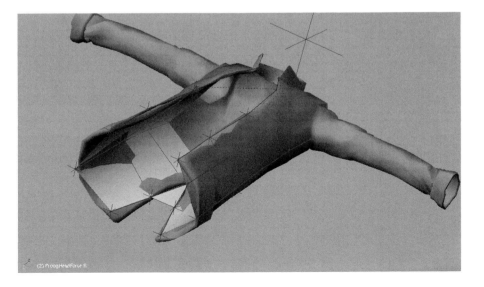

Figure 14.16
An empty is vertex-parented to the tail of the lining.

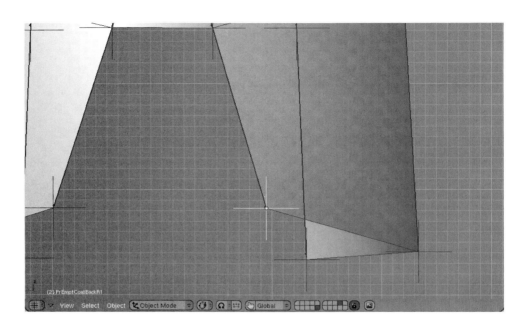

Figure 14.17
The empty is then made the IK target for the tail bone of the jacket.

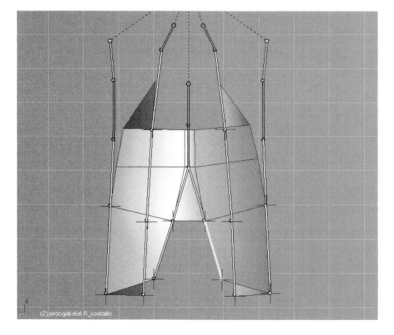

Texturing Proog

Without a doubt, on of the most striking and distinguishing features of *Elephants Dream* is the almost obsessive attention to textures. Well-done texturing adds an entirely new dimension of realism to any 3D scene, and it's clear that the creators of *Elephants Dream* were keenly aware of the increase in production value that can be attained by texturing.

I recommend exploring the machine textures and matte paintings in the Orange files included on the DVD; there is some beautiful work to be found. In terms of the characters, Emo's texturing is probably the most immediately obvious because of its strange discoloration and incongruous wrinkling, which is striking on such a young-looking face shape, but it is the more subtle and natural texturing of the Proog character that I find particularly interesting.

In Figure 14.18, you see the three main texture images for Proog's head: the color texture (unfortunately reproduced here in black and white), the bump map texture, and the specularity texture. In the color texture, various pinks, reds, and blues lie over a layer of pinkish skin tone. Veins are drawn lightly in blue, and light and dark areas represent variations in skin stress.

The bump map texture shows areas of depression and elevation on the face, creating wrinkles, bumps, and indentations. The light veins in the forehead coincide with the blue-tinted veins in the color map to raise them slightly from the surface. Neutral gray has no effect on the normal value of the base mesh.

The light areas on the specularity map appear in the final render as shinier than the dark areas. When creating this texture, the artist took into account factors such as oiliness of skin, tautness of skin, and closeness of skin to bone. This texture follows the other two, but is less highly contrasted than the bump map. Also, attention is given to areas such as the rims of the ears, which will have a slightly higher specularity than other areas but are not of particular interest for bump mapping.

Figure 14.18

Texture images for Proog's head: color; bump-mapping; specularity

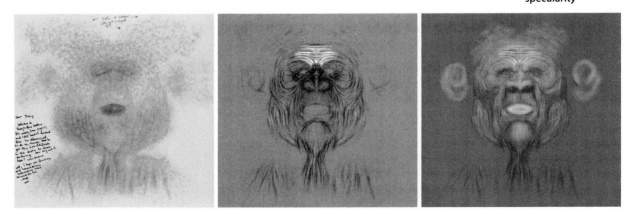

Ways of Walking: Following a Path vs. a Manually Keyed Walk

Modeling and rigging are not the only areas in which the study of *Elephants Dream* can yield interesting insights. The animation in the film is also well worth a close analysis.

In Chapter 7, I mentioned that there are times when it is better to have a character follow a path with a walk cycle, and times when it is better to have the character's movements keyed by hand as the character progresses. The "typewriter" scene in *Elephants Dream*, shown in Figure 14.19, provides a vivid example of the use of these two methods to accomplish the same thing with very different dramatic effects. In this case, both characters are traversing the same chasm by stepping on mechanical typewriter keys that rise from the depths to meet their feet with each step. Proog, apparently aware of and somewhat stimulated by this perilous situation, crosses acrobatically, even breaking into a kind of dance, suggesting that he is keenly aware of cheating death with each step. Emo, on the other hand, is ignorant of the keys. He strolls across them as if he were walking down a street, in calm and even strides.

Emo's walk is a perfect example of an appropriate use of the follow path option in Blender's NLA editor. To see the action first hand, open the file `ORANGE/production/04_typewriter/04_09.blend`, which corresponds to this shot. As you can see in Figure 14.20, Emo is constrained to a stride path (as was discussed in Chapter 7).

Figure 14.19

The "typewriter" scene

Figure 14.20

**Emo follows a
stride path**

Proog, on the other hand, is keyed by hand, enabling him to strike all kinds of wild poses, such as the one shown in Figure 14.21, in which he breaks into something like a Russian folk dance while crossing the chasm.

Figure 14.21

Proog's dance

Figure 14.22

Nonlinear animation of the typewriter scene

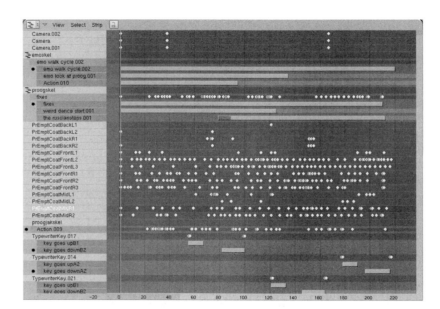

The NLA Editor display for this shot can be seen in Figure 14.22. (It has been truncated for display here; in fact, more channels exist for the other typewriter keys.) You can check the Action editor also to see that Emo's walk cycle is an ordinary short walk cycle that repeats over and over again, whereas the two actions that make up Proog's traversal of the typewriter keys are both extended, nonrepetitive actions. Note also how many keys are required to get his jacket to move nicely. It is not entirely clear from the evidence here whether the jacket empties were set by hand or whether the keys were created by baking procedural animations, such as softbodies, into a set of fixed keys.

Tips on Studying the *Elephants Dream* Files

The Orange team buried a lot of amusing surprises in these files, which makes studying the files all the more fun, but there are many more benefits to be gotten by careful analysis of the files than just the fun of a treasure hunt. If you are interested enough in character animation with Blender to have gotten this far in this book, you owe it to yourself to spend some quality time with the *Elephants Dream* .blend files.

Clearly, I have barely scratched the surface in looking at these .blend files and pointing out noteworthy and illuminating features of this production. Rumor has it that the Orange team is considering plans to release a "workbook" to accompany the film, which would certainly be a great resource to the Blender animation community. As you can already see, there is more than enough material to fill a book of its own. In the meantime, however, you have the .blend files with which you can continue your Blender animation education. Diving into the .blend files for *Elephants Dream* on your own can be daunting at first, but with a little patience you'll begin to find your way around them.

My first suggestion is for those accustomed to ignoring "readme" files: change your policy this time and start with the readme.rtf file located in the top-level ORANGE directory. This file contains necessary information about where things are located and how the contents of the directories are organized. You can ignore the file if you want, but reading it will save you a lot of poking around.

An important thing to remember as you look into the files is that important information is often hidden from immediate view, either by using layers or by using Blender's hide function. Use the Outliner window to get a clear idea of what objects and datablocks are actually present in the files. If you can't find something, you can press Alt+H to unhide it, but be sure to check all the layers. Also, don't forget the bone display layers. Remember that they are distinct from ordinary layers, and you will not get a clear idea of how an armature works without being able to view all its bones.

Another place where interesting material might be hidden is in different *scenes*, which can be accessed using the scene drop-down menu at the top of your screen. In particular, many of the files use a separate scene to store the compositing information. To see the 3D objects and animation in these files, you will need to change scenes.

The film uses a number of techniques that I did not have space to cover thoroughly in this book: force fields; dupligroups, a method of animating multiple instances of the same object; and node-based compositing, a set of tools for putting images together that are much more powerful than the simple alpha-overlay compositing you looked at in Chapter 11. For further information on these and other techniques and tools available in Blender, you should investigate the resources for further learning described in Chapter 18.

CHAPTER 15

Feifi the Canary: *Plumiferos* Takes Wing

In this chapter we have a very special opportunity to take a glimpse inside the commercial feature film *Plumiferos,* which is currently in production as I write this. The creators have kindly allowed me access to the rig of Feifi the canary, one of the main characters of the film, and I am very pleased to present an overview of this excellent example of cartoon-style rigging.

- Introducing Feifi

- Facial Deformations with Lattices

- Rigging a Cartoon Bird

Introducing Feifi

It's hard to imagine a better counterpoint to the Proog and Emo rigs discussed in Chapter 14 than the character of Feifi the Canary. Although the two protagonists of *Elephants Dream* are eminently unlovable, Feifi and the other birds of *Plumiferos* are as cute and charming as Proog and Emo are unsettling. For these reasons of character and for stylistic reasons, the modeling and rigging of Feifi are carried out in very different ways from those of *Elephants Dream.*

Stylistically, *Elephants Dream* is realistic and artificial in a way almost diametrically opposed to the way in which *Plumiferos* is cartoony and naturalistic. The creators of *Plumiferos* have created a natural-looking, convincing world in which they can tell their story. Lighting in *Plumiferos* is painstakingly naturalistic, whereas *Elephants Dream* is full of surreal glows and emanations. The directing style and camera work in *Plumiferos* is unobtrusive, whereas *Elephants Dream* often uses dramatic framing and camera angles to enhance the feeling of danger and unease in the film. In other important respects, however—particularly as discussed in this chapter—*Plumiferos* is far less realistic and far more cartoony than *Elephants Dream.* This cartoon-quality completely informs the way the rig is set up, as you will see in this chapter.

Figure 15.1 shows some *Plumiferos* character sketches.

Feifi Mesh

Looking at the wireframe contours of the mesh in Figure 15.2, the differences in style and character between Feifi and the *Elephants Dream* protagonists are immediately clear. Feifi is rounded and smooth, with none of the jaggedness and incongruity of those characters.

Figure 15.1

Designs for one of the avian protagonists of *Plumiferos*

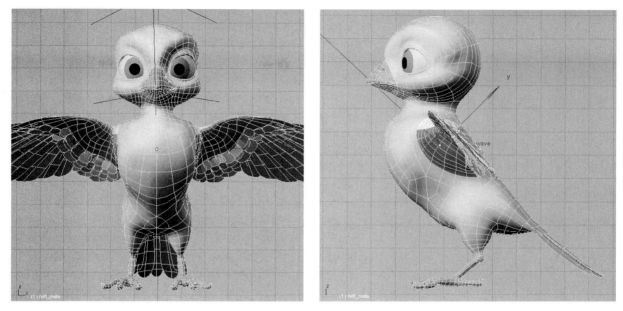

Feifi is a classically cute cartoon character, complete with a large head and very large eyes, puffy cheeks, a small chin and mouth (in this case, a beak), and a small rounded body. The mesh of the body is smooth, clean, and at first glance appears comparatively simple.

In fact, however, although Feifi's head is clearly cartoony in its proportions, the body is not very exaggerated at all. The torso, legs, and feet are highly naturalistic. The most significant and complex concessions to naturalism in the mesh are probably to be found in the wings, shown in their rest position in Figure 15.3. Clearly they are based on considerable study of actual bird wings, and the component feathers are painstakingly organized to yield a naturalistic structure that can be animated in a convincing way, although, in keeping with the film's cartoon style, these wings are in fact far more versatile and expressive than truly natural bird wings.

Feifi is not a single unbroken mesh. The wings and tail are built up of many mesh parts representing features that have been modeled separately and placed together, as can be seen in the exploded image of the Feifi mesh shown in Figure 15.4. These segments were modeled separately for several reasons. First, this

Figure 15.4

**Separate feathers
that make up
the wings**

Figure 15.4

Separate feathers that make up the wings

approach is more modular than to have all the mesh pieces attached; similar wing structures are used for many of the bird characters in *Plumiferos*, and it is easier to reuse wing parts if they are separate. Also, using multiple mesh parts enables more materials to be applied to an object. Each unbroken mesh is limited to 16 different materials in Blender, which is generally not a particularly limiting restriction, in part because it is easy to use separate mesh segments within an object, as is done here.

Finally, it turns out that modeling each of the large features that make up the wing separately yields very nice results and also facilitates some interesting possibilities for wing posing, which you will look at a bit later in this chapter.

Cartoon Facial Deformations with Lattices

Chapter 10 looked briefly at the use of lattices and their applicability to cartoon-style effects. One of the drawbacks of using lattices in the current version of Blender is that it can be difficult to animate them because of their reliance on the deprecated relative vertex key system rather than shape keys, which are much easier to use and are typically used with meshes. The Feifi rig takes the idea of using lattices for cartoon distortion to its logi-cal extreme. A considerable amount of mesh posing is done with lattices, and very little is done with shape keys. Even traditional armature deformation is kept to a minimum, particularly in the face area. Furthermore, Feifi makes use of hooks and bone parenting to enable complex lattice deformations to be controlled by armature, analogously to the way other meshes have done, but without the use of either shape keys or driven Ipos. In complex rigs such as this one, in which there are many deformers involved, it is very important to keep track of what is parented to what. Bone parenting, empties, hooks, vertex parenting, and ordinary object parenting are all employed in important ways here.

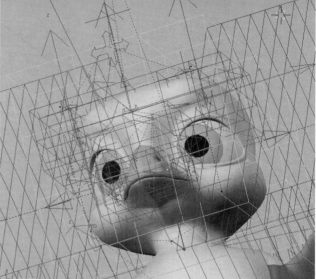

Figure 15.5 shows a view of Feifi's head with a complex scaffolding of multiple lattices. Each lattice covers a specific portion of the mesh and influences the part of the mesh defined by the vertex group named in the VGroup field in the lattice modifier, shown in Figure 15.6. Parts of the lattice that will be deformed are connected to a hook by selecting in Edit mode the lattice verts that are to be influenced by the hook, and pressing Ctrl+H to create a hook. By default, a new empty will be created as the hook object. (The process is the same for adding hooks to mesh vertices.) This empty is then bone parented to the appropriate controller bone.

Figure 15.5
Lattices modifying Feifi's head

Feifi's lips are deformed using a lattice deformed by a curve. Control points in the curve are controlled by hooks, which in turn are parented to bones in armature. This setup makes it possible to control a wide range of curvy poses for the lips.

This approach results in a remarkably expressive face rig. In Figure 15.7, you see a small sample of the kinds of deformations and facial expressions possible with this approach. The only portion of the face rig that involves weight-painted, bone-deformed mesh is the lower beak portion, which is opened by means of a bone. The only shape keys used are for opening and closing the eyelids. In these examples, once again, you see the potential for lattices to cre-ate exaggeration, and hence cartoon style.

Figure 15.6
Lattice modifier applied to the Cabeza ("head") vertex group

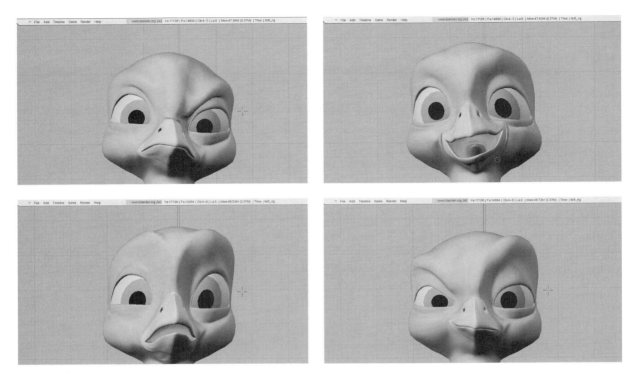

Figure 15.7

Facial expressions with a lattice/armature combination

Rigging a Cartoon Bird

The rest of the Feifi rig is equally interesting. You can see the entire bone armature structure in Figure 15.8. Although it is not clear from the black and white image, the CVS Blender version currently used by the *Plumiferos* team enables custom bone colors as well as shapes. In the Feifi rig, the left wing ("plegar") and foot bone setups are colored red and the right wing and foot are in blue. Animators often need to work in wireframe mode or without the mesh visible, and it can be difficult to tell right from left when viewing the armature from the side. For this reason, using colored bones to distinguish the sides can be very useful. Expect this feature to be available soon in an official Blender release.

The rigging of Feifi's torso also takes a different approach from those discussed elsewhere in this book. Although it looks like one at first glance, the spine isn't really an ordinary IK chain. In fact, the bones aren't connected at all. There is a series of unconnected deform bones, each of which is parented to a control bone (with a circular custom bone shape). These control bones are the ones used for posing, as shown in Figure 15.9. The whole spine is a targetless IK chain. Thus, you can pose it first by manipulating the neck control and then tweak all rotations of every single control bone along the spine, not only the hip bone. Moreover, you can translate each segment along the Y normal axis to get

Figure 15.8
Feifi armature

Figure 15.9
Posing Feifi's torso

 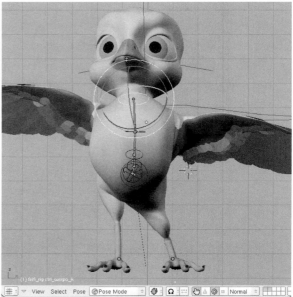

squash and stretch effects for the body, resulting in a very flexible and precisely controlled cartoon spine. This area and the main posing bones for the head and legs are skinned in a straightforward way using weight painting, as shown in Figure 15.10.

Wings

A place where the Feifi rig is especially interesting is in the wings. Modeling and rigging wings and feathers present a number of challenges that are not easily addressed using traditional armature-mesh deformation.

The Feifi rig breaks wing movement into components that can be described as flap, curl, and fan, with each of these components controlled mostly independently from the others (as can be seen in Figure 15.11). The angle of Feifi's wing to his body is determined by the rotation of a circular dial-like custom bone located over his shoulder. The curl within the wing is controlled by a chain of FK bones extending horizontally from the shoulder area; this setup enables much more flexible posing than a natural bird wing would be capable of, which is appropriate to a cartoon bird character who will likely have

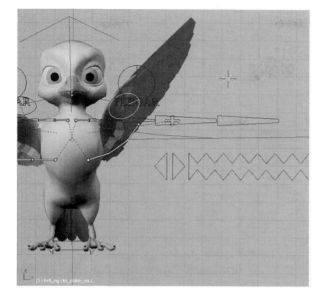 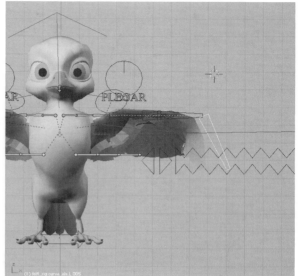

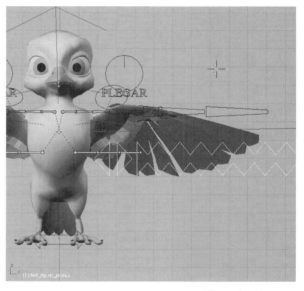

to use his wing as a hand from time to time. Finally, the fanning of the wing feathers, a key element of expressive wing posing, is controlled by *scaling* the accordion-shaped custom bones positioned horizontally beneath each wing.

This kind of flexibility would be difficult to accomplish using only weight painting and armature deformation. In fact, most of Feifi's wing posing is not accomplished with weight painting. Instead, as in the case of the facial deformations, much of the solution to rigging Feifi's wings is found in the use of lattices. Feifi's wings are each modified by two lattices: one that controls flap and one that controls the curl of the wings. The lattices in turn are controlled by using hooks parented to the faces of an auxiliary mesh that follows the B-bone segments of control bones to enable the lattices to most accurately reflect the behavior of the B-bones because simple bone parenting would not represent flexing of the bone itself. A single wing's curl lattice is influenced by 25 separate hook modifiers. Figure 15.12 shows a wing pose, the accompanying lattice deformations, and a full view of all layers of the armature.

Figure 15.11

Main components of Feifi's wing movement: flap, curl, and fan

Figure 15.12

Posed mesh, lattices, and full armature

The only part of the wing's pose that is not controlled by lattices is the fanning mechanism. To fan the feathers, traditional armature deformation is used, in that each separately modeled feather is fully assigned to its own bone, as can be seen in Figure 15.13. Each feather follows the movement of its governing bone, while remaining stiff.

Figure 15.13

Feather mesh segment fully assigned to a deform bone

The fanning itself is controlled by a very clever example of a kind of mechanical rigging that does not often find its way into character armatures. To understand how it works, it is helpful first to look at the setup in its rest position in Edit mode, as shown in Figure 15.14. Located at the tip of each deform bone is a small control bone (the bones named with the prefix `tar_roja`). These bones have no direct relationship via parenting to the feather deform bones; they are simply placed at their tips. The parent of the control bones is the `str_proha.L` bone.

In Pose mode, each of the feather deform bones is constrained using a Lock Track constraint to point toward the location of its respective control bone. Scaling the parent of this set of bones has the effect of scaling the control bones and their distances from

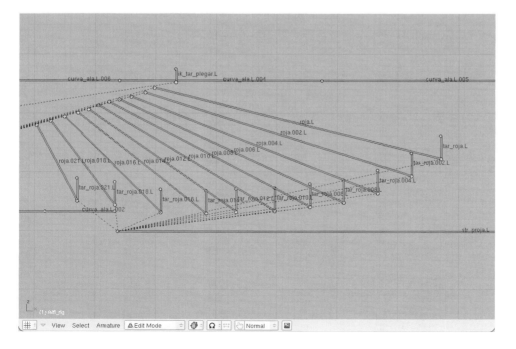

Figure 15.14

Wing-fanning mechanism in Edit mode

each other, while also changing the location of the point to which they are parented. As this happens, the tracking of the feather deform bones toward the control bones results in the deform bones spreading apart from each other, as can be seen in Figure 15.15.

Figure 15.15

Feather-fanning mechanism in action

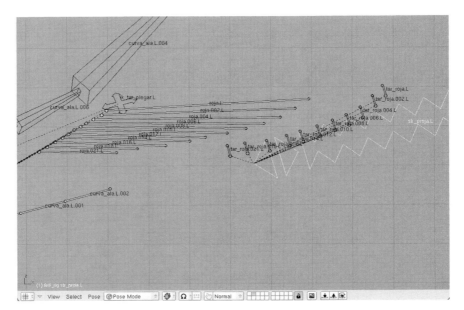

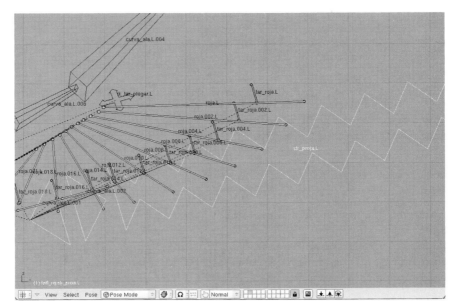

Workflow for wing posing is as follows: for acting purposes, the dial-controlled bones should be in a horizontal flat position. From this position, moving the tip of the wing main controls creates the basic pose. The pose can be refined by rotating each segment until the desired final pose is arrived at. Scaling the "accordion" bone poses the feathers. When folding the wings, the steps are opposite. The main wing control chain should be in a flat horizontal position, and the dial can be used from that position to fold the wing.

For flight shots, a wave deformer affecting the wings is used to simulate wind. This cannot be turned on and off in the middle of an animation, but it results in a convincing appearance of the wings being buffeted by wind during flight.

As you can see, in spite of the apparent simplicity of the Feifi character, the rig is a fairly complex construction. The result is a very expressive, poseable character that can enable an animator to create a wide range of actions and emotions quickly and easily. Although some of the techniques used in this rig certainly deserve to be described in greater depth, I hope that the approaches overviewed in this chapter will help to give you an idea of the variety of possibilities available in Blender for rigging characters and perhaps point you toward some solutions of your own for your specific rigging needs.

CHAPTER 16

Blender in the Pipeline

Any fully realized animation project involves numerous steps to complete its production. *Elephants Dream* and *Plumiferos* have seen Blender's fullest integration into the production pipeline of such large-scale projects so far, and both of them represent rites of passage for Blender as a production tool. This chapter looks a bit at Blender's place in the production pipeline and some of the tools it employs to make it more useful in a production environment. Many of these tools have been developed as a direct result of the Orange Project, so it's very clear how actual use of Blender in a production environment has helped feed its development as an industrial-strength CG solution.

- **Production Pipeline**
- **Using Libraries**
- **Collaboration with Subversion and Verse**
- **…and Back into Blender**

Production Pipeline

The core Orange Team consisted of eight individuals, including the soundtrack composer/sound designer. The other seven on the team all worked with Blender as producer, director, art director, technical director, and three lead artists. In addition to these production team members, several other people are credited with contributing smaller amounts of artwork, animation, and assistance in texture creation.

The *Plumiferos* production team consists of about 28 people, about 19 of whom work specifically with Blender in some capacity. The team consists of the following:

5 art, concept, and storyboarding

4 production

7 material, textures, and lighting

9 animators

1 Python scripting

1 director

1 animation supervisor

Both production teams also relied heavily on the Blender developer community at large.

In any production, the process begins with a concept. The Orange Project and *Plumiferos* took different approaches in this regard. In the case of the Orange Project, the concept for *Elephants Dream* was arrived at in a very collaborative way by the creative team after the project already began. With *Plumiferos,* much of the broader conception of the picture had to be done in advance of securing financing to have a viable, interesting project to pitch to prospective investors.

Nevertheless, in all cases, the preproduction phase is an important period, in which artists and technical workers must get together and decide on many aspects of how the film will be made and what it will look like. 2D artists are important at this point for drawing initial conceptions of characters, props, and locations (see Figure 16.1).

Figure 16.1

Several stages in creating a character

The open source 2D software Gimp played an important role at this stage in both productions. Both productions also used clay to create 3D models of their main characters in advance of modeling them on the computer (see Figure 16.2).

Most medium- and large-scale productions map out their sequence of shots graphically with a storyboard, which is the best way for the director to communicate ideas and intentions visually to the animators. This process can be achieved by using 2D drawing software such as Gimp or simply drawn on paper (see Figure 16.3). In the case of *Plumiferos,* storyboarding was followed by the creation of a 2D animatic, which is a very rough animated version of a storyboard, to help to visualize how the onscreen elements will move in relation to each other. The *Plumiferos* team created this 2D animatic with Blender. *Elephants Dream* did not use a 2D animatic.

After the movement in the film has been sketched out in a 2D animatic, the process of creating the 3D world begins. By this time, modelers are working on creating the rigged models and sets that will be used in the final film. By using Blender's capability to append and link datablocks between files, it is possible for a team to work on different aspects of the film

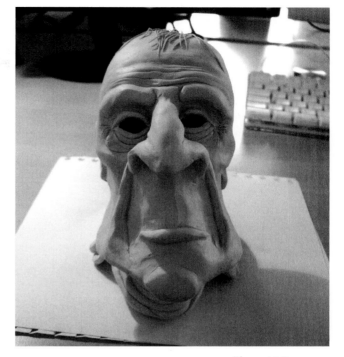

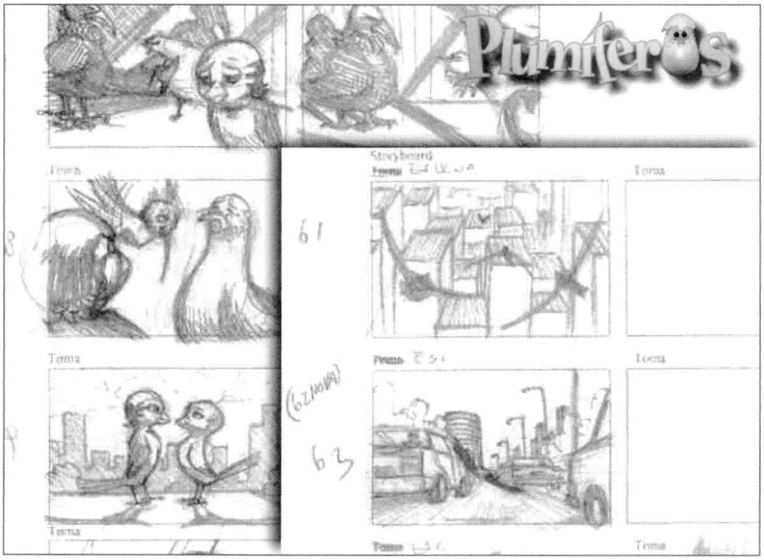

Figure 16.2
Proog in clay

Figure 16.3
**Storyboard images
for *Plumiferos***

in parallel and bring them together later in the process. At this stage, camera positions and movement are decided upon, blocking is worked out in detail, and a 3D animatic is created. The *Elephants Dream* source files have several examples of 3D animatics among them. 3D animatics incorporate simplified rigs and movements, but give a much more detailed view of the relations between objects and the camera that is possible in the 2D animatic. 3D animatics are of course created in Blender, as are all sets, props, and character models. Blender's usefulness in creating 3D animatics has been recognized even in Hollywood. 3D animatics artist Anthony Zierhut has written about how he used Blender to aid with visualization on the production *Spider-Man 2*. (You can find his article on the Blender website at `http://www.blender.org/cms/Animatics_for_Motion_P.393.0.html`.)

Eventually, the final animation work is begun by using fully rigged characters, although modeling work might still be progressing with the final rigs. Texturing, in particular, must be done in conjunction with lighting because the appearance of textures depends closely upon the lighting of a scene. It is very important to plan the workflow so that multiple threads of production can be carried out simultaneously.

The final steps of production involve compositing, adding various visual effects, and finally rendering. Blender's compositing system is used to do the compositing and can be used in conjunction with other software to create effects. In *Elephants Dream*, the rendering was done using Blender's internal renderer, which is optimized for speed, especially for use in animations. *Plumiferos* is also planned to be rendered entirely with the Blender internal renderer.

Animation productions of even fairly small scales are likely to need render farm support, and midsize or large productions cannot be carried out without significant computing resources. Typically, this means a Linux cluster with a large number of parallel compute nodes. *Elephants Dream* used the DrQueue open-source render farm manager to distribute rendering tasks across the machines on the cluster.

Figure 16.4

A rendered frame

When shots have all been rendered, it is time to do postprocessing and editing. Blender can play an important role in this part of the pipeline, but as discussed in Chapter 11, it has some limitations, particularly regarding its handling of sound. Audio/video editing for *Elephants Dream* was done primarily using the Linux-based Blender build with ffmpeg support, which is also playing an important role in the *Plumiferos* production.

Using Libraries

In any production large enough to require extensive reuse of models, Ipos, or other data-blocks, using libraries is a must. A character, for example, might feature in numerous shots. It is important that changes made to the character model at any stage in the production be reproduced for all instances of the model throughout the film. Doing this by hand in a large production is out of the question, so the typical solution is to use libraries of models and other datablocks that can then be appended or linked to whatever scene they are needed in.

Chapter 1 looked at the usefulness of the Append function. By default, Append creates a new copy of the appended datablock in the current file. When the link button is selected in the Append datablock browser, the added datablock is linked to the original datablock in the original file. Changes made to the original datablock are also implemented in all linked instances of the datablock in other files.

Any datablock can be appended, including groups. An object can be added to a group by selecting Add To Group in the Object (F7) buttons. It is common, for example, to represent a single character with a group that includes the character mesh; the character armature; and whatever empties, curve guides, or other incidental objects are considered to be part of the character. In this way, all these objects can be appended at one stroke. Characters that need to be deformed by an armature or shapes should be appended, not linked. Linking should be reserved for objects that do not deform.

The production libraries for *Elephants Dream* can be found in the `/ORANGE/production/lib/` directory.

Collaboration with Subversion and Verse

Although creating an animated film is not the same as developing a piece of software, many aspects of the digital production pipeline bear similarities to a software development environment. For this reason, tools originally designed to assist collaborative software development can be useful and even necessary for digital productions in which it is necessary for a number of people to access and modify common files. Subversion is an open-source version management system for collaboration between programmers. It keeps a central copy of all files and enables users to maintain their own local copy of the files that they need to work with, and to make changes independently of other users.

When users make changes that they want to apply to the central copy of the file, they commit changes which are logged by Subversion and applied to the central file. Other users' copies are then updated to reflect the change. If two users commit changes at the same time, Subversion can identify where the changes are made and integrate them into the same new file. If the two changes affect the same part of the file, Subversion requires clarification about how to proceed, and the users have to make their changes agree with each other. Also, Subversion maintains a complete history of all commits, allowing access to any previous version.

The *Elephants Dream* team used Subversion to manage its digital assets for the production. The team opted for this for several reasons. First, Subversion is free/open-source software and so fit with the mission of the Orange Project. Second, several of the creators are programmers, so they were comfortable with this way of working. For nonprogrammers, using a software version control system to manage digital assets might be confusing. There are, of course, a variety of commercial digital asset management tools available.

Verse is another tool to assist in real-time collaboration. The idea is to allow multiple people to work simultaneously on the same 3D or 2D environment over a network. At present, Verse has severe limitations in the kind of 3D objects it can handle and in the operations allowed. Verse is not used in the *Plumiferos* production, although some use was made of it on *Elephants Dream,* and the Blender Foundation is active in supporting its development.

...and Back Into Blender

The many features that were developed as a result of the Orange Project have already been documented and released in the current version of Blender. Likewise, Blender's integration into the *Plumiferos* production pipeline is already resulting in numerous developments to Blender, some of which are already available in the CVS repository. Among the highlights that have already been developed are as follows:

- The Frame Stamp render option, allowing information such as time code, frame number, camera, scene number, file name, and other texts to be printed over the render
- New constraints available for bones and objects, providing tighter control and greater ease of animation
- New tools for organizing and editing shape keys
- New tools for selecting and editing keyframes and actions
- Shape keys for lattices and vertex groups within lattices
- Numerous new nodes and compositing tools
- New tools for adjusting playback and rendering in the Sequence Editor

Some of them, such as time code burn-ins, address specific needs in a production environment, whereas many of the others are of use to animators in all environments. Other anticipated changes include an update of action constraints and other constraints to make them more intuitive, improvements to the Ipo driver system, speed control in the Sequence Editor, a search function in the Outliner to enable objects or datablocks to be found quickly, and improvements in the way mesh modeling tools interact with meshes with shape keys defined.

It should be clear that being used in production has as much to offer to Blender as Blender has to offer to a professional pipeline. As a broadly supported open-source package, Blender's development is fast and organic. It develops quickly in the ways that are most needed, and its development responds well to the challenges of a professional pipeline. As more and more small studios and independent films adopt Blender as their primary 3D animation tool, Blender will continue to become increasingly well-suited to high-end professional productions.

In Part IV, "Beyond Blender," I will point you toward a number of resources outside of Blender that might be useful in your animation work. I will suggest some software that complements Blender's functionality and extends the possibilities of what you can create. I will also recommend several books and websites in which you can learn more about Blender, character animation, and related CG tasks.

PART IV

Blender and Beyond

This material covered in this book is far from the end of the story for aspiring Blender animators. In this last part, you look briefly at some of the areas that might be worthy of further study. Your work will benefit greatly if you have an understanding of other available software tools to complement Blender's functionality, and this book offers a survey of some of the best free software options available. There is also a lot to learn about the craft of creating animation (this book only scratches the surface), so a small selection of recommended further reading on the topics of traditional animation and related CG techniques is also included.

CHAPTER 17

Other Software and Formats

As powerful and versatile as Blender is, no one program can do everything that the CG animator needs to do. Certain tasks, such as creating 2D textures or editing sound, require a completely different sort of software. Even for things that can be done by Blender—such as editing, UV unwrapping, compositing, and so forth—some people prefer to use several 3D applications for different tasks. This chapter takes a brief look at Blender's interaction with other software. First you will look at a variety of file formats that can be imported and exported to and from Blender. The second section surveys recommended open-source software packages for various tasks in creating fully developed CG animations.

The chapter concludes with some changes currently in the works for Blender itself. Blender's development waits for no one; by the time this book is published, it is likely that a new version will have been released or will be scheduled to be released very soon. Here, you'll learn about scheduled updates and improvements so you have an idea of what to expect and how it relates to the version included on the DVD.

- **Importing and Exporting Other File Formats**

- **Useful Open-Source Software for Blender Artists**

- **Blending into the (Near) Future**

Importing and Exporting Other File Formats

Blender has script-based import and export support for a wide variety of formats and software. Some of these scripts might be somewhat deprecated for use with the current Blender release, however, so care should be taken in using them, as always. You should, of course, thoroughly test any scripts you intend to use before planning to place them into a production pipeline.

Support for importing into Blender is available for the following formats:

- VRML 1.0
- DXF
- VideoScape
- STL
- 3D Studio (.3ds)
- AC3D (.ac)
- COLLADA 1.3.1 (.dae)
- COLLADA 1.4 (.dae)
- DEC Object File Format (.off)
- DirectX (.x)
- Google Earth (.kml/.kmz)
- LightWave (.lwo)
- MD2 (.md2)
- Nendo (.ndo)
- OpenFlight (.flt)
- Paths (.svg, .ps, .eps, .ai, Gimp)
- Pro Engineer (.slp)
- Radiosity (.radio)
- Raw Faces (.raw)
- Stanford PLY (.ply)
- TrueSpace (.cob)
- Wavefront (.obj)

Support for exporting from Blender is available for the following formats:

- VRML 1.0
- DXF
- Videoscape
- STL
- 3D Studio (.3ds)
- AC3D (.ac)
- COLLADA 1.3.1 (.dae)
- COLLADA 1.4 (.dae)
- DEC Object File Format(.off)
- DirectX (.x)
- LightWave (.lwo)
- Lightwave Motion (.mot)
- MD2 (.md2)
- Nendo (.ndo)
- OpenFlight (.flt)
- OpenInventor (.iv)
- Radiosity (.radio)
- Raw Faces (.raw)
- SoftImage XSI (.xsi)
- Stanford PLY (.ply)
- TrueSpace (.cob)
- VRML97 (.wrl)
- VideoScape with Vertex Colors (.obj)
- Wavefront (.obj)
- X3D Extensible 3D (.x3d)
- xfig (.fig)

There is some limited support available for importing and exporting BVH motion capture files, but imported BVH files are not integrated into the Blender animation system, so this is not very useful for Blender animators. Fully integrated support for BVH files will likely be implemented after currently planned modifications to the Python API are completed.

Useful Open-Source Software for Blender Artists

There is a huge amount of software available these days that can be useful at some point in a full 3D content creation pipeline—far more applications than I can cover here. Partly for space reasons, I am limiting this list to the most significant open-source applications. I also assume that readers are familiar with at least the most well-known proprietary options in such areas as 3D content creation, image manipulation, and nonlinear video editing, so I don't need to list them explicitly.

Most of what a 3D animator needs to do can be done using some combination of the software listed here. These aren't all recommendations, as you'll see, but a very brief overview of open-source alternatives in various areas.

Modeling

These applications all have functions or capabilities that can be used to augment Blender's own modeling capabilities. Although there are others available that might be useful, the following are the ones that seem to me to have the most to offer to Blender users.

Wings3D Wings3D is an open-source 3D modeling packaging with a lot of overlap in functionality with Blender's modeling capabilities. The interface is different, and some people find it to be easier to use. Wings3D allows polygons with more than four sides, whereas Blender is restricted to quads and tris for its polygons. This allows for more flexibility in modeling, but the geometry must be converted for the meshes to be used in Blender.

SharpConstruct SharpConstruct is a displacement painting application, similar in concept to a simplified version of the proprietary ZBrush application and to the Blender B-Brush Sculpter displacement painting Python script mentioned in Chapter 12. Although Sharp-Construct currently counts as a separate software application, SharpConstruct's chief developer, Nicholas Bishop, has been working on implementing SharpConstruct's functionality directly into Blender in the form of a Sculpt mode as part of his Google 2006 Summer of Code–sponsored coding project. It is likely that an official Blender release will be available with the functionality of SharpConstruct fully integrated by the time this book hits the stores, so check `www.blender.org` for the latest version.

MakeHuman MakeHuman is not a traditional modeling package; it is an application that enables you to create a model of a human being by selecting from a large number of available attributes and values for the figure, which is then created automatically by the program. The meshes it outputs are good-quality quad meshes, and it is a good solution if you need a convincing figure model to certain specifications but do not want to do the modeling yourself. The software is still in beta, so its behavior might be erratic.

Texturing and 2D

Texturing is a crucial area of 3D modeling that cannot be satisfactorily done within Blender itself (or with any 3D modeling application in general). Although Blender can create a variety of procedural texture effects, realistic textures require the use of photo manipulation software. Also, there are cases (for example, the logo on Captain Blender's costume) in which 2D images must be created. These situations can call for a vector graphics application.

Gimp, GimpShop Gimp is the premier open-source, image-manipulation software. It is a powerful application with all the functionality you need to use photographs or images to create textures. It is often compared with Photoshop, the proprietary standard for image manipulation, whose functionality Gimp largely emulates. I don't intend to try to make a point-by-point comparison between the two applications here; if you are in a position of having to decide which of these packages to use in a professional setting, I recommend that you research the issue thoroughly. However, if you are interested in trying Gimp but have been put off by its un–Photoshop-like interface, GimpShop might be a solution. GimpShop is a modification of Gimp that deliberately mimics the look and feel of Photoshop in response to complaints that Gimp's own interface was willfully unintuitive (read: not the same as Photoshop's). Indeed, for users accustomed to Photoshop, GimpShop represents a big improvement in the usability of Gimp.

Inkscape If Gimp/GimpShop is the open-source answer to Photoshop, Inkscape represents the open-source community's stab at Illustrator. Inkscape is a 2D vector graphics illustration package. Although not as established as Gimp, Inkscape is growing in popularity and does a good job of covering the core functionality needed in a vector illustrations application. Inkscape certainly enables you to do more sophisticated work than the logo on Captain Blender's costume.

Sound and Lip Sync

If you want to do fully realized animations, you should integrate sound. The following are a few applications to help you deal with sound.

Audacity Audacity is an excellent comprehensive sound editor. Its bare-bones interface is very easy to use and it enables you to edit and convert sound files quickly and simply. Along with Blender and Gimp, it represents one of the high points of open-source multimedia software. If you plan to work with sound using open-source software, you need Audacity.

JLipSync JLipSync is a Java-based application for creating and exporting a timeline of phonemes based on a sound file. It is very similar to the proprietary software package called Magpie and is also similar to the free (but non–open-source) lip sync software Papagayo, which provides a function to try to automatically guess phonemes based on sound waves.

These software packages can be used in conjunction with the BlenderLipSynchro Python script mentioned in Chapter 12.

Nonlinear Video Editing and Compositing

If you want to create fully developed animated shorts or features, a full nonlinear editing system is a requirement. The proprietary standards are Adobe Premier and After Effects, Final Cut Pro, and Avid. Blender's Sequence Editor is getting closer to being a viable alternative for some of the functionality of these packages, but it is not a general solution.

Unfortunately, Sequence Editor might be the closest thing that open-source software has to offer at present. A good open-source alternative for nonlinear video editing has been a dream of open-source users for a long time, but realizing that dream has been easier said than done.

The usual suspects in open-source video editing and compositing are the following:

- Cinelerra
- Kino
- Jahshaka
- Positron
- VirtualDub

Each has quirks and drawbacks that prevent it from being a viable, general-purpose, video-editing alternative. Cinelerra and Kino both have their fans, but neither package is available for most Blender users because they are released for Linux only. Lately, Cinelerra has stopped providing binary installers altogether, even for Linux; the only way to use Cinelerra is to compile it yourself on Linux from the source code, making it the least-accessible option available. There does not seem to be interest at present in porting either package to other platforms.

Jahshaka has a different problem. The software is well-known and has a slick, eye-catching interface and ports to all major platforms. However, at the time of this writing, there seems to be widespread consensus among open-source users that the software itself is lacking in stability, at least for Windows and Mac. Nevertheless, the software has a lot of potential and seems to be a promising candidate if its stability problems can be rectified.

Positron is essentially a stagnated branching-off of the Blender Sequence Editor. Originally intended to build on the potential of the Sequence Editor to create a video editing suite, Positron development seems to have gotten hung up, whereas the Blender Sequence Editor has continued to improve.

In the midst of this morass of nonfunctioning or semifunctional software, it's probably worth mentioning that a useable, free, but non–open-source alternative for Windows users is Wax, which has basic nonlinear editing capabilities and runs relatively smoothly.

VirtualDub is also useful (for Windows users) for certain video- and audio-processing tasks. The functionality is far too limited to begin to compare with the proprietary NLEs, but you can string video and audio sequences together and export them, and using VirtualDub alongside the Blender Sequence Editor can yield a pretty satisfactory package. VirtualDub itself does not have nonlinear editing capability (it has only linear editing capacity), but if the nonlinear editing is done in Blender, VirtualDub can be useful for putting the final video and audio files together.

By the time you read this, however, the nonlinear editing capabilities of all these packages will probably be surpassed by the Blender Sequence Editor, which, with ffmpeg support in Linux, is already the best option in the Linux environment. If you need more NLE functionality than that, you probably have to turn to a proprietary solution.

Video Playback

To play back the wide variety of video files available, you need a codec package and probably also need QuickTime installed—although you do not necessarily need to use the QuickTime player. If you are using Macintosh, the QuickTime player is probably the best option, but if you are using Windows or Linux, there are several better alternatives.

There are several free video players available, but MediaPlayer Classic is an excellent player for Windows that is capable of handling a wide range of codecs and, in my experience, playing back QuickTime files more smoothly than QuickTime itself (provided that QuickTime is installed). Mplayer and VLC Media Player are cross-platform players capable of supporting a variety of codecs.

Collaboration

The following software packages are for use in collaborative projects, in which more than one person is involved in the work and potentially more than one application is being used.

Collada Collada is an XML-based format intended to be useable as an open standard, general representation schema for 3D information to allow the free exchange of this information between various applications. Using Collada (and the associated Blender-specific plugins), it should be possible to share data between Blender and Maya, 3D Studio Max, Softimage XSI, and a number of other supported applications.

Verse Verse is a tool for setting up a protocol to allow real-time interaction between various 3D environments, such as those of the software packages just mentioned. Collada and Verse are complementary in their goals and approaches. A Verse-based content-creation environment can use Collada as its format, enabling users of multiple, 3D content-creation applications to work on the same data simultaneously over a network. The Blender Foundation is actively involved in promoting development in Verse.

Blending into the (Near) Future

This section takes a quick look at changes expected over the next few Blender releases. Depending on the progress of the development, they might not all make it into the next release, but they are all on the table for likely inclusion in the future. Some of these features are already available in CVS builds available at `www.graphicall.org`, and will most likely be in an official release by the time this book is out. (It is no problem to run multiple versions of Blender side by side on the same machine, so if you want to experiment with a CVS build, you can do so without abandoning the release you have installed).

Reading about some of these features and changes will hopefully help ease the culture shock of entering into the fast-paced world of Blender. After you get up to speed with the current version, you will be chomping at the bit for the next release.

Orange Project

Most of the significant advances in Blender software produced for the Orange project were incorporated into the 2.42 release, resulting in a huge leap in functionality. Many features, such as the node-based compositing and rendering system, were a result of this work, along with some of the armature-related features I have covered. Probably the most notable exception was ffmpeg support for non-Linux platforms, which has not yet made official release. It is certainly one of the most eagerly awaited features among non–Linux-based Blender users.

Google Summer of Code 2006

The Google Summer of Code grants for 2006 fund three projects: an implementation of the SharpConstruct sculpt tools by Nicholas Bishop (mentioned previously in this chapter), an upgrade of the modifier stack by Ben Batt, and tools for generating 3D sky effects by Dmitriy Mazovka.

The sculpt tools will be accessible in a new mode called Sculpt mode and will be similar to the tools currently available in SharpConstruct. This project will also aim to add multiresolution modeling to allow Blender to treat an object as a highly subdivided mesh in certain circumstances and as a comparatively low poly mesh in others.

The modifier stack upgrade will involve many internal changes to the modifier stack, which should improve the performance and make its use more intuitive and free. This work will also add some new modifiers, which will move some functionality from other areas in Blender and implement it in the form of modifiers. Any of the functionality discussed in this book will probably not be relocated.

The sky generator will add completely new functionality, but does not seem likely to alter anything as currently implemented in Blender.

Other Developments

A wide variety of projects are underway, including UV mapping improvements; ocean, cloth, and better-integrated rigid body physics simulations; a number of improved scripting tools and options; and a complete refactoring of the Blender event-handling system, which promises closer integration of scripts into the Blender interface and the possibility of user-configurable keyboard shortcuts. Some of them will clearly be longer-term projects, but the changes are happening fast, and each Blender release is sure to give users a lot of new toys to play with.

One especially exciting development in the works for character animators will be a much more powerful and precise way to control walk cycles by use of improved Action cycling options and new Action Modifiers that will become available in the NLA Editor. One of these Action Modifiers currently under development will allow any Armature Bone path to be deformed by a curve, enabling you to make characters walk over complex paths, including up and down hills, all without any foot slippage. This will be much more powerful and much easier to set up than the stride bone, and will probably replace the functionality of the stride bone entirely.

For information on all new features, go to the downloads area at www.blender.org and check the release logs for the latest release. You can also learn more from the "Changes since last version" section on the main development page of the same website.

In the final chapter, I'll tell you more about where to go to learn how to use the parts of Blender, present and future, that have not been covered in this book, so that you can fully take advantage of all the features that Blender has and will have to offer.

CHAPTER 18

Resources for Further Learning

At this point, you should know all you need to get started with character animation in Blender. There's plenty more to learn, though, about both Blender and character animation. This chapter directs you to resources to continue your study of these topics.

The first section is a rundown of freely available online tutorials in Blender. Some of the introductory tutorials overlap in coverage with this book and might provide another angle to learn from. Most of the intermediate-level tutorials and resources I'll be pointing to, however, cover aspects of using Blender that I haven't been able to address at all in this book. Becoming familiar with these resources can also help you to stay on top of new features and functionality of future Blender releases.

The second section directs you to a few of what I think are truly indispensable books on CG and on animation. If you are an experienced 3D animator already, you probably have all these books on your bookshelf; if not, you should. If you are just beginning in the field, these books will prove to be invaluable references.

- **Selected Online Resources**
- **Recommended Books**
- **On Becoming a Blender Master**

Selected Online Resources

Perhaps more than with any other software of its kind, Blender's users so far have depended on freely available online resources. Although the situation with books is changing (this book being one example), in the past there was very little published information available for learners of Blender. In fact, the one book that was available, the Blender 2.3 guide, was basically a printed version of the same guide available online.

This dearth of printed information sources, combined with the free and open spirit of the Blender development model and the extraordinary passion that Blender users have for sharing their knowledge, has resulted in an extremely rich supply of online learning resources for Blender. Neither quality nor quantity has ever been a problem; instead, the difficulty has been in ensuring that the wealth of documentation and tutorials available were all easy to find and up to date. The Blender community has done an admirable job in accomplishing this, and after you know where to look you will find that the mysteries of Blender will be quickly revealed.

Official Documentation

The official website for Blender is `www.blender.org`. You can download the software here, and it is also home to an excellent gallery of Blender artwork. But the place you want to start for documentation is in the Blender Wikibook here:

        `http://mediawiki.blender.org/index.php/Main_Page`

You should bookmark this page because you will be returning to it a lot if you use Blender. This documentation changes rapidly to stay up-to-date and is currently undergoing a major overhaul as a result of the Blender Foundation's Summer of Documentation project, which promises a wealth of new documentation on many of the new Blender features. Here you find in-depth tutorials on Python scripting, the Game Engine, Blender's physical simulation, materials and procedural texturing, lighting, modeling, and the Blender database functionality, as well as a number of great tutorials geared specifically to character animation. Ryan Dale's excellent *Introduction to Character Animation* tutorial has quickly become an indispensable resource for beginning animators. It covers the basics of building a rigged character mesh and is definitely worth checking out here:

        `http://mediawiki.blender.org/index.php/BSoD/Introduction_to_Character_`
        `Animation`

At a more advanced level, Robert Christian has written an *Introduction to Rigging* that is turning out to be an absolute must-read for any reader of this book. It covers rigging in Blender in considerable detail and offers examples of a variety of different professional-quality rigging solutions, covering a number of armature features not covered in this book and discussing the pros and cons of each approach. You'll find this fantastic resource here:

        `http://mediawiki.blender.org/index.php/BSoD/Introduction_to_Rigging`

Finally, William Padovani Germano is in the middle of his work on the Summer of Documentation tutorial *Introduction to the Principles of Animation*. This document will cover many of the fundamental points about animation that I touched on in this book and expand on some points that I have not discussed much. Although it is only partially completed at the time of this writing, it looks sure to be a very informative and useful complement to the material in this book. That tutorial can be found here:

```
http://mediawiki.blender.org/index.php/BSoD/Introduction_to_the_Principles_
of_Animation
```

All the Summer of Documentation tutorials appear to be coming along beautifully, and the breadth and depth of this documentation will make it required reading for Blender users of all skill levels. In addition to the Summer of Documentation tutorials, the Blender Wiki has loads of excellent tutorials in the Noob to Pro Wiki Book. I particularly recommend Andy Dolphin's tutorial on lip sync with shape keys.

BlenderArtists Forum, BlenderNation, and Blender Professionals Portal

Blender has a very active, enthusiastic, and helpful community of users at `http://blender-artists.org/forum/`. This is where you should go first for technical questions about using Blender or any other Blender-related help. Use the search function first, and you will probably find the answer to your question immediately. Otherwise, post your question in the appropriate forum and an answer will certainly come quickly, often within minutes.

BlenderNation at `http://blendernation.com` is a regularly updated source of Blender news. This is a good place to look to keep up with what's happening in the Blender world. It also has one of the best collections of tutorials and video tutorials available anywhere for Blender.

The Blender Professionals Portal at `http://www.blenderpro.com` is a new online resource that provides a variety of tools for professional Blender users and employers to get in contact with each other and to keep abreast with developments, both in the CG industry in general and in the Blender community. Blender Professionals also serves as a repository for scripts and provide up-to-date CVS builds with special features not yet available in official Blender releases.

Other Recommended Tutorials and Online Resources

There are a huge number of tutorials and learning resources available for Blender on the Web, and more are popping up daily. It is inevitable that I will fail to mention many excellent ones, but you will surely come across them if you read and search for specific topics in the BlenderArtists forum. Still, there are a few that I want to mention: those that offer interesting alternatives to approaches I've taken in this book and those that I am particularly indebted to and want to acknowledge here.

Tutorials and Sample Blend Files

The *Elephants Dream* website at `http://www.elephantsdream.org` is a great resource for finding information on advanced animation and film production with Blender. Many "making-of" videos, tutorials, and production notes make this site a real gold mine for the Blender animator. One of the great things on offer there is the Mancandy character rig created by Bassam Kurdali. The direct link to the Mancandy page is here:

`http://orange.blender.org/blog/mancandy-updated`

Mancandy (see Figure 18.1) is one of the quintessential Blender practice rigs and one of the best examples available of how rigging should be done in Blender. Mancandy is included on the DVD accompanying this book, but the notes on the web page are very informative.

Figure 18.1

Bassam Kurdali's annotated Mancandy rig

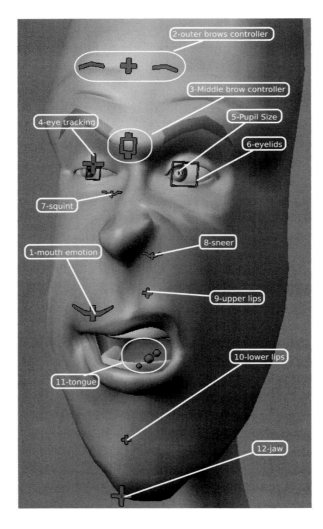

Blenderart magazine is a freely available, bimonthly PDF magazine covering all aspects of creating art in Blender. *Blenderart* has featured dozens of articles and tutorials on modeling, animation, texturing, rendering, and scripting contributed by some of the most skilled Blender users around. You can download all the issues that have come out so far at `http://www.blenderart.org`.

Although Jason Pierce's Ludwig rig itself is included on the DVD for this book, Ludwig's own homepage is also well worth checking out:

> `http://www.cs.unm.edu/~sketch/gallery/resource/ludwig/ludwig.html`

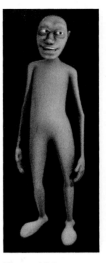

In addition to the Ludwig rig (see Figure 18.2), you'll also find several sample animations using the rig. A very nice and understandable tutorial by Nathan Dunlap for making a walk animation with the Ludwig rig can be found at

> `http://www.nathandunlap.brickfilms.com/tutorials/wt01b.html`

Colin Lister's web page for his work in progress film *Cog* is an excellent resource for tutorials on texturing and creating a variety of interesting effects, including realistic smoke and water effects. His web page is here:

> `http://www.cogfilms.com/tutorials.html`

Figure 18.2
Ludwig by Jason Pierce

Calvin's Simple Page has an excellent set of Blender character animation tutorials, including an introduction to Ipo Drivers and Shape keys, a tutorial on making cartoon-style eyes, and a very interesting foot rig that replicates the functionality of the Ludwig rig described in this book, but does so without using action constraints. There are several other interesting tutorials there, and the site is updated regularly. You can find that site at `http://www.blenderprojects.com/calvin/`. Calvin's all-armature approach to rigging a mouth is also well worth checking out, and you can find blend files and a discussion on that here:

> `http://blenderartists.org/forum/showthread.php?t=70892`

Jorge Rocha's website includes a section on tutorials on advanced rigging tricks and also includes a free rigged model of a realistic clothed woman (see Figure 18.3) that you can find on the DVD. He also has some useful Python scripts available. His website can be found at `http://kokcito.tk`.

Colin Levy has several very nice advanced tutorials on animation, scene creation, and camera mapping on his website. The website is located here:

> `http://www.peerlessproductions.com/tuts.html`

Gimble has written a very in-depth stride tutorial that goes into considerably more depth about that feature than I've gone into. The URL for that website is the following:

> `http://www.telusplanet.net/public/kugyelka/blender/tutorials/stride/`
> `stride.html`

Figure 18.3

**Jorge Rocha's rigged
female character**

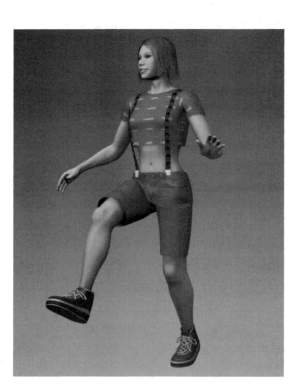

Video Tutorials

A lot of people find video tutorials particularly useful. Greybeard's video tutorials have become a venerable institution for Blender learners, and the videos hosted on his site cover a wide range of topics in Blender use. This is the best single collection of video tutorials I know of, and it can be found at `http://www.ibiblio.org/bvidtute`. There is also a video tutorial section on the official Blender site here:

`http://blender3d.org/cms/Video_Tutorials.396.0.html`

BlenderNation also has a section devoted to video tutorials. Regardless of how you learn, you'll find countless helpful Blender resources available on the Web. If you start with what I've listed here, you will be a pro at all aspects of Blender in no time.

Recommended Books

CG animation is one of the most multidisciplinary art forms there is. To be a good CG animator, you must be technically inclined and also artistically gifted. You have to master modeling, texturing, posing, timing, lighting, rendering, and many other skills. And in addition to talent and practical skill, there is also a wealth of knowledge that you must have. These books are a small selection of what I consider to be required reading for anyone wanting to create animations with Blender.

Character Animation

Animation has been around for about as long as cinema, but the art of character animation was perfected by the Disney studio in the 1930s and has not changed much since then. The techniques used to express motion and emotion in *The Incredibles* are not appreciably different from those used in *Snow White and the Seven Dwarves*. These books cover the principles of character animation, regardless of the technical tools you use to implement it.

Animation by **Preston Blair** (Walter T. Foster, current ed. 1987) First published in 1948, this book is pretty much the classic text on character animation. Almost everything in this book has since appeared elsewhere dozens of times, and anybody who grew up on Saturday morning cartoons has probably acquired most of the content of this book unconsciously by sheer osmosis. It has stood for half a century as an indispensable guide to the basics of character motion and an important document of the period when animation came into its own as a fully developed art form.

The Illusion of Life by **Frank Thomas and Ollie Johnston** (Disney Editions, revised ed. 1995) This is a beautifully illustrated, hard-bound coffee table book that also happens to be very informative for animators. It presents the origins and methods of animation as created and used by Walt Disney and the Disney studio. It's interesting not only as a historical document of the art of animation but also as a guide to the principles and the ideas behind them. There's plenty in here that is not at all pertinent to CG work, but if you have any interest at all in how animation used to be done before the dawn of the Ipo curve, this is required reading.

The Animator's Survival Kit by **Richard Williams** (Faber & Faber, 2002) This book covers many of the same principles dealt with by the two other books I listed here, but it stands out in the wealth of visual examples included. There's hardly any printed text in the whole huge book. Every page is filled with drawn animation sequences with text handwritten on the illustrations. Richard Williams is a true master of the art of animation, and this is likely the closest most of us will ever get to peering over the shoulder of the likes of him.

CG-Related

I am deliberately leaving out references to a number of general digital character animation books because although there are many of them, I think that studying old-school character animation, combined with mastering one's own chosen software package tends to make these books somewhat redundant. There are a lot of specific digital techniques which do need expanding on, though, so here I list a few CG books that mostly deal with issues not covered by this book or the tutorials I've referred to.

Stop Staring by **Jason Osipa** (Sybex/Wiley, 2nd ed. 2007) This is the quintessential book on facial modeling and animation in 3D. Lip sync and emotional facial expressions are all dealt with in depth and in a way that is very practical for the digital artist.

***Building a Digital Human* by Ken Brilliant** (Laxmi Publications, 2005) This book covers polygon modeling of a human figure from beginning to end in great detail. Realistic organic modeling with polygons is far from trivial and this book does a good job of explaining the practice and the theory behind it.

***Digital Lighting and Rendering* by Jeremy Birn** (New Riders, 2nd edition 2006) This book does a great job of covering the topic of lighting and rendering. Pretty much everything you need to know about lighting and lights is in here and most of it is fully applicable to Blender's lighting system. With regard to rendering, this book will leave you with a much clearer idea of the strengths and weaknesses of the Blender internal renderer and an understanding of the differences between the various rendering engines and ray tracers. The book also does an excellent job of highlighting the similarities and differences between digital lighting and traditional film lighting, and is terrific-looking to boot. The book's sister volume *Digital Texturing and Painting* by Owen Demers is also a beautiful and inspiring book, but in my opinion it lacks the practical focus of *Digital Lighting and Rendering*.

***Inspired 3D Short Film Production* by Jeremy Cantor and Pepe Valencia** (Course Technology, 2004) This book gives a nice overview of the full process of producing a 3D animated film. Although it doesn't go into the individual steps in great detail, it will give you an idea of what the process is and has a number of practical tips for people trying to get started with a 3D short. Even if you have no intention of doing all the work yourself, this book will help to give you an idea of where the animator fits into the larger scheme of such a project. It's also a nice-looking book with an accompanying DVD filled with entertaining and inspiring short animations.

On Becoming a Blender Master

If you've followed the steps in this book, sought help on the BlenderArtists forum, and investigated some of the other resources mentioned in this chapter, you are, without a doubt, well along the path to becoming a master of Blender. As your own skills improve, bear in mind that as a free software application with still limited industry support, Blender relies heavily on the energy and enthusiasm of its users. Your own contributions to Blender and the community have a special weight. These contributions might come in a variety of forms. If you are a top-notch coder in C or Python, you might consider getting involved in coding Blender or creating useful scripts. Creating good, clear tutorials is also an excellent way to contribute to the community (and to learn!). Likewise, making yourself available at the BlenderArtists forum to answer questions from people less experienced than you is also an important contribution. And as an artist, simply creating work in Blender and letting that be known has great value for the Blender community at large.

I hope that you've gotten something out of what I have attempted to contribute with this book. I'm looking forward to seeing your work.

Happy Blendering!

Index